Guide to Microsoft® Windows 2000® Core Technologies

Ed Tittel
James Michael Stewart

ONE MAIN STREET, CAMBRIDGE, MA 02142

Australia • Canada • Denmark • Japan • Mexico • New Zealand • Philippines
Puerto Rico • Singapore • South Africa • Spain • United Kingdom • United States

Guide to Microsoft Windows 2000 Core Technologies is published by Course Technology.

Associate Publisher	Kristen Duerr
Senior Acquisitions Editor	Stephen Solomon
Product Manager	David George
Production Editor	Daphne Barbas
Quality Assurance Manager	John Bosco
Associate Product Manager	Laura Hildebrand
Marketing Manager	Susan Ogar
Text Designer	GEX, Inc.
Composition House	GEX, Inc.
Cover Designer	Efrat Reis

© 2000 Course Technology, a division of Thomson Learning.

Thomson Learning is a trademark used herein under license.

ALL RIGHTS RESERVED. No part of this work may be reproduced, transcribed, or used in any form or by any means—graphic, electronic, or mechanical, including photocopying, recording, taping, Web distribution, or information storage and retrieval systems—without prior written permission of the publisher.

Disclaimer

Course Technology reserves the right to revise this publication and make changes from time to time in its content without notice.

The Web addresses in this book are subject to change from time to time as necessary without notice.

For more information, contact Course Technology, One Main Street, Cambridge, MA 02142; or find us on the World Wide Web at *www.course.com*.

For permission to use material from this text or product, contact us by

- Web: www.thomsonrights.com
- Phone: 1-800-730-2214
- Fax: 1-800-730-2215

ISBN 0-619-01549-7

Printed in Canada
1 2 3 4 5 WC 04 03 02 01 00

BRIEF CONTENTS

TABLE OF CONTENTS v

PREFACE xiii

CHAPTER ONE
What Is an Operating System? 1

CHAPTER TWO
Examining the Parts of an Operating System 25

CHAPTER THREE
Key Windows 2000 Components 51

CHAPTER FOUR
Allocating and Managing Operating System Resources 87

CHAPTER FIVE
Hardware and Device Management in Windows 2000 121

CHAPTER SIX
Data Storage 147

CHAPTER SEVEN
Storage Management 181

CHAPTER EIGHT
Networking Basics 211

CHAPTER NINE
Network Identification 241

CHAPTER TEN
Organizing Network Resources 271

CHAPTER ELEVEN
Sharing Network Resources 295

CHAPTER TWELVE
Securing Network Resources 329

CHAPTER THIRTEEN
Fault Tolerance 361

CHAPTER FOURTEEN
Disaster Recovery Mechanisms. 395

CHAPTER FIFTEEN
Troubleshooting Windows 2000 417

APPENDIX
Windows Scripting Host . . . . App 1

GLOSSARY   Glossary 1

INDEX   Index 1

TABLE OF CONTENTS

TABLE OF CONTENTS	**v**
PREFACE	**xiii**

CHAPTER ONE
What Is an Operating System?   1

Operating System Design Objectives	2
Evolution of Operating Systems	3
Embedded Commands	3
Control Programs	4
Batch Systems	4
Single Task or Single User?	4
Multiprocessing	5
Key Operating System Functions	9
Operating Systems Sit Between Applications and Hardware	9
Operating Systems Ensure a Robust, Secure Environment	11
Operating Systems Define Consistent Interfaces	12
Operating Systems Manage Resource Allocation	12
Types of Operating Systems	13
End User or Single User	13
Server-Oriented	13
Comparing Windows 2000 Professional and Windows 2000 Server	13
Windows 2000 Professional	14
Windows 2000 Server	16
Windows 2000 Advanced Server	17
Windows 2000 Datacenter Server	18
Chapter Summary	18
Key Terms	19
Review Questions	21
Hands-on Projects	23
Case Projects	23

CHAPTER TWO
Examining the Parts of an Operating System   25

General Principles of Modern Operating System Architecture	26
Environmental Subsystems	28
Executive	32
The Kernel	35
Hardware Abstraction Layer	37
Device Drivers	37

Outline of Win2K Architecture	38
User Space and Kernel Space	38
Pieces Found in Each Space and Their Relationship to Each Other	40
Chapter Summary	41
Key Terms	41
Review Questions	43
Hands-on Projects	45
Case Projects	49

CHAPTER THREE
Key Windows 2000 Components — 51

Important Files and Subsystems	52
Bootstrapping	53
Device Drivers	54
Base Operating System Loaders	55
The Windows Registry	58
HKEY_LOCAL_MACHINE	61
HKEY_CLASSES_ROOT	63
HKEY_CURRENT_CONFIG	63
HKEY_CURRENT_USER	64
HKEY_USERS	65
Protecting the Registry	65
Base System Functionality	67
Writing to Disk	67
Allocating Memory	67
Allocating CPU Time	68
Handling Data-Processing Requests	69
Error Handling	69
Network Functionality	70
Interprocess Communications (IPCs, RPCs)	70
Messaging	71
Terminal Services	71
Tools Found in Windows 2000 Server	72
Chapter Summary	74
Key Terms	74
Review Questions	76
Hands-on Projects	79
Case Projects	85

CHAPTER FOUR
Allocating and Managing Operating System Resources — 87

Distributing CPU Cycles	88
Understanding Multitasking Types	89
Thread Scheduling Basics	90
Memory Management	100
Earmarking Memory for Processes	101
Sharing Memory Among Processes	102
Using the Paging File	103
Reading Data from Memory	103

Object Manager	105
Executive Objects	106
Setting Object Security	107
Chapter Summary	108
Key Terms	108
Review Questions	110
Hands-on Projects	112
Case Projects	120

CHAPTER FIVE
Hardware and Device Management in Windows 2000 — 121

An Overview of Hardware Management	122
Hardware and Devices: Which Is Which?	123
How Windows 2000 Manages Devices and Resource Allocation	124
How Windows 2000 Communicates with the CPU and Other System Resources	125
The Four Components of Hardware Management	126
Win32 Driver Model and Windows 2000 Architecture	126
The WDM Layered Driver Approach	127
Power Management and the OnNow System	129
Hardware Devices	130
System Buses	131
Configuring User Input, Display Devices, and Power Management	133
Configuring Display and Input Devices	133
Power Management and Configuration	135
What if It Breaks? Troubleshooting Devices in Windows 2000	136
One Thing at a Time	136
Document, Document, Document	137
General Troubleshooting Tips	138
Chapter Summary	139
Key Terms	140
Review Questions	141
Hands-on Projects	144
Case Projects	146

CHAPTER SIX
Data Storage — 147

Understanding Disk Architecture	148
Physical Disk Divisions and Important Files	148
Logical Disk Divisions	150
Understanding Windows 2000 File Systems	155
FAT16	155
FAT32	157
NTFS	157
Chapter Summary	163
Key Terms	163
Review Questions	166
Hands-on Projects	168
Case Projects	180

CHAPTER SEVEN
Storage Management — 181

- Organizing Disk Space — 182
  - Basic Disks — 182
  - Dynamic Disks — 184
  - Fault-Tolerant Volumes — 188
- Applying User Quotas — 191
  - Why Use Disk Quotas? — 191
- Archiving Data — 194
  - Backup Methods — 195
- Chapter Summary — 196
- Key Terms — 196
- Review Questions — 197
- Hands-on Projects — 199
- Case Projects — 210

CHAPTER EIGHT
Networking Basics — 211

- Principles of Networking — 212
  - LANs, WANs, and MANs — 212
- OSI Reference Model — 212
  - Application Layer — 213
  - Presentation Layer — 213
  - Session Layer — 214
  - Transport Layer — 214
  - Network Layer — 214
  - Data Link Layer — 214
  - Physical Layer — 215
- Putting It All Together — 215
- Role of Protocols and Services — 217
  - NetBEUI — 217
  - IPX/SPX — 218
  - TCP/IP — 218
  - Services — 218
- Normal and Network Operating System Basics — 223
- Windows 2000 Networking Model — 224
- Routing and Remote Access — 225
  - IP Routing — 225
  - Remote Access — 227
- Server Versus Client Roles — 228
- Chapter Summary — 229
- Key Terms — 230
- Review Questions — 232
- Hands-on Projects — 234
- Case Projects — 240

CHAPTER NINE
Network Identification   241

User Identification Versus Computer Identification	242
Users	242
NetBIOS Names	242
Machine Identification and Name Resolution	242
Domain Name Service	242
Windows Internet Name Service	247
Dynamic Host Configuration Protocol	250
Network Organization	255
Subnets and Gateways	255
Domains	256
Chapter Summary	257
Key Terms	257
Review Questions	258
Hands-on Projects	260
Case Projects	270

CHAPTER TEN
Organizing Network Resources   271

User and Resource Identification	272
Preparing for Active Directory	277
Upgrading an Existing Windows NT Network	277
Installing a New Windows 2000 Network	279
Designing Directory Structures	280
Troubleshooting Active Directory	281
Active Directory Files	282
Backing Up the Active Directory	283
Recovering and Restoring the Active Directory	284
Chapter Summary	284
Key Terms	285
Review Questions	286
Hands-on Projects	287
Case Projects	294

CHAPTER ELEVEN
Sharing Network Resources   295

Resource Sharing Basics	296
Finding Resources	296
Connecting to Resources from the Client	298
Device Sharing	299
Using Windows Explorer and My Network Places	299
File and Folder Sharing	303
Distributed File System	304
Printer Sharing	306
Printing in Windows 2000	307
IntelliMirror for Application Distribution	311
IIS for Web Serving	312
Configuring Folders for IIS Access	313

Terminal Services	316
Setting Up Terminal Services	316
Administration Tools	317
Chapter Summary	318
Key Terms	319
Review Questions	320
Hands-on Projects	322
Case Projects	328

CHAPTER TWELVE
Securing Network Resources — 329

Application and Client Licensing	330
Per-Seat Versus Per-User Licensing	330
Types of Licenses Required	331
User and Group Rights and Permissions	333
Server Accounts Versus Domain Accounts	333
User Authentication Methods	334
NTLM	335
Kerberos	335
Certificates	336
User Profiles and Group Policies	337
User Profiles	337
Group Policies	338
Data Encryption	341
Symmetric Encryption	341
Public Key Encryption	341
Data Encryption in Windows 2000	342
Encryption Tools in Windows 2000	343
Enforcing Encryption	344
Protecting Encryption Keys	344
Chapter Summary	345
Key Terms	345
Review Questions	347
Hands-on Projects	350
Case Projects	357

CHAPTER THIRTEEN
Fault Tolerance — 361

What Is Fault Tolerance?	362
Backing Up and Restoring Data	362
Backup Tools	363
Backup Schemes	365
A Quick Tour of Backup Media Supported in Windows 2000	369
Using Fault-Tolerant Disk Configurations	369
RAID Levels Supported in Windows 2000	370
Creating Fault-Tolerant Volumes with the Disk Management Tool	374
Server Clustering	375
Clustering Terminology	375
How Clustering Works	380
Client–Cluster Communications	380
Requirements for Clustered Applications	381

Chapter Summary	382
Key Terms	382
Review Questions	384
Hands-on Projects	387
Case Projects	395

CHAPTER FOURTEEN
Disaster Recovery Mechanisms — 395

What's Happening During the Boot Process?	396
Loading Basic Hardware Support	396
Loading Ntldr	397
Detecting Hardware	397
Loading the Windows 2000 System Kernel	398
Advanced Options Menu	399
Safe Mode Options	400
Boot Logging	400
Enable VGA Mode	401
Last Known Good Configuration	401
Directory Services Restore Mode	403
Debugging Mode	403
Repairing a Damaged Operating System	404
Emergency Repair Disk	404
System Recovery Console	404
Restoring a Server	406
Chapter Summary	407
Key Terms	407
Review Questions	408
Hands-on Projects	411
Case Projects	415

CHAPTER FIFTEEN
Troubleshooting Windows 2000 — 417

General Principles of Troubleshooting	418
Computer Information File	418
Common-Sense Troubleshooting	420
Troubleshooting Installation Problems	421
Troubleshooting Tools	422
Event Viewer	422
Computer Management	423
The Registry	425
About Value Entries	429
Registry Storage Files	430
The Registry Editors: REGEDIT and REGEDT32	432
Registry Size Limitations	433
Backing Up the Registry	434
Restoring the Registry	435
Windows 2000 Resource Kit Registry Tools	436
Troubleshooting Boot Failures	437
Advanced Start-up Options	437
Start-up File Repair	438

Troubleshooting Printer Problems	439
Troubleshooting RAS Problems	440
Troubleshooting Network Problems	440
Troubleshooting Disk Problems	441
Miscellaneous Troubleshooting Issues	441
Permissions Problems	441
Master Boot Record	441
Dr. Watson	441
Applying Service Pack Updates	442
Installing and Uninstalling a Service Pack	443
Verifying Service Packs	443
Using Microsoft References for Troubleshooting	444
Chapter Summary	445
Key Terms	446
Review Questions	448
Hands-on Projects	451
Case Projects	455

APPENDIX
Windows Scripting Host — App 1

Command-Based Scripting	App 2
Windows-Based Scripting	App 3
Manually Registering Script Engines	App 4
Sample Script	App 4

GLOSSARY — Glossary 1

INDEX — Index 1

Preface

INTRODUCTION

Welcome to *Guide to Microsoft Windows 2000 Core Technologies*! This book offers you real-world examples, interactive activities, and hundreds of hands-on projects that reinforce key concepts and help you understand the underlying components of Windows 2000. This book also features troubleshooting tips for solutions to common problems that you will encounter in the realm of Windows 2000 administration.

This book offers in-depth study of all the salient functions and features of installing, configuring, and maintaining Windows 2000 Server. Throughout the book, we provide pointed review questions to reinforce the concepts introduced in each chapter. In addition to the review questions, we provide detailed hands-on projects that let you experience first hand the processes involved in Windows 2000 configuration and management. Finally, to put a real-world slant on the concepts introduced in each chapter, we provide case studies to prepare you for situations that must be managed in a live networking environment.

THE INTENDED AUDIENCE

This book is intended to serve the needs of those individuals and information systems professionals who are interested in learning more about Microsoft Windows 2000, as well as individuals who are interested in obtaining Microsoft Windows 2000 certification.

Chapter 1, "What Is an Operating System?," introduces the basic principles that govern the design of an operating system and explains the fundamental roles that an operating system must play. In addition, it addresses how an operating system works with hardware and other software and enables users to access a computer's services and resources. It also teaches you how to recognize the key components that make up an operating system and how they relate to one another, as well as provides an overview of the various Windows 2000 family members.

In **Chapter 2**, "Examining the Parts of an Operating System," we discuss the purpose of operating systems, list the parts of a modern operating system, and explain how the pieces of an operating system relate to one another. In addition, we describe the difference between kernel mode and user mode and explain why there's a difference and relate this information to the Windows 2000 architecture.

In **Chapter 3**, "Key Windows 2000 Components," we recount the basic startup process for Windows 2000 and provide an overview of the Windows 2000 Registry. In addition, we describe the Windows 2000 base functionality so that you can recognize and use the basic administrative tools included with Windows 2000.

In **Chapter 4**, "Allocating and Managing Operating System Resources," we explain what applications, processes, and threads are and how they fit together, and provide you with the information needed to understand how different server types have different priorities. In addition, we explain how memory management works. Finally, we list the kinds of objects found in Windows 2000 and explain how Windows 2000 object-level security works so that you may better understand the role of the object manager in Windows 2000.

Chapter 5, "Hardware and Device Management in Windows 2000" discusses the differences between hardware and devices, and how the operating system manages devices and resource allocation. We also examine how devices communicate with the CPU and other system resources. In addition, we list the four components of hardware management in Windows 2000 and how they interact. We conclude this chapter with a discussion of how the new Win32 Driver Model (WDM) fits into the Windows 2000 architecture and provide information on Windows 2000's support for Power Management, the OnNow system, and hardware devices and system buses.

Chapter 6, "Data Storage," explains how physical disks are organized, describes how Win2K reads disks to circumvent the logical limit to partition size, and explores how the physical structure of a hard disk relates to its logical organization. Additionally, we list the types of volumes supported by Windows 2000 and discuss the role of a file system in an operating system. Finally, we describe the features of each file system that Windows 2000 supports, and examine the advanced features of NTFS.

Chapter 7, "Storage Management," explores how data is managed in Windows 2000. This discussion includes how to create and manage basic and dynamic disks using Windows 2000 disk management tools. In addition, we explore the different Windows 2000 volumes, including simple, spanned, striped, mirrored, and RAID 5 volumes, as well as how to recover from failed mirrored and RAID 5 volumes in Windows 2000. Finally, we show you how to assign quotas for all users and for individual users. We also discuss how to upgrade a basic disk to a dynamic one, and extend an NTFS volume to include extra disk space.

In **Chapter 8**, "Networking Basics," we examine the seven layers of the OSI model, the role of protocols and services in networks, and how those protocols are based on this networking model. Finally, we explain the differences between a normal operating system and a network operating system and list the differences between client and server roles.

Chapter 9, "Network Identification," takes a look at the naming protocols used in Windows 2000 Server, as well as how to configure the Microsoft Domain Name Service (DNS) for Windows 2000 Server. Additionally, we discuss how to install and manage the

Microsoft Windows Internet Name Service (WINS) for Windows 2000 Server. We also show you how to assign TCP/IP addressing information to your clients dynamically using the Microsoft Dynamic Host Configuration Protocol (DHCP) service for Windows 2000 Server and create DHCP scopes, Superscopes, and Multicast Scopes. We conclude this chapter with a discussion of the basic concepts of TCP/IP subnets and domains.

In **Chapter 10**, "Organizing Network Resources," we explore the differences between an Active Directory domain and a Windows NT domain, and explore Active Directory organizational units, domains, trees, and forests, as well as how to maintain and control the Active Directory. We also explore how Active Directory maintains its files and logs, how to complete a backup of the Active Directory, as well as recover and restore the Active Directory in case of failure.

Chapter 11, "Sharing Network Resources," explores resource sharing and the steps necessary to share resources, files, folders, and printers on a Windows 2000 Server. We also discuss IntelliMirror and the software installation and maintenance features. This chapter also examines how to install and configure Internet Information Services for sharing Web resources, as well as how to install and configure Windows 2000 Terminal Server.

Chapter 12, "Securing Network Resources," explains how an operating system and applications are licensed. We also tell you how to edit the rights and permissions associated with groups, or create your own groups with special rights and explain the various methods of user authentication available in Windows 2000. Finally, we explore how to distinguish policies and profiles and explain how each are used in Windows 2000 and discuss the encryption methods employed by Windows 2000.

Chapter 13, "Fault Tolerance," defines the parts of an operating system that make it fault tolerant and explains how the various kinds of backup operations work. We also list the backup media supported by Windows 2000 and explain what RAID is and how the various forms of RAID supported by Windows 2000 contribute to its fault tolerance. This chapter concludes with a discussion of clustering and how it works.

Chapter 14, "Disaster Recovery Mechanisms," describes what happens during the Windows 2000 boot process. In addition, we explore how the tools in the Advanced Option menu work to repair a damaged operating system and define how the Emergency Repair Disk and the Recovery Console can recover Windows 2000 settings or fix a problem. Finally, we explain how the restoration process works to restore a server back to its original condition.

This book concludes with **Chapter 15**, "Troubleshooting Windows 2000." Here, we show you how to troubleshoot general problems with Windows 2000, introduce you to some of the troubleshooting tools of Windows 2000, and examine how to work with advanced boot options. We also discuss how to troubleshoot the Windows 2000 Registry, back up data and settings, and recover a Windows 2000 Professional client's applications and data. We conclude with how to create and use an Emergency Repair Disk, and install and use the Recovery Console. We also describe remote operating system installation and how it can be used with IntelliMirror to recover an entire PC remotely.

Additionally, the **Appendix**, "Windows Scripting Host," discusses how to handle scripting in Windows 2000 using two scripting tools: the DOS-based Cscript.exe and the Windows-based Wscript.exe.

FEATURES

Many features in this book are designed to improve its pedagogical value and aid you in fully understanding Windows 2000 concepts.

- **Chapter Objectives** Each chapter begins with a detailed list of the concepts to be mastered within that chapter. This list provides you with a quick reference to the contents of the chapter as well as a useful study guide.
- **Illustrations and Tables** Numerous illustrations of networking components help you visualize common networking setups, theories, and architectures. In addition, tables provide details and comparisons of both practical and theoretical information.
- **Chapter Summaries** The text of each chapter concludes with a summary of the concepts it has introduced. These summaries provide a helpful way to recap and revisit the ideas covered in each chapter.
- **Key Terms** Following the summary, a list of new networking terms and their definitions encourages proper understanding of the chapter's key concepts and provides a useful reference.
- **Review Questions** End-of-chapter assessments begin with a set of review questions that reinforce the ideas introduced in each chapter. These questions not only show you whether you have mastered the concepts, but are written to help prepare you for the Microsoft certification examination.
- **Hands-on Projects** Although it is important to understand the theory behind networking technology, nothing can improve upon real-world experience. Each chapter provides a series of exercises aimed at giving students hands-on implementation experience.
- **Case Projects** Finally, each chapter closes with a section that proposes certain networking situations. You are asked to evaluate the situations and decide upon the course of action to be taken to remedy the problems described. This valuable tool will help you sharpen your decision-making and troubleshooting skills, which are important aspects of network administration.

Text and Graphic Conventions

Wherever appropriate, additional information has been added to this book to help you better understand what is being discussed in the chapter. Icons throughout the text alert you to additional materials. The icons used in this book are described here:

 Tips give extra information on how to attack a problem, time-saving shortcuts, or what to do in certain real-world situations.

 Note icons are used to present additional helpful material related to the subject being discussed.

 Important information about potential mistakes or hazards is highlighted with a Caution icon.

 Each step-by-step Hands-on Project is marked by the Hands-on icon.

Where Should You Start?

This book is intended to be read in sequence, from beginning to end. Each chapter builds upon those that precede it, to provide a solid understanding of Windows 2000 concepts. After completing the chapters, you may find it useful to go back through the book and use the review questions and projects to solidify this knowledge. Readers are also encouraged to investigate the many pointers to online and printed sources of additional information that are cited throughout this book.

Acknowledgments

Ed Tittel: I would like to thank my co-author, James Michael Stewart, for shouldering the burden of this book, and for helping us to meet an aggressive schedule. Your work continues to improve, Michael—please keep it up! I'd also like to thank Dawn Rader for her tireless efforts in coordinating this project on the LANWrights side. I'd also like to thank my family and friends for their continued support for my oh-so-interesting career, especially Mom, Kat, Robert, Blackie, and the Big Babboo.

Michael Stewart: Thanks to my boss and co-author, Ed Tittel, for including me in this book series. To my parents, Dave and Sue, thanks for your love and consistent support. To Mark, it seems that the stars are stacked against us, our plans to hang always seem to get foiled! To HERbert, why is it that only an hour after I clip your nails they are sharp as needles again!?!? And finally, as always, to Elvis—I recently was blessed with a sighting of your holy visage, wait a sec, that was just Earlvis, darn.

Collectively: Both of us would like to thank the crew at Course Technology for making this book possible, including Stephen Solomon, our acquisitions editor; Dave George, our project editor; Daphne Barbas, our production editor; and all the other people at Course Technology who helped with the book. A great deal of thanks goes out to Christa Anderson, Barry Shilmover, Earl Follis, and David Johnson for their contributions to this book. We'd also like to thank Carole McClendon our agent at Waterside Productions, for helping us to cement a business relationship that has proved so worthwhile to everyone. Thanks to one and all!

CHAPTER 1

WHAT IS AN OPERATING SYSTEM?

> **After reading this chapter and completing the exercises you will be able to:**
> - Understand the basic principles that govern the design of an operating system
> - Explain the fundamental roles that an operating system must play
> - Describe how an operating system works with hardware and other software
> - Recognize the key components that make up an operating system and how they relate to one another
> - Understand how an operating system enables users to access a computer's services and resources
> - Differentiate between the various Windows 2000 family members

Basically, an operating system is a special-purpose program that operates a computer and allows other programs to run. In fact, without an active operating system of some kind, a computer is nothing more than a very expensive paperweight. An operating system makes it possible for a computer to provide services, run applications, and deliver resources. All of these activities are essential for any user to take advantage of the speed and power that modern computers have to offer.

An operating system performs the following primary tasks:

- Creates an operating environment in which one or more applications can run
- Provides basic access to system hardware, such as keyboard, mouse, display, and disk drives
- Allows applications to access hardware resources

In addition to these primary tasks, modern operating systems provide many more services and conveniences for users and software developers alike. For example, the graphical user interfaces (GUIs) that operating systems such as Windows and the Macintosh offer make it easy for users to navigate their desktops and the applications they find there. At the same time, the operating system defines a consistent graphical environment that developers can exploit to create powerful applications. In fact, this same graphical environment also permits the operating system itself to present the same face to users that applications do. Therefore, all elements of the desktop (whether an application or a system component) use identical graphical symbols and navigation techniques.

In this chapter, you will learn what functions an operating system performs and what kinds of services and interfaces it can make available to applications. Along the way, you will learn to recognize the key components that make up an operating system and the kinds of access and activities it can support. In particular, you will explore these fundamentals as they apply to the Windows 2000 product family.

OPERATING SYSTEM DESIGN OBJECTIVES

One of the main tasks of an operating system is to bridge the gap between the applications running on the system and the hardware that is installed within it. As you will see, operating systems have come a long way from what they were a few years ago. Whereas in the past the application was responsible for communicating with, for example, the modem or the printer, today the operating system performs that task. This evolution in operating system design has enabled software developers to concentrate on creating the applications, rather than on "teaching" the applications to communicate with the hardware devices on the system. Given the huge number of devices on the market today (such as modems), it would be almost impossible for a developer to write an application that can communicate with all of them.

As operating systems have evolved, they have become increasingly reliable. This evolution partly reflects the way in which the applications, the operating system, and the hardware communicate. As operating systems become more complex, the interface between the application and the hardware disappears. This structure allows for tighter control over how the hardware is accessed and therefore forces the applications to communicate with the operating system.

If it were not for the operating system, all applications would need to include all the code that would be required to communicate with all types of hardware. For example, without an operating system, a network-based program would need to include support for all protocols that could potentially be used to communicate on the network as well as drivers for all possible network cards that could be installed in the system. As you can imagine, creating such support would very quickly become an impossible task for any application developer.

Another drawback of older or "legacy" operating systems was their lack of control over applications. If a misbehaving application corrupted part of the memory or rendered a network card inaccessible, all other applications would suffer the same fate. Today's operating systems manage how and when applications interact with each other. For example, Windows 2000 runs 16-bit applications in separate memory spaces so that if the 16-bit application fails, other system processes are protected from the application failure.

Finally, operating systems provide application developers with a consistent standard for connecting with networks, printers, and hardware devices, and for displaying information on the screen. Before Microsoft Windows 3.0 became available, most personal computers ran some form of the DOS operating system. Although primitive, the DOS operating system was extremely small and would run off a single floppy disk. Many administrators continue to use DOS-bootable disks for troubleshooting purposes. A major limitation of the DOS operating systems was that each application had to control the system itself. For example, if you installed word processing software on your system and you needed the application to print a document, you had to use the drivers that were supplied to you by the company that released the application. Thus, if you purchased and installed a new printer, you needed to wait for the word processor's developer to release a new driver that supported your new printer. Even worse, if you had multiple applications running on the system, you needed to install a driver for each application that needed to print; each of these drivers would be proprietary and would not work with other applications. The same was true when displaying any type of interface. If you wanted an application to have menus and windows, your application would have to tell the video card how to draw a box, a menu, and so on.

With the release of Windows, users had a common platform on which to work. Now if you want an application to print to a printer installed on the system, you just send a "print" command and the operating system takes care of the rest. You simply install the printer driver at the operating system level rather than at the application level. This approach "teaches" the operating system how to print. Any application that knows how to send a print job to the operating system can then have it sent to the printer.

EVOLUTION OF OPERATING SYSTEMS

Early computers had no operating systems per se. All system control instructions and application activity were mixed together. The applications were responsible for communicating with some of the devices that existed on the system. The process of evolution has separated system control from applications and provided increasingly complex capabilities. Parallel evolution has provided complex system services, interfaces, and resources for applications. Over time, operating systems have become larger, more complex, and more comprehensive.

Embedded Commands

The earliest computers couldn't even store programs. It was necessary to flip switches to enter instructions one at a time. This simple-minded form of operation virtually dictated that control and application instructions be mixed together as needed. As programmers of these early systems gained additional experience and insight into their work, they realized that certain sequences of control instructions were necessary to start programs, to perform common activities, and to manage program behavior.

The origin of computer operating systems derived from the separation of common control sequences from specific applications. To make their jobs easier, these early programmers collected program elements that occurred in the majority of their programs and figured out how to reuse them as needed. Over time, these elements were separated from individual applications to remain available—if not running—on such computers purely for convenience. These elements ultimately defined the key components that remain at the heart of most modern operating systems.

Control Programs

The next step in the evolution of the computer operating system involved packaging those common control elements that were eventually recognized within standalone applications and regularly including them with applications in separate form. These elements would precede an application to establish an operating environment in which applications could run; likewise, other such elements might follow an application by cleaning up after it or preceding yet another application. In computer jargon, this kind of software environment, which is an important part of any operating system, is known as a **runtime environment**.

The separation of control elements from application elements and the regular reuse of such control elements provided the impetus for the development of operating systems as you know them today. As operating systems have evolved, their control functions have been augmented with all kinds of services, user interfaces, and other functions. Nevertheless, maintaining control over a computer's hardware and providing a runtime environment for applications remain the key functions that any operating system must provide.

Batch Systems

A **batch system** creates a runtime environment in which one program or application follows another in sequence. Because such sequences may be defined in advance, then submitted for execution on a computer as a single task, such collections are called **batch jobs**. A batch system is a kind of operating system that is constructed to support the execution of batch jobs.

Some experts believe that batch systems represent the earliest kind of computer operating system, because in addition to providing control over the hardware and a runtime environment for applications, batch systems were the first to support a command language. A **command language** provides a collection of terms, some of which take modifiers or parameters, that allow a user to tell the operating system what to do in the simplest terms. To this day, most operating systems, including Windows 2000, support a command language. Most operating systems also support one or more forms of batch-mode operation. In Windows 2000, command scripts and the Scheduler service combine to create a relatively powerful batch system.

Single Task or Single User?

Early computers were both incredibly expensive and labor-intensive. Although such systems could handle only one program at a time, the advent of batch systems meant that sequences of programs quickly became commonplace. Competition for scarce computing resources soon meant that users had to schedule when they would be allowed to access these primitive, but powerful computing behemoths. As the number of potential users for such systems increased and each user's runtime requirements inevitably diverged, computer system developers quickly realized that creating multiple user identities was a good idea.

The introduction of the notion that multiple users might share a single machine added considerably to the kinds of control that an operating system must provide on a computer. For example, if user A and user B share access to the same machine, it's not necessarily a good idea for user A and user B to automatically share access to the same files and applications. If user A works in the Engineering Department and user B works in the Accounting Department, it should be readily apparent that there are all kinds of reasons why restricting such access might be wise. Therefore, identifying users has also come to mean identifying which system resources those users may or may not access and what kinds of operations they may perform. This relationship represents a crude but accurate foundation for computer and operating system security, which is covered in greater detail in Chapter 12.

Multiprocessing

Multiprocessing is a term that supports several interpretations. It can refer to any of the following:

- A system that contains more than one **central processing unit (CPU)** and can therefore execute more than one application at a time
- A system that supports multiple simultaneous users, so that more than one user can execute an application or access a resource at the same time
- A system that allows more than one task to be active at any given moment, which presents the appearance that more than one application is active at the same time
- A system that allows any task to create multiple subtasks (for example, a spelling checker that runs in the background for a word processing application can run as a thread separate from the main text entry window) so logically disjoint activities can proceed in parallel

In fact, even though each of these capabilities can be explained and understood separately, modern operating systems tend to support all of these capabilities. The following sections explore each of them in detail. It is important to remember that all of these capabilities can and do function together in most operating systems.

Multiple CPUs

One way to increase processing power is to add more CPUs to a single computer. Theoretically, multiple CPUs are better than one. For each additional CPU that's added to a computer, however, an increasing amount of that CPU's capabilities is taken up by the coordination effort with the other CPU. Therefore, although adding a second identical CPU to a computer with only a single CPU installed can increase performance by as much as 85 percent, adding a third CPU seldom increases performance by more than 60 percent. Not only is the law of diminishing returns at work here, but this sort of scheme also exacts an increasing toll for each additional CPU that's added to a multiprocessor system. As this paragraph is being written, computer manufacturers such as Dell and Compaq are releasing the first generation of mass-produced, eight-way systems. As time goes by, an increasing number of CPUs in servers will become more common and this number should continue to increase.

For an operating system to use multiple CPUs, it must be constructed to recognize and utilize such additional resources. For example, Windows 2000 Professional supports 1 or 2 CPUs, Windows 2000 Server supports a maximum of 4 CPUs, and more advanced versions of Windows 2000 support as many as 8 (Advanced Server) to 32 CPUs (Datacenter Server). Nevertheless, for Windows 2000 to recognize an additional CPU on any given machine, it may be necessary to reinstall the software. Other modern operating systems, such as any of the many flavors of UNIX or other similar systems, also support multiple CPUs.

Adding multiple CPUs to a computer increases the complexity of the operating systems that seek to use those resources. In particular, such operating systems must be able not only to recognize multiple CPUs, but also to schedule tasks or threads to occupy as many CPUs as possible at any given moment. The upside is that a computer with multiple CPUs can truly execute multiple activities at the same time. The downside is that the operating system must be able to juggle those CPUs, and to coordinate their access to memory, storage, and other system resources. The reason that the performance boost for each additional CPU declines as more CPUs are added is that the juggling act becomes increasingly difficult as the number of CPUs grows.

As another way of increasing the available processing power, modern operating systems often support a facility called **clustering**. Instead of adding more CPUs to a single computer, clustering allows multiple servers to function as a single, logical server. A clustering facility permits tasks and threads to be distributed among the servers in a cluster in much the same way that an operating system that supports multiple CPUs distributes threads and tasks on a single multiprocessor machine. In fact, clustering services appear in more advanced versions of Windows 2000 Server as part of their incremental increases in capability. Likewise, other operating systems such as UNIX support clustering in high-end implementations.

Multiple Users

By the 1960s, computers had become both pervasive and powerful enough to support multiple users at the same time. This evolution led to the advent of multiuser operating systems, wherein protecting the operating system from the users and protecting the users from each other became serious concerns. Over time, operating systems have acquired capabilities aimed at serving individual users that go well beyond basic hardware controls and managing user security. Because so many of these new capabilities—including graphical interfaces, user profiles, e-mail, and other personalized directories—are aimed at personalizing computing experience for individual users, many capabilities that users take for granted on modern networks have been designed specifically to support their needs.

In fact, the operating system capabilities required to support multiple simultaneous users have driven much of the development work involved in building modern operating systems. When multiple individuals can request the same resources, it becomes necessary to synchronize access to those resources, particularly when more than one user wants to change his or her contents. Likewise, there are some resources (for example, employee directories) that many users may want to access but that only a few users should be allowed to change. Although these two scenarios illustrate only a few of the coordination issues that emerge when managing access to shared resources, they capture the kinds of synchronization that operating systems must deliver at the barest minimum.

In addition, when multiple users share access to a single system (or a single network), they expect to share all kinds of information and services as well. These features include items as mundane as shared files and printers as well as more exotic and complex services, such as e-mail and Web sites. Modern operating systems must therefore be able to communicate across networks to synchronize and coordinate multiple copies of the same information, as readily as they must be able to keep user A out of user B's files and vice versa. Support for networking is no longer optional in any operating system, be it on a desktop or a server. Nevertheless, such support is especially important on server machines where services and information must be shared to justify their presence. Windows 2000 offers excellent user and group management options. For example, each user has a profile and security identifier that tells the system the resources to which the user has access as well as the limit on disk space allocated to that user. User and group management is discussed in detail in Chapter 12.

Multiple Tasks

When a runtime environment must be created in which multiple users can share access to a computer, it should be obvious that the system must include some mechanism to support the apparent operation of multiple tasks. Until recently, even the most powerful mainframes supported only a single CPU, yet many such systems provided support for simultaneous access from multiple users. Although a computer with a single CPU can really execute only one task at a time, a bit of technological sleight-of-hand called **virtual multitasking** makes it appear that the computer is executing more than one task at a time.

The sleight-of-hand involved in virtual multitasking exploits the differences in time scale between computer operations and human perception. Fundamentally, virtual multitasking relies on a combination of what computer scientists call **time slicing** and some kind of scheduling system. The scheduling system permits a single task to occupy the CPU for a fixed length of time (called a time slice), after which that task must make way for whatever task is scheduled to occupy the CPU next.

Much of the work involved in designing a robust and fair operating system centers on how tasks are scheduled for operation and what kinds of events or incoming messages are allowed to interrupt a task that may be executing at any given moment. Modern operating systems schedule tasks according to multiple levels of priority, allowing higher-priority tasks access to the CPU on a more or less preferential basis. To prevent low-priority tasks from being permanently denied access to the CPU, such low-priority jobs have their priorities raised over time to ensure that they will ultimately be completed. In addition, when the computer's hardware requires handling, or when an error occurs, it is possible that even the highest-priority tasks will be momentarily interrupted to accommodate such time-sensitive events. In fact, such events are often called **priority interrupts** (or more simply, interrupts) for this very reason.

Multitasking may be virtual (as it must be on a computer with only a single CPU) or real (as it must be on a computer with multiple CPUs). This technique explains how operating systems are able to execute multiple applications at the same time and to support interaction with multiple users at any given moment. Support for multiple users is far more important on servers than on desktop machines, but is a hallmark of most operating systems, including Windows 2000 and UNIX. In most cases, users will "own" unique sessions whenever they access an operating system that supports multiple users. Therefore, some correspondence exists between multitasking and support for multiple users, because each such session invariably runs within its own task.

When a user session is established within the context of a particular task, whenever that session launches an application, or accesses a service, it is customary for the operating system to **launch** (or **spawn**) another task to accommodate that activity. For Windows 2000, such spawned tasks inherit security characteristics from their parent user session. In other operating systems, such as UNIX, a different set of security characteristics may be associated with a spawned process. Although some experts believe that the Windows technique is more secure, others suggest that this strict notion of inheritance is too restrictive, especially when it comes to performing system management tasks. This debate is unlikely to be settled any time soon, but it is important to understand that only the most extreme contortions will permit a system manager to bypass this mechanism on a Windows 2000 machine.

Multiple Threads

Threading is a relatively new execution mechanism in operating systems. In building support for multiple users, operating system designers learned that the overhead involved in stopping one task and starting another could sometimes be prohibitive. This kind of operating system activity, called **context switching**, involves saving the state of the running task, loading in the state of the pending task, and then starting execution of that pending task. In runtime environments where execution of a single instruction occurs in microseconds, it is not uncommon for a context switch to take several milliseconds. As a consequence, operating system designers needed a mechanism to permit related activities to occur more efficiently than by spawning entirely new tasks. This mechanism, which is called **threading**, defines a way for a single task to operate multiple related activities in parallel without imposing the delays associated with a typical context switch when changing from one thread to another. (For example, a background spelling checker in the context of a word processor is an excellent case in point.)

Modern operating systems, including Windows 2000, Windows 98, UNIX, and others, invariably support some kind of threading mechanism. In fact, many modern programming languages, such as Java, also support built-in threading mechanisms. Particularly where network services (such as Web access, file transfers, or e-mail) are concerned, threading provides an extremely efficient way to support a large number of simultaneous users without requiring each user to incur the overhead associated with context switching. This fact explains why so many network services rely heavily on threading as the primary mechanism to support heavy use.

Operating systems themselves, especially modern ones, also rely heavily on threading to allow them to efficiently handle many types of activities at the same time. Developers must therefore write applications that use threading mechanisms explicitly to exploit the potential performance improvements that threading can provide. The trend toward threading helps explain why newer, 32-bit versions of typical productivity applications (for example, word processors, spreadsheets, and so forth) are often more efficient than their older, more compact counterparts.

Key Operating System Functions

Our examination of the evolution of various aspects of modern operating systems has set the stage for our discussion of those functions that any operating system must provide.

At present, you have merely skimmed the surface of the concepts involved and the technologies that underlie them. This section of the chapter examines these concepts and technologies in greater detail.

Operating Systems Sit Between Applications and Hardware

To understand how the operating systems communicate between the applications and the hardware, you need to understand some of the main components of a computer system. These components include the following items:

- Central processing unit (CPU)
- Memory
- Storage
- Input/output (I/O) devices

Each of these components is covered in detail in the following sections. Also discussed is how an operating system communicates between the applications and these components.

Central Processing Unit

The CPU is the brains of the operation. Until recently, it performed all tasks that the system needed to process. You can now get video cards that offload the processing normally performed by the CPU to a processor on the video card. The same is true for some network interface cards.

The processor performs all computations and calculations and communicates with all of the components in the system. The operating system uses the processor or processors to allow multiple applications to request information from the system.

Before more advanced operating systems (such as Windows 2000) became available, operating systems could allow only one application to communicate with the processor. Thus you could run only a single application at a time. With DOS programs, once the program was executed, control was not returned to you until the application ended its run. An exception to this rule was Terminate and Stay Resident (TSR) programs, which executed and left a component of themselves running in memory. Unfortunately, it does not take many of these applications to completely use up the available memory in the computer.

Windows 2000 permits multitasking to take place. With multitasking, multiple applications can execute at the same time. The operating system juggles between them and the processor.

Memory

Memory is what makes your computer work. Without it, the system would be slower than slow, because memory tends to be much faster than hard disks (nanoseconds versus milliseconds)—which also explains why memory is much more expensive than hard disks. When was the last time you bought 13 GB of RAM? The operating system controls how each application talks to memory. To accomplish this task, each application is given its own virtual memory space (for example, 2 GB). As far as the application is concerned, it has the 2 GB of memory all to itself. The same is true for all applications running on the system. You might ask, "But what if my system does not have 2 GB of memory?" Remember that this system involves virtual memory. What this concept really means is that the operating system simply gives the application addresses for 2 GB of memory. When the application writes data to a memory address, the operating system intercepts this request and stores it in a real memory location in physical memory. It then maintains a list of the mapping between the virtual memory address and the real one. It does the same for every application running on the system.

If it runs out of physical memory, the operating system stores the information in a special location on the hard drive (known as the swap file). When the operating system notices that all of physical memory is full, it will find data that has not been accessed for the longest time and write the information to the swap file in **pages** (which are simply sections of memory). When a system is "paging," it transfers data from the physical memory to the swap file and back. Because physical memory is much faster than hard disks, this process slows down the system considerably.

 As a general rule, the more memory you have in your computer, the more information can be stored in memory; therefore, the faster the computer runs. Generally, a memory upgrade shows a larger, noticeable improvement of speed over a processor upgrade.

Storage

Like memory, storage makes a server operate as a server. Most servers fill some sort of file and resource access role. To operate efficiently, the file server must have enough disk space to hold all of the client information that is needed. Today, hard disks are fairly inexpensive. Even some of the high-end SCSI drives have dropped in price considerably over the last few years.

The operating system efficiently accesses the storage resources on the system and allocates some of those resources to users and applications. In Windows 2000, quotas can be set for individual users for directories and disks. This restriction ensures that no one user will take more than his or her fair share of the server resources. To enforce this limitation, Windows 2000 uses the NTFS file system. This file system gives the operating system the ability to assign users and groups permissions to individual files or directories. Unlike with older operating systems, such as Windows 98, multiple users can use the same system without ever having access to each other's files.

Some operating systems—namely, the Windows 2000 Server family—also use the available disks to create fault-tolerant file systems that will survive a single hard disk failure. They accomplish this goal by logically creating a single drive from multiple disks. The disks are then presented to the applications as a single volume.

Input/Output (I/O) Devices

The I/O devices allow applications to communicate with the external world. They can include modems, mice, keyboards, scanners, printers, video displays, and multimedia devices. The operating system creates a generic interface for such applications. Before modern operating systems became available, the individual applications were charged with the role of communicating with each device. Because no standards existed, every device had to have a driver installed in the application for it to work. Advanced operating systems have since taken over the role of communicating with the devices. Today, the application simply issues the operating system commands such as "dial this number on the modem" or "display a window 100 pixels by 100 pixels."

To make this process become a reality, device drivers are installed on the operating system. The operating system learns how to communicate with the device, which allows all the applications that are installed on the system to communicate with the device as well. Installing a new device is easy. Simply install the physical device, and then install the device driver in the operating system, and the device becomes available to all the applications. When a new version of the device driver is released, you simply update the driver at the operating system level and all the applications will be able to use the new drivers.

Operating Systems Ensure a Robust, Secure Environment

One of the biggest advantages to running an operating system such as Windows 2000 is its built-in security. It uses multiuser security to control which users have access to system resources. Multiple users can log into the system at the same time, while the operating system maintains a list of the permissions that are assigned to each user and group on the system. With this kind of security, an administrator can really customize how users access resources on the system.

A major drawback of installing new operating systems is the need to support existing applications. As Microsoft evolved its operating systems, the company maintained some level of backward compatibility. If this compatibility did not exist, many applications would not run on the new operating systems, and the operating systems might not receive the industry acceptance that is needed to support them. To accomplish this goal, Windows 2000 creates **virtual machines** to emulate the older operating systems. With a virtual machine, the application running on a particular machine believes that it is running on, for example, an

MS-DOS machine or a Windows 3.1 machine. The fact that it is running on a Windows 2000 system remains completely hidden from the application. The only issue with this process is that Windows 2000 does not allow applications to directly communicate with any of the system devices, such as memory and storage. Any application that attempts to access the hardware directly is terminated, which is necessary to protect the system from instabilities that can occur by having applications communicate with hardware inappropriately.

Operating Systems Define Consistent Interfaces

Applications share many similar requirements, such as window interfaces or access to the I/O devices. Operating systems provide common services and activities for these applications. For example, any DOS application that needed to display graphics on the screen had to do so by itself. It needed the driver for the video card, and it had to "teach" the display how to draw the window and any menus that would appear in the windows. The same was true for every application that was running on the system. As you can see, many of the processes run on an older operating system, such as MS-DOS, were duplicated by every application that was running on the system.

Graphical and other metaphors define a user interface. By "teaching" the operating system how to display information on the screen, that task was taken away from the applications. Because of the many different views on how the interface should look, developers could never agree on a common interface. It therefore became the job of the operating system to display information. Now when an application needs to open a file, it makes a call to the operating system, which can open a window that allows the user to browse to the correct location and open the file.

Operating Systems Manage Resource Allocation

Mediation is the key to successful system operation. If applications are not controlled, they can corrupt the system. This problem was especially noticeable in Windows 3.1 and Windows 95. A badly written application could bring the entire system crashing down. Because any application could communicate with the hardware on the system, when applications tried to access the hardware at the same time or modified another application's properties, the system could crash.

To prevent this problem from happening in Windows 2000, Microsoft introduced two modes: the user mode and the kernel mode. The user mode is where the applications reside, and the kernel mode is where the operating system exists. Any application that needs to communicate with any of the system's hardware must do so through the kernel mode. This restriction allows the operating system to control how and which applications communicate with the hardware. For this control to take place, the application must be written to use this type of a model. These modes of operation and the ways in which they function in Windows 2000 are discussed in detail in Chapter 2.

Types of Operating Systems

Operating systems can be classified into two categories: operating systems designed for individual users and operating systems designed for a multiuser environment. These two types of operating systems are covered in the following sections.

End User or Single User

A single-user operating system is optimized for foreground applications, and allows any application that is running on the desktop to use more resources than an application that runs on the network. This approach allows applications to run on the system more efficiently. These types of operating systems, such as Windows 2000 Professional, are designed to run applications such as word processors and spreadsheets.

Server-Oriented

A server-oriented operating system is optimized to run back-end applications, such as e-mail services, naming servers, Web services, and file and print services. Processes running in the background get precedence over ones that run in the foreground. For this reason, word processor and spreadsheet applications run more slowly on a server than on a workstation.

Comparing Windows 2000 Professional and Windows 2000 Server

With Windows NT, Microsoft originally offered two versions of the operating system: Windows NT Workstation and Windows NT Server. Windows NT Workstation was designed as a secure, robust, business-geared operating system. It was Microsoft's vision that the corporate desktop would run this operating system rather than Windows 95 or 98. At the same time, Windows NT Server was designed to run the back-end applications of the organizations, such as e-mail, database, and Web servers. More advanced features, such as server clustering, were eventually introduced in a third version known as Windows NT Enterprise Server. This version of the operating system was aimed at high-end, large implementations of messaging and database systems.

With Windows 2000, Microsoft changed its focus slightly. Four different versions of the Windows 2000 operating system exist:

- Windows 2000 Professional
- Windows 2000 Server
- Windows 2000 Advanced Server
- Windows 2000 Datacenter Server

The following sections cover each of these operating systems, including their uses and functions.

Windows 2000 Professional

As stated earlier, this version of Windows 2000 replaces Windows 95, Windows 98, and Windows NT Workstation and is designed for the business-based desktop. It incorporates the security and stability of Windows NT with the Plug and Play capabilities of Windows 95 and Windows 98. Windows 2000 Professional includes several new features:

- **Virtual private network (VPN) support.** This option provides secure connectivity to an internal network using a public network such as the Internet.

- **Offline folder.** This new feature in Windows 2000 allows you to store commonly accessed network documents on your workstation so that they will be available when your system is not connected to the network. Modified files are automatically synchronized when you connect to the network and log on.

- **Internet Printing Protocol (IPP).** This new protocol allows clients to connect to a printer that is connected to a Windows 2000 network using a URL, to download and install drivers over the Internet, and to view the printer status in a Web browser, such as Internet Explorer.

- **Add/Remove Hardware Wizard.** Windows 2000 introduces a Control Panel applet that was badly missed in Windows NT. This applet allows the operating system to detect and install new hardware devices.

- **Disk duplication.** This feature allows for the duplication of system hard drives for use with third-party disk imaging software.

- **New Backup application.** Unlike its Windows NT predecessor, the Windows 2000 Backup program has many new, advanced features, such as the ability to back up to any media, not just to tape.

- **FAT32 file system support.** Windows 2000 now supports the FAT file system, which is used in newer versions of Windows 95 and in Windows 98.

- **New security features.** Windows 2000 supports more security options than any previous versions of Windows, including **Kerberos security**, Smart Card support, **Internet Protocol Security (IPSec)**, and **Encrypted File System (EFS)**.

Table 1-1 outlines the component requirements for Windows 2000 Professional on two types of systems.

Table 1-1 Component requirements for Windows 2000 Professional

Component	Intel Platform	Alpha Platform
CPU	Minimum: 133 MHz Pentium Processor Recommended: 300 MHz Pentium II Processor	Compaq Alpha Processor
Memory	Minimum: 64 MB Recommended: 132 MB	Minimum: 64 MB Recommended: 132 MB
Disk space	2 GB hard drive with 1 GB free space. (Additional free hard disk space is required if you are installing over a network.)	2 GB hard drive with 1 GB free space. (Additional free hard disk space is required if you are installing over a network.)
Networking	A network interface card (NIC) that appears on the Hardware Compatibility List (HCL) with the appropriate Intel-based drivers	A network interface card (NIC) that appears on the Hardware Compatibility List (HCL) with the appropriate Alpha-based drivers
Input devices	Keyboard and mouse	Keyboard and mouse
Additional	CD-ROM drive 16× or faster recommended	CD-ROM drive 16× or faster recommended.
Display	Minimum: VGA-compatible video card and monitor (640×480) Recommended: SuperVGA-compatible video card and monitor (800×600 or 1024×768)	Minimum: VGA-compatible video card and monitor (640×480) Recommended: SuperVGA-compatible video card and monitor (800×600 or 1024×768)

Microsoft maintains a database of all devices that have been tested with Windows 2000. These devices are the only ones for which Microsoft provides support if you should run into problems. This database is known as the Windows 2000 Hardware Compatibility List (HCL). You should verify that all components in your systems are listed on the HCL. A copy of the HCL is found on the Windows 2000 CD-ROM in the \support\hcl.txt file. Remember, however, that this file is only as current as the Windows 2000 CD. With today's rapidly changing computer world, this list will quickly become obsolete. For this reason, Microsoft maintains an ever-changing, online, searchable version of the HCL. The online version of the HCL can be found at *http://www.microsoft.com/hcl*.

As stated earlier in the chapter, Windows 2000 Professional can support a maximum of two processors. If your system has a single processor but is upgraded to a two-processor system, you may need to reinstall Windows 2000 or run a Resource Kit tool to make the change.

Windows 2000 Server

Windows 2000 Server is Microsoft's entry-level server solution. Most organizations will run this version, which, closely ties in with Windows 2000 Professional to create a stable and secure business-networking environment. Windows 2000 Server includes all of the features found in Windows 2000 Professional, plus the following:

- **Active Directory.** This feature offers support for Microsoft's new directory service.
- **Remote Computer Management.** This service, which is also included with Windows 2000 Professional, adds the capability to configure the properties of any server service or application that may be installed on a remote system.
- **Remote Installation Service (RIS).** RIS allows for the remote installation of Windows 2000 Professional systems from a central networked location.
- **Group policies.** With this service, an administrator can control the amount of access that users have to applications and systems based on the users' permissions.
- **Terminal services.** This set of services provides the Windows 2000 Server system with the ability to support multiple client sessions running on a single computer. It greatly reduces the total cost of ownership (TCO) by minimizing the amount of hardware and software upgrades that need to be done on each individual client system.
- **Remote storage.** An administrator can configure this service to automatically migrate files that are not commonly accessed to a remote storage device, such as a tape backup system, so as to free disk space for applications and services that require it.
- **Services for Macintosh.** This service connects Apple Macintosh systems to a Windows 2000 system and allows for file and print sharing to take place.
- **Gateway Services for NetWare (GSNW).** This service allows multiple Windows clients to access file and print resources on one or more Novell NetWare servers without the need to reconfigure all clients to log into the NetWare network.
- **Disk quotas.** With Windows 2000 Server's new NTFS file system (Version 5), as an administrator you can now assign users quotas on folders, volumes, or disks. This assignment ensures that a single user does not monopolize the hard disk space that exists on your server.

Table 1-2 outlines the component requirements for Windows 2000 Server on two types of systems.

Windows 2000 Server supports a maximum of four Symmetric Multiple Processor (SMP) systems. If you install Windows 2000 Server on a new system or install a fresh copy on an existing system, however, you can get only two processors at a maximum. The only way that you can run Windows 2000 Server on a four-processor system is if you have Windows NT 4.0 installed on the system with four-way SMP support and you upgrade the system.

Table 1-2   Component requirements for Windows 2000 Server

Component	Intel Platform	Alpha Platform
CPU	Minimum: 133 MHz Pentium Class Processor Recommended: 400 MHz Pentium II Processor	Compaq Alpha-based Processor
Memory	Minimum: 128 MB for servers supporting 5 or fewer clients Recommended: 256 MB for servers supporting more than 5 clients	Minimum: 96 MB Recommended: 128 MB or higher
Disk space	Minimum: 685 MB for the partition where the Windows 2000 operating system files reside Recommended: 1 GB for the partition where the Windows 2000 operating system files reside	Minimum: 367 MB for the partition where the Windows 2000 operating system files reside Recommended: 1 GB for the partition where the Windows 2000 operating system files reside
Networking	One or more NICs that appear on the HCL with the appropriate Alpha-based drivers	One or more NICs that appear on the HCL with the appropriate Alpha-based drivers
Input devices	Keyboard and mouse	Keyboard and mouse
Additional	12× CD-ROM drive or higher	12× CD-ROM drive or higher
Display	Minimum: VGA-compatible video card and monitor (640×480) Recommended: SuperVGA-compatible video card and monitor (800×600 or 1024×768)	Minimum: VGA-compatible video card and monitor (640×480) Recommended: SuperVGA-compatible video card and monitor (800×600 or 1024×768)

Windows 2000 Advanced Server

The third member of the Windows 2000 family is Windows 2000 Advanced Server. This operating system provides you with all the features of Windows 2000 Server, but is designed to run on large enterprise systems. This version stems from Microsoft's belief that some of the most advanced features should exist only on the high-end server solutions (and the company can charge more money for these solutions, of course). Microsoft started this trend with the release of Windows NT Server Enterprise Edition. Windows 2000 Advanced Server is designed to run on some of the new-wave eight-way SMP servers. As well as supporting a large number of processors, it also supports internal system memory of as much as 64 GB.

Following are some of the services that are included in Windows 2000 Advanced Server:

- **Network load balancing.** This service allows you to configure your network so that some network-based servers, such as Web services, are available during most of the time. These services can therefore be shared between two or more Windows 2000 Advanced Server systems and fail over between them automatically.

- **Windows clustering.** This feature allows for the implementation of Windows 2000 clusters. A cluster can automatically detect if an application, service, or server fails and then migrate the failed component to another system in the cluster. This system is designed for mission-critical applications and servers.

Windows 2000 Datacenter Server

Rounding up the Windows 2000 Server family is Microsoft's Windows 2000 Datacenter Server. This server is designed as the powerhouse of Windows 2000 networks. It contains all of the components in Windows 2000 Advanced Server, but allows for more processor and memory to be accessed by the operating system. The regular shipping version of Windows 2000 Datacenter Server will support a maximum of 16 processors, whereas the original equipment manufacturer (OEM) versions will support as many as 32 processors in a single system. (Windows 2000 Advanced Server also includes more advanced clustering components to allow for larger and more stable Windows 2000 clusters to be designed, implemented, and maintained.)

One of the most impressive new features of Windows 2000 Datacenter Server is its ability to assign processors and memory to individual applications or groups. For example, if your organization purchases an eight-way SMP system for the Human Resources and the Payroll Departments (with 16 GB of RAM), you can assign four processors and 8 GB of RAM to the Human Resources department and the same amount to the Payroll Department. If the Human Resources applications exceed their processors and memory, they will not be allowed to use the processors and memory assigned to the Payroll Department.

As you can well imagine, this system is not for everyone. Along with the increased cost of the operating system, 16-way (or higher) SMP systems are not cheap. This solution is designed for extremely large implementations, such as online transaction systems and very large data warehouses.

CHAPTER SUMMARY

- Operating systems are designed to bridge the gap between the applications and the hardware. They have continued to evolve over the last few years and will continue to do so for many years to come. One benefit of this evolution is the fact that operating systems have become more reliable and more stable.

- Early computers did not have operating systems at all. They simply ran commands in sequence to accomplish their goals. Some of the first computers used switches to receive the commands, or special cards that were fed into the system.

- It is important to understand how the operating system communicates with each of the different hardware components that exist in all systems, such as the CPU, memory, storage, and I/O devices. New versions of operating systems, Windows 2000 included, isolate these components from the applications. This structure makes the operating system much more stable than older systems, because a single application cannot corrupt the entire system.

- Microsoft released four versions of Windows 2000: Professional, Server, Advanced Server, and Datacenter Server. Windows 2000 Professional is the business desktop solution that replaces Windows NT Workstation and Windows 95/98. The Server version is designed for use with most server-based systems and offers a robust, scalable operating system. With Windows 2000 Advanced Server, Microsoft has included advanced support for more processors, more memory, and clustering capabilities. Rounding up the Windows 2000 family, Datacenter Server is designed for extremely large enterprise implementations of Windows 2000.

KEY TERMS

Add/Remove Hardware Wizard — A Control Panel applet introduced in Windows 2000 that was badly missed in Windows NT. This applet allows the operating system to detect and install new hardware devices.

batch jobs — Sequences that are submitted for execution on a computer as a single task.

batch system — A runtime environment in which one program or application follows another in sequence.

central processing unit (CPU) — The "brains" of the computer. The components that complete most of the calculations on a system.

clustering — The ability of multiple servers to function as a single, logical server. A clustering facility allows tasks and threads to be distributed among the servers in a cluster in much the same way that an operating system that supports multiple CPUs distributes threads and tasks on a single multiprocessor machine.

command language — A collection of terms that allow a user to tell the operating system what to do.

context switching — The process of saving the state of the running task, loading the state of the pending task, and then starting execution of that pending task.

disk duplication — A feature that allows for the duplication of system hard drives for use with third-party disk imaging software.

disk quotas — A feature available with Windows 2000 Server's new NTFS file system (Version 5). As an administrator, you can now assign users quotas on folders, volumes, or disks. This feature ensures that a single user does not monopolize the hard disk space that exists on your server.

Encrypted File System (EFS) — A system for encrypting files on a Windows 2000 system to protect them from unauthorized access.

Gateway Services for NetWare (GSNW) — A service that allows multiple Windows clients to access file and print resources on one or more Novell NetWare servers without the need to reconfigure all clients to log into the NetWare network.

group policies — A service that allows an administrator to control the amount of access that users have to applications and systems based on the users' permissions.

Internet Printing Protocol (IPP) — A new protocol that allows clients to connect to a printer that is connected to a Windows 2000 network using a URL, to download and install drivers over the Internet, and to view the printer status in a Web browser, such as Internet Explorer.

Internet Protocol Security (IPSec) — A new, secure, industry standard implementation of the popular TCP/IP protocol.

Kerberos security — An industry standard form of security authentication that is used by Windows 2000.

launch — The process of executing an application.

multiprocessing — A system with multiple CPUs installed.

network load balancing — A feature that allows you to configure your network so that some network-based servers, such as Web services, are available most of the time. These services can therefore be shared between two or more Windows 2000 Advanced Server systems and fail over between them automatically.

offline folder — A new feature in Windows 2000 that allows you to store commonly accessed network documents on your workstation so that they are available when your system is not connected to the network. Modified files are automatically synchronized when you reconnect to the network and log on.

pages — Sections of memory used by an operating system to transfer data from the physical memory to the swap file and back. Because physical memory is much faster than hard disks, paging slows down the system considerably.

priority interrupts — A way for hardware devices to notify the CPU that they need its attention.

Remote Computer Management — A service, also included with Windows 2000 Professional, that adds the capability to configure the properties of any server service or application that might be installed on a remote system.

Remote Installation Service (RIS) — A service that allows for the remote installation of Windows 2000 Professional systems from a central networked location.

remote storage — A service that an administrator can configure to automatically migrate files that are not commonly accessed to a remote storage device, such as a tape backup system, so as to free up disk space for applications and services that require it.

runtime environment — The packaging of common control elements for applications to use.

Services for Macintosh — A service that connects Apple Macintosh systems to a Windows 2000 system and allows file and print sharing.

spawn — Same as *launch*. The process of executing an application.

terminal services — A service that provides Windows 2000 Server systems with the ability to support multiple client sessions running on a single computer. This feature greatly reduces TCO by minimizing the amount of hardware and software upgrades needed for each individual client system.

threading — A way for a single task to operate multiple related activities in parallel without imposing the delays associated with a typical context switch.

time slicing — A fixed length of time that the system allows a single task to occupy the CPU.

virtual machines — A way for Windows 2000 to let non-Windows 2000 applications run on the system. It emulates the native operating system of the application.

virtual multitasking — A way of making a computer appear as if it is executing more than one thing at a time.

virtual private network (VPN) — A way to connect to an internal network securely through a public network, such as the Internet.

Windows clustering — A feature that allows for the implementation of Windows 2000 clusters. A cluster can automatically detect if an application, service, or server fails and then migrate the failed component to another system in the cluster. It is designed for mission-critical applications and servers.

REVIEW QUESTIONS

1. Which Windows 2000 version or versions support disk quotas? Choose all that apply.
   a. Professional
   b. Server
   c. Advanced Server
   d. Datacenter Server

2. Which version or versions of Windows 2000 support clustering? Choose all that apply.
   a. Professional
   b. Server
   c. Advanced Server
   d. Datacenter Server

3. All versions of Windows 2000 Server support at least four-way processing. True or False?

4. Multitasking is defined as the ability to communicate with multiple processors at the same time on a single system. True or False?

5. Under Windows 2000, applications are allowed to communicate directly with the hardware. True or False?

6. All applications under Windows 2000 run in which mode?
   a. Protected
   b. Real
   c. Kernel
   d. User

7. Which version or versions of Windows 2000 will run on the Compaq Alpha platform? Choose all that apply.
   a. Professional
   b. Server
   c. Advanced Server
   d. Datacenter Server

8. A Windows 2000 system must have a CD-ROM drive before the operating system can be installed. True or False?

9. When Windows 2000 runs legacy applications, it emulates them by running which of the following?
   a. Virtual system
   b. Virtual machine
   c. Spawned application
   d. The application in real mode

10. Operating systems today give application developers a standard interface with which to work. True or False?

11. In a single-user operating system, which is true?
    a. Foreground applications get more resources.
    b. Background applications get more resources.
    c. Networking is not an option.
    d. Background and foreground applications get resources assigned to them equally.

12. Which version or versions of Windows 2000 support a maximum of 32 processors?
    a. Professional
    b. Server
    c. Advanced Server
    d. Datacenter Server

13. In a server-oriented operating system, which of the following is true?
    a. Foreground applications get more resources.
    b. Background applications get more resources.
    c. Networking is not an option.
    d. Background and foreground applications get resources assigned to them equally.

14. The operating system itself runs in which mode?
    a. Real
    b. Protected
    c. Kernel
    d. User

15. Services for Macintosh makes a Windows 2000 server appear like a Macintosh server to Apple Macintosh clients. True or False?

16. All versions of Windows 2000 support Remote Installation Services. True or False?

17. Which version or versions of Windows 2000 are designed as desktop operating systems?
    a. Professional
    b. Server

c. Advanced Server

d. Datacenter Server

18. All versions of Windows 2000 support offline folders. True or False?
19. Windows 2000 will run on a Pentium 166 system with 16 MB of RAM. True or False?
20. Terminal services are supported under Windows 2000 Professional. True or False?

HANDS-ON PROJECTS

Project 1-1

To search for a hardware component in the online version of Microsoft's Hardware Compatibility List:

1. Open your browser and go to *http://www.microsoft.com/hcl/*.
2. Enter a product description in the **Search For The Following** field.
3. Choose a product category from the drop-down list.
4. Click the **Go** icon.
5. A list of all supported platforms appears.

Project 1-2

To find more information about the different Windows 2000 versions:

1. Open your Web browser and go to
   http://www.microsoft.com/windows/professional/default.asp (the Windows 2000 Professional page).
2. Open your Web browser and go to *http://www.microsoft.com/windows/server/default.asp* (the Windows 2000 Server page).

CASE PROJECTS

1. Your organization would like to purchase a single system with 16 processors and have the processors and memory assigned to individual departments with no overlap. Which version of Windows 2000 does your organization need?
2. A client of yours would like to implement a Windows 2000 cluster. Which Windows 2000 solution would you recommend?

CHAPTER 2

EXAMINING THE PARTS OF AN OPERATING SYSTEM

> **After reading this chapter and completing the exercises, you will be able to:**
> - Explain the purpose of operating systems
> - List the parts of a modern operating system
> - Explain how the pieces of an operating system relate to one another
> - Describe the difference between kernel mode and user mode and explain why the difference exists
> - Relate this information to the Windows 2000 architecture

The basic functions of an operating system are to create an operating environment for applications and to provide those applications with some base functionality. Technically speaking, an operating system isn't strictly necessary. You *could* design an application to interact directly with computer hardware, reading and writing data to disk and displaying it on the monitor. An old version of WordPerfect did something similar, bypassing DOS to pull data from the keyboard buffer so that it could display user input more quickly than could applications that relied on the operating system. Designing such an application would be difficult, however, because it would require application designers to build code to interact with system hardware into the applications. It would also mean that the designers would have to create a different version of the application for every hardware version— something that is very difficult to do. Rather than design applications to interact with system hardware, operating systems now handle that task. Of course, operating systems provide other important functionality.

Another reason to prevent applications from communicating directly with hardware is that separating the two keeps applications from messing up the hardware in a way that crashes the system. Games supply a prime example of this kind of problem. Imagine that you're running around in MechCommander, or some other game, under Windows 98, about to capture the fort . . . and then the music begins droning a single note and the screen freezes. Some kind of communication with the sound card has caused not only the game but also the entire operating system to crash. If you press Ctrl+Alt+Delete to bring up the task list, nothing happens—the mouse and keyboard no longer respond. There's nothing left to do but press the Reset button on the computer and reboot. If the operating system handles all communication between applications and hardware, however, then communication with hardware happens in a standard way and this kind of scenario becomes much less likely.

Some operating systems, such as Windows 9x, permit applications to have some communication with hardware, but Windows 2000 (Win2K) and its Windows NT predecessors do not. For this reason, some games do not run under Windows NT or Win2K—they need to access system hardware to work. The Win2K insistence that it handle all communication between applications and hardware limits the set of applications that will run under the operating system, but also makes Win2K more robust (that is, less likely to crash) than operating systems that do permit such communication.

This chapter discusses the parts of a modern operating system, using Windows 2000 as a model, and then shows you how Win2K organizes those parts into a coherent whole and uses them to support applications and user needs.

GENERAL PRINCIPLES OF MODERN OPERATING SYSTEM ARCHITECTURE

Traditionally, operating systems were monolithic. All of the **helper** parts of the operating system—the parts that allowed applications to communicate with hardware—were lumped together in a single unit and communicated with each other in a separate area of memory, away from applications. As shown in Figure 2-1, these parts were interdependent, which meant that changing one part—such as the way device drivers worked—meant that you might have to update the rest of the operating system so that it would continue to function properly. Unfortunately, the fact that all parts of the operating system were designed to run in the same memory space meant that one part of the operating system could corrupt another part. For example, if the first part was badly designed, it might do something it wasn't supposed to do, such as editing the data accessible to the second part.

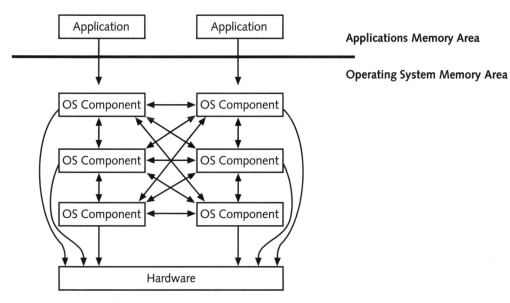

Figure 2-1 A model of a monolithic operating system

Because of these drawbacks, modern operating systems are inclined to take a different approach, using a layered model or a client/server model. In the layered model (see Figure 2-2), the operating system is divided into modules that are layered on top of each other like a wedding cake. Also like a wedding cake, the pieces are interdependent to some degree—if you remove the bottom layer, the layer on top of it will collapse. They are also modular, however. To continue with the wedding cake analogy, if the original operating system were all vanilla and you replaced layer 3 with a chocolate layer, the whole thing would still work together—you wouldn't have to redesign the other layers to work with the chocolate layer. In a layered operating system, each module contains code that the other layers can talk to so as to communicate with that layer or transfer data between the layers.

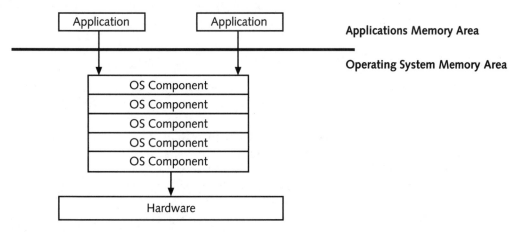

Figure 2-2 A model of a layered operating system

The client/server operating system model (shown in Figure 2-3) divides the operating system into a number of server processes, each of which implements a part of the operating system, such as memory management or accessing hard disks. The **client** (an application or another server process) sends a message to the server process to do something. A messaging part of the operating service passes the message to the server process, which then does whatever the client requested. The messaging part of the operating system then passes the results back to the client. The only disadvantage of the client/server model is that, in its pure form, it's very slow because of the messaging back and forth that is needed to get anything done.

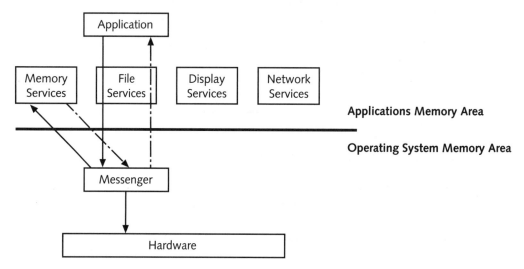

Figure 2-3   A model of a client/server operating system

Windows 2000 combines the layered model and the client/server model. It is designed as a collection of discrete modules that can communicate with each other either directly or via the messaging component mentioned earlier; the modules are layered so that they support each other as well. The remainder of this chapter first discusses the parts of Windows 2000 and then considers how those parts fit together.

Environmental Subsystems

For applications to execute in an operating system, they must have access to those pieces of the operating system that contain the functions they need, such as functions providing for allocation of CPU time or use of RAM for storing data. The part of an operating system that enables such access is called the **environmental subsystem**. Different environmental subsystems expose different parts of the core operating system capabilities. Consequently, applications, which are built to expect a certain kind of support from their operating environment, can run only in that environment. For example, UNIX applications can't run in Windows because the UNIX and Windows operating environments are different. The only way that you can run an application in an operating environment for which it wasn't built is via a mechanism called **emulation**. Emulation creates a compatible operating environment for the application, then translates the application's requests so that the local operating environment can execute them. Because of the overhead incurred in the translation process, emulation is slow.

Windows 98 supports only a single environmental subsystem, which you see when you start up the computer. Win2K supports three such subsystems: the 32-bit Windows (Win32) subsystem you see when you start the computer, POSIX, and, on x86 systems, OS/2 1.0. (The most recent version of OS/2 is 3.0.) You can review all of the current subsystem information by using the Win2K Registry Editor, which displays a graphical image of all operating system information. As you can see in Figure 2-4, the Win32 subsystem starts by default and is necessary to the operating system, whereas the OS/2 and POSIX subsystems are optional and don't start unless you specifically run them. The "Required" values mean that the Debug and Windows subsystems must be loaded for Win2K to work. Debug is blank because it's used for internal Microsoft testing; Windows is defined as being Csrss.exe, which is the executable name of the Win32 subsystem. To start a subsystem, you must run it like a program, much as you might type Winword.exe at the command prompt to run Microsoft Word. When it's loading, Win2K runs Csrss.exe automatically.

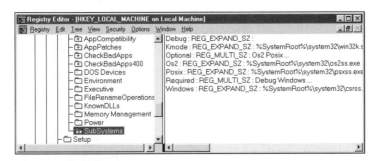

Figure 2-4 Registry values for environmental subsystems

 A 32-bit operating system supports 32-bit instructions, which is the technical way of saying that every communication it makes with a computer's hardware contains 32 bits of data. The larger each instruction is, the more capabilities the operating system has, because it can tell the hardware to do more things in a single instruction. Win2K is a 32-bit operating system, as is the Windows environmental subsystem. The OS/2 and POSIX environmental subsystems are 16-bit, which makes them slightly slower than the other subsystems.

How do applications use the subsystems to communicate with the operating system's capabilities? Each subsystem contains a collection of **function calls**, which are predefined messages that the subsystem can use to communicate with the core operating system functions. (They're referred to as "calls" because a program "calls" a function to use it.) A subsystem's communications are limited to those function calls, just as a person who speaks only English is limited to expressing the thoughts for which English words exist.

In Win2K, function calls can't be mixed between subsystems. That's because although two subsystems may share some capabilities, they don't use the same function calls—they don't speak the same "language." For this reason, an application designed to use a particular set of function calls can't run under a subsystem that doesn't support them. This fact explains why the POSIX and OS/2 environmental subsystems aren't good for much—they're very abbreviated versions of the environmental subsystems and don't support many of the function calls used by other versions of these subsystems. Consequently, you can't even run all OS/2 applications in the OS/2 subsystem because the subsystem doesn't support all of the OS/2 function calls. Not all OS/2 functions are included in the environmental subsystem, although most of the functions required to run and display OS/2 applications are. Thus, unless you must support POSIX or OS/2 applications, use of these subsystems is not recommended.

Win2K has two classes of functions: those that call parts of the core system services, and those that call a support function, such as a part of the Win32 subsystem or the heap service that allocates resources to applications. Both types of function calls are part of **dynamic link libraries (DLLs)**, which are essentially function-specific collections of functions that an environmental subsystem supports. The Win32 subsystem, for example, supports Gdi32.dll, which is the dynamic link library that contains all of the functions needed to support graphical output. Collectively, an environmental subsystem's DLLs that provide a standard interface to the core operating system functions are called its **application programming interface (API)**. That is, the API provides applications with a standard interface to the workings of the computer. It makes it possible to change the inner workings of the operating system without affecting the applications, so long as the function calls remain the same.

A good analogy is driving a car. Because cars have a standard API (steering wheel, clutch, windshield wipers, and so forth), once you learn how to drive a car, you can drive any vehicle that works like the one on which you learned to drive, whether it's a Hyundai or a Porsche. The interface for the cars remains the same even if the inner workings do not. Along these same lines, if an API of an OS has changed, the OS itself remains largely the same, but functions differently under the hood. Consider the Telephony API (TAPI). Because communications carriers' technology changes frequently, the API must change to provide the most efficient method for communication between the carrier and the operating system. Users remain largely unaware of these changes, because they just connect to the Internet in the way they always did through the operating system.

 Not all DLLs reside in the environmental subsystems. Ntdll.dll is a collection of two classes of system functions: one to call core operating system functions and one to call functions that are part of subsystems.

Win32 Subsystem

The Win32 subsystem is the most important environmental subsystem for Win2K, because the rest of the operating system depends on it to expose the necessary parts of the core operating system. As noted earlier, the other two subsystems start only on demand, when you run an application that requires their support. The Win32 subsystem, in contrast, must always be running. If the environmental subsystem crashes, or you stop it, then the entire operating system will crash and you must restart the computer.

The Win32 subsystem contains the following features:

- The environmental subsystem process (Csrss.exe), supports display of text windows (such as the Win2K command prompt), provides the ability to create processes and threads, and offers some support for creating the Virtual DOS Machines that Win2K uses to support DOS and Windows 3.x applications.
- The Win32K.sys device driver contains the Windows Manager, which is responsible for displaying window-based applications (which means any Windows application) and collecting user input, and the graphical device interface (GDI), which creates printer and monitor output.
- Subsystem DLLs translate application calls directed to the API to the core operating system components.
- Graphics device drivers take the graphical instructions that Gdi32.dll puts together and pass them to the video and printer drivers that constitute the software interface to the video boards and printers.

If you wanted to run Microsoft Word application, for example, you'd run it in the Win32 subsystem that's already running, because Microsoft Word requires some function calls found only in this operating environment. When you click the Microsoft Word icon to start the application, Csrss.exe starts the application, User.dll draws the application's windows and buttons, and Gdi32.dll sends the windows and buttons to the monitor for display. When you save a document, another one of the subsystem .DLLs calls the operating system's ability to write data to a file on the hard disk.

Win32 applications are not the only ones to use the Win32 subsystem. If you run a Win16 or DOS application on a Win2K machine, when it starts the application, Win2K creates a special operating environment to accommodate the legacy application. This operating environment runs in the Win32 subsystem, rather than directly in the Win2K operating environment.

POSIX Subsystem

The Portable Operating System Interface (based on) UNIX (POSIX) is a collection of international standards for UNIX-like operating system interfaces. The idea is that, if the vendors creating operating systems follow a standard, then applications built for one version of POSIX will work on all versions of POSIX. This standardization is necessary because of the plethora of essentially incompatible UNIX versions that exist.

The Win2K POSIX environmental subsystem is based on one of the many POSIX standards (implying that this idea of creating a standard interface doesn't seem to have worked so well): POSIX.1. Microsoft included POSIX in the original design of Win2K mainly to satisfy a U.S. government requirement for POSIX support. POSIX.1's API is very limited, however, and requires some support from the Win32 subsystem for display and communication between applications.

OS/2 Subsystem

The OS/2 environmental subsystem is based on an old version of OS/2— that is, version 1.2. Like the POSIX subsystem, its capabilities are limited even for those who would like to run OS/2 applications. This subsystem is supported only on x86 systems, not the Alpha chips used in high-end servers. More important, it supports only OS/2 1.2 character-based applications; it cannot handle the graphical OS/2 applications. (An add-on to the subsystem can display the OS/2 2.1 graphical interface, but the OS/2 API still supports only character-based applications.) Even those applications are limited in their functionality, however. As noted earlier, for security reasons, Windows NT-based operating systems don't allow applications to directly access hardware, so OS/2 applications that use a technique called advanced video (which directly communicates with the video card) aren't supported in the Win2K environment. Like POSIX, the OS/2 environmental subsystem is largely a decorative add-on to Win2K, rather than a useful component.

Executive

The executive portion of Win2K is loaded with a file called Ntoskrnl.exe, which you can find in the %*systemroot*%\system32 folder (WINNT\system32 on most computers). The executive component of the operating system is modular by nature and contains the following major items:

- Process and Thread Manager
- Virtual Memory Manager
- Security Reference Monitor
- Input/Output (normally shortened to I/O) Manager
- Cache Manager

The following sections discuss each of these modules in detail.

Process and Thread Manager

The Process and Thread Manager creates and terminates **processes** and **threads**. Processes and threads are discussed further in Chapter 4, "Allocating and Managing Operating System Resources." The basic idea is that the executable files on your system—files such as Sol.exe—don't actually do anything. These files are known as **executable images**. When you start an executable image, Win2K first determines what kind of file it is and what kind of environmental subsystem it requires. The Process and Thread Manager then creates a process for that image; this process defines the relative importance of the functions that the executable is supposed to carry out, gives it some virtual memory areas in which to store data, and defines the operating environment available to the image.

 Typically, but not always, the ratio of processes to executable images is 1:1.

One part of the process is called *a thread*, which is the executable element of the image. Every process always has at least one thread, though it may spawn more to support the application as necessary. Threads are allocated CPU time based on their relative importance and are the "worker bees" that allow the executable file to carry out its intended tasks.

As each thread finishes, it terminates and releases its resources back to the process pool. When the last thread in a process terminates, the Process and Thread Manager ends the process and releases all of the process's resources so that other processes can allocate them to their threads.

Although the processes themselves don't execute, people—and the Win2K diagnostic tools—often refer to processes running on the server, rather than threads. It's a convenient form of shorthand that refers to all threads in a process.

Win2K has another process-related structure that's new to the Windows NT environment: **jobs**. A job controls certain attributes of the processes associated with it, such as the default working set (the amount of process-related data that the process gets to keep in RAM, rather than have paged to disk; the next section provides a brief introduction to virtual memory) allowed by each process within the job, its total CPU time limit, the per-process CPU time limit, the maximum number of processes associated with the job, the priority class for the processes, and the processor affinity, if any (that is, the preferred processor to use in a multiprocessor computer). The main function of a job is to allow Win2K to deal with certain processes as groups, rather than as separate tasks. This functionality is new to Win2K, and few applications currently take advantage of it.

Virtual Memory Manager

One of the resources that a process makes available to its threads is a set of virtual memory addresses. **Virtual memory** is a method of using both physical memory (RAM) and a paging file stored on the hard disk for data storage. Data that processes are currently using is stored in RAM where the processes can access it quickly and is called the processes' **working set**; data that the processes have used but are not currently manipulating is stored in the paging file.

Storage of data by the Virtual Memory Manager can be compared to clothing storage. Data in RAM is analogous to the clothes in your closet—the things that are currently in use or frequently accessed. Data in a paging file (stored on the hard disk) is analogous to the clothes you store in your attic—not in current use or used less frequently. The Virtual Memory Manager stores less frequently used data on disk in a paging file and more frequently used data in RAM. Just as it takes longer to retrieve clothing from the attic than from your closet, it takes longer to pull data from the paging file (milliseconds, or thousandths of a second) than from RAM (nanoseconds, or billionths of a second). The advantage of using an attic (or paging file) is that it provides more storage space.

Each process running on a Win2K computer has 4 GB (gigabytes—that's billions of bytes) of virtual memory that it can see. Of this memory, 2 GB consist of system memory addresses, which core Win2K functions use to store data and which are common to all processes running on the system. The other 2 GB are reserved for the use of the threads running in that particular process. This statement doesn't mean that the process has 2 GB of RAM reserved for it—even the most heavily loaded Win2K servers max out at 1 GB of RAM. Instead, it means that the process can see 2 GB of personal addressable memory spaces in which to store data. Other processes will also see 2 GB of personal addressable memory spaces. One of the jobs of the Virtual Memory Manager is to keep straight how these virtual memory addresses map to physical memory—RAM and the paging file—and to retrieve data requested by processes. Chapter 4 discusses memory management in more detail.

Security Reference Monitor

The Security Reference Monitor is responsible for enforcing the security settings defined in the security subsystem. Security settings in Win2K are a matter of rights (what actions you can perform) and permissions (what objects you can access). Each user or predefined group of users has a **security ID (SID)** associated with it. Chapter 12, "Securing Network Resources," discusses Win2K security systems in detail. For now, suffice it to say, that, when you log onto the domain, the operating system evaluates your SID and gives you an access token based on your SID, which is in turn determined by the security restrictions of the user group to which you belong and any settings that the administrator has applied directly to your account. The access token acts like a pass; it details the things that you're allowed to do on the network.

Each object on the network (each file, application, shared resource, and so on) also has an **access control list (ACL)** that defines the permissions or rights needed to use that resource and specifies precisely how each permission set allows that object to be used. For example, the file object Mydoc.doc could have an ACL that says, "Members of the Users group can read this document, members of the Administrators group can read and edit this document, and members of the Guests group can't see it, let alone read or edit it."

When you try to access an object on the Win2K domain, the Security Reference Monitor compares your access token to the information in the object's ACL. Based on the results of the comparison, you're either permitted a degree of control over that object or told that you're not allowed to use it. If auditing is turned on, then the Security Reference Monitor not only will decide who gets access to what, but will also record successful and failed attempts to access objects or change security settings—and record who instigated those attempts.

I/O Manager

I/O covers how data gets into the computer and how it gets out. The I/O Manager is the piece of Win2K that implements all I/O—no matter what kinds of devices are involved (printers, hard disks, microphones, keyboards)—and communicates with the device drivers that handle the actual communication between the operating system and the hardware. Because I/O is a major part of any operating system, it is discussed in many places throughout this book.

Cache Manager

The Cache Manager is in charge of the **file system cache**, which is a range of virtual memory addresses reserved for storing recently used data related to file sharing from any storage medium (hard disk, CD-ROM, network-accessible drives). This cache holds data related to file reads and writes—not only the file contents themselves, but also a catalog of disk structure and organization (so file-based I/O is faster). In addition, it holds disk updates in RAM for a brief period, writing them to disk when the system is less busy. The Cache Manager oversees all of these operations, telling the I/O Manager when to retrieve recently used data from the file system cache instead of from the hard disk and ensuring that the contents of the cache are written to the hard disk periodically so that they will not be lost if the server crashes. Because it must shuffle data between RAM and the hard disk, the Cache Manager relies on the Virtual Memory Manager to help it with these tasks.

Other Executive Support Functions

Besides these main groups, the executive part of Win2K includes some functions that support them and, in some cases, work with device drivers. The two most important are the **Object Manager** and the **local procedure call (LPC) facility**. The Object Manager creates the objects that represent executive-level operating system structures such as processes and threads (which are then managed by the Process and Thread Manager). The LPC facility handles interprocess communications—messaging between client and server processes on the local computer (this messaging piece allows the parts of a client/server operating system to communicate). Other functions handle the basic processing required to convert data from one format to another, to organize the security structure, and to allocate memory to Win2K core functionality.

The Kernel

The most important part of Win2K is the kernel, which is the other half of Ntoskrnl.exe and the part that juggles all of the low-level scheduling required in the operating system. The threads that the Process and Thread Manager creates are scheduled for CPU cycles by the kernel. Likewise, the interrupts that I/O devices use to tell the CPU that they have data to process are handled by the kernel. When a process asks the Virtual Memory Manager to retrieve a piece of data that's been swapped out to the paging file, the kernel provides the core functionality that allows the Virtual Memory Manager to realize what it must do to transfer the data to the process. The kernel doesn't make policy—that's up to the subsystem and executive parts of Win2K that have already been discussed. It also doesn't do any error checking to verify that a subsystem is allowed to do what it's trying to do. Rather, it carries out the support functions that allow the executive and the environmental subsystems to operate.

Because the kernel is so crucial to Win2K, it's different from other parts of the operating system. Most of the operating system has pieces that can be paged in and out of RAM, being retrieved from the paging file when they're needed. The kernel is different—it's *always* stored in RAM or, as it is commonly referred to, *resident in memory*. Kernel threads have a higher priority than other threads; therefore, although it will relinquish CPU time so that the CPU can handle interrupts, the kernel won't be interrupted in any of its functions to let other threads run.

Another difference between the kernel and the rest of Win2K relates to the kernel's simplicity. The kernel is designed to do its job as quickly as possible. For this reason, it must leave all policymaking to the other parts of the operating system. If a user wants to run an application, the kernel isn't concerned with who the user is or whether that person has the right to run that application. It just creates the threads, schedules CPU time for them, and assumes that the Security Reference Monitor has already checked the permissions.

Broadly speaking, the kernel has two main goals: to provide control objects that carry out the functions ordered by the subsystems and executive, and to create a uniform interface that the executive and system device drivers can use to interact with the hardware architectures (meaning x86-based computers or Alpha-based computers).

The Puppet Masters: Kernel Objects

Why does the kernel need to create objects (such as threads) if a part of the executive is already creating them? The answer is, because the executive isn't making them, or isn't making them complete and able to control themselves. The Process and Thread Manager issues instructions to create a thread. Those instructions, in turn, are passed to the kernel to execute. The executive part of the operating system represents threads and other shareable resources as objects. Objects have attributes, such as security settings (ACLs), resource quotas that must reflect the amount of resources used by the object, and handles that allow other objects to manipulate them. All in all, an object represents a formidable amount of bookkeeping. To make Win2K more responsive, the kernel manipulates these complicated objects with simpler **kernel objects** that contain no security information or other attributes, but nevertheless help the operating system organize and time the execution of the executive-level objects. Most executive level objects are linked to one or more kernel objects that manipulate the executive-level objects.

There are two kinds of kernel objects. One type, called **control objects**, controls various operating system functions, such as running the kernel process (recall that the executable image Ntoskrnl.exe that supports the kernel and the executive doesn't do anything; it's just a framework for processes and the threads inside them) and handling hardware interrupts. The second type, dispatcher objects, synchronizes events on the computer and affects thread scheduling. Chapter 4 covers more details about how control objects and dispatcher objects make Win2K work.

Kernel-Level Hardware Support

The second major job of the kernel is to keep the executive and subsystems from having to worry about the kind of hardware on which they're running. To achieve this goal, the kernel has to smooth out any variations in the way that different architectures handle such events as hardware interrupts and page faults. If the kernel didn't take care of this job, then variations in the hardware platform would create similar variations in the executive and subsystems. That said, the kernel itself doesn't really change much to reflect different hardware. It will vary occasionally depending on the hardware installed in the computer on which you install Win2K. For example, the kernel for an Alpha-based machine is different from the kernel for an x86-based machine, because the CPU cache in an Alpha chip works differently from the one in an x86 chip. Nevertheless, the kernel is designed to make it as portable across different hardware as is possible.

The kernel does not interact directly with computer hardware or provide a consistent interface between the operating system and the hardware. That's the job of the hardware abstraction layer (HAL), discussed in the next section. The hardware interactions that are truly hardware-specific and can't be smoothed over with the kernel are included in the HAL.

Hardware Abstraction Layer

When Windows NT was first designed, a crucial element of its design was portability, or the ability to be used on more than one hardware platform. Not all operating systems are portable, and some are more portable than others. In an earlier version, Windows NT was actually more portable than it is now. Windows NT 4 would run on x86-based computers, Alpha-based computers, and computers based on the MIPS and PowerPC chips. Microsoft dropped support for the latter two platforms when the MIPS chip was discontinued and the PowerPC version of Windows NT didn't sell. Win2K runs on only the Alpha and x86 platforms.

The hardware abstraction layer is a key component to making Win2K portable. This loadable kernel-level DLL (called Hal.dll; stored in the *%systemroot%*\system32 folder on a Win2K computer) provides the low-level interface to the hardware of the computer on which Win2K is installed. It hides all hardware-dependent details, such as I/O interfaces, interrupt controllers, and support for multiprocessor computers, or any mechanism that varies significantly with the hardware in the computer. Win2K supports many HALs, but installs only the one you need for your hardware platform. In some cases, the computer manufacturer must provide the HAL (for example, for computers that have more than four processors).

To keep from having to provide numerous versions of the executive component of Win2K, Microsoft maintained portability in Win2K by having the executive call HAL routines when they are needed to access hardware. This approach is roughly equivalent to the way that applications call on the Win2K environmental subsystem DLLs to access core Win2K functionality. The HAL is Win2K's API to the hardware and, as such, the only part of Win2K that interacts directly with system hardware. Even device drivers must call on the HAL.

Because they must interact with hardware directly, HALs are written in a low-level programming language called assembler, rather than the higher-level C in which the rest of Win2K is written. Assembler language code executes more quickly than C code because it has less overhead associated with it. Writing C code is much simpler, however. Although the syntax for assembler language is cryptic, with a little practice, you can read C code to see what it's doing even if you can't program in it.

Device Drivers

Device drivers are modules in the kernel that act as go-betweens for the I/O subsystem and the HAL. There are several types of device drivers:

- **Hardware device drivers**, such as printer drivers, write data to or retrieve it from a physical device or network, manipulating the hardware via the HAL. These are the device drivers you probably think of first.

- **File system drivers** are how Win2K translates file-oriented I/O requests and communicates them to a hard disk or other storage media, like a tape drive or CD-ROM.
- **Filter drivers** intercept I/O requests and perform some processing on them to make the requests intelligible to the receiving devices. For example, if you've logically merged two physical disks into a single volume, any I/O requests to that disk must be translated so that the HAL knows with which physical disk it must communicate. Some quota management software is also based on filter drivers, because the quota system must see the available capacity of the hard disk before permitting anyone to write to it.
- **Network redirectors and servers** are file system drivers that transfer data to and from network-accessible drives. In fact, when a Win2K computer is set up for networking, the redirector intercepts all file read or write requests and examines them to see whether they need the redirector's help. If the I/O request is intended for a locally accessible hard drive, then the redirector relinquishes the request to the file system driver.

Win2K loads device drivers when you boot up the computer, but the drivers don't actually do anything until they're called. If a thread initiates an I/O function (such as a request to retrieve a file from disk) or a piece of hardware interrupts the CPU with a request to process some data, the appropriate device driver communicates with the HAL to retrieve the necessary data.

OUTLINE OF WIN2K ARCHITECTURE

To really understand how the pieces of Win2K interoperate, you need to see how they fit together. This chapter has discussed some of the communication that takes place between some parts of the operating system (like the device drivers depending on the HAL to actually communicate with hardware, rather than doing it themselves). The following sections will describe the organization of the Win2K pieces in more detail.

User Space and Kernel Space

Before you can understand how Win2K is organized, you must recognize the difference between user space and kernel space. To prevent user applications from accessing or corrupting data that Win2K needs, Win2K uses two processor access modes: **kernel mode** and **user mode**. User application code runs in user mode; operating system code, such as device drivers, runs in kernel mode.

The basic difference between the two modes is the degree of access that processes are granted to the system. Kernel-mode processes (that is, processes that run in kernel mode) can use any CPU instruction and can read or write on any part of system memory (that is, the 2 GB of virtual addresses shared among all processes). User-mode processes, on the other hand, can use only a subset of CPU instructions and can read and write only to the 2 GB of virtual memory addresses private to them. The two modes give Win2K the power it needs yet prevent user applications from crashing the operating system. Although an application running in one of the environmental subsystems can still crash itself, it won't take down the rest of the operating system with it.

Kernel mode is sometimes referred to as *privileged mode* because of the privileged position occupied by any code executing in that mode.

Virtual memory is divided into pages (sections that an application can use to store data). Win2K tags each page to indicate what access mode the processor must be in to read and/or write to that page. Threads can access pages in system space (with addresses ranging from 800000000 to FFFFFFFF) only when they're running in kernel mode. Threads running in user mode can access only the pages in user space (with addresses ranging from 00000000 to 7FFFFFFF). Figure 2-5 illustrates this distinction.

		7FFFFFFF
User Mode	2 GB	
		800000000
		FFFFFFFF
Kernel Mode	2 GB	
		00000000

Figure 2-5 Kernel-mode and user-mode virtual memory addresses

The numbering employed by operating systems typically takes the form of a base-16 numbering system called hexadecimal (or just "hex"). The decimal system to which you're accustomed uses one or more of 10 digits to represent any number: 0, 1, 2, 3, 4, 5, 6, 7, 8, 9. Hexadecimal uses those digits as well, but adds a few more: . . . .9, A, B, C, D, E, F. Thus 15 decimal is F hexadecimal. Why use hexadecimal? It's a really convenient way to translate from the binary numbering system that computers read and, with a little practice, hex notation is much easier to read than binary notation.

Threads of user applications switch from user mode to kernel mode depending on what they're doing, using privileged mode when they need to call a system service. For example, if you're running Microsoft Word and try to open a file, the thread responsible for opening that file must call the executive routine that handles file opening. This routine runs in kernel mode. Word itself continues to run in user mode, but gives some time to a system process so that the executive routine will open the file you requested. When the system service is finished, the CPU switches back into user mode (a move called a **context switch**, which is discussed more in Chapter 4) and then gives control back to the Word thread. Thus Win2K never runs in kernel mode when the user application has control.

That's the difference between user mode and kernel mode. Figure 2-6 indicates which parts of Win2K are in each mode.

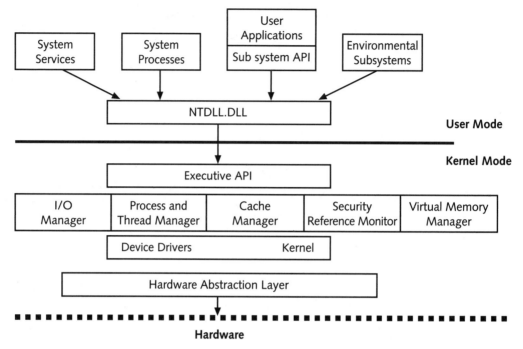

Figure 2-6 A simplified Win2K structure

 A thread supporting a user application normally spends some time running in kernel mode and some time running in user mode, depending on what it's doing. For example, if a thread is waiting for user input, it runs in user mode. If the thread is actually performing a computational function, it operates in kernel mode.

Pieces Found in Each Space and Their Relationship to Each Other

The user mode/kernel mode design has several implications. User applications, environmental subsystems, and Win2K services run in user mode and do not communicate directly with the executive, which runs in kernel mode. Rather, the subsystem DLLs—the API—pass information to the executive part. System processes, such as the logon process that passes your user name and password to the security subsystem and that determines whether you're allowed to log onto the computer, run in user mode but can pass information to the executive services without relying on the subsystem DLLs. The kernel and device drivers support the executive, and the HAL performs all communication with hardware that Win2K needs.

The graphics services in kernel mode are actually part of the Win32 subsystem, Microsoft puts them in kernel mode, however, to make Win2K draw windows more quickly.

Chapter Summary

- This chapter introduced the general principles of operating system architecture with a focus on the Windows 2000 (Win 2K) architecture.

- The Windows 2000 virtual memory model combines the use of physical RAM and paging files into a demand paging mechanism so as to maximize memory use and efficiency. Windows 2000 is easy to use, offers new storage capabilities, provides improved Internet access, and maintains strict security.

- Windows 2000 is based on a modular programming technique. Its main processing mechanism is divided into two modes: user mode and kernel mode. User mode hosts all user processes and accesses resources via the executive.

- The separation of modes provides for a more stable and secure computing environment. It supports the application subsystems that enable Windows 2000 to execute DOS, Win16, Win32, POSIX, and OS/2 software.

- The kernel mode hosts all system processes and mediates all resource access. Its executive manages operations such as I/O, security, memory, processes, file systems, objects, and graphical devices.

Key Terms

access control list (ACL) — The list that defines the permissions or rights needed to use a system resource and specifies precisely how each permission set allows that object to be used.

application programming interface (API) — The entire set of DLLs that an environmental subsystem supports to request kernel-mode services.

client — The computer or user that requests information from a server.

context switch — The action that takes place when a processor switches from kernel mode to user mode.

control object — A kernel object that controls various operating system functions, such as running the kernel process.

device driver — A kernel-mode module that acts as a go-between for the I/O subsystem and the hardware abstraction layer.

dynamic link library (DLL) — A specific set of function calls that allows executable routines to be stored as files and to be loaded only when needed by a program that calls them.

emulation — A mechanism by which an environmental subsystem supports applications for which it doesn't have an API.

environmental subsystem — The part of an operating system that provides an interface to the functions that an application needs to support user requests. Win2K supports three environmental subsystems: Win32, POSIX 1.0a, and OS/2 1.0.

executable image — The name of an application or a logical construct for the processes and threads that actually execute the application.

file system cache — A range of virtual memory addresses reserved for storing recently used data related to storage I/O.

file system driver — A device driver that translates file-oriented I/O requests for the hardware abstract layer to pass to storage media.

filter driver — A device driver that intercepts file I/O requests and processes the request to make it intelligible to the receiving device.

function call — A predefined request for a kernel-mode action that the environmental subsystem can call at the request of an application.

hardware device driver — A module that writes data to or retrieves data from a physical device or network, manipulating the hardware via the hardware abstraction layer.

helper — Parts of the operating system that allow applications to communicate with hardware. Originally, these parts were lumped together in a single unit and communicated with each other in a separate area of memory, away from applications.

job — A collection of processes with certain common characteristics, such as the working set and the amount of CPU time that the threads in the process get.

kernel mode — A processing mode that gives complete access to all writable addresses in the system process area. Kernel objects run in kernel mode. Because this mode allows access to the operating system, only code that must interact with the operating system directly runs in kernel mode.

kernel object — An object that exists only in kernel mode and with which the kernel manipulates executive-level objects such as processes and threads. Kernel objects contain no security information or other attributes, so they don't incur the same kind of policy-based overhead that executive objects do.

local procedure call (LPC) facility — The Win2K messaging mechanism that allows client and server processes to communicate.

network redirectors and servers — File system drivers that transfer data to and from network-accessible drives.

object manager — The part of the executive that creates the objects representing executive-level structures such as processes and threads.

process — The context for an executable thread. Processes define the priority, available resources, virtual memory settings, and other settings for the threads executing in the context of that process.

security ID (SID) — The unique identifier that is determined by the security restrictions of the user group to which you belong and any settings that the administrator has applied directly to your account.

thread — An entity within a process for which Win2K schedules CPU time to execute a function of some kind. When a thread has finished its job, it terminates.

user mode — A restricted kind of access to CPU functions and virtual memory. User mode limits user applications to using per-process virtual memory addresses and a subset of CPU functions, allowing them to request kernel-mode functions but not to read or write data in system areas.

virtual memory — A method of using both hard disk space and physical RAM to make it appear as though a computer has as much as 4 GB of RAM.

working set — Data that the thread in a process is currently using and that is stored in RAM.

Review Questions

1. No modern operating systems permit applications to directly access system hardware. True or False?
2. The collection of core system operations on which an environmental subsystem can call are individually known as _____ and collectively known as the environmental subsystem's _____.
3. Which of the following is a group of related function calls?
   a. Dynamic link library
   b. Application programming interface
   c. Environmental subsystem
   d. Operating environment
4. Which environmental subsystem(s) is (are) loaded when Win2K starts up?
5. The OS/2 subsystem is supported only on Alpha Win2K systems. True or False?
6. With which file is the executive portion of Win2K loaded?
   a. Ntldr
   b. Ntdll.dll
   c. Ntoskrnl.exe
   d. Both A and B
7. Which of the following is not part of the Win2K executive?
   a. Win32 subsystem
   b. I/O Manager
   c. Process and Thread Manager
   d. Ntdll.dll
8. The _____ is responsible for storing recently used file data in memory.
9. Every thread has at least one process, but it may spawn more processes to support the actions of the person using an application. True or False?
10. What is a Win2K job?
11. A process's _____ is the set of data that the process currently has stored in physical memory.
12. Memory access times are typically measured in _____; disk access times are measured in _____.
13. Win2K supports _____ of virtual memory addresses.
    a. 2 GB
    b. 3 GB
    c. 4 GB
    d. As much as you install in the computer (typically a maximum of 1 GB in modern computers)

14. How are ACLs used in the Win2K executive? Which part of the executive uses them?
15. Users get _____ based on their security identifiers (SIDs).
16. Which part of the Win2K executive manages the problem of how data gets into the computer and how it gets out?
    a. Security Reference Monitor
    b. Cache Manager
    c. I/O Manager
    d. Device drivers
17. In Win2K, the part of the executive that handles communication between client and server processes on the same computer is called the _____.
18. The Process and Thread Manager creates its own processes and threads. True or False?
19. Which two components of Win2K does Ntoskrnl.exe load?
20. The _____ handles all low-level scheduling for Win2K.
    a. Executive
    b. Kernel
    c. Process and Thread Manager
    d. None of the above
21. The scheduling component of Win2K is always resident in memory. True or False?
22. Which part of Win2K interacts directly with system hardware?
    a. Device drivers
    b. Executive
    c. Kernel
    d. None of the above
    e. Hardware abstraction layer (HAL)
23. List the platforms on which Win2K runs, and compare them with the platforms on which Windows NT 4 ran.
24. _____ are the parts of the kernel that act as go-betweens for the I/O subsystem and the part of Win2K that interacts with hardware.
25. A network redirector is a file system driver. True or False?
26. On what kind of device drivers might quota management software rely?
    a. Filter drivers
    b. File system drivers
    c. I/O drivers
    d. None of the above
27. In Win2K, applications execute in _____ mode.
28. How do user-mode and kernel-mode processes use memory differently?

29. Device drivers run in _____ mode; the executive runs in _____ mode.

30. What is it called when the CPU changes from handling kernel-mode processes to handling user-mode processes?

    a. Context switch
    b. Working set
    c. Paging operation
    d. Local procedure call

Hands-on Projects

Project 2-1

The Win32 subsystem is generated when Win2K runs the executable image Csrss.exe at startup time. Win2K depends on the Win32 subsystem to provide basic functionality to the operating system. In this demand, the Win32 subsystem is different from the OS/2 and POSIX subsystems, which are loaded only if you run an application that requires them.

To manipulate any process, you need to know its image name or its process ID (PID; the number identifying it). You already know the image name of the Win32 subsystem; you will find its PID with a tool called the Task Manager.

Many tools will supply you with a PID, not just the Task Manager. Because the Task Manager will be referred to again in the course of this book, you should become familiar with it now.

To find the process ID of the Win32 subsystem:

1. To run the Task Manager, press **Ctrl+Alt+Delete** to open the Windows Security dialog box. You'll have a choice of actions: log off the system, shut down, lock the computer, change the password, and open the Task Manager. Click the **Task Manager** button to open the Task Manager.

2. Click the **Process** tab of the Task Manager, as shown in Figure 2-7.

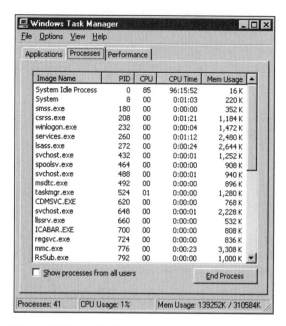

Figure 2-7 List of processes running on the computer

3. Find the **Csrss.exe** image in the list of running processes. When you find it, look at the number opposite it in the PID column. Write down this PID for your instance of the Win32 subsystem—you'll need it for the next exercise.

Project 2-2

If you could stop Csrss.exe from running, you'd crash the entire operating system. In Windows NT 4, you could stop the Win32 process, which would cause a "blue screen of death" and require you to restart the computer. Win2K protects itself from crashing. To see what happens when you try to crash it, follow these steps:

To observe the importance of the Win32 subsystem:

1. Open the **Win2K Resource Kit**, which is in the **Programs** section of the **Start** menu.

2. In the Resource Kit, click the folder for **Tools A to Z**, so that the screen looks like the one in Figure 2-8.

Hands-on Projects

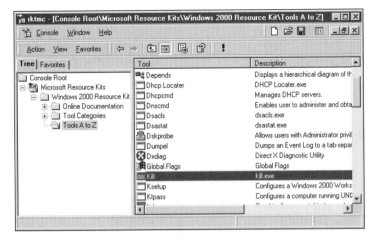

Figure 2-8 The Kill tool in the Resource Kit

3. Double-click the **Kill** tool. You'll open a command-line window that looks like the one in Figure 2-9.

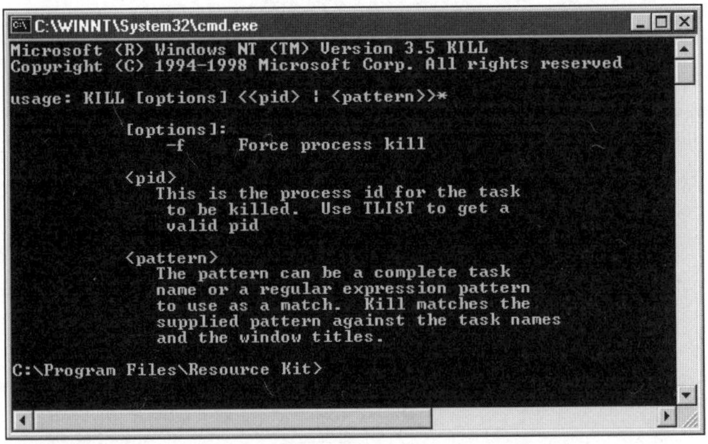

Figure 2-9 Command-line options for the Kill utility

4. Type **KILL** *PID*, where *PID* is the process ID you wrote down in Hands-on Project 2-1.
5. Note that you receive the following message:

    ```
    process csrss.exe (204) - '' could not be killed
    ```

    Even if you add the –f switch to KILL, which should force a process to end, you'll get the same message.

Project 2-3

You can use the Win2K Performance Monitor to observe many things about your computer, including the amount of time it spends executing user code versus kernel code. To see this difference, follow these steps.

To find out how much time your computer spends in kernel mode and in user mode:

1. Click Start, Run, and type **perfmon**. When you see a dialog box indicating that the Performance Monitor has been replaced by the System Monitor and telling you to click OK to start the System Monitor or Cancel to start the Performance Monitor, click **Cancel**. (The System Monitor includes support for the Performance Monitor, but keep the interface simple for now.) You'll see a screen like the one in Figure 2-10.

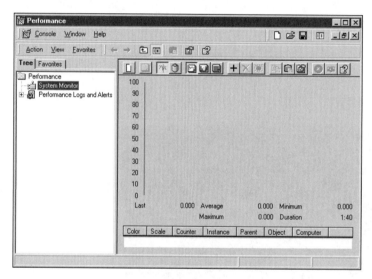

Figure 2-10 Performance Monitor

2. Click the button that has the plus sign (called the Add button) on it to open the dialog box shown in Figure 2-11 (You can also right click the chart and select Add Counters from the resulting menu.)

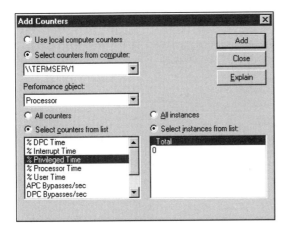

Figure 2-11 Add Counters dialog box

3. In the Performance object field, select the **Processor** object. It should already be visible.
4. In the Select counters from list field, choose **% Privileged Time**. Click **Add**. Choose **% User Time**. Click **Add**.
5. Click **Close** to close the Add Counters dialog box.

A key at the bottom of the Performance Monitor shows you the colors used for each mode of execution. When you do anything on the computer—save a file, move the mouse, open an application—you'll see both chart lines spike. On average, however, the computer spends more time in privileged mode (recall, that's another name for kernel mode) than in user mode.

CASE PROJECTS

1. You're installing Win2K on one new computer with 128 MB of RAM and on a second computer with 256 MB of RAM. Otherwise, the two computers are identical. How will the virtual memory address range available differ on these two computers, and why? Will this amount change if you install more memory on one of the computers without reinstalling the operating system?

2. You've installed a new word processor and a new network card driver on your computer on the same day. A few minutes later, when you open a file stored on a network-accessible drive, Win2K crashes. Which of the two new items on your computer is more likely to be responsible for the crash, and (specifically) why?

CHAPTER 3
KEY WINDOWS 2000 COMPONENTS

> **After reading this chapter and completing the exercises, you will be able to:**
> - Recount the basic start-up process for Windows 2000
> - Understand the Windows 2000 Registry
> - Appreciate the Windows 2000 base functionality
> - Recognize basic administrative tools included with Windows 2000

Like most operating systems, Windows 2000 is made up of multiple files, each of which serves a specific purpose to create a workable computing environment. These files range from memory managers and hardware drivers to management components and interface translators. This chapter looks at the important files and components found in Windows 2000.

Important Files and Subsystems

Windows 2000 contains dozens of files that initiate its core components, which in turn load additional files that control such things as the user interface, security, and hardware support. These files help establish a workable runtime environment for Windows 2000. Each of these files is discussed in detail throughout this chapter.

Microsoft took a "divide and conquer" approach when designing Windows 2000 (and its predecessor, Windows NT). That approach shows clearly in the **modular architecture** depicted in Figure 3-1. The system is divided into two distinct operating modes: user mode and kernel mode. Each of these modes is further divided into single-function or special-purpose modules. Each module is independent, which means that program code is not shared across any two modules. In some instances, module independence increases the overall operating system size because of the need to maintain duplicate code. User and kernel modes were discussed in Chapter 2. On the other hand, this design offers improved reliability, performance, and fault tolerance, all of which outweigh the costs of a larger system footprint.

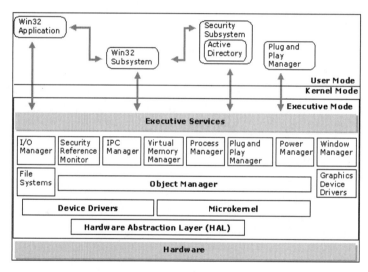

Figure 3-1 Windows 2000 architecture

A modular operating system design, like that characterizing Windows 2000, has several important benefits. Each module can be replaced or repaired without affecting other modules. As long as communication interfaces between modules remain the same (or functionally equivalent), each module can be replaced with either an updated version from Microsoft or a module from a third-party vendor. Modules cooperate to create networking, communications, and application environments, which in turn support tasks and applications involved in general computing activities.

Before you examine the details of the components in an active operating system, you need to explore the process by which the operating system is loaded. The following sections discuss the **bootstrapping** (or just "boot") **files**, the **core system files**, and other key elements in a Windows 2000 system.

Bootstrapping

The **bootstrapping** process encompasses the initial activities that occur before an operating system can load. This process basically transforms a hunk of metal and plastic into a computing device ready to accept instructions.

The following initial activities make up the bootstrapping process:

- Powering on the computer: Bootstrapping first provides power to the computer, usually when a user flips the power button on the box.

- **Power On, Self-Test (POST)**: This internal diagnostic ensures that all required core hardware is present and operating properly. The Basic Input/Output System (BIOS) embedded on the motherboard and on other expansion cards, such as video adapters and Small Computer System Interface (SCSI) adapters, initiates the diagnostic tests. These tests appear on the monitor as vendor banners, memory counts, hard drive initializations, SCSI card and device enumerations, and listings for known ports, addresses, and **interrupt requests (IRQs)**. The POST also checks for the presence of floppy drives, a keyboard, and, in some cases, a mouse.

- Boot disk access: The bootstrapping process accesses the **master boot record (MBR)** on each hard drive. The MBR contains a copy of the partition table, which maintains or defines logical divisions on a hard drive. The partition table information is used to locate the active partition, also known as the **system partition**. The active partition contains the files used to load or initiate an operating system. In addition, the MBR defines which file (or files) should be loaded to initiate an operating system. After the computer hardware locates the active partition and the operating system loader, it transfers execution to that file (or files).

On most systems, the complementary metal oxide semiconductor (CMOS) looks for a bootable floppy before starting from a hard drive. If a floppy is present, the computer attempts to start from that floppy. If an MBR is not present on the floppy, a "Non-system disk or disk error; Replace and press any key when ready" error occurs.

Next, the computer launches the operating system initialization files, thereby ending the bootstrapping process. Depending on the system configuration, the initialization files either launch a single operating system or enable the user to choose from several operating systems (known as a **multiboot system**). Windows 2000 supports multiboot capabilities with most other Microsoft operating systems without requiring additional software. A multiboot system that includes a non-Microsoft operating system, however, usually requires a partition management tool such as Partition Magic from PowerQuest (*http://www.powerquest.com/*) or System Commander from V Communications (*http://www.v-com.com/*).

It is important to identify Microsoft-specific terminology when talking about operating system components. In Microsoft terms, the system partition contains the files used to initialize the Windows 2000 load process; the boot partition contains the main Windows 2000 directory and the pagefile. The system partition must be active. Although the boot partition can be the same partition as the system partition, it is typically located elsewhere on either the same or a different physical drive. Under Windows 2000, a boot partition can be transformed into a dynamic storage device, whereas a system partition must remain a standard basic storage device. On Alpha systems (which are RISC-based systems), a system partition must be formatted using file allocation table (FAT). On Intel systems, a system partition can be formatted with a FAT, FAT32, or New Technology File System (NTFS).

If no active partition exists on a hard drive, if the active partition is not the system partition, or if the files defined in the MBR are not present, any of several error messages can appear:

- Invalid partition table
- Error loading operating system
- Missing operating system

These error messages typically indicate that a functional operating system is not present on the computer. In some cases, they may signal that the hardware is not functioning properly or that the hard drive's partition table has failed or become corrupted. To fix these errors, you need to use some type of partitioning, configuration, or formatting tool. Luckily, the installation routines found on the four Windows 2000 setup boot disks include these functions.

Device Drivers

As mentioned in Chapter 2, a device driver is a small program designed to grant a specific operating system the ability to interact with and manipulate a device. An operating system requires device drivers to perform actions involving hardware access. Such actions include processing commands through the CPU, storing data in memory, reading input from a keyboard or mouse, reading data from a hard drive, creating a graphical display on a monitor, moving data across a network, and creating hard copy on a printer.

Windows 2000 includes most core device drivers (such as those for the CPU, memory, motherboard, PCI bus, and so forth) as part of the **hardware abstraction layer (HAL)**. Other hardware drivers, such as video system, audio, printer, network interface, and drive controller drivers, are easier to add, update, and change because they're not hardwired into (that is, permanent parts of) the HAL. After the initial installation of Windows 2000 is complete, you can modify or replace these drivers with newer, more powerful software.

Two types of device drivers operate in the Windows 2000 environment: **device class drivers** and **individual device drivers**.

Device class drivers supply basic driver interfaces and functions that define broad parameters for specific types of devices. Examples include Telephony Application Programming Interface (TAPI) modem drivers, graphic-rendering drivers within the printer subsystem, and

Integrated Drive Electronic (IDE) drivers for drive controllers. Individual device drivers are device- and model-specific programs that define the exact capabilities and functions of a particular device down to the make and model level; they allow the operating system to access the device's functions. These types of drivers are provided by the manufacturer whey you buy a new peripheral device, such as a printer, fax machine, or network interface card.

After a device driver is installed, it appears in the list of devices (the device and the driver are seen as the same object) within the Device Manager. The Device Manager (see Figure 3-2) is accessed either from the Hardware tab in the System applet (Start, Settings, Control Panel, System) or through the System Tools node in the Computer Management interface (Start, Programs, Administrative Tools, Computer Management).

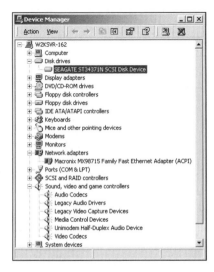

Figure 3-2 The Windows 2000 Device Manager

For more details on device drivers, see Chapter 5, "Device Management."

Base Operating System Loaders

After the computer identifies an active partition, the operating system launch procedure begins. This procedure varies with different operating systems, primarily because of the use of different filenames and the various tasks or functions assigned to files. Windows 2000 shares a common boot process and boot filenames with its predecessor, Windows NT. The boot process includes the following files, which are located in the root directory of the system partition (see Figure 3-3):

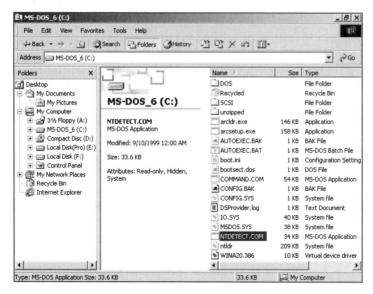

Figure 3-3 The files in the root directory of the system partition

- **Ntldr** is the operating system initialization file launched by the computer upon completion of the bootstrapping process. This file is responsible for loading Windows NT or other operating systems when they are present on a multiboot system. Ntldr uses the Boot.ini file to present a boot menu, which you use to select the operating system that should be launched.

- **Boot.ini** defines all relevant host partitions and the primary executables for those operating systems present on a computer. It also defines the default system to load when the boot menu display timer expires.

- **Ntdetect.com** executes before the Windows 2000 executable files are loaded from the boot partition. It performs hardware detection to create an inventory of devices and their configurations. A detected configuration is used to select a hardware profile, if more than one configuration is defined. The selected hardware profile determines which device drivers are loaded.

- **Ntbootdd.sys** appears only on systems with SCSI controllers that do not use an on-board BIOS translation. This file enables the drive controller system on the motherboard to control a SCSI adapter and its attached hard drives.

- **Bootsect.dos** is present only on a multiboot system where another Microsoft operating system, such as Windows 95/98, or a clone operating system, such as DOS, appears. This file establishes a boot environment more conducive to non-Windows 2000 and non-Windows NT operating systems.

- **Osloader.exe** appears only on Alpha systems. It replaces all of the preceding files that may be found on Intel machines by combining their functions into a single file. Alpha systems do not support multiboot systems.

When you select Windows 2000 from the boot menu or the boot menu timer expires with Windows 2000 as the default operating system, the Ntldr file executes Ntdetect.com. The latter file inspects the current state of hardware and attempts to match it with a known hardware profile. If the system cannot make a match, the user is prompted to select an alternative hardware profile. Hardware profiles are typically used on portable computers whose hardware devices change often, such as docking stations or network connections. After a hardware profile match is made, Ntldr launches **Ntoskrnl.exe** without releasing control of the system.

Ntoskrnl.exe is the Windows 2000 kernel, which is the core of the Windows 2000 operating environment. It controls the loading of all other files involved in establishing the computing environment. This file resides on the boot partition in the \Winnt\System32 folder (assuming you accept the default name for the system root during installation).

In addition to the Ntoskrnl.exe file, the boot process loads the Hal.dll file into memory. The Registry System key determines the system configuration and the order in which to load device drivers. Each driver required at start-up is loaded into memory (the progress of the loading process is indicated on the black screen by the display of several dots in the upper-left corner of the screen) and the Ntoskrnl. launches. When this operation is successful, the "Microsoft (R) Windows 2000 (TM) Server (Build 2072); 1 System Processor (128 MB Memory)" (or some equivalent) blue screen appears.

Next, the following system initialization functions occur:

1. All device drivers loaded into memory start.
2. Another Registry scan looks for the next set of device drivers to load (those required by the system but not required to initialize the kernel). These drivers are loaded and initialized.
3. The Session Manager (Smss.exe) launches to load and manage all services.
4. The BootExecute items launch. The Session Manager executes these commands before any services are loaded. BootExecute items include Autochk.exe (the Windows 2000 equivalent of the Windows NT Chkdsk.exe), which scans disks for problems or errors.
5. The Session Manager initiates the pagefile settings required by the Virtual Memory Manager.
6. The DOS Devices key is parsed to define all symbolic links to map to physical I/O ports, mail slots, named pipes, and so on.
7. The Windows 32-bit subsystem launches and initiates all I/O processes and the video display.

After all required drivers and files load and are initiated without significant problems, Winlogon.exe launches and starts the Local Security Administration (Lsass.exe). Next, the Begin Logon dialog box prompts the user to press Ctrl+Alt+Delete to log on. The start-up process is considered complete only after a successful logon.

The Windows Registry

The **Registry** is a hierarchical database that stores the configuration and parameter details that govern Windows 2000 operation (see Figure 3-4). Windows 2000 also maintains text-based initialization files, such as Win.ini and System.ini, for backward compatibility, but these files are not required for Windows 2000 to run. Instead, the Registry handles the configuration and parameter details for the operating system and applications in the native Windows 2000 environment.

 Microsoft recommends that you avoid direct interaction with the Registry whenever possible. In many situations, however, editing the Registry directly is the only possible way to solve a problem. Always back up the Registry and proceed with extreme caution whenever you find it necessary to modify the Windows Registry.

The Registry does not provide an exhaustive list of all applicable Windows 2000 configuration settings; rather, it lists only the exceptions to ordinary default settings for most entries. Defaults govern nearly all Windows 2000 behaviors unless a value in the Registry defines an alternative or additional setting. This approach creates a configuration environment in which some settings might not appear in the Registry; you must therefore change a built-in default manually. To make any changes to the Registry, you must be familiar with the exact syntax, spellings, path specifications, and valid values for Registry items. The Registry's structure is designed for system use and is not particularly user-friendly (as shown in Figure 3-4). The basic architecture of the Registry may be described as follows:

- The Registry is divided into five subtrees (listed on the left side of Figure 3-4).
- Each subtree is divided into keys.
- Each key is divided into subkeys.
- Any particular key can contain one or more layers or levels of subkeys. One or more value entries can occur within any key or subkey. A value entry includes a named parameter and one or more associated items of configuration data.
- Each value entry consists of three components: a name, a data type, and one or more actual data values.
- The data associated with any value entry describes its actual meaning or setting; the name identifies that setting; and the type indicates how the data entry should be interpreted.
- Registry data can be one of several types, including binary, decimal, text string, and hexadecimal.

The Windows Registry

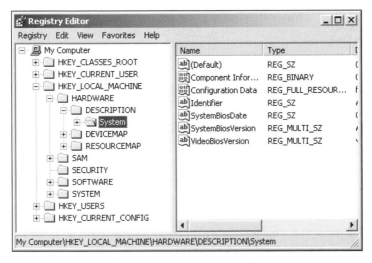

Figure 3-4 The Registry as seen through REGEDIT

The Windows 2000 Registry includes five subtrees:

- HKEY_LOCAL_MACHINE: This subtree includes the parameters that control the local computer system—specifically, hardware devices and device-dependent operating system components. The settings in this subtree are independent of users, applications, and processes.

- HKEY_CLASSES_ROOT: This subtree includes the parameters that control the relationships between file format types and applications. This relationship is based on the file extension (the characters to the right of the last period in a filename, such as "doc" in "Readme.doc"). The HKEY_CLASSES_ROOT subtree also maintains information about object linking and embedding, COM objects, and file-class associations.

- HKEY_CURRENT_CONFIG: This subtree contains the parameters that control the environment for the currently active hardware profile. Its contents are built or copied each time the system is started just after a hardware profile is selected. The contents are copied from the appropriate subtree of the HKEY_LOCAL _MACHINE\ System\CurrentControlSet\HardwareProfiles\ subtree. The HKEY_CURRENT_CONFIG subtree is actually a compromise intended to maintain compatibility with Windows 95 applications that reference this subtree, instead of the HKEY_LOCAL_MACHINE subtree, so as to obtain configuration information.

- HKEY_CURRENT_USER: This subtree includes the parameters that control the user environment for whichever user account is currently logged into a Windows 2000 system. This subkey is loaded into memory from the Ntuser.dat (or Ntuser.man) file found in a user's profile. The most recent copy of the user's profile information is copied from HKEY_USERS key, if that user's profile data is present; otherwise, the default user profile is loaded.

- HKEY_USERS: This subtree includes profile information settings for all users who have logged into this computer, along with the default user profile.

The Registry items that actually define or change the way in which objects, services, and functions operate are found in the Registry value entries. As noted earlier, each value entry has three components: name, data type, and value. A value entry name often consists of a capitalized phrase with no embedded spaces, such as DefaultUserName. The data contained in a value entry is stored in one of five primary data types:

- REG_BINARY: Binary format for arbitrarily large amounts of Registry data.
- REG_DWORD: Binary, hexadecimal, or decimal format for a maximum of 32 bits of Registry data.
- REG_SZ: A Unicode text string format for Registry data.
- REG_MULTI_SZ: A Unicode text string containing multiple values separated by NULL characters.
- REG_EXPAND_SZ: An expandable text string containing variables (such as %systemroot%) to be replaced by an application.

You must explicitly define the data type used to store data when creating a value entry. It is not possible to transform a value entry from one data type to another. To change the data type of a value entry, you must delete the entry and re-create it using a new data type.

The term hive often crops up in discussions of the Registry. A **hive** is a section of the Registry that is stored in a separate file. Hives are permanent structures; they are saved each time that the system shuts down and reloaded each time the system powers up. Hives are not rebuilt or constructed each time that Windows 2000 boots. These sections are stored in one of two locations: %systemroot%\System32\Config (all hives) and \Documents and Settings\%username% (only Ntuser.dat, or Ntuser.man). Table 3-1 lists the hives stored by Windows 2000 and their related filenames.

Table 3-1 Filenames of Registry hives

Registry Hive	Filenames
HKEY_LOCAL_MACHINE\SAM	Sam, Sam.log, Sam.sav
HKEY_LOCAL_MACHINE\Security	Security, Security.log, Security.sav
HKEY_LOCAL_MACHINE\Software	Software, Software.log, Software.sav
HKEY_LOCAL_MACHINE\System	System, System.alt, System.log, System.sav
HKEY_CURRENT_CONFIG	System, System.alt, System.log, System.sav
HKEY_USERS\.DEFAULT	Default, Default.log, Default.sav
(Not associated with a hive)	Userdiff, Userdiff.log
HKEY_CURRENT_USER	Ntuser.dat, Ntuser.dat.log

As you can see from Table 3-1, several types of files are used to store the Registry hives. The four main file types are as follows:

- No extension indicates the hive file itself.
- .alt indicates a back-up copy of the hive file. Only the System hive has an .alt file.
- .log indicates a log of all transactions or changes made to a hive.
- .sav indicates a copy of the hive file created at the end of the text portion of the initial setup process.

The Registry layout, structure, and files are complex. Nevertheless, the design of the Registry makes it easy for the operating system to use the Registry from memory and to provide basic fault tolerance. Each time the system starts, the entire Registry is loaded into memory; while the system is running, however, only this memory-resident version of the Registry is used. Changes to the Registry are made to the memory-resident version and become effective immediately (when the changes affect a core process, the system must be restarted). The transaction logs record all changes made to the memory-resident Registry. When the system shuts down, the transaction log is used to implement the same net changes to the hive file (the hive file is not copied from memory to the hard drive). When the system is started again, the log file is used to verify that the changes it recorded were made into the hive file: the log file is then cleared.

Because the System hive is extremely important, changes are made to its main hive file, then to its .alt file. This approach ensures that a functioning hive file remains available even if the change process is interrupted.

The Windows 2000 Registry has only five default subtrees (described in the following sections). Installing some Windows 95 or Windows 98 software can result in the creation of a sixth subtree, HKEY_DYN_DATA. This subtree does not really exist. Instead, Windows 2000 creates a virtual link to other areas of the Registry that already support the data structure represented by this key in Windows 95/98. This process maintains compatibility for older Win32 applications.

HKEY_LOCAL_MACHINE

The HKEY_LOCAL_MACHINE subtree, shown in Figure 3-5, contains device configuration data. This information is independent of users, applications, and processes. Applications, device drivers, and kernel services use this data to load and configure device-dependent functions, objects, and services. The key is divided into five subkeys: Hardware, SAM, Security, Software, and System.

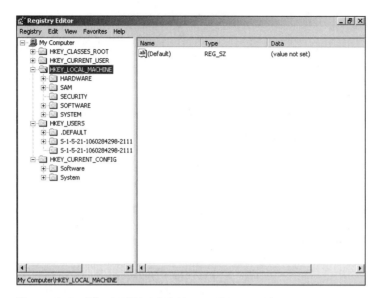

Figure 3-5 The HKEY_LOCAL_MACHINE subtree

HKEY_LOCAL_MACHINE\Hardware

The Hardware subkey of HKEY_LOCAL_MACHINE stores data specific to current hardware attached to the local computer, including physical settings, I/O ports, memory requirements, driver mappings, and IRQ settings. The data in this subkey is regenerated by the Ntdetect.com utility each time that the system starts and is not saved to a hive file whenever a shutdown occurs.

HKEY_LOCAL_MACHINE\SAM

The Security Accounts Manager (SAM) subkey of HKEY_LOCAL_MACHINE stores security-related data, including the SAM database and information about user accounts and groups. Most experts recommend that you never edit the data in this subkey directly. Use the Windows 2000 Active Directory, accounts, and group management tools to manage this sensitive and important system data instead.

HKEY_LOCAL_MACHINE\Security

The Security subkey of HKEY_LOCAL_MACHINE stores data specific to security policies (that is, group policies and local security policies). Most experts recommend that you never edit the data in this subkey directly; use the Windows 2000 Policy Editor and related tools to manage this sensitive system data instead.

HKEY_LOCAL_MACHINE\Software

The Software subkey of HKEY_LOCAL_MACHINE stores data related to installed software components. It is usually subdivided into subkeys, with one subkey for each software vendor with one or more products installed. For example, all Microsoft software information is stored in the HKEY_LOCAL_MACHINE\Software\Microsoft subkey.

HKEY_LOCAL_MACHINE\System

The System subkey of HKEY_LOCAL_MACHINE stores data related to the Windows 2000 start-up process, including start-up parameters, initialization instructions for device drivers, service parameters, and descriptions of basic operating system behaviors. The data in the System subkey are divided into control sets. A **control set** is a hardware profile-specific collection of start-up process parameters. The CurrentControlSet is a link to the ControlSet### subkey that contains data that describe the current active session. The numbered subkeys that appear beneath the System subkey, such as ControlSet001 and ControlSet002, represent unique hardware profiles and backups of previous successful system starts.

HKEY_CLASSES_ROOT

The HKEY_CLASSES_ROOT subtree, shown in Figure 3-6, contains mappings between application file extensions and data essential to COM objects and maintains a copy of the information in the HKEY_LOCAL_MACHINE\Software\Classes subtree. This subtree provides backward compatibility with Windows 95/98 applications.

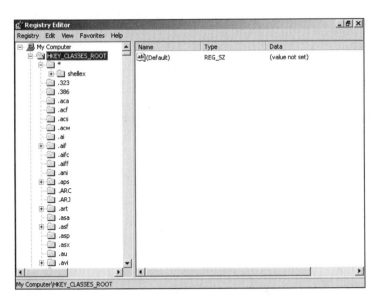

Figure 3-6 The HKEY_CLASSES_ROOT subtree

HKEY_CURRENT_CONFIG

The HKEY_CURRENT_CONFIG subtree, shown in Figure 3-7, maps to the current control set used by the system, which appears in HKEY_LOCAL_MACHINE\System\CurrentControlSet\Hardware Profiles\Current. This subtree supports backward compatibility with Windows 95/98 applications.

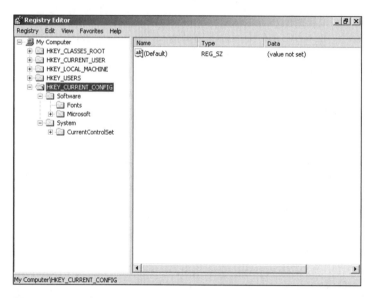

Figure 3-7 The HKEY_CURRENT_CONFIG subtree

HKEY_CURRENT_USER

The HKEY_CURRENT_USER subtree, shown in Figure 3-8, contains the current user's profile and is created whenever a user logs onto a Windows 2000 machine. It is created by copying profile data from HKEY_USERS and loading the Ntuser.dat file, or by duplicating the default user profile from HKEY_USERS if no profile for that user appears in Ntuser.dat.

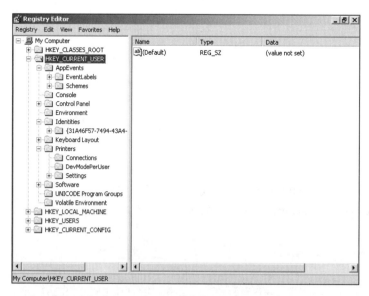

Figure 3-8 The HKEY_CURRENT_USER subtree

HKEY_USERS

The HKEY_CLASSES_ROOT subtree, shown in Figure 3-9, contains user profiles for all users who have logged onto this computer at any time in the past. It also includes a default user profile that is invoked whenever an existing user profile is not available.

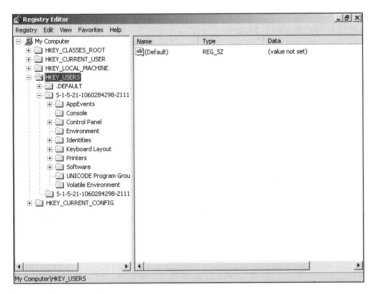

Figure 3-9 The HKEY_USERS subtree

Protecting the Registry

Protecting the Windows 2000 Registry involves following two essential rules. First and foremost, avoid editing the Registry directly. Instead, use an interface such as an administrative tool, a Microsoft Management Console (MMC) snap-in, or some other utility that edits the Registry.

Second, back up the Registry whenever it is altered. You can then restore the back-up copy if the original becomes damaged or corrupted.

Backing Up the Registry

You can back up the Registry in any one of the following ways:

- Use back-up software designed for Windows 2000 that includes Registry backups with full system data backups.
- Use Microsoft's REGEDIT or REGEDT32 tools to create Registry backups manually (see Hands-on Project 3-6 to see how this backup is done).
- Use a Support Tools utility designed to back up the Registry (REG COPY, REG SAVE, or REG BACKUP).

The emergency repair disk (ERD) that Windows 2000 creates as a system repair tool no longer contains a copy of the Registry. For this reason, the ERD is not considered a valid way of maintaining even a partial Registry backup.

If a Windows 2000 Registry becomes corrupted, you might be able to restore the system to normal activity through one of several repair maneuvers. The first such maneuver involves the Last Known Good Configuration start-up option, which attempts to restore the Registry to its (presumably working) state at the time of the last successful logon. The second maneuver is to use the Windows 2000 Safe Mode boot option, which boots the system using only basic drivers and required system files. The third maneuver is to restore all or part of the Registry from a backup. Try these repair strategies in the order they are presented here, because the amount of work and time required to complete each one increases from first to last. Refer to Chapter 15, "Troubleshooting Windows 2000," for more information on how to perform these procedures.

Modifying the Registry

If you must edit the Windows 2000 Registry directly, you can use one of two editors: REGEDIT and REGEDT32. You can launch these tools manually from a command prompt or by using the Run command. REGEDIT is a 16-bit application, and REGEDT32 is a 32-bit application.

REGEDIT, which originally appeared in Windows 95, displays all Registry subtrees in a single window and allows exhaustive searching of the entire Registry's contents. In contrast, REGEDT32 displays each subtree in its own cascading window. Its primary benefit is improved controls for security settings and the ability to audit Registry access on a subtree, key, subkey, or value entry basis.

Either Registry editor can be used to add, modify, and delete value entries and subtrees, import and export all or part of the Registry, and access and edit Registries on remote systems. When using either Registry editor, however, you risk damaging the Registry. Because the Registry is the primary control mechanism for Windows 2000, it is possible to destroy an installation because of a minor editing mistake. Whenever you edit the Registry directly, remember to do the following:

- Create a back-up of all Registry keys to be edited.
- If possible, back up all data on another computer to prevent loss of access to back-up data if the system fails.
- Perform only a single change at a time.
- Reboot the system between changes, even if not prompted to do so.
- Test changes on nonproduction systems before altering a mission-critical system or deploying wholesale changes on numerous systems.

- Use REGEDT32 in read-only mode when you are exploring the Registry to prevent accidental changes or damages.

For more information on the Registry, consult the Windows 2000 Support Tools. For details on individual value entries, consult the REGENTRY tool on the Windows 2000 installation CD in the Support\Tools directory.

BASE SYSTEM FUNCTIONALITY

As discussed in Chapter 1, any operating system must support some essential operations. In the following sections, these basic operations are covered in more detail as they relate to Windows 2000.

Writing to Disk

Writing to disk is a key function that allows data to be retained even when a computer is not running. In this process, information that is stored in memory becomes recorded on a physical disk drive or some other persistent storage medium (such as a CD-ROM or tape drive). Data stored in memory is considered transitory, because all data in memory is lost when power is not available. Data stored on a physical drive is considered permanent, because the information is retained even when power is no longer available.

The Windows 2000 system writes data, including page swapping, Registry changes, and user profile changes, to disk for several reasons. Most often, disk writing activities are initiated by user applications to record data relevant to the application in the form of one or more specially formatted data files. For Windows 2000, writing to disk involves the File Systems Manager module in the **executive services** portion of the kernel, because such activity usually requires accessing one or more files. The following executive services modules can be involved as well:

- The Object Manager handles the initial request for which file object (or objects) may be requested for access.
- The Security Reference Monitor is called, because the Object Manager inquires whether access to the requested object and related service may proceed.
- The I/O Manager handles access to the device class driver and the actual device driver for the physical drive that is accessed, if the Object Manager calls it to do so. (By implication, the Security Reference Monitor must have granted access to the object for whatever service is requested.)

When virtual memory is accessed, the Virtual Memory Manager may instigate writing to the disk as well, if the operating system needs to read from or write to the **paging file** stored on disk. (A paging file—also known as a pagefile—is temporary storage space on a hard drive.)

Allocating Memory

As discussed in Chapter 2, memory allocation is the process whereby sections of memory are assigned to a process or device driver for its exclusive use. This function is important; without it, processes and device drivers might interfere with each other's operations by overwriting data stored in memory.

Windows 2000 employs **virtual machines** whenever possible, even on systems with ample amounts of physical RAM. Each virtual machine can access as much as 4 GB of address space. The Windows 2000 executive services Virtual Memory Manager juggles address spaces for all virtual machines, mapping all used address spaces to actual memory pages. The Virtual Memory Manager allocates memory dynamically, based on availability and use. When a process requires such a memory page, the page is loaded into physical RAM (if it is not already present). When a page is not in use, it can be pushed out to the pagefile to release physical RAM for other uses, such as other processes or threads that are active on the same machine at roughly the same time.

On the one hand, some device drivers—specifically, real-mode device drivers—require fixed, predetermined physical memory allocations to work. On the other hand, protected-mode device drivers can reside in areas of memory that might not always be present in physical RAM. Fortunately, the Virtual Memory Manager is aware of those memory areas that real-mode drivers must use exclusively and will not page those sections to disk or map them into virtual machine address spaces.

Allocating CPU Time

Allocating CPU time means controlling when and how much execution time is granted to processes. Most modern operating systems grant access to the CPU for a maximum fixed time interval known as a time slice (this operation is sometimes called time slicing). CPU allocation is important in a multithreaded operating system because it prevents any single thread from dominating access to the CPU. By assigning explicit execution priorities to processes and by limiting the maximum amount of time that the process is allowed to access the CPU before stepping aside for another process, more than one process can appear to be active simultaneously, even on a single-CPU system. That's because humans are so much slower than computers. Although a process might be able to accomplish significant work before its time slice expires and other processes become active, to ordinary mortals all processes that are sharing the CPU appear to be active at the same time.

Windows 2000 uses a scheduling algorithm for the CPU called **preemptive multitasking**. In plain English, even though a process may expect to occupy the CPU for an entire time slice, once it becomes active, it can be preempted at any time when a higher-priority task requires service. This task-switching capability lets Windows 2000 maintain the operating system kernel, control hardware access, sustain virtual machines, and allow user-mode processes to execute, all apparently simultaneously. In reality, of course, the operating system executive is scheduling processes, monitoring their progress, and switching them out continuously, depending on elapsed time or the arrival of higher-priority processes or tasks.

Windows 2000 also supports a different scheduling regimen called cooperative multitasking for Windows 16-bit applications. The original environment of Windows 16-bit applications allowed processes to retain access to the CPU until those processes voluntarily relinquished such access. Thus those processes were designed to surrender possession of the CPU on a cooperative basis to permit other tasks to execute.

Because cooperative multitasking is fundamentally incompatible with preemptive multitasking, Windows 2000 provides a runtime environment that emulates cooperative multitasking within the context of a single virtual machine. By default, Win16 applications operate within the same virtual machine. Within that virtual machine, the Win16 processes follow the cooperative multitasking native to such applications, which allows Windows 2000 to support what appears to be cooperative multitasking in a preemptive multitasking environment. In reality, the single virtual machine in which Win16 applications execute is subject to the time slice limitations, execution priority settings, and possibility of preemption by other processes, just as all other Windows 2000 virtual machines are.

The allocation of CPU time is managed primarily by the scheduling and priority management aspects of the operating system kernel, which is always resident in memory. Although the Process Manager is also involved, it is responsible for maintaining active virtual machines, not allocating CPU access.

Handling Data-Processing Requests

Handling data-processing requests basically means responding to resource requests that originate in a particular process that is active at the time the request is made. The operating system must direct that request to the proper provider, possibly instructing that provider to respond to the request. For example, when an application requests a file, the request is captured by the virtual machine, routed to the kernel's executive services, and processed by the Security Reference Monitor, the Object Manager, and the File Systems Manager. Ultimately, that request is routed to the drive where the file resides through the agencies of the I/O Manager, and its contents are obtained. This information then follows the same trail in reverse, going back to the requesting process.

Resource requests can include requests for memory, CPU access, files, graphical objects or information, and keyboard input or output. Without the ability to handle such requests, any operating system, including Windows 2000, is useless. This point explains the fundamental impetus for the Windows 2000 architecture, especially the executive services components and their modular design. Each of those modules is designed to handle particular kinds of resource requests or to expedite the process of handling resource requests in general. Their modularity helps ensure that individual components can change to improve their capabilities or performance without materially affecting other aspects of the system. In this respect, Windows 2000 resembles a complex machine made of interlocking parts, all of which are necessary for the operating system to do its job.

Error Handling

Error handling involves recognizing and averting the effects of invalid data or attempts to execute illegal actions before they can damage a system or the resources managed by that system. It also requires generating a system response—perhaps an error message to users and some kind of post-error cleanup behavior. In turn, this step requires dealing with issues specific to the context within which errors occur and responding with the appropriate action.

Error handling is primarily a defensive reaction to an anomalous system or application condition. From an operating system perspective, error handling applies to its kernel, subsystem modules, and utilities and device drivers. At this level, the primary function of error handling is to prevent system crashes by redirecting problems to an error mechanism rather than attempting to continue processes or operations with incorrect data or to execute illegal or invalid instructions.

Within Windows 2000, errors are handled by suspending the process associated with the error in noncore system code. Because processes remain isolated from one another, the failure or suspension of a single process should not cause the entire operating system to crash. If an error can be resolved, the suspended process can be released to continue functioning. If it cannot be resolved, the offending process is usually terminated. The worst-case scenario for an application error is that the application in which the error occurred terminates, losing whatever data that has not yet been saved to disk.

On the other hand, if an error occurs in some component of the operating system itself, a so-called STOP error occurs. (Because these types of errors are reported in a special format on an all-blue, character-only screen, they are called the "blue screen of death," abbreviated as BSOD.) STOP errors cause the operating system to halt and cease its operations. It is possible to configure STOP error management to record details about whatever event triggered the error, to restart the system, and even to write the current contents of memory to a dump file for debugging inspection by a system professional.

Network Functionality

Network functionality is the ability to communicate with other computers across some kind of communications medium. This capability relies on a shared protocol (communication language), a shared physical medium (cable, telephone wire, infrared, microwaves, and so on), and a network interface (often an expansion card or PC Card with its related device drivers).

Windows 2000 includes network functionality as a basic element of its design. The ability to communicate over a network permits the sharing of resources and distribution of the workload. In addition, it simplifies interpersonal communications, promotes centralized administration and control, and offers a broader range of access to resources—from across the room to across the world. With the phenomenal rise of the Internet, no operating system released in the latter part of the 1990s can be considered complete if it does not offer built-in networking support. In fact, the last operating system from Microsoft that failed to include built-in networking functionality was Windows 3.1 (released in 1990).

Interprocess Communications (IPCs, RPCs)

In the Microsoft environment, interprocess communication (IPC) employs a proprietary but well-documented API that processes use to exchange information. In more general terms, IPC defines a mechanism that allows one active process to exchange data with another process. If both processes are active, information can move more or less directly from sender to receiver. If the receiving process is unavailable or inactive, however, an intermediary is required to store the information for delivery to the receiver if and when the receiver becomes active. Handling these kinds of complexities is what makes IPC so interesting and the software that implements IPC so challenging to create.

In the Windows 2000 environment, IPC allows programmers to employ well-defined query and response mechanisms without requiring them to develop these mechanisms themselves. IPC enables the kernel, executive services, virtual machines, and user processes to function as they do—that is, to communicate with each other so as to direct activity within the operating system.

Remote process communication (RPC) is similar to IPC; it allows processes running on different machines to communicate. RPC occurs across local networks or wide area network (WAN) links. This fundamental technology enables client-server applications to operate and distributed computing to occur.

Messaging

In general, messaging allows operating systems to communicate across a network or over a remote access link. It relies on a server service that listens on a specific port address to which clients direct resource requests across the network.

Messaging is a generalized concept that includes both IPC and RPC mechanisms. In Windows operating systems, messaging also includes esoteric mechanisms such as named pipes, mailslots, and NetBIOS interfaces. Windows 2000 takes advantage of this capability, especially with powerful clients. When either Windows 2000 Professional or Windows NT 4.0 Workstation operates as a client, the messaging features of Windows 2000 support a much broader range of interaction, control, and resource access.

Terminal Services

Terminal Services refers to a class of computer services that traditionally describes a mechanism that permits a so-called **smart terminal**—not much more than a monitor and a keyboard with a network attachment—to access and use the services of an operating system across a network.

In their earliest manifestations, terminals defined a typical user interface for mainframes and minicomputers. In such environments, the computer was a large, exotic, and expensive collection of equipment kept behind locked doors and maintained to by a specially trained staff. Ordinary users could access the computer only through a terminal, which gave them the ability to input data and queries and to view the results of their work, but included little or no additional computing abilities.

Today, two distinct categories of Terminal Services persist: client emulation and remote control. Although it remains possible to use Terminal Services with nothing more than a smart terminal and keyboard, client emulation allows PCs and other stand-alone computers to act as if they were nothing more than smart terminals from the serving computer's point of view.

Windows 2000 includes an add-on that supports Terminal Services, and both types of clients (smart terminals and PCs that are emulating smart terminals) can take advantage of its services.

Remote control, on the other hand, gives one operating system the ability to control a remote system or to use that remote system's full client capabilities as if it were physically present. This feature simplifies administration by allowing a single client to control systems throughout a network. In either case, the remote control aspect of Terminal Services allows an entire desktop environment to be maintained in a virtual machine on a server that any client can access across the network (even if that client is not a Windows machine).

Microsoft designed its Terminal Services with a particular class of desktop computers in mind—**thin clients**, also known as **network computers**. Both terms refer to a configuration similar to the original smart terminal in the mainframe and minicomputer eras: a low-cost, low-powered desktop environment. For the more modern implementations, this configuration consists of a networked computer with just enough CPU power and memory to handle local input and output tasks. This client machine relies on a server elsewhere on the network to run applications, provide storage, and supply the many services that workplace users expect today, such as e-mail, Internet access, and productivity applications.

Terminal Services allow inexpensive client devices to deliver all of the high-powered, complex services and applications that can run on today's high-performance servers. It also allows organizations to control client desktops much more rigorously and makes these desktops much easier to maintain and update in a rapidly changing technological landscape. Although it's not clear whether this kind of computing will ever rule the world again, as it did in the 1960s when mainframes and minicomputers were the norm, it does offer an attractive option for some organizations. Clearly, this kind of computing works better than using stand-alone PCs (primarily for cost and control reasons) for certain applications—such as point-of-sale devices ("smart" cash registers), factory floor monitors and devices, and loading dock systems. Such computing is expected to remain in active use for the foreseeable future.

Microsoft apparently agrees with this analysis, because Windows 2000 Server includes Terminal Services as an add-on element. This feature allows lower-end PCs or thin clients to participate in the rich environment of Windows 2000 without meeting the hardware requirements needed for installing Windows 2000 Professional on those client machines. Terminals or thin clients with access to Terminal Services need little more than a bootstrap mechanism to access the network and a Windows 2000 Server running the right software. After they're connected, the Terminal Services process maintains the user environment, transmitting only the graphical display information and receiving only the input from the keyboard or mouse that the client needs to manage local input and display information.

TOOLS FOUND IN WINDOWS 2000 SERVER

Windows 2000 Server offers a wide variety of system control, administration, and management tools. These tools allow you to fine-tune, control, and manipulate all aspects of the operating system. In an effort to standardize control interfaces, Microsoft introduced the Microsoft

Management Console (MMC) in Internet Information Server 4.0. With the release of Windows 2000, the MMC becomes the operating system's standard management interface.

The MMC is a standardized graphical interface into which control modules called snap-ins can be loaded to provide administration and control functionality over specific types or groups of objects within the Windows 2000 environment. The MMC provides no control functions itself; rather, it merely defines an environment and a set of well-documented mechanisms to control underlying systems, related subsystems, and operating system objects of many types.

In fact, the Windows 2000 administration and control tools combine MMC snap-ins, multi-tabbed dialog boxes, and step-by-step software wizards. You can access all of these control utilities through the Windows 2000 Control Panel. Some of the more important tools in this collection include the following:

- Add/Remove Hardware: Use this wizard to install drivers for new hardware, remove drivers for hardware to be removed from the system, and troubleshoot malfunctioning hardware.

- Add/Remove Programs: Use this tool to change or remove installed applications, setup new applications, and alter the installed components of Windows 2000.

- Network and Dial-Up Connections: Use this tool to configure all network communications, including settings for NICs, services, and protocols. This interface manages both direct cable connections, such as those used in a LAN, and remote links, such as those created over telephone or ISDN lines.

- System: Use this multitabbed dialog box to change network membership and computer name, access the Device Manager, define hardware profiles, create roaming user profiles, define performance options, set pagefile settings, define environmental variables, and define start-up and recovery options.

- Active Directory Users and Computers: Use this tool to define and manage user accounts and groups. You access this tool via the Start menu or the Administrative Tools icon in the Control Panel.

- Computer Management: Use this tool to access the Event Viewer, obtain system information, review performance, manage shared folders, access the Device Manager, manage physical disks, and manage system services, such as Dynamic Host Configuration Protocol (DHCP), telephony, Internet Information Services (IIS), and Domain Name Service (DNS). Access it via the Start menu or the Administrative Tools icon in the Control Panel.

- Distributed File System: Use this tool to create a single-access-point, single-hierarchy system for a shared resource on a network when the resources are hosted by multiple servers. Access it via the Start menu or the Administrative Tools icon in the Control Panel.

- Routing and Remote Access: Use this tool to manage multihomed server-based routing and remote access to and from the server. Access it via the Start menu or the Administrative Tools icon in the Control Panel.

Many of the tools found in Windows 2000 are MMC snap-in transformations of previous controls found in Windows NT or tools migrated and improved from Windows 98. The result is a set of powerful, easy-to-use tools that manage and control every aspect of the Windows 2000 environment.

CHAPTER SUMMARY

- An operating system consists of a collection of files, such as Ntoskrnl.exe, DLLs, and device drivers. Specific files are required during start-up to establish the environment so that the operating system as a whole can be loaded and maintained.

- Windows 2000 employs a modular approach in its system architecture that results in a stable and functional system. The major functions and capabilities of Windows 2000 are delegated to and managed by the executive services. The Registry contains configuration and operational settings that Windows 2000 uses to control its environment.

- Windows 2000 demonstrates all of the basic system functionalities that a modern operating system must support. Various administration and management utilities control the environment of Windows 2000, primarily those found in the Control Panel and under the Administrative Tools menu.

KEY TERMS

Boot.ini — A file that defines the host partitions and the primary executables of the operating systems present on the computer. Boot.ini also defines the default operating system that loads when the customizable boot menu display timer expires.

boot partition — On a Windows 2000 system, the partition that contains the main operating system directory and the pagefile. The boot partition can be the same as the system partition, but most often is located elsewhere, either on the same drive or on a different physical drive.

Bootsect.dos — On a multiboot system with another Microsoft, clone, or near-equivalent operating system such as DOS or Windows 95/98, a file that is used to establish a start-up environment more conducive to these older Microsoft operating systems.

bootstrapping — The initialization process that a computer goes through to inspect its hardware and locate the boot files for an operating system on the active partition of a hard drive.

bootstrapping files — Computer files required to initiate loading and launching an operating system. Also called boot files.

control set — A hardware-profile-specific collection of boot process parameters.

core system files — Those files that make up the core components of an operating system. If these files become corrupted or damaged, the operating system cannot function.

device class driver — A piece of software that supplies basic driver interfaces and functions that define broad parameters for specific types of devices.

executive services — The collection of all intermediary and management components for all resources, security, and communications in the Windows 2000 environment.

User-mode processes do not actually interact with executive services; rather, they interact with APIs defined for their application subsystems. The virtual machine in which the calling application runs then redirects such API calls to the kernel, where they are routed to the appropriate executive service.

hardware abstraction layer (HAL) — The only module of Windows 2000 that is hardware-specific. The HAL is built to match the type and state of the hardware during installation.

hive — A section of the Registry that is stored in a separate file. Hives are permanent structures that are saved each time the system is shut down, and reloaded each time the system is powered up.

individual device driver — A device- and model-specific program that defines the exact capabilities and functions of a particular device down to the make and model level, and allows the operating system to access the device's functions.

interrupt request (IRQ) — A special, high-priority communications channel through which a hardware device informs the CPU that it needs to perform some action or respond to some condition.

master boot record (MBR) — The section on a hard drive where the partition table and other key descriptive information are stored.

modular architecture — A method of programming where multiple separate components are combined into a single logical whole. Each component handles a specific task or a small set of related tasks. Windows 2000 uses such architecture in its kernel mode, particularly for the components that make up its executive services.

multiboot system — A computer that contains two or more operating systems and allows the user to select which operating system to start during each initial system start-up cycle.

network computers — See thin clients.

Ntbootdd.sys — A file that appears on Windows 2000 and Windows NT systems with SCSI controllers that do not have an on-board BIOS translation enabled or present. It enables the drive controller system on the motherboard to control a SCSI adapter and its attached hard drives.

Ntdetect.com — A file that is invoked just prior to loading the Windows 2000 executable files from the boot partition. It performs a hardware inspection to create an inventory of devices and their configurations. The configuration that is detected is used to select a hardware profile, which in turn determines which device drivers are loaded.

Ntldr — The operating system initialization file that the computer launches upon the completion of the bootstrapping process. It is responsible for loading Windows NT or other operating systems when it appears on a multiboot system. Ntldr uses the Boot.ini file to present a boot menu, which in turn is used to select the operating system to be launched.

Ntoskrnl.exe — A file that contains the Windows 2000 kernel, which is the core of the Windows 2000 operating environment. It controls the loading of all other files involved in establishing the computing environment. Ntoskrnl.exe resides on the boot partition in the \Winnt\System32 folder (assuming the default name for the system root is accepted during installation).

Osloader.exe — A file that appears only on Alpha systems. It replaces all of the various files found on Intel machines by combining their functions into a single file.

paging file — See pagefile.

pagefile — Temporary storage space on a hard drive.

Power On, Self-Test (POST) — An internal diagnostic that a computer performs during the earliest phases of the bootstrapping process.

preemptive multitasking — Type of multitasking in which the memory manager controls who has control of the CPU, rather than giving the responsibilities to the applications.

Registry — The configuration and parameter details that govern how Windows 2000 operates. The Registry is stored as a single hierarchical database.

smart terminal — A computer that has only a monitor and a keyboard with a network attachment.

system partition — The partition that contains the files used to initialize the Windows 2000 loading process.

thin clients — A low-cost, low-powered desktop environment with just enough CPU power and memory to handle local input and output tasks.

virtual machine — A software construct that creates a computer environment for each process, so that the process appears to be the exclusive resident of the physical machine. In Windows 2000, application subsystems construct virtual machines for processes. When a process requests access to a resource (whether memory, CPU time, keyboard input, display changes, or hard drive resources), the virtual machine relays that request to the application subsystem in which the virtual machine resides. This subsystem, in turn, passes the request to the appropriate executive service in the kernel mode.

REVIEW QUESTIONS

1. Which of the following statements are true? (Choose all that apply.)
   a. MS-DOS requires several specialized files to load itself as an operating system.
   b. Windows 2000 is a monolithic code block.
   c. Modular architecture improves fault tolerance.
   d. Individual modules of Windows 2000 cannot be replaced.

2. What happens immediately after a computer's power is turned on?
   a. The Registry is loaded.
   b. Boot.ini is read.
   c. POST takes place.
   d. Ntoskrnl.exe is launched.

3. Which of the following actually determines from where the computer attempts to load an operating system?
   a. Active partition
   b. Partition table
   c. Registry
   d. File system

4. Windows 2000 cannot exist on a computer in a multiboot configuration. True or False?
5. In the Windows 2000 context, the active partition is also the _____ partition.
6. On Alpha systems hosting Windows 2000, the system partition must be formatted with which of the following?
   a. FAT
   b. FAT32
   c. NTFS
   d. HPFS
7. What tool can you use to partition a hard drive?
   a. Registry
   b. Setup Boot disks
   c. MBR
   d. Boot Manager
8. Windows 2000 and Windows NT have nearly identical boot methods. True or False?
9. Which Windows 2000 boot file is the operating system initialization file that the computer launches upon the completion of the bootstrapping process?
   a. Ntldr
   b. Boot.ini
   c. Ntdetect.com
   d. Ntbootdd.sys
10. Which Windows 2000 boot file appears only on multiboot systems?
    a. Boot.ini
    b. Ntdetect.com
    c. Ntbootdd.sys
    d. Bootsect.dos
11. Osloader.exe replaces the functions of Ntldr and Ntdetect.com and can be used on either Intel or Alpha systems. True or False?
12. Before the Ntoskrnl file is given control of the computer, several DLLs, the HAL, and other device drivers are loaded into memory. True or False?
13. What is the last component launched before the logon dialog box is displayed that prompts you to press Ctrl+Alt+Delete?
    a. Winlogon.exe
    b. Lsass.exe
    c. Ntoskrnl.exe
    d. Hal.dll

14. The Windows 2000 environment is divided into two sections: the user mode and the kernel mode. True or False?

15. Why does Windows 2000 have two operational modes? (Choose all that apply.)
    a. The two modes are used to allocate execution time based on importance and priority.
    b. The two modes prevent nonsystem code from interacting with hardware.
    c. The two modes allow core environment-maintaining operations to function as background tasks.
    d. The two modes maintain the integrity of the security system.

16. All processes in the user mode function within a virtual machine. True or False?

17. Which of the following are true of user-mode processes? (Choose all that apply.)
    a. They can address 4 GB of memory.
    b. They have direct hardware access.
    c. Executive services provide proxied resources.
    d. They can be of five application types.

18. Which application types supported by Windows 2000 are actually emulations based on another application subsystem? (Choose all that apply.)
    a. Win32
    b. Win16
    c. DOS
    d. POSIX
    e. OS/2

19. Which executive service is involved whenever a user attempts to access a resource, no matter what the resource is?
    a. IPC Manager
    b. Security Reference Monitor
    c. Virtual Memory Manager
    d. File System Manager

20. Although the Registry is the primary means of storing configuration data for Windows 2000, several text-based initialization files are required as well. True or False?

21. When it is necessary to make system changes, which of the following tools does Microsoft recommend? (Choose all that apply.)
    a. Active Directory Users and Computers
    b. Computer Management
    c. REGEDIT
    d. System applet

22. The Registry is a list of exceptions instead of an exhaustive collection of contr meters. True or False?
23. Which of the following are true in regard to the Registry? (Choose all that apply.)
    a. A single change can cause system failure.
    b. A backup of the Registry is the only protection against invalid values.
    c. The Registry is self-repairing.
    d. Changes to the Registry take place only after a restart of the system.
24. The base functionality of network communications includes the ability to interact with other systems over physical connections as well as temporary remote access connections. True or False?
25. The base functionality of memory allocation involves which of the following items or components? (Choose all that apply.)
    a. Virtual Memory Manager
    b. Real-mode device drivers
    c. Virtual machines
    d. Process priorities

HANDS-ON PROJECTS

Project 3-1

To explore the Registry via REGEDT32:

1. Open the Run dialog box (**Start, Run**).
2. Type **REGEDT32**. Click **OK**.
3. Select **Read Only Mode** from the **Options** menu.
4. Select the **HKEY_LOCAL_MACHINE** subtree window.
5. Double-click the **Software** subkey.
6. Locate and double-click the **Microsoft** subkey. See Figure 3-10.
7. Locate and double-click the **Windows NT** subkey.
8. Double-click the **CurrentVersion** subkey.
9. Locate and select the **WinLogon** subkey.
10. Locate and double-click the **DefaultUserName** value entry.
11. Because you are in read-only mode, a message appears stating that your changes will not be saved. Click **OK**.
12. You see the data of the DefaultUserName value entry. Click **OK**.
13. Close REGEDT32 by selecting **Exit** from the Registry menu.

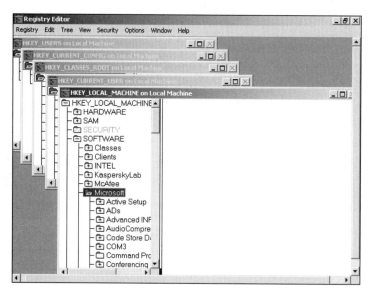

Figure 3-10 Exploring the HKEY_LOCAL_MACHINE\Software\Microsoft subkey

Project 3-2

To explore the Active Directory Users and Computers tool:

1. Open the Active Directory Users and Computers tool (**Start**, **Programs**, **Administrative Tools**, **Active Directory Users and Computers**).
2. Double-click the node named after your domain. (It should have a .local extension.)
3. Click the **Users** node. See Figure 3-11.
4. Double-click the **Administrator** user account in the Details pane.
5. Explore the multitabbed user properties dialog box, but do not make any changes.
6. Click **Cancel** when complete (this action discards your changes if you made any).
7. Select the **Computers** node. All nondomain controller systems are displayed in the Details pane.
8. Select the **Domain Controllers** node. All domain controller systems are displayed in the Details pane.
9. Click the **Builtin** node. All of the existing groups are displayed in the Details pane.
10. Double-click the **Administrators** group. Explore the multitabbed group properties dialog box, but do not make any changes.
11. Click **Cancel**.
12. Close the Active Directory Users and Computers tool by selecting **Exit** from the **Console** menu.

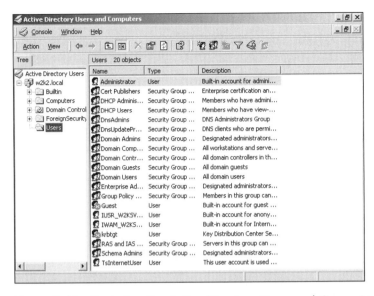

Figure 3-11 Exploring the Active Directory Users and Computers tool

Project 3-3

To explore the Computer Management tool:

1. Open the Computer Management tool (**Start**, **Programs**, **Administrative Tools**, **Computer Management**).

2. Click on the plus signs to the left of the **System Tools**, **Storage**, and **Services and Applications** nodes to expand their contents (if not already expanded). See Figure 3-12.

Figure 3-12 Exploring the Computer Management tool

3. Select the **Event Viewer** below the **System Tools** node.
4. Double-click the **System Log** in the Details pane.
5. Double-click an event detail.
6. After reading the detail, click **OK** to close it.
7. Select the **System Information** node below the **System Tools** node.
8. Double-click **Hardware Resources**, and then **IRQs**. This choice shows the IRQs currently in use. See Figure 3-13.

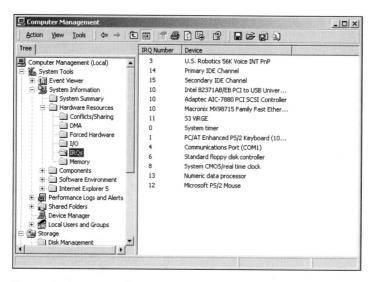

Figure 3-13 Using the Computer Management tool to determine the IRQs in use

9. Select the **Shared Folders** node.
10. Double-click the **Shares** detail. It reveals all of the current shares from this system.
11. Select the **Device Manager** node. It shows the categorized list of installed devices.
12. Select **Disk Management** below the **Storage** node. It displays the physical configuration of hard drives.
13. Select the **Disk Defragmenter** node. It is used to initiate defragmentation.
14. Select the **Logical Drives** node. It lists all local drives and mapped shares.
15. Select **Services** below the **Services and Applications** node. It lists all of the installed services and their current status.
16. Close **Computer Management** by clicking the **Close** button in the top-right corner of the window.

Project 3-4

To explore the Task Manager:

1. Launch the **Task Manager** (right-click over an empty area of the taskbar, then select **Task Manager** from the resulting menu).
2. Select the **Applications** tab. It lists all active applications and their status. See Figure 3-14.

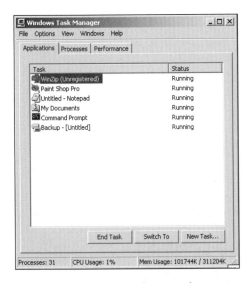

Figure 3-14 The Windows Task Manager

3. Select the **Processes** tab. It lists all active processes and related data such as CPU time, process ID, and memory usage. This tab can display more than a dozen different data items for each process.
4. Notice some of the core system files listed, such as Winlogon and Lsass.
5. Select the **Performance** tab. It displays real-time data about CPU and memory usage.
6. Close the Task Manager by selecting **Exit Task Manager** from the **File** menu.

Project 3-5

To explore the Control Panel:

1. Open the Control Panel (**Start**, **Settings**, **Control Panel**).
2. Double-click the **Add/Remove Hardware** applet to open it.
3. Click **Next** on the Welcome screen.
4. Select **Add/Troubleshoot a device**. Click **Next**.
5. After the wizard completes its search for devices, click **Cancel** to exit the wizard.
6. Double-click the **Add/Remove Programs** applet to open it. Notice the list of installed applications. See Figure 3-15.

Figure 3-15 The Add/Remove Programs applet

7. Select the **Add New Programs** item. Notice the controls used to launch installation of a new application.
8. Select the **Add/Remove Windows Components** item.
9. Scroll down the list of installed and available Windows components.
10. Click **Cancel** to exit this wizard.
11. Click **Close**.
12. Double-click the **System** applet to open it.
13. Select the **Hardware** tab. Notice the links to install new hardware, access the Device Manager, and configure hardware profiles.
14. Select the **Advanced** tab. Notice the links to performance options, environmental variables, and start-up and recovery options.
15. Click **Cancel**.
16. Close the Control Panel by selecting **Close** from the **File** menu.

Project 3-6

To back up the Registry:

1. Launch the Registry Editor (**Start**, **Run**, **REGEDIT**).
2. Select **Export Registry File** from the Registry menu.
3. Provide a location to which to export the file.
4. Provide a name for the exported file. "W2Kserver-Registry" was chosen in Figure 3-16.

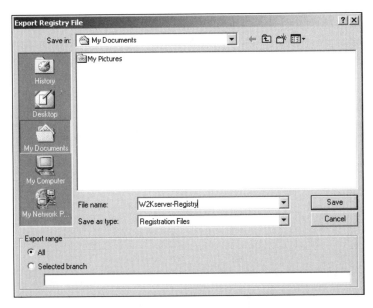

Figure 3-16 Exporting the Registry using REGEDIT

5. Select the **All** radio button in the **Export range** field. Click **Cancel**.
6. Select **Exit** from the Registry menu to close the Registry Editor.

CASE PROJECTS

1. Describe the files involved with the initialization of the Windows 2000 operating system that are active between bootstrapping and the prompt to log on.
2. Describe at least five basic functions of an operating system and explain how Windows 2000 demonstrates these functions.
3. Describe the process of bootstrapping and the problems that can occur before an operating system is launched.
4. Describe the Windows NT Registry. Be sure to mention its structure, purpose, layout, fault-tolerant mechanisms, and editing practices.

CHAPTER 4

ALLOCATING AND MANAGING OPERATING SYSTEM RESOURCES

> **After reading this chapter and completing the exercises, you will be able to:**
> - Explain what applications, processes, and threads are and how they fit together
> - Understand how different server types have different priorities
> - Explain how memory management works
> - Understand the role of the Object Manager in Win2K
> - List the kinds of objects found in Win2K
> - Explain how Win2K object-level security works

Modern operating systems such as Windows 2000 (Win2K) are multitasking, which means that more than one application can run at the same time. (In single-tasking operating systems like DOS, only one application can run at a time.) If you look at the taskbar in your Win2K computer, you'll likely see a number of application icons representing running applications. Many applications are running simultaneously—for that matter, many parts of the operating system are running simultaneously—and these contending tasks must all compete for CPU time so that they can carry out their duties. One fundamental problem that any operating system must address is how to allocate system resources among all applications running on the computer—not to mention the various parts of the operating system itself.

For any multitasking operating system, resource management is key to its success. If resource management is done well, then applications and the parts of the operating system that need to process data will work together to make it appear that the computer is doing many things at once. If resource management is done badly, then tasks don't finish, applications hang, and users get cranky. This chapter discusses the mechanics of how Win2K manages resources to make the operating system run as smoothly as possible, allocating resources where they're needed without starving less important functions. To manage these resources, Win2K represents them as objects for the convenience of the parts of the executive component that must manipulate them.

DISTRIBUTING CPU CYCLES

The central processing unit (CPU) is the brain of the computer and is its most important part. Everything else in the computer—disks, memory, cards, and so on—is either storage or a means of getting data to the CPU for processing. Once the CPU processes the data, something happens: letters appear on the monitor, a file is saved to disk, or data are moved from the paging file to **physical memory**. In all cases, however, the CPU must be involved.

Some computers with multiprocessing capabilities contain more than one CPU, implying that no single processor is central. (If more than one processor in a computer is running Win2K, then the processors are equal in status; under normal circumstances, one isn't preferred to the other.) For this reason, you'll sometimes hear the CPU in a machine referred to as the processor. Both terms refer to the same piece of the computer.

The operating system controls how that CPU time is distributed among the applications and the operating system. The problem is that the CPU can do only one thing at a time. Even in multitasking operating systems, which may have dozens of applications running at the same time, the CPU can crunch numbers for only one of those applications at any given moment. Thus the CPU's time is divided into **cycles**, which are discrete chunks of time that the CPU can dedicate to any given application's needs. The trick is to distribute those cycles in such a way that the computer seems as responsive as possible, giving the most time to applications running in the foreground without starving the applications running in the background.

Recall from the discussion of the Process and Thread Manager in Chapter 2 that Win2K doesn't really recognize applications as such. When you run an application, the Win2K Process and Thread Manager creates a **process**, which defines the resources available to that application. Among these resources are the following:

- The importance of this process (and thus of the threads within it) relative to the other processes running on the computer.

- The virtual memory addresses in which the threads belonging to this process can store data.

- In multiprocessor systems, the preferred processor that threads in that process should use, if any.

- The location of the page directory for virtual memory dedicated to that process. The page directory is required when translating virtual memory addresses to physical memory addresses.

If a process is set up to prefer using one processor over another, then the process is said to have an **affinity** for that processor. Normally, the threads in a process use whichever processor is least busy. In some cases, however, the person who wrote the application may direct the process to have an affinity for a certain processor, so that threads belonging to that process will run only on that processor unless explicitly directed otherwise, even if another processor is less busy.

The process also contains at least one **thread**, which is the executable part of the application. That is, a thread is responsible for carrying out a task. The system contains a thread for accepting keyboard input, a thread for saving data to disk, and so forth. The Process and Thread Manager creates threads only as they're needed to complete a task; it then deletes each thread as its task is completed and returns the resources used by that thread to the process's pool of resources. Basically, the application is the user's front end to all threads that are running and to the process that defines how those threads will get storage space and CPU cycles. You interact with the application; Win2K interacts with the processes and threads that make the application do whatever it does.

As you can see, then, the problem lies not in getting CPU cycles to applications, but in getting them to the threads that support the tasks that the applications are supposed to complete. That's a somewhat complicated chore, and the subject of the following section.

Understanding Multitasking Types

Resource management in a multitasking operating system such as Win2K is geared toward making it *appear* to the user as though all programs are running concurrently without interfering with each other. Strictly speaking, running multiple applications simultaneously isn't possible from the point of view of Win2K. The CPU can do only one thing at a time, so some form of multitasking is needed.

There are three main kinds of multitasking in the Windows world. A simple multitasking environment performs **task switching**, in which multiple applications may be open at a single time, but only the **foreground application**—those being used at the moment—gets any CPU cycles. The **background applications**—those opened but not receiving input—stop working until they're in the foreground again.

A more even-handed approach is **cooperative multitasking**, which is used in Windows 3.x. This mechanism gives all applications access to the CPU for a set period in round-robin format. The "cooperative" part comes from the fact that the applications are supposed to cooperate with each other and voluntarily relinquish the CPU when their time for using the CPU is up. It doesn't always work this way, however. A misbehaving application or an application performing an especially complicated calculation may not relinquish the CPU, thus freezing all other applications in place until the misbehaving application comes to its senses or you restart the machine.

To avoid this problem, Win32 operating systems, including Win2K, use **preemptive multitasking**. This method basically takes control of the CPU away from the applications and gives it to a part of the operating system. Rather than being dependent on the goodwill of the running applications to relinquish the CPU to other applications, preemptive multitasking can interrupt a running application to give CPU time to an application currently running in the background, even if it's not currently getting user input.

Thread Scheduling Basics

Win2K uses a priority-driven preemptive multitasking system to allocate CPU time to threads. Thus the thread with the highest priority that's ready to run always gets the CPU. If more than one thread has the same priority, then those threads share CPU time among themselves in round-robin fashion, so that they all get equal time. If a thread with a certain priority is running and a thread with a higher priority becomes ready to run, then the thread with the higher priority displaces the running thread (more precisely, Win2K displaces the running thread) and gains control of the CPU. The threads that are ready to run may belong to the same process or to different processes. Scheduling happens at the thread level and is unrelated to the processes, except in terms of how process priority affects thread priority.

When a thread is ready to run, it continues for a preset number of CPU cycles called a **quantum**. A quantum is the length of time that a thread is allowed to run before Win2K interrupts the thread to see whether any other threads with the same priority are ready to run. The quantum isn't consistent for all threads; as you'll see, the number of cycles in a quantum can vary from thread to thread and also depending on whether you're running Windows 2000 Server or Windows 2000 Professional. No Registry setting controls quantum length. Instead, each thread has a quantum value that represents the number of CPU cycles in its quantum. Threads running under Windows 2000 Server have a longer quantum than threads running under Windows 2000 Professional. The reasoning behind this difference is as follows: Any task you ask a server to perform is probably urgent and should be completed all at once. The longer quantum is intended to make it more likely that the task will be completed in a single quantum.

Whenever a thread begins running, the CPU must load that thread's **context**, or the information defining its operating environment. What priority is the thread? In which addresses can it store data? What resources does it have available to create other threads or processes, if necessary? This information is recorded in the thread's context. When the CPU loads a new thread's context into memory, this procedure is called **context switching**.

If two threads from the same process get the CPU in succession, then no context switching is necessary. The information is already loaded.

As you may recall from Chapter 2, the part of Win2K that takes responsibility for scheduling the threads lies in the kernel. The kernel does not contain a single scheduling mechanism. Rather, the code is spread through all parts of the kernel that interact with threads, with the code segments collectively being called the kernel's **dispatcher**. The kernel's dispatcher has much the same function as the dispatcher for a taxi company: it keeps track of all units (taxicabs or threads) and organizes them.

The dispatcher is triggered by any of the following events:

- A thread becomes ready to run.
- A thread stops running because it has finished its quantum, the thread terminates, or the thread waits for other input without which it can't continue.

- A thread's priority changes.
- In multiprocessor systems, a running thread's **processor affinity** changes.

In any of these cases, Win2K must determine which thread should next get the CPU. As mentioned earlier, it will be the thread of highest priority that's ready to run on that CPU.

> If no thread is ready to run, then the idle thread gets the CPU. The idle thread isn't really a thread, but more of a placeholder—the cybernetic equivalent of the CPU twiddling its thumbs while waiting for something to do. The idle thread isn't perfectly idle, as it keeps an eye on the system to see whether any real work becomes available, but it doesn't do anything itself.

Understanding Thread States

A thread may not be ready to run because of its **thread state**. A thread may be in any of the following states:

- *Ready:* A ready thread isn't waiting on anything and is, as the name implies, ready to execute. The dispatcher considers only ready threads when looking for threads to give CPU cycles.

- *Standby:* The thread has been selected to run next on a particular processor. When the running thread stops, the dispatcher performs a context switch to this thread. Only one thread may be in the standby state for each processor in the computer—essentially, it's the next thread in line.

- *Running:* Once the dispatcher has performed the context switch to load a thread's process information, the thread starts its quantum and gets CPU time. It continues to run until one of the following events happens: its quantum ends, the dispatcher stops the thread to run another thread with a higher priority that's entered the ready state, the thread terminates, or the thread voluntarily enters the wait state because it needs more information.

- *Waiting:* A waiting thread has been running but is now on hold, either waiting for more data or having been pulled from the running state to let another thread execute. When a thread exits the waiting state, depending on the circumstances it may either resume running or return to the ready state, where it may be chosen to run.

- *Transition:* A thread is ready to run but some of its kernel resources have been paged out of memory so that the CPU can't execute the thread's task due to incomplete information. Once a thread exits the transition state, it is in the ready state.

- *Terminated:* A thread has finished executing. The Process and Thread Manager may delete this thread or, if it might be needed again, may keep it around and reuse it in the same process later.

A thread's life cycle might look like the following example: A process has created Thread Alpha, with a priority of 8. Thread Alpha is now ready to run. When the dispatcher examines the threads in the ready state, it picks Thread Alpha as having the highest priority and puts

Alpha into the standby state for the processor, poised to take over the CPU when the currently running thread finishes its quantum. The running thread terminates, and Alpha enters the running state, getting all of the CPU's time.

But wait! Thread Beta, with a priority of 12, jumps into the fray. This thread has just entered the ready state. The dispatcher, which is responsible for ensuring that the CPU is always busy with the most important task available, puts Alpha into the standby state and gives the CPU time to Beta. When Beta finishes its quantum, the dispatcher examines the available threads. Because Alpha is in the standby state and no threads with a higher priority are ready, the dispatcher lets Alpha go back to the running state, where it finishes its quantum.

When Alpha finishes its quantum, it also completes its job, so the dispatcher puts Alpha into the terminated state. From here, the Process and Thread Manager can either delete Alpha or keep it around in case it needs another thread object. This situation implies a tradeoff. On the one hand, keeping the thread object uses up some of the resources allocated to the process to which the thread is related, while making those resources unavailable to other threads that the process might need to create. On the other hand, it saves time if the process needs a new thread, because it doesn't have to go through the (fairly lengthy) process of creating a thread when it needs one.

Thread and Process Priority

Priority is the key to how threads get CPU time. Consequently, it's important to understand how priorities are set and how they work. When a process is created, it's assigned a priority that reflects its importance. Each thread that's created in the context of this process has a priority influenced by, but not necessarily identical to, its process's priority. A thread's starting priority—its **base priority**—matches that of its process. Win2K may raise or lower that priority for some threads under certain conditions.

Most threads are **variable priority threads**, which means that Win2K can raise or lower their priorities as circumstances dictate. Exceptions include the important system threads that belong to a different class of processes, called real-time processes, which have a higher priority than all user application threads. Any thread with a real-time priority level keeps its original priority.

 Although Win2K has such "real-time" processes, this terminology is something of a misnomer. Win2K is not a real-time operating system because it has no way to ensure that a thread executes at a certain time—a requirement of a true real-time operating system. Win2K uses thread priority to do its best to ensure that important threads run as often as possible, but that is the limit of its ability.

Applications are designed to run at a given priority level, usually normal. You can tweak the priority for user applications, however, if you start them from the command prompt. Using the start command, you can make an application run as a high-priority or even real-time priority process. For example, to run Solitaire in real time, you would type start /realtime sol. You can also change process priorities from the Task Scheduler. There is a catch: if you run applications in real time, Win2K essential services may be less responsive, because more threads will contend for CPU time.

Scheduling Scenarios

So far, you have learned about the possible states of threads and the dispatcher's scheduling of threads to run based on their relative priority. You will now look at how this system can work in practice, based on a few possible scenarios:

- Quantum end
- Voluntary switching
- Preemptive thread scheduling
- Thread termination

Quantum End Recall that every thread running under Win2K has a quantum based both on the thread and on the version of Windows 2000 you're running—Server or Professional. When the running thread finishes its quantum, Win2K must decide whether its priority should be reduced and, if so, whether another thread should run.

Why would Win2K reduce a thread's priority? The operating system will sometimes raise a thread's priority to ensure that it receives CPU time—the priority-driven scheduling makes Win2K vulnerable to starving low-priority threads for CPU cycles. Once the thread has had some time to run, Win2K may lower its priority back to its original level.

If Win2K lowers the thread's priority, the dispatcher runs the thread currently in the standby state, if no other thread with a higher priority has become available in the meantime. The thread that had been running goes to the back of the line of threads that are in the ready state and that share the same priority, as shown in Figure 4-1.

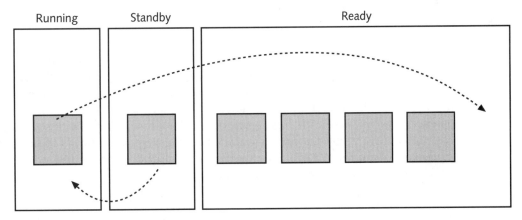

Figure 4-1 When a thread has finished running, it goes to the back of the line of ready threads of the same priority

Voluntary Switching Just because a thread has a quantum doesn't mean that it will always finish that quantum. A thread might leave the running state and enter the waiting state, either voluntarily or when preempted by the thread dispatcher.

If a thread is waiting for something else to happen, then it will voluntarily enter a waiting state, as shown in Figure 4-2. This situation might happen, for example, if the thread needs some I/O to complete before it can complete its own task. A thread isn't penalized for its "generosity" in relinquishing the processor. If it gives up the processor to another thread that's ready to go, then the waiting thread receives a priority boost when it's ready again so that it gets the processor immediately (instead of having to wait for the thread to which it yielded the processor to complete its quantum). It will also be allowed to restart its quantum.

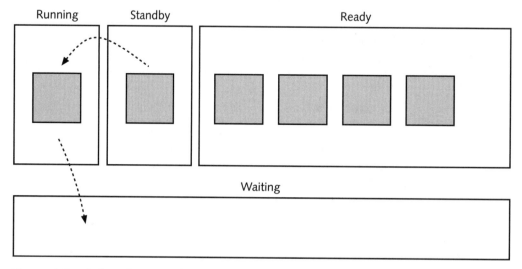

Figure 4-2 A thread waiting for something will go into a waiting state and yield the CPU to the next waiting thread

Preemption Even if a thread doesn't wait voluntarily, it may end up waiting anyway. If a thread is running and a thread with higher priority becomes available, then the running thread will be preempted and the higher-priority thread will get the CPU. This situation works somewhat differently than voluntary switching. First, as you can see in Figure 4-3, the preempted thread does not enter a waiting state. Rather, the preempted thread enters the standby state so that when the higher-priority thread finishes, it will be next in line. Its priority does not rise; instead, it merely waits for the higher-priority thread to finish so that it can resume its quantum. Second, the preempted thread does not restart its quantum, but rather completes the quantum it had already started.

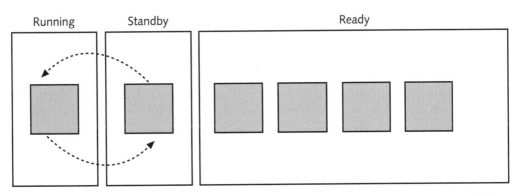

Figure 4-3 A thread preempted by another thread will enter the standby state until the second thread finishes its quantum

Termination As explained earlier, when a thread finishes its task (not just its quantum), it goes into the terminated state, as shown in Figure 4-4. If the thread object is no longer needed by any running process or thread, then it is deleted and its resources go back into its process's resource pool. If the thread isn't deleted, its priority remains unchanged, but it won't get CPU cycles until it's reinitialized and sent back to the ready state.

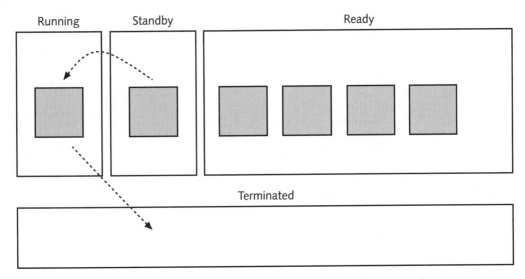

Figure 4-4 A thread that finishes its assigned task enters the terminated state

Adjusting Thread Scheduling

To make the system more responsive, Win2K may edit thread priority or extend a thread's quantum. These adjustments may include any of the following:

- Boosting priority for foreground applications
- Boosting thread priority for threads that have stopped waiting for interrupts to be processed

- Boosting thread priority for threads entering a waiting state
- Boosting thread priority for threads not getting CPU time

Priority Boost for Foreground Applications The simplest way that Win2K can ensure that a thread gets enough time is to give it a slight priority boost. Depending on how Win2K is set up, the foreground application may receive a slight or not-so-slight priority boost.

You can set up your Win2K computer to run applications more efficiently (this strategy is recommended for Windows 2000 Professional or for Windows 2000 Servers supporting terminal session clients). With a system configured in such a way, user applications running in the foreground get a priority boost of 12 when they're accepting input, then drop to a priority of 11 at intervals when they're in the foreground but not immediately receiving user input. (Unless you're copying something previously written, it's unlikely that you'll be constantly inputting data into an application.) If you've set up the Win2K computer as a server, so that it gives more or less equal time to all applications, the foreground application *still gets a priority boost*, albeit a smaller one than it would on a machine optimized for running applications. In this case, the foreground application's priority is boosted from the usual 8 to 10 while the application is actively accepting input, but drops to 9 periodically if you stop entering data into the application. In either case, as soon as another application enters the foreground, the first application's priority reverts to its base priority of 8. (Priority settings range from 1 to 15.)

To edit or check the setting, open the System applet in the Control Panel and access the Advanced tab. If you click the Performance Options button, you'll see a dialog box like the one shown in Figure 4-5. If you set the application response to optimize performance for running applications, then the foreground application gets a longer quantum; if you set it for background services, then all applications have the same quantum. This information is recorded in the Registry under HKEY_LOCAL_MACHINE\System\CurrentControlSet\Control\Priority Control\Win32PrioritySeparation. If you change the setting, it's reflected immediately in the Registry—you do not have to restart the computer.

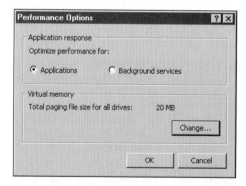

Figure 4-5 Options for treating foreground applications

Priority Boosting After Waiting for I/O Operations If a thread has gone into a waiting state because it needs some I/O operation (such as reading from a disk) to complete, then Win2K will give that thread a priority boost when the operation is finished and the thread is ready to run again. As a result, the threads will run, complete what they were doing, and finish their quantum so that other threads can run.

The actual degree of priority boost depends on how long the thread had to wait for the I/O operation to finish. With a short wait, the thread gets a small boost in priority; with a long wait, it receives a larger boost. Thus threads waiting on relatively fast devices, such as locally accessible CD drives or hard disks, will experience a smaller priority boost, and threads waiting on slower devices, such as the keyboard, will have a much larger one. The idea is that the priority should increase in line with the performance hit that the thread experienced while waiting. The actual priority is determined by the device driver used to access the I/O device. Thus the dispatcher doesn't evaluate the length of the wait, but rather the device on which the thread was waiting. For example, a thread that had been waiting for the end of an I/O operation that depended on the hard disk driver would get a temporary priority boost of 1. A thread waiting on keyboard input would receive a temporary priority boost of 6.

Only threads with priorities in the variable range will get a priority boost. They'll also be boosted only up to the top of the variable range. In other words, a priority boost will not suddenly give a variable thread real-time priority. For example, if a thread has a base priority of 8 (normal for user applications), a priority boost of 8 will give it a priority of 15, which is the top priority for variable priority threads. A thread with a base priority of 15 would receive no boost at all, because its priority is already as high as it can go.

After its priority is boosted, the thread can run one quantum at the increased priority level. When that quantum ends, the dispatcher reduces that thread's priority by one level—to use the usual jargon, decrements it by 1. If the thread is still the highest-priority thread available, then it gets another quantum, after which it's decremented again. This process, which is illustrated in Figure 4-6, continues until the thread reaches its original priority.

Priority Boosts After Waiting for User Input or User Messages Users are a lot slower than disks. To help threads waiting for user input before they can continue what they were doing, the Win2K dispatcher raises the priority of threads waiting for user responses or for window messages once the threads have received this input and are ready to start again. It also doubles the next quantum for that thread, so that the thread has a chance to finish the task that required user input.

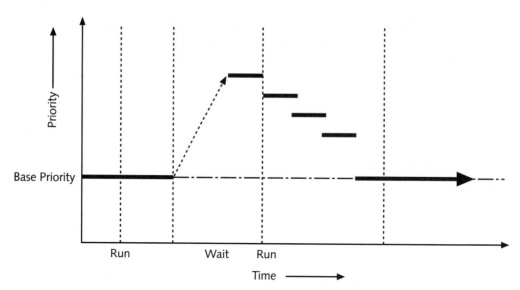

Figure 4-6 The dispatcher raises the priority of waiting threads to an amount based on the device for which they were waiting

As shown in Figure 4-7, this priority boost works somewhat differently from the priority boost that threads can gain after their I/O-based wait ends. First, it is always the same amount. Second, it doesn't last as long as the I/O-based boosts do, because the boost caused by waiting for user input persists for only a single quantum. When that quantum has finished, the thread drops back immediately to its base priority.

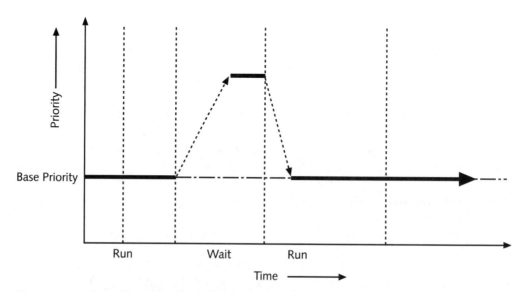

Figure 4-7 Threads waiting for user input get a single big boost after the wait ends, then drop to their base priority

Distributing CPU Cycles   99

Priority Boosts to Rectify CPU Starvation Many threads are interdependent. It's perfectly possible—and quite common—for one thread to depend on output from another thread's execution.

But consider the following: A thread with a priority of 12 is running, keeping a thread with a priority of 8 from getting any CPU time. A thread with a priority of 14 needs the priority-8 thread to finish, however, before it can complete its own task. Although the priority-14 thread should be able to bump the priority-12 thread, it can't, because the priority-8 thread must finish first. The priority-4 thread will never finish, however, because the priority-12 thread is getting all of the CPU time while the priority-14 thread remains in the waiting state.

To resolve this situation, a part of Win2K called the **balance set manager** must become involved. Although the balance set manager is mostly concerned with memory management functions, it has one scheduling trick: It scans the queue of ready threads, looking for those that have been ready to run but haven't been able to do so for longer than a few seconds. If it finds such a thread, the balance set manager will boost the thread's priority to 15—the highest priority available to a variable priority thread—and give it double the normal quantum. Effectively, this action not only gives the starved thread immediate control of the CPU, preempting the priority-12 thread that originally caused the trouble, but also gives the starved thread a longer period to complete its task. Once this long quantum ends, the thread's priority reverts to its original base priority. If the two quantums weren't sufficient to allow the thread to finish its job, then the thread returns to the ready queue, waiting for the balance set manager to notice that it's not running and to give it another doubled quantum. Figure 4-8 illustrates this scenario.

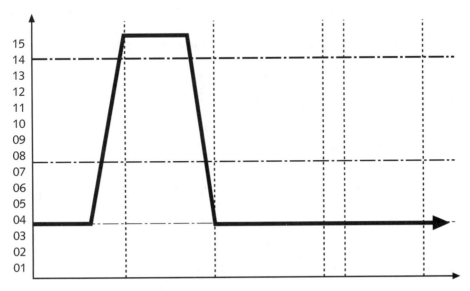

Figure 4-8   The balance set manager gives CPU-starved threads both a high temporary priority and a doubled quantum

This mechanism won't always immediately resolve bottlenecks caused by high-priority threads that depend on low-priority ones. Eventually, however, it will get the low-priority threads out of the way so that the threads dependent on them can execute.

CPU time is merely one resource that Win2K must control to make applications run well. Another resource is virtual memory, which is controlled by the Virtual Memory Manager (VMM).

Memory Management

Even in these days of servers with 1 GB of physical RAM installed, no server has enough memory to keep up with the demands of all applications running on it. Therefore, Win2K uses disk space to emulate physical memory, essentially "faking out" the applications and operating system by storing only the data they currently need to operate; the rest is stored in the paging file, a location on the hard disk. When the application needs data in the paging file, Win2K brings it back into physical memory. To the application, it appears that the data was always stored in RAM, with the only difference being that, if the data appeared in the paging file, its retrieval takes a bit longer. This emulation allows all active processes to think that they have 4 GB of memory in which to store data (4 GB is the maximum amount of memory that Windows 2000 will support).

As you can see in Figure 4-9, this 4 GB is divided into two halves: system space (kernel) and per-process space (virtual memory). The kernel is the part of the operating system that supports items such as boot drivers, the system cache, and other elements that every process will need. It claims the upper 2 GB of memory. This part of the **virtual memory** address space is shared among all running processes. The lower 2 GB of virtual memory is reserved for user-specific applications and is private to each process.

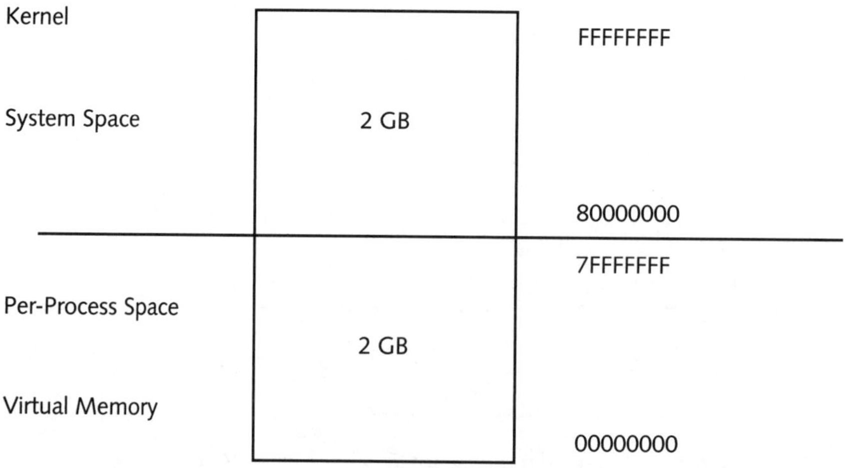

Kernel System Space	2 GB	FFFFFFFF 80000000
Per-Process Space Virtual Memory	2 GB	7FFFFFFF 00000000

Figure 4-9 Distribution of virtual memory addresses

Virtual address space is merely a list of storage spaces available to the threads running within a process, like an inventory sheet for a warehouse. The physical organization of the warehouse may not map precisely to the inventory sheet, but so long as everyone knows that Entry 5 on the inventory sheet corresponds to Bay 20 in the warehouse, it doesn't matter. The Win2K memory manager takes charge of keeping track of the process's inventory lists so that they don't try to store data in the same location in physical memory.

Win2K includes support for terminal services, a way of letting network clients run applications on the server while seeing the application interface on their computer. Because terminal services imply that many people are running applications on the same computer, Win2K needs a way to keep these applications sorted out so that it can tell which applications are associated with each person. Each client connection is called a session. Each time a remote user connects to a Win2K terminal session, a new session ID is generated. All of the processes created to run within that session are associated with that particular session ID. This approach keeps Win2K from becoming confused as to which process in which session asked for what data.

Keeping track of how virtual memory and physical memory are used is a big job. To achieve this goal, you need a device that will send data to disk when it's not being used, but then retrieve the information when the process refers to that data again. That is, you need a method of translating the virtual memory addresses to the physical memory where the data is actually stored. You need some mechanism for reserving memory for certain processes and for preventing processes from corrupting each other's memory. All these jobs are handled by a part of the Win2K executive called the Virtual Memory Manager.

Earmarking Memory for Processes

When a process is created, Win2K must allocate some virtual memory addresses to that process for its exclusive use. The operating system supports a two-stage approach to memory allocation. First, processes can reserve free (unused and unreserved) memory addresses. Second, they can commit that allocation by backing those addresses with some storage. You can't put anything in an address any more than you could live in a new housing development that consisted of only empty plots with addresses attached to each plot. To live there, you'd need to build a house. Likewise, to store memory at an address, a process must have storage to which that address refers.

Reserving memory is simply a way for a thread to say, "I'd like to use these virtual memory addresses at some point in the future." **Reserved memory** doesn't take up any room in the paging file or in RAM, because the process isn't actually using the memory. Before the process can store memory in that range of addresses, it must commit it. **Committed memory** reserves a space in the paging file for that process's exclusive use.

Why bother with this two-step approach? Two reasons explain its attractiveness. First, it's handy for processes that need a large chunk of virtual memory addresses next to each other—they can reserve them all at once and then commit later. Second, this method can reduce paging file usage by not committing any space in it to the virtual memory addresses until this space is actually needed.

Memory is reserved—and therefore committed—in multiples of the **system page** size. (A page is an area of memory; all processors deal with memory in pages, with the size of the page varying with the processor type.) For example, on x86 systems, processes must reserve memory in 4 KB increments, because x86 systems process memory requests in 4 KB chunks. If a process attempts to reserve 18 KB of virtual memory addresses, the actual amount reserved would be 20 KB because the amount of space used must be a multiple of 4.

Sharing Memory Among Processes

Sometimes it makes sense for processes to share data. First, processes may share even process-specific data, rather than loading identical copies of the same material into memory. Second, under normal circumstances, all processes share a common view of the lower 2 GB of virtual memory addresses.

Copy-on-Write Protection

When you launch an application, you actually load certain data into memory that the threads must reference to do their work. For example, if you run WordCruncher 98, files A through E are loaded into memory to provide basic functionality. If you start a second instance of WordCruncher, is it really necessary to load all of those files into memory again? You could, but it would consume a lot of memory. If you let all instances of WordCruncher use the same copies of A through E, however, then one instance that needs to overwrite part of that information will affect all other instances.

To circumvent the wasted space/data corruption dilemma, Win2K uses a technique called **copy-on-write data sharing**. Basically, it means that if more than one application is referencing data on a read-only basis, as many applications as need to and are able to may reference the same data loaded into the same part of memory. If an application writes to that data, however, the Virtual Memory Manager will copy the edited data to a new location.

Protecting System Memory

Although all processes share a common view of the lower 2 GB of virtual memory addresses, you still need some mechanism to protect the data there, thus ensuring that a process (or even the operating system), doesn't have its data corrupted. Win2K includes some measures to prevent such corruption.

First, only kernel-mode threads can access data in the system's virtual address areas. As discussed in Chapter 2, when a user-mode thread needs to manipulate the kernel, it doesn't actually perform the manipulation itself. Rather, the executive accepts the request and uses a kernel-mode thread to interact with the system memory areas. User-mode applications cannot directly modify or even access system data.

Second, threads don't actually interact with virtual memory addresses—the Virtual Memory Manager handles that task for them. When a thread tries to read or write the contents of virtual memory, the Virtual Memory Manager intervenes to handle the address translation. In that way, Win2K ensures that threads belonging to one process don't accidentally access memory pages belonging to another process.

Third, memory areas are protected. Memory areas may have different permissions attached to them (making some read-only and some read-write, just like disk space). Shared memory areas are protected with normal Win2K access control lists that control access to all objects. When a thread attempts to access an area of virtual memory, the Security Reference Monitor in the executive checks the permissions associated with that thread against the permissions required to access that memory. If the thread doesn't have the appropriate permission set, access is denied.

Using the Paging File

For virtual memory to work, you need a paging file—that is, an area of hard disk space reserved for data that processes load into memory. Committed memory is memory that has space in the paging file reserved for it. Processes can't use RAM without having a location to which to transfer their data if RAM becomes too full.

Unfortunately, no matter how much RAM is installed in the machine, it will become full sooner or later. Every time you run an application, you start at least one process. That process, in turns, starts threads. All of those threads need some data in memory—collectively called the process's **working set**—to work. Once you start loading user files into memory as well, things get crowded very quickly.

You may recall that the balance set manager was responsible for making sure that low-priority threads got some CPU time. This same balance set manager has another job: making sure that only the data processes need most actually takes up room in physical memory. If physical memory gets too full, the balance set manager **trims** each process's working set, sending nonessential data to the paging file. Which data? The Win2K Virtual Memory Manager uses one of two algorithms for this kind of operation: **Least Recently Used (LRU)** or **First In, First Out (FIFO)**. The LRU algorithm discards the data that's been in memory for the longest time without being used; FIFO discards the data that's been in memory for the longest time, regardless of when it was last used. Multiprocessor computers and all Alpha-based computers use FIFO, whereas single-processor x86 computers use LRU. LRU is somewhat more responsive to the needs of the user and the operating system, but FIFO is faster, because it doesn't require the Virtual Memory Manager to determine which data was least recently used.

Reading Data from Memory

Now you know how data gets into memory—but how does it get out when a process needs to use some of that information? The Virtual Memory Manager acts as an intermediary between application threads and the physical memory, both for security reasons and because virtual memory addresses don't necessarily have any relationship to the location in RAM where the data is actually stored. To retrieve data from memory, the Virtual Memory Manager must perform **address translation** to convert the virtual memory addresses into physical memory addresses.

Virtual addresses are not mapped directly to physical ones—no direct correlation exists between virtual address C80000 and physical memory address 65, for example. Instead, virtual memory addresses are associated with a structure stored in a non-pageable part of system memory, known as a **page table entry (PTE)**. The PTE contains the physical address to which the virtual address is mapped. Mapping addresses via the PTE intermediary means that if the data is paged to disk and then back to a different area of RAM, the virtual memory address need not be updated to reflect the change in location—only the PTE requires updating.

Of course, the procedure is actually more complicated. If the Virtual Memory Manager had to sort through 4 GB of PTEs to find the one that translated a virtual memory address into a physical memory address, it would take forever. For this reason, PTEs are organized into **page tables**, and the page tables are gathered into **page directories**. Essentially, this setup is analogous to the drive/folder/file structure that file systems use to help you organize your data.

Each virtual memory address is 32 bits long. Although you normally see these addresses written in hexadecimal for ease of use, it's easier to understand how address translation works if you write the address in the binary format that the operating system uses internally. For example, imagine that a thread has asked for the data in virtual memory address 8000A500. In binary notation, this address is written as 10000000000000001010010100000000.

The reason for writing out this address the long way is that virtual memory addresses are interpreted as three separate components: 1000000000 0000001010 010100000000. Counting from the left, the first 10 bits of the virtual address point to the proper page directory. The second 10 bits point to the proper page table in that page directory. The final 12 bits point to the byte of data within the page.

Using this information, the process of translating memory addresses is as follows:

1. The Virtual Memory Manager finds the page directory for the current process. The current process is the one that owns the thread that's currently using the CPU; the location of the page directory is part of the thread's context and is therefore loaded into memory when the thread starts running.

2. The Virtual Memory Manager reads the page directory to find the page table that holds the required PTE.

3. The PTE is read to map the virtual address to a page in physical memory.

4. The byte index is used to find the desired data within the physical memory. If the data currently resides in memory, the Virtual Memory Manager retrieves the information for the thread.

If the data *isn't* currently in memory, the Virtual Memory Manager executes a **page fault** to find the data in the paging file and send it back to physical memory. The **page fault handler** searches the paging file for the desired data (all of which is cataloged so it can be easily retrieved) and puts it back into physical memory.

The page fault handler puts not only the requested data back into memory, but also the data around it. It assumes that if the application is using one part of data, it might need the data close to it as well.

If physical memory is full, then the balance set manager evaluates process data and trims the working set according to the appropriate algorithm. The PTE will be updated to reflect the new physical address, and the Virtual Memory Manager can retrieve the data for the thread.

By this point, you should have a good idea of how Win2K manages CPU time and virtual memory. The brains behind both operations is the Object Manager, which is the subject of the next section.

OBJECT MANAGER

The core of all resource management in the Win2K is the Object Manager, which creates and destroys the objects that represent system resources, thus allowing all resource management to be performed from a single point in the operating system instead of making each part of Win2K handle its own resource management. Basically, each kind of object represents a specific kind of computing resource, user data, or part of the computer. For example, a file object represents the data in a user file, a device object might represent a floppy disk drive, and a process object represents a process.

The environmental subsystems in which you run applications interact with objects to gain access to resources in the same way that you use a mouse to move the insertion point across the screen. You do not actually move the insertion point: in fact, even the mouse doesn't actually move the insertion point. Instead, the mouse is a controllable representation of the internal mechanism that moves the insertion point.

Microsoft designed the Object Manager with the following goals in mind:

- To provide a consistent mechanism for managing system resources
- To manage all object security from a single point in the operating system
- To supply some mechanism for charging processes for the resources they use
- To allow one process to inherit resources from another process that created it
- To supply a mechanism for keeping an object available until all processes are finished with it

Recall from Chapter 2 that the core operating system contains two main parts: the executive and the kernel. The executive runs in user mode, giving the environmental subsystems access to core operating system functions and making policy decisions about who is allowed to do what in the operating system. The kernel runs in kernel mode and synchronizes the parts of Win2K to make them cooperate.

To keep consistent with this division of labor, Win2K has two kinds of objects: executive objects and kernel objects. The parts of the executive (Process and Thread Manager, Virtual Memory Manager, I/O Manager, and so on) use executive objects, which include policy information. Kernel objects are implemented within the Win2K kernel and provide the timing mechanisms that Win2K uses to keep the parts of the executive working together.

Executive Objects

Executive-mode functions need executive objects to give the functions access to system resources or parts of the computer. Executive objects are the user-mode representations of kernel-mode object functions, so an executive object may actually supply executive functions with access to a number of kernel functions. The kernel functions, in turn, may create executive objects while using kernel objects to keep track of how those executive objects are being used. For example, imagine that you're running Microsoft Word in the Win32 environmental subsystem and you tell Word to create a new file. Word asks the Win32 subsystem to create the file (remember—applications can't actually do anything; they just ask the operating system to do it for them). The Win32 subsystem takes the request and calls on the executive-level function CreateFile. The executive, in turn, verifies that this request is permitted and then passes it to the kernel-mode function that creates files. The kernel creates an executive-level file object that the Win32 operating system can use to manipulate the data in that file.

Figure 4-10 illustrates the three parts of an executive object: the labeling information that the object manager uses to keep track of the object; the kernel component; and the executive component. As you can see, when part of the operating system manipulates an executive object, it automatically manipulates the kernel object nested within the executive object, even if that part of the operating system is unaware of the kernel objects.

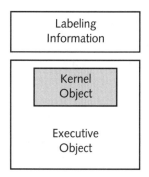

Figure 4-10 An executive object containing a kernel object

Many kinds of executive objects exist. You don't need to know the names of all of them, but some of the more important ones will come up in the discussion of how Win2K manages resources. A thread, as discussed in Chapter 2, is an executable part of an application that has a certain job to do. All threads in the same application are part of one process that describes the conditions under which the threads run: virtual address areas available to them, priority, and so forth. Processes communicate with each other via ports. All processes and threads have **access tokens** that contain their security profiles. Each profile consists of an identifying name and a set of rights and permissions based on the rights and permissions of the person who initiated the action that led to the process being created initially (for example, starting an application).

As discussed earlier in this chapter, all threads in all processes contend for CPU time, so some timing objects are also important. Mutants are responsible for ensuring that only one thread at a time accesses a resource that can't handle multiple simultaneous requests. For resources that can handle more than one simultaneous thread request, but not an unlimited number, semaphores allow only a certain number of threads to reach the resource. A timer tells a thread when a specified period of time has elapsed.

Calling All Objects!

Most Win2K objects have names that other objects (such as process objects) can use to get their attention. (Objects without names can't be called and are very rare.) The Object Manager also uses these names to keep track of objects. When a process creates an object or refers to an existing object by name, the process receives a **handle** to that object. It's faster for a process to refer to an object by its handle than by the object's real name. To understand why, consider this analogy: once a process has a handle to an object, it's like having a red telephone on that object's desk. The process dials the red telephone, and the object is connected to the process instantly. The Object Manager, which would normally have to find the object for the process, never becomes involved. Because it's so much more efficient to call a process via its handle than through the Object Manager, threads in a process cannot communicate with an object until that process has established a handle with the object.

Because the Object Manager is responsible for creating and deleting all object handles, it can keep track of which user-mode processes are trying to access objects and determine whether the security profile of that process permits the kind of access to the object that the process is seeking. This concept leads us to object security.

Setting Object Security

When you log onto a Win2K computer, the Security Reference Monitor compares your user name and password with the security database contained on the Win2K domain controller. Based on the rights and privileges associated with your user name, you—and the objects you create—have a certain set of rights, represented by an access token attached to the object. When an object you create attempts to access another object, the Security Reference Monitor checks the **access control list (ACL)** of the object, which lists who's allowed to do what to the object. For example, a file object's ACL might permit members of the Everyone group to read the file, but restrict members of the Account Operators group to editing the file. The Security Reference Monitor compares the data in the ACL with the information in the access token. If the access token lists the appropriate permissions, then the object gets the access. If it doesn't, then access is not allowed and you receive an Access Denied error.

Chapter Summary

- In any multitasking operating system, the biggest headache lies in making sure that each part of the operating system gets enough CPU time and memory to be responsive, but not so much that other parts that also need those computing resources are starved.

- This chapter explored how Win2K divides applications and the operating system itself into discrete parts, then assigns resources to each of those parts.

- This chapter also discussed how Win2K uses objects to represent computing resources and how it manages security for those resources.

Key Terms

access control list (ACL) — A list associated with an object that defines the rights that groups and individuals have to the object. The ACL is used by the Security Reference Monitor to protect objects from unauthorized access.

access token — An identifier given to an object upon its creation. Based on the identity of the person who created it (or who created the object that created it), an object has certain rights, which are listed in its access token. The Security Reference Monitor compares the data in the access token with that required by the ACL to determine what kind of access the object may have to a particular object.

address translation — The act of converting virtual addresses to physical addresses. This conversion is necessary because the operating system deals entirely in virtual addresses, leaving physical memory addresses to hardware. The two types of addresses don't necessarily bear any relation to each other.

affinity — The term used when a process is set up to prefer using one processor over another.

background application — An application that is running but not currently receiving user input.

balance set manager — The part of Win2K responsible for trimming process working sets to free physical memory as well as for identifying low-priority threads that aren't receiving CPU cycles.

base priority — The priority with which a thread starts after its creation. The base priority of a thread is always equal to that of the process that created it.

committed memory — Memory allocated to a process that is backed with the necessary amount of space in the paging file. Processes must commit memory before they can store data in it.

context — The information describing the operating environment for all threads in a particular process.

context switching — The act of setting aside one thread's context for that of another thread, when the second thread starts using the CPU.

cooperative multitasking — A type of multitasking in which all applications in turn get some CPU time and are supposed to relinquish the processor when their time is up.

copy-on-write data sharing — A form of shared memory protection. Copy-on-write allows multiple processes to read the same bit of data stored in physical memory. If one of the processes attempts to change the data, however, the Virtual Memory Manager copies the edited data to a new location and the process uses the copy. This approach keeps the editing process from corrupting the data that other processes are using.

cycles — Discrete chunks of time that the CPU can dedicate to any given application's needs.

dispatcher — A set of routines in the Win2K kernel that governs thread scheduling.

First In, First Out (FIFO) — An algorithm that marks the oldest data in RAM to be sent to the paging file. The balance set manager uses this algorithm on Alpha and multiprocessor x86 computers.

foreground application — The application currently receiving user input.

handle — A connection to an object that allows one object to manipulate another.

idle thread — A low-priority thread that runs whenever no other threads are running on the CPU. The idle thread watches for events that will require CPU time, but doesn't actually do anything with the CPU itself.

Least Recently Used (LRU) — An algorithm that marks the least recently used data in RAM to be sent to the paging file. The balance set manager uses this algorithm on single-processor x86 computers.

page directory — A collection of page tables for a particular process.

page fault — An event in which the Virtual Memory Manager must retrieve data from disk to put it back into RAM for a process.

page fault handler — The part of the Virtual Memory Manager that finds the data that's been paged to disk so as to put that data back into RAM.

page table — A list of page table entries, used to map virtual addresses to storage areas in physical memory.

page table entry (PTE) — The entry on a page table that contains the mapping of physical storage to virtual memory addresses.

physical memory — The memory chips installed in the computer that are used for temporary storage of process data. Synonymous with random access memory (RAM).

preemptive multitasking — A type of multitasking in which the Virtual Memory Manager controls who has control of the CPU, rather than giving this responsibility to the applications.

process — The environment defining the resources available to threads, which are the executable parts of an application. Processes define the memory available, any processor affinities, the location where the process page directory is stored in physical memory, and other information that the CPU needs to work with a thread.

processor affinity — In multiprocessor systems, a feature that may be used to tell all threads in a process that they should use one processor in preference to another, even if the preferred processor is busier than the alternative processors.

quantum — The number of CPU cycles that a thread gets to use when executing. During its quantum, a thread gets all of the CPU's attention.

reserved memory — Virtual memory addresses set aside for a particular process but not yet committed—that is, no space in the paging file has been reserved for them.

system page — Chunks of memory, as viewed by a processor. The system page for an x86 machine is 4 KB in size; for an Alpha machine, it is 8 KB in size.

task switching — A method of multitasking in which the user may switch between applications. The application in the foreground gets all CPU cycles; the background applications get none.

thread — The executable element of an application.

thread state — Any one of five states that a thread may be in, defining its readiness to use the CPU.

trim — The procedure in which some of a process's working set is moved to the paging file to free room in physical memory.

variable priority thread — A thread with a base priority from 1 to 15 that may have a higher priority if the dispatcher thinks it appropriate. A variable priority thread may never have a priority higher than 15.

virtual memory — A mechanism by which RAM is supplemented with disk space to make it appear that the computer has more memory installed than it really does.

working set — The data that the threads in a process have stored in physical memory. The working set may grow or shrink depending on how much physical memory is available, but the process may not use any data that is not in its working set.

REVIEW QUESTIONS

1. Win2K is a(n) _____ operating system; DOS is a(n) _____ operating system.

2. A processor in a computer running a multitasking operating system such as Win2K can execute more than one application at a time. True or False?

3. If the threads in a process are designed to prefer one processor over another (in a multiprocessor computer), then those threads are designed to have a(n) _____ that processor.

    a. preference for

    b. affinity for

    c. association with

    d. None of the above

4. In any multitasking operating system, the application in the foreground is the one that receives most of the CPU cycles. True or False?

5. Describe how an application in a cooperative multitasking operating system can cause all applications to hang, and explain how a preemptive multitasking operating system can prevent this event from happening.

6. What is a quantum?

7. What is context switching?
   a. The act of loading one process's environment information into memory and setting aside the environment information of another process
   b. The act of moving from kernel mode to user mode, or vice versa
   c. The act of shifting working set data from main memory to the paging file
   d. The act of changing a thread's priority to help it gain CPU cycles
8. Which part of Win2K holds the dispatcher?
   a. Executive
   b. Win32 subsystem
   c. HAL
   d. Kernel
9. When a thread is scheduled to be run next on a particular CPU, but is not presently running, then the thread is said to be in the _____ state.
10. A preempted thread goes into the waiting state. True or False?
11. What is the usual base priority of a thread associated with a user application?
    a. 5
    b. 8
    c. 12
    d. 24
12. Explain why Win2K is not a true real-time operating system.
13. Threads that voluntarily relinquish the processor get a boost in priority once they're ready to start running again. True or False?
14. If you configure a Win2K machine to give all applications equal access to the CPU, then the foreground application does not receive a priority boost. True or False?
15. A thread awaiting an I/O operation exits the waiting state when the I/O operation is complete. How is the priority boost given to this thread determined?
16. Which part of the Virtual Memory Manager is involved both in scheduling threads and in conserving system RAM?
17. When old data in a process's working set is sent to the paging file, this is known as _____ the working set.
18. Explain how a faster hard disk could improve virtual memory performance.
19. What does a PTE do?
20. When a process marks a set of virtual memory addresses for its own use, it is said to be _____ this memory. When the process backs these addresses with space in the paging file, those addresses are said to be _____.

HANDS-ON PROJECTS

Project 4-1

Win2K boosts the priority of the foreground application to make it as responsive as possible. The amount of the boost depends on whether the Win2K machine is optimized for running applications or for serving client requests. In either case, however, the active application is boosted. In this exercise, you'll optimize the server for running applications and then watch the thread associated with that application have its priority raised and lowered.

To watch a thread's priority change as its application moves from foreground to background:

1. Make sure that the computer is optimized for running applications. Open the **Control Panel** and run the **System** applet. Access the **Advanced** tab, and click the **Performance Options** button you see there. You should see a dialog box like the one shown earlier in Figure 4-5.
2. Close the **Performance Options** dialog box.
3. Run **FreeCell**, a game in the **Games** folder of the **Accessories** menu. (This application has only a single thread.)
4. Run **Performance Monitor** (**Start**, **Run**, **perfmon**). Click the button with the + sign on it to add a new counter.
5. Scroll down the list of performance objects until you find the **Thread** object. Scroll down in the list of counters until you see the counters for **Priority base** and **Priority Current**. Hold down the **Ctrl** button, and click the counters to select both. In the list of instances, choose **FreeCell**. There should be only one thread for that application. When you finish making the selections, your screen should look like Figure 4-11. Click **Add**, then click **Close** to close this dialog box and return to the chart.
6. Right-click the graph numbers on the left of the chart and select **Properties** from the resulting menu.
7. Select the **Graph** tab and change the Maximum value for Verticle scale to **20**.
8. Click **OK**.

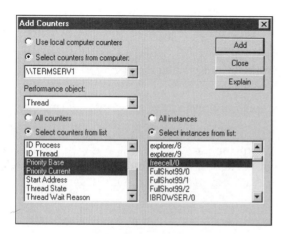

Figure 4-11 Choose to display the current and base priority for the FreeCell thread

9. Experiment with FreeCell. Notice that when you're actively clicking on the game, its priority is 12. When you click **Performance Monitor** to move that application to the foreground, but leave FreeCell up and open, FreeCell's thread priority drops to 10. When you minimize the game, the thread's priority should drop to 8. Figure 4-12 shows the changes in thread priority.

10. Close all open applications.

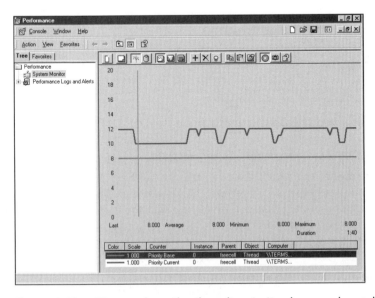

Figure 4-12 Observe how the thread's priority changes depending on how you're interacting with the game

Project 4-2

You can also use Performance Monitor to see the state of a thread at any given time. Just as the application you have open is idle more often than not, a thread is waiting for input more often than it's running. Although the Performance Monitor's documentation of the Thread State counter is slightly off, you can still use it to determine how much time an active application's threads are running as opposed to waiting for input.

To determine how much time a thread spends waiting as opposed to running:

1. Open **FreeCell**.
2. Open **Performance Monitor**, click the **Add** button (the one with a plus sign on it). As in Project 4-1, scroll down the list of performance objects until you come to the **Thread** object. In the list of Thread counters, find **Thread State**. In the list of objects to monitor, find FreeCell. When you've made all of the selections so that your screen looks like the one in Figure 4-13, click **Add**, and then click **Close**.

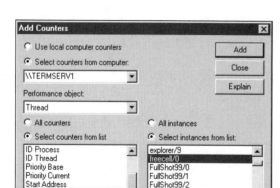

Figure 4-13 Make these selections to monitor the state of the FreeCell thread

3. Repeat steps 6 through 8 in Hands-on Project 4-1.
4. With **Performance Monitor** still open, start playing FreeCell. Watch how the value of Thread State flips between 1 (running) and 5 (waiting). The performance chart should look like the one in Figure 4-14. Notice that the game is spending much more time waiting for user input than running.
5. Close FreeCell and Performance monitor.

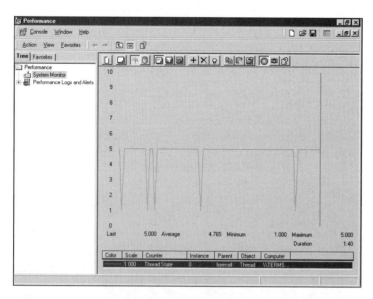

Figure 4-14 A thread in a user application generally spends more time waiting than executing

Although the explanation for the Thread State counter says that a value of 1 for the thread state indicates that the thread is ready, it actually corresponds to a running thread. From time to time, you'll come across these discrepancies when using Performance Monitor.

Project 4-3

 User applications are not system-critical, so they run in the normal range of priority and their threads have a base priority of 8. You can specify that an application's process—and thus the threads running within the context of that process—should have an abnormally high priority, however. To do so, you need to know the application's program name. In this exercise, you'll start FreeCell with an abnormally high priority, then compare its priority with that of a normal instance of FreeCell.

To start an application with an abnormally high priority:

1. From the **Accessories** section of the **Programs** folder, choose **Command Prompt**.
2. At the command prompt, type **start/realtime freecell**. FreeCell will start normally.
3. Run the **Process Viewer** (Pviewer) in the Win2K Support Tools, and scroll down the list of running processes to find the one for **FreeCell**. Your screen should look like Figure 4-15. Notice that the dynamic priority for FreeCell is 24 (in the real-time range).
4. Close Process Viewer.

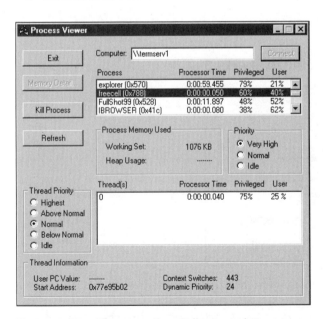

Figure 4-15 If you run FreeCell as a real-time process, then it will have a higher dynamic priority than it would otherwise

116 Chapter 4 Allocating and Managing Operating System Resources

You should install the Support Tools included on the Windows 2000 CD—this collection of tools can come in handy. After you've installed the Support Tools, the Programs folder will include a menu item for it.

Keep this instance of FreeCell open—you'll need it for Project 4-4.

Project 4-4

In Project 4-1, you watched the priority of an application's thread change when that application was in the foreground and you were interacting with it. The dispatcher won't boost all priorities, however—just those of threads belonging to variable-priority processes. If a process has a real-time priority, then its threads will not be boosted even when you're typing into them.

To observe that only variable-priority processes change priority when in the foreground:

1. Use the command-prompt **start** command to start **FreeCell** with a high priority, if you haven't already done so.

2. In **Performance Monitor**, click the **Add** button (the one with the plus sign on it) and scroll to the **Thread** performance object. Choose the counters for the Priority Current and Priority Base, and the FreeCell instance. When your screen looks like Figure 4-16, click **Add**, and then click **Close**.

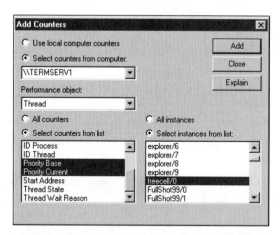

Figure 4-16 Choose the counters to monitor the FreeCell thread

3. Start **FreeCell** from the **Accessories** section of the **Programs** folder.

4. Repeat Step 2 for the new instance of **FreeCell** (it will be labeled freecell/0#1), and add the base and current priority for the normal instance of FreeCell to the chart.

5. Play with each instance of FreeCell, noticing what happens to the base and current priority of each instance of the game. As shown in Figure 4-17, you should see the priority for the normal instance of FreeCell go up and down as you use and minimize the application, respectively, but the priority of the real time instance of the game will remain constant at 24.
6. Close all open windows.

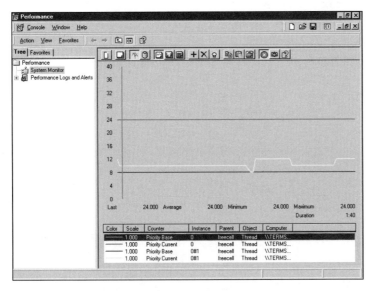

Figure 4-17 Only the variable priority instance of FreeCell will fluctuate in priority as it moves from foreground to background

Project 4-5

You can have more than one paging file set up on your system. Win2K will accept one paging file per logical drive (that is, per drive letter). In this exercise, you'll view and edit the paging file settings.

To view and edit the paging file information for your computer:

1. Run the **System** applet in the **Control Panel**. From the **Advanced** tab, click the **Performance Options** button to open the dialog box shown earlier in Figure 4-5.
2. The Performance Options dialog box will display the current size of the paging file. To change this amount or to see how it's distributed among logical drives, click the **Change** button to open the dialog box shown in Figure 4-18.
3. To view the paging file information for a particular drive, highlight that drive in the top box. The minimum and maximum size of the paging file for that drive will be displayed below. To change the value, type in a new minimum or maximum, being careful not to set the maximum size of the paging file smaller than the recommended size (based on the amount of physical memory installed).

Make the minimum size of the paging file close to the recommended size of the paging file, if possible. Although Win2K will extend the paging file as needed (up to the amount of room on the disk), enlarging the paging file is a time-consuming process, and one you can skip by making the paging file big initially.

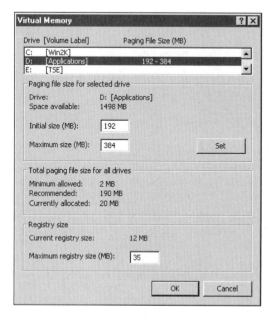

Figure 4-18 The Virtual Memory settings show how the paging file is distributed on your computer

4. When you have finished making changes, click **Set**, and then click **OK** to finalize the changes.

Project 4-6

The set of data that a process maintains in physical memory is called its working set. When you're using an application, the process will attempt to build its working set as large as possible, so that it has all of the data that it might need readily at hand. If data that the process has used is not in the working set, it resides in the paging file: thus, if the process needs that data, a delay will occur while the page fault handler retrieves the data. When you're not actively using an application, there's no need for its working set to take up RAM, so the balance set manager trims the working set when applications are idle. In this exercise, you'll watch as an application builds its working set, loading as much data into RAM as it can. You'll also see how the balance set manager trims the working set when you minimize an application, then how the working set is rebuilt when you start using the application again.

To watch a process's working set change as you use the application associated with that process:

1. Make sure that **FreeCell** is running, but minimize it.

2. In the **Performance Monitor**, click the **Add** button (the one with the plus sign on it) and scroll to the **Process** performance object. Choose the **Working Set** counter and the **FreeCell** instance. When your screen looks like Figure 4-19, click **Add**, and then click **Close**.

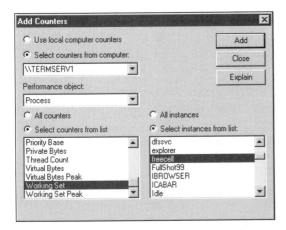

Figure 4-19 Monitor the working set for the FreeCell process

3. Start playing FreeCell, but keep an eye on the process working set. It should start from almost nothing, then increase as you continue using the application. The longer you play the game, the larger the process's working set will be.
4. Minimize FreeCell and watch the size of the process's working set drop immediately.
5. Start playing the game again, and notice how the working set increases. Your performance chart should look something like the one in Figure 4-20.

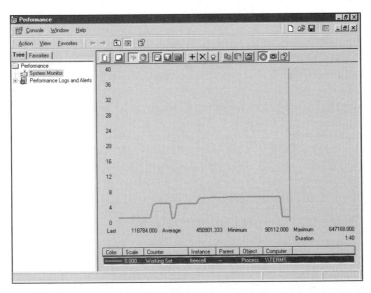

Figure 4-20 The process working set reflects how the application is being used

Case Projects

1. Your computer has been running low on virtual memory. In an effort to fix the problem, you add more physical memory. This step helps, but you still keep getting "Low on Virtual Memory" warning messages. How could you resolve the shortage of virtual memory without adding more physical memory?

2. Thread A needs information read from the hard disk to continue running, and so voluntarily gives up the CPU to Thread B, the next thread in line. What state was Thread B in, and what state does Thread A go into? When does Thread A start running again?

3. Explain the difference between task switching, cooperative multitasking, and preemptive multitasking, and explain which one Win2K uses and why.

4. Is it better for performance for Win2K to run multiple threads from the same process in succession? If it makes a difference, why?

CHAPTER 5

HARDWARE AND DEVICE MANAGEMENT IN WINDOWS 2000

> **After reading this chapter and completing the exercises, you will be able to:**
> - Differentiate between hardware and devices
> - Describe how the operating system manages devices and resource allocation
> - Examine how devices communicate with the CPU and other system resources
> - List the four components of hardware management in Windows 2000 and describe how they interact
> - Describe how the new Win32 Driver Model (WDM) fits into the Windows 2000 architecture
> - Understand Windows 2000 support for Power Management and the OnNow system
> - Describe Windows 2000 support for hardware devices and system bases
> - Demonstrate the device and power management configuration tools within Windows 2000
> - Troubleshoot Windows 2000 device drivers and hardware

Hardware management is an important facet of any operating system—and Windows 2000 is no exception. The ability to smoothly and efficiently handle a large number of hardware devices, from that old 14.4 Kbps modem to the latest DVD disc player, is one of the shining achievements of Windows 2000. As we look into the internals of Windows 2000, you will see that Microsoft has built in a large amount of hardware support that device manufacturers once provided via very complex device drivers. Hardware management in Windows 2000 is divided into four distinct yet interdependent components: **Win32 Driver Model (WDM), power management, hardware devices,** and **system buses.** We will examine the design and operation of each of these components in detail as we take an overall view of how hardware and device management is handled in Windows 2000.

An Overview of Hardware Management

Our first task is to distinguish between hardware and devices. As shown in Figure 5-1, hardware is a physical component (or peripheral) and a device is a generic operating system term for the entire stack of software that supports and maintains the hardware. For example, you can install hardware such as a VGA display adapter in a Windows 2000 computer. The supporting drivers for that hardware present a device with standardized application programming interfaces (APIs), I/O ports, and memory ranges available for use by the operating system. As such, device drivers provide an important avenue of communications between the physical hardware and the various pieces of the operating system.

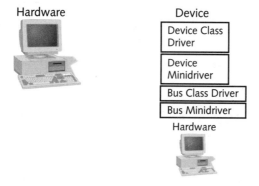

Figure 5-1 A device consists of hardware and supporting device drivers needed for use by the operating system

With the release of Windows 98 and Windows 2000, Microsoft radically changed the internal operations and design of device drivers. The new device driver design is called the WDM. Although the new WDM concepts are quite similar to both the **VxD driver** concepts used in Windows 95 and the existing "NT-style" device drivers used in Windows NT 4.0/3.51, there are significant implementation differences between these driver technologies. In particular, installation and device detection is handled is quite differently between the older driver specifications and the new WDM model. The new WDM architecture supports the **Plug and Play** standard, whereas the older Windows NT-style drivers do not. Although most Windows NT- and VxD-style device drivers operate satisfactorily under Windows 2000, a wealth of new features and capabilities are available to the enterprising developer who embraces the WDM architecture.

One of the most important benefits of the WDM design is that, in most cases, device drivers written under WDM can be deployed without any modification in both Windows 98 and Windows 2000 environments. This standardization should significantly ease the development burden for device manufacturers and driver developers.

A primary advantage of the original Windows NT operating system is the hardware abstraction layer (HAL), which acts as a buffer to keep ill-behaved applications from crashing the entire operating system by accessing the hardware directly. HAL is still around in Windows 2000. Applications continue to pass hardware calls through the driver stack to the HAL, which then passes those requests to the hardware itself (theoretically), protecting the operating system from application-induced crashes. This approach of buffering the hardware from direct application access works very well in Windows 2000, even if it's not quite foolproof. Accommodations must be made in the device driver coding, however, to account for the fact that the HAL protects devices from direct access by the operating system components and application software running on the machine.

The new WDM architecture also includes a layered approach to device drivers, which provides some of the base functionality in built-in WDM class drivers that ship with Windows 98 and Windows 2000. This layered approach means that for broad classes of standard hardware and peripheral devices [like hard drives or **Universal Serial Bus (USB)** devices], only a small piece of code, called a minidriver, needs to be developed by device manufacturers. Microsoft has already provided the many basic driver capabilities in the standard Windows 2000 bus class drivers.

Windows 2000 includes extensive built-in support for advanced power management features, such as *suspend* and *resume*, for every piece of system hardware and all attached peripherals. This expansion of power management capabilities is part of the PC industry's efforts to make PCs as easy to use and as quick to turn on as the average toaster. The only way to accomplish such a feat with a PC is to keep the computer and all peripherals in a low-power suspend mode, which we like to call "the big sleep." Much like the Monty Python "Dead Parrot" sketch, the PC isn't really dead, it's just resting.

In addition, the Windows 2000 architecture supports multiple system buses and a wide variety of devices in an effort to give the user total hardware management. The system buses include **IEEE 1394 Serial Bus (FireWire)** and USB support native to the operating system. Windows 2000 also offers direct support for many newfangled technologies, such as DVD (Digital Versitile Disk), imaging, multiple display adapters, and digital audio devices.

The following sections discuss, in considerable detail, hardware and device management in Windows 2000. They then explain how you can apply this in-depth knowledge to understand and troubleshoot hardware problems in Windows 2000.

HARDWARE AND DEVICES: WHICH IS WHICH?

What's the difference between hardware and devices? As this chapter was being written, that very question kept popping up again and again. After reviewing numerous Microsoft Web sites and documentation, we finally have an intelligent answer that attempts to differentiate between the two terms. Hardware means just that: a physical piece of computer equipment, such as a motherboard, modem, or peripheral. Windows 2000 communicates with and manages hardware via defined devices. A device is a combination of hardware and the supporting software—device drivers, class drivers, minidrivers, and so on—used to make the hardware available for use by the operating system. If you peruse the Windows 2000 **Device Manager** (Start, Settings, Control Panel, System, choose the Hardware tab, and click the Device Manager button), you will see a list of all available devices, as shown in Figure 5-2. If you double-click a particular device, you can read the driver details for the software supporting that device. You can think of devices as a package of physical hardware and the software used to make that hardware useful to the operating system. In reality, the two terms are frequently used interchangeably.

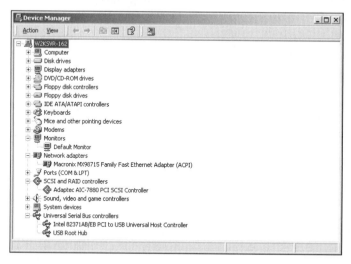

Figure 5-2 The Device Manager provides a list of all system hardware

HOW WINDOWS 2000 MANAGES DEVICES AND RESOURCE ALLOCATION

During the past five years, the proliferation of adapters using the **PCI bus** standard and the popularity of Plug and Play hardware has greatly altered the way in which an operating system manages devices. The original motivation for the PCI bus was twofold: to provide for software configuration (that is, no jumpers to set on the boards) of hardware adapters, and to increase the clock speed and throughput of the primary system bus in PCs. The impetus for Plug and Play was to allow the computer to intelligently choose a harmonious configuration for all compliant devices in a PC. As hardware is added or removed from a personal computer, the **Plug and Play Manager** automatically updates the system configuration, resource allocation, and device drivers to reflect the device changes.

The process by which Windows 2000 discovers which devices are installed and which resources are being used by those devices is called **enumeration**. In enumeration, each installed device is polled and a hardware tree is built in the Registry to reflect the machine's configuration. The Plug and Play Manager provides the arbitration process for resource allocation, and enumeration is the method by which Windows 2000 discovers the installed devices and resources in use. After enumeration is complete, the Plug and Play Manager modifies the Registry by creating a device tree on a bus-by-bus basis. This device tree includes a branch for each device, the unique device identification, a list of resources required by the device, and a list of resources allocated to the device. You can view the current hardware tree in the Control Panel, System applet by clicking the Device Manager button on the Hardware tab. Figure 5-3 shows one such Device Manager hardware tree.

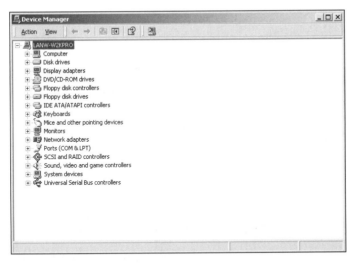

Figure 5-3   Enumeration creates a hardware tree in the Registry, which can be displayed in the Device Manager

Another important part of the enumeration process is the loading of device drivers. Once again, the Plug and Play Manager has a role. It dynamically loads and unloads the appropriate device drivers based on the findings of the enumeration process. Because of the highly evolved functionality of Plug and Play adapters and the **Advanced Configuration and Power Interface (ACPI) specification**, little or no user configuration is required when adding new devices to your Windows 2000 system.

How Windows 2000 Communicates with the CPU and Other System Resources

We are now ready to take a quick look at the actual path that Windows 2000 uses in communciations involving the operating system, system devices, and memory. The following sections go into some detail about how hardware and devices are recognized and managed under Windows 2000. Figure 5-4 shows a simplified rendition of the various communication pathways between devices, device drivers, and system resources, such as RAM and the CPU.

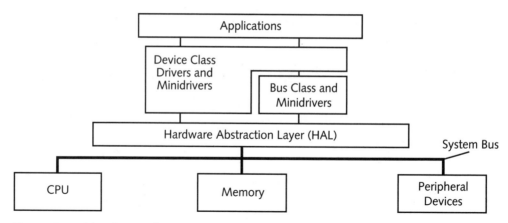

Figure 5-4 The data path among system components is dependent on the system bus

THE FOUR COMPONENTS OF HARDWARE MANAGEMENT

As mentioned earlier, the four primary components of hardware management implemented in Windows 2000 are WDM layers, power management, hardware devices, and system buses. Each hardware management component provides specific services and capabilities within the operating system. Although we discuss each of these components as if they are separate and distinct, in reality these components are very tightly integrated into the operating system—and into each other—to provide a comprehensive method for managing hardware. WDM is the glue that holds the overall hardware management components together. It also provides an exciting new standard method for implementing device drivers, moving a large portion of device communications into standard class drivers provided with the operating system and thereby greatly easing the burden of driver developers.

WIN32 DRIVER MODEL AND WINDOWS 2000 ARCHITECTURE

The new WDM device driver specification represents a major leap in device management and driver design. Traditionally, device drivers had to take into account myriad details and functions to manage installation, communication, and maintenance between hardware and the underlying operating system. The development effort required was quite large because all device drivers had to control and track all user configuration information, hardware communication, API calls, and any required services. By transferring a large number of the low-level device management to standardized Windows 2000 class drivers, Microsoft has enabled faster device driver development, greater standardization in the interaction between drivers and the operating system, and increased usability because WDM is supported by both Windows 98 and Windows 2000.

The WDM Layered Driver Approach

The WDM architecture allows for a layered approach in which the majority of the layers for most devices are supplied by the Windows 2000 operating system. Figure 5-5 illustrates an example of the layered approach to device drivers implemented in the WDM. Your actual layers might differ according to the configuration of your particular machine.

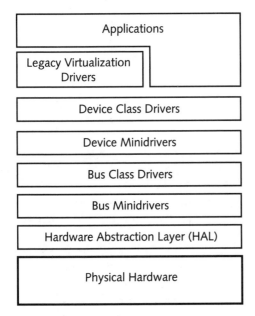

Figure 5-5 WDM layers include class drivers and Device Minidrivers

Applications communicate either with the legacy virtualization layer (discussed later) or directly with a **device class driver**. Device class drivers are standard drivers provided by WDM. A device class driver talks to a **device minidriver**, which is provided by each device manufacturer or driver developer and is specific to a particular piece of hardware. Depending on the hardware supported, the device minidriver might pass instructions and information to the **bus class driver**, which would communicate with the **bus minidriver**, which would in turn communicate with the HAL, as shown in Figure 5-5.

Class and Bus Drivers Built into Windows 2000

Hardware devices supported directly under the WDM specification include the following:

- Power management
- USB
- Plug and Play
- Digital audio
- Imaging (still image and video capture)

- Human Interface Device
- IEEE 1394 Serial Bus (FireWire)
- DVD

If you are developing a device driver for hardware in one of these categories, a minidriver is all that's required in most instances. WDM and Windows 2000 handle the majority of the driver functions through either built-in class or bus drivers, or both, depending on your specific device requirements.

If, for example, you were writing a driver to provide support for a FireWire-based keyboard device under Windows 2000, you would have to develop a device minidriver to interact with the human interface device class *and* a bus minidriver to interact with the IEEE 1394 bus class driver of WDM. API support and resource management are built into the device class and bus class drivers, and development of the two minidrivers to support your new FireWire keyboard will be reasonably simple. Compared with older device driver techniques, in which developers included sophisticated code for management of resources, communications, and device housekeeping, minidrivers are a snap. In fact, the Windows 2000 class and bus drivers often provide enough support to enable all of the standard tasks and resources for a particular device. For example, a standard VGA adapter operates quite well with the built-in class.

The Legacy Virtualization Drivers Layer of WDM Although the WDM device drivers are the preferred method of implementing hardware support in Windows 2000, older VxD-style drivers are also supported in the new architecture so as to maintain some backward compatibility with existing hardware and software. The **legacy virtualization drivers layer** provides that compatibility support. Looking back at Figure 5-5, you can see this layer near the top of the **driver stack**, just under the Applications layer. The legacy virtualization drivers provide support for older VxD drivers by intercepting API and functions calls that, for example, might access a mouse or other input device hardware directly in flight simulation software running in a **Virtual DOS Machine** of Windows 98. As the application tries to access hardware via the VxD driver, the legacy virtualization drivers intercept those requests and map them to the appropriate class or bus drivers in Windows 2000. In the case of the flight simulator example, user input requests would be mapped to the **human interface device class**, which supports hardware, such as keyboards, mice, virtual reality gloves, and joysticks.

The legacy virtualization drivers layer provides another important service to VxD-style device drivers: it acts as a legacy device "traffic cop." Some legacy device drivers are accustomed to taking full control of any hardware used by the driver and accessing that hardware directly by design. The legacy virtualization drivers layer provides a seamless method of allowing multiple VxD-style device drivers to share the same hardware or software without conflicts. This device time-sharing process is accomplished by monitoring and maintaining the proper state of hardware devices as the various drivers gain and relinquish control through the legacy virtualization drivers layer. This task is much more difficult than it appears at first glance, because different drivers expect the same device to be in different states of operation. For example, if device driver 1 is accumulating mouse input and device driver 2 interrupts that operation for its own input purposes, the virtualization drivers must fool driver 1 into believing that the device is still operating under the control of driver 1. While driver 2 has control of the mouse, the virtualization drivers maintain the state of the mouse hardware expected by driver 1. After driver 2 completes its use of the mouse input, the virtualization drivers restore the mouse to the proper state necessary for driver 1 to continue using the mouse without failure or timeout of the device driver.

POWER MANAGEMENT AND THE ONNOW SYSTEM

Windows 2000 provides power management through the integrated **OnNow system**, which governs the power states and requirements for all aspects of a Windows 2000-based PC. OnNow works in conjunction with an Advanced Configuration and Power Interface (ACPI)-enabled BIOS to gather motherboard and BIOS information regarding power management and Plug and Play device configuration. This granular approach to power management allows OnNow to put individual devices within a system into a reduced-power mode while they are not actively being used. This innate ability to turn devices on as needed and to put them to "sleep" when idle requires some changes to the operating system and applications. The developers of many popular applications will undoubtedly modify their products to conform to the OnNow specification as Windows 2000 gains acceptance. Figure 5-6 shows the architecture of the OnNow system components.

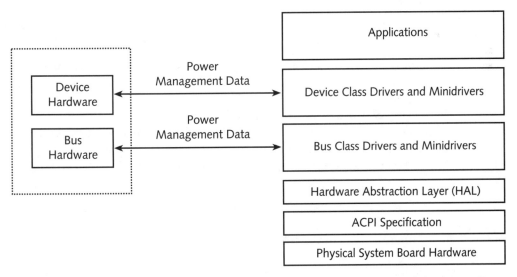

Figure 5-6 The OnNow system defines a power management data path between the driver stack and the physical hardware

Many current applications assume that all attached system devices and peripherals are always up and running. Consequently, applications such as fax software or backup software will need to be rewritten to add OnNow support for sophisticated device power management. For example, applications running under OnNow must take into account that an idle device might be automatically put into sleep mode by Windows 2000 and that OnNow will need some time to "wake up" the hardware before the device can be accessed by the application. This latency characteristic would crash most current applications that access hardware on a regular basis. WDM supports OnNow by defining specific driver interfaces called **device driver interfaces (DDIs)**, which can detect idle services and handle power state changes at the device level.

HARDWARE DEVICES

The third component of the Windows 2000 operating system is hardware devices. As mentioned earlier in our discussion of device and bus class drivers built into Windows 2000, several broad categories of hardware devices are supported directly by Windows 2000 and WDM:

- human interface device
- Multiple display support
- Video capture
- Still image capture
- Digital audio
- DVD
- AGP (Accelerated Graphics Port)

Our earlier discussion of these device classes considered them in relation to the WDM device class and minidriver model. Now let's look at each class of hardware device in more detail.

The human interface device class represents the new standard method by which input devices interact with Windows 2000. It includes such input devices as a mouse and other pointing devices, game controllers, keyboards, and virtual reality controllers. How will device class drivers and bus class drivers interact for most hardware devices? The majority of devices supported under the human interface device class will use the new USB bus as an input interface into the PC. Hence, a USB-based human interface device input device will require the use of both the human interface device class driver and the USB bus class driver.

Multiple display support is now native to the operating system with Windows 2000. Although various manufacturers have implemented proprietary multiple display support for several years, Windows 2000 now implements this feature as an integral part of the operating system. You can define as many as nine monitors easily under Windows 2000 and specify the starting-point and end-point coordinates for each monitor. Figure 5-7 shows a typical multiple monitor setup under Windows 2000.

Configuration of multiple displays is handled through the Control Panel, Display applet (Start, Settings, Control Panel, Display, choose the Settings tab, then click Identify). You may be thinking, "How in the world can I install and configure nine display adapters in my PC?" Don't forget that the FireWire bus can support 127 devices, and many display manufacturers are including a FireWire interface in their new monitors.

Virtual Desktop

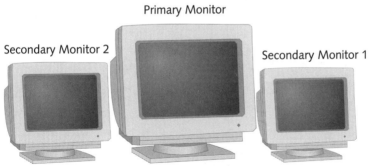

Your desktop can be displayed across monitors of varying resolutions using a screen coordinate system

Figure 5-7 Win2K supports as many as nine displays using a coordinates system to map the virtual desktop

SYSTEM BUSES

A bus is simply a communication pipeline between various hardware components of a PC. Windows 2000 includes native support for four system buses:

- PCI bus
- PC Card and CardBus
- IEEE 1394 bus (FireWire)
- USB bus

Each bus serves a different, distinct purpose in the PC. For example, the **CardBus** supports laptop add-in cards in a manner similar to the older PCMCIA (Personal Computer Memory Card International Association) specification, but at much greater throughput and with enhanced Plug and Play capabilities. This new-specification laptop adapter is referred to as a **PC Card**. The PCI bus is now the standard high-performance bus used to connect system memory, the CPU, system cache, add-in adapters, and other system buses. FireWire is a relatively new serial bus standard that allows much greater throughput, hot-swap capabilities, device daisy-chaining, and easier device configuration than the older RS-232 serial standard. USB is also a new serial bus standard, although USB and FireWire are optimized for different classes of devices.

FireWire supports as many as 63 devices per bus and is designed for efficient connection of high-bandwidth consumer electronics, such as digital, still, and video cameras, high-speed scanners and printers, and DVD drives. You can also interconnect as many as 1023 FireWire buses to support a massive total of more than 64,000 devices. That should be enough for even the most ardent computer gadget freak! Figure 5-8 shows an example of a typical FireWire bus. Note that multiple computers can share a FireWire device, such as a printer, by using a FireWire splitter. Obviously, the printer in this example is designed for shared access from multiple computers.

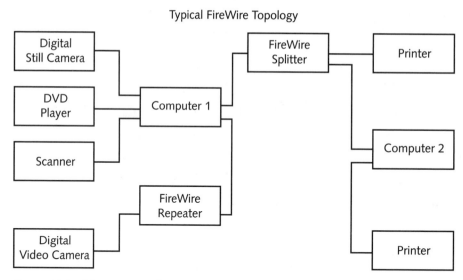

Figure 5-8 The FireWire bus supports repeaters and splitters

USB serves as a single port connection that can support multiple system input devices, such as a mouse, keyboards, joysticks, and digital audio playback, all on the same bus. This bus supports 127 devices in a tiered topology. Figure 5-9 shows an example of a typical USB topology.

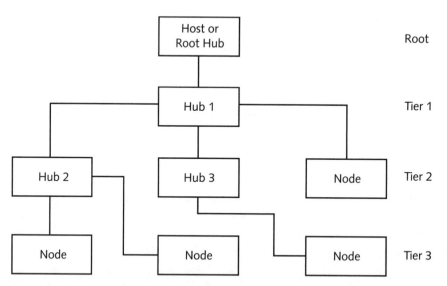

Figure 5-9 The USB bus features a tiered topology

 Even though we have not mentioned support for some other very popular PC system buses (such as ISA, EISA, and SCSI), Windows 2000 does accommodate devices utilizing these buses, as well. These buses are not directly and natively supported along with the other bus class drivers primarily because of architectural issues and the need for manual configuration of adapters using these buses.

By now, you can probably see a pattern on the part of Microsoft—it has tried to make installation and configuration of hardware as easy as those processes are under the Apple Macintosh architecture. Windows 2000 and Windows 98 clearly emphasize technologies such as Plug and Play because of their ease of use for operating system users. Older technologies and buses are still supported, but not as directly or as elegantly as the new technologies are. Hardware manufacturers have been served notice by Microsoft where to direct their new product development efforts and are being actively enticed by the WDM architecture. Microsoft knows that the best way to speed adoption of new technologies is to make them very cost-effective for the manufacturer while showing end users the clear benefits of upgrading.

CONFIGURING USER INPUT, DISPLAY DEVICES, AND POWER MANAGEMENT

Even the best-laid plans of the Plug and Play Manager can sometimes go awry. Where do you turn when you want to change your device's configuration? How do you adjust your display settings or calibrate an input device? The Control Panel is the right place to start. See Figure 5-10.

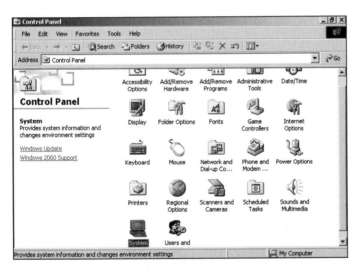

Figure 5-10   The Control Panel is the starting place for most device and operating system configuration actions

Configuring Display and Input Devices

When you look at the various standard applets under the Control Panel in Windows 2000, you will certainly notice the Display applet. Using this applet, you can perform myriad display configuration tasks, such as changing the system display resolution, configuring a screen saver, configuring the power management options of your monitor, and changing the appearance of your Windows desktop. For configuration of input devices, you have several pertinent applets, depending on the type of input device. For instance, the Game Controllers applet configures joysticks, and flight simulation yokes, as shown in Figure 5-11.

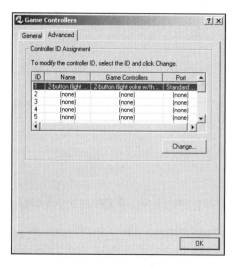

Figure 5-11 The Game Controllers applet controls configuration and calibration of game input devices

The Keyboard applet allows you to configure the typematic rate—how quickly characters are repeated when you hold a key down, the rate of blinking for the system cursor, and the language and layout of the keyboard. The Mouse applet is one of the most used of the input device applets. It allows you to configure your mouse as left- or right-handed, specify how quickly you must click for the operating system to recognize a double-click, change the sensitivity of mouse motions, and set the shape and size of your system pointers. You can also select pointer schemes that change the pointer appearance based on the task being performed. Figure 5-12 shows the Mouse applet.

Figure 5-12 You can control mouse actions and pointer appearance through the Mouse applet

Power Management and Configuration

Another important applet in the Windows 2000 Control Panel is the Power Options applet. This applet enables you to configure the amount of time that must pass before the system "automagically" turns off the monitor or hard drive (see Figure 5-13). You can also enable "hibernation mode," which is the precursor to the OnNow system—it puts the computer into a very low-power suspended state after a set interval of inactivity.

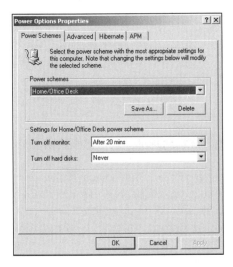

Figure 5-13 You can configure the many power management options of Win2K with the Power Options applet

 The appearance of the Power Options applet may differ on your computer based on its power manageability features. In the case of the Windows 2000 PC in Figure 5-13, the motherboard supports the older Advanced Power Management (APM) standard and you can enable APM features by clicking a check box. If you install Windows 2000 on a PC that does not support APM, you will not see this tab. Conversely, if you install Windows 2000 on a PC that supports ACPI management, you will see additional tabs and options in this applet.

Help Right Where You Need It

One of the most welcome additions to the Control Panel applets is a new Troubleshoot button, shown in Figure 5-14, which is located on the Settings tab of the Display applet.

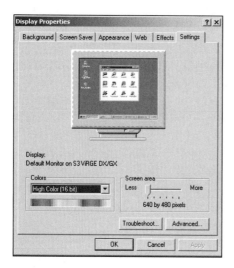

Figure 5-14 Notice the Troubleshoot button in the Display applet, Settings tab

You will also find a Troubleshoot button on all of the input device applets, the Phone and Modem applets, and the Scanners and Cameras applets. Clicking a Troubleshoot button takes you directly to the Windows 2000 Troubleshooting Wizard, which walks you through the troubleshooting process by asking a few simple questions that describe the type of problem(s) you are having and suggesting possible solutions. We'll talk about these new troubleshooting buttons at length in the next section.

WHAT IF IT BREAKS? TROUBLESHOOTING DEVICES IN WINDOWS 2000

As good as Windows 2000 is as an operating system, there is always the possibility that it might stop working correctly at some time. In particular, as you add and remove hardware from your PC, you might find yourself in the unenviable position of having to troubleshoot the hardware, drivers, and operating system configuration to resolve such problems. The bad news is that troubleshooting the complex combinations of hardware and software common to today's PCs remains more art than science. The good news is that Microsoft has given you invaluable ammunition in your troubleshooting battle in the form of expanded device help topics and new troubleshooting wizards. We'll examine the specific techniques you will use for troubleshooting Windows 2000 in detail, but first, let's look at some standard operating procedures for resolving hardware and driver problems.

One Thing at a Time

The most often given—and most often ignored—advice for troubleshooting hardware is to change only one parameter, setting, or configuration option at a time whenever possible. When you adjust multiple variables at once, you have several possible outcomes—none of which is desirable: You might compound the problem instead of fixing it; you might accidentally fix the problem but have no idea which of your changes produced the favorable results; or you might do no harm and no good but lose track of your original settings along the way. All in all, it's best to stick to one change at a time. That is, if you suspect an IRQ conflict, make all possible IRQ changes to resolve the conflict *before* proceeding to I/O port changes or memory range changes.

Document, Document, Document

Carefully document your current configuration settings *before* beginning to make changes. Granted, documenting your configuration prior to making changes isn't really troubleshooting, but it is certainly a critical step in the troubleshooting process. The more cumulative changes you make, the more likely that you will not remember your original device settings when you try to undo all of your troubleshooting efforts.

The easiest way to document your computer settings prior to a foray into the wilds of troubleshooting is with the **MSInfo32** tool, also called the System Information tool. To access the System Information tool, select Start, Programs, Administrative Tools, Computer Management, expand the System Tools icon, and select System Information. As shown in Figure 5-15, the System Information utility contains a tree view in the left pane with which you can navigate among the four components of system information. Using this tool, you can print any component summary from the File menu.

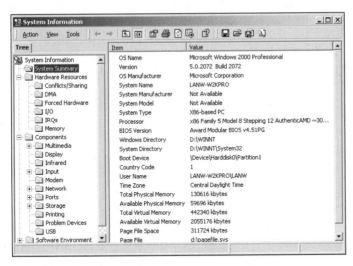

Figure 5-15 The MSInfo32 utility offers a plethora of hardware and software configuration information

Another tool for documenting system configuration information is the Device Manager applet under the System utility in the Control Panel. To start the Device Manager, click Start, Settings, Control Panel, System, choose the Hardware tab, and then click the Device Manager button. Once in Device Manager, click the View menu and select **Print**. You can print this system summary on your default printer or send it to a text file.

Yet another option for documenting the system configuration prior to troubleshooting a hardware problem is to use third-party utilities. Many third-party utilities, such as the popular Norton Utilities, offer an option to document every detail and configuration setting for your Windows 2000 system.

General Troubleshooting Tips

The following is a list of general hardware troubleshooting steps for Windows 2000—or any operating system, for that matter:

> For additional information on troubleshooting Windows 2000, go to the online help for the operating system, or look at the Windows 2000 documentation. In addition, more detailed troubleshooting advice appears in Chapter 15.

- **How do I know that there is a problem?** If something isn't working correctly, it is usually good sign that a resource conflict, driver problem, or other anomaly is present. Always check the Device Manager in the Control Panel, System applet when you suspect a hardware problem. Any unresolved resource conflict will be prominently marked with a red X next to the device in question.

- **How do I resolve the problem?** You can modify some device settings in the Device Manager. Note that manual modifications of resource assignments should be used only as a last resort because of the automatic conflict resolution of Plug and Play hardware. One of your first steps should be to verify that you are using the latest device driver for every piece of hardware. You can download current drivers from most manufacturers' Web sites.

- **How can I avoid hardware problems to begin with?** Always be sure to use the latest device drivers for your hardware. Verify that your hardware is using the latest hardware BIOS updates. Many hardware manufacturers update the onboard code or BIOS for their hardware as problems are resolved or features are added.

Troubleshooting the Universal Serial Bus

By design, there are no user-configurable resource settings for USB devices. As a result, typical USB problems are usually related to physical connections. Be sure to comply with the cabling type and distance limitations and to set up the hub placement and hierarchical structure according to the USB specification. If a USB device is failing, try connecting the device to another known-good USB port. If the malfunctioning USB device is bus-powered, try connecting the device directly to a USB controller. Frequently, USB hubs do not support bus-powered devices that draw a large amount of current. As a last resort, you can delete the USB host controller under the Device Manager, restart your PC, and allow the operating system to redetect and reinstall the USB drivers. Also, be sure to use the latest drivers if your USB manufacturer offers specific drivers newer than those shipping with Windows 2000.

Troubleshooting the FireWire Bus

Similar to the USB bus and devices, the FireWire bus and devices should be self-configuring. In the event of FireWire-related problems, check your physical connections, cabling, and distance limitations. Updating FireWire drivers may also resolve FireWire-related problems.

Troubleshooting the PCI Bus

The PCI bus uses software-configurable hardware in lieu of dual inline package (DIP) switches and jumpers. The combination of PCI bus components and Plug and Play capabilities should prevent any hardware configuration and resource conflict problems. Some hardware permits you to set IRQ, I/O ports, media type, and memory address manually via manufacturer-provided software configuration utilities.

Troubleshooting Fatal Exception Errors

Typically, fatal exception errors are caused either by an incorrect device driver that does not correspond to the hardware installed or by an internal problem (such as a bug) related to poor device driver design. Either way, verifying that you have installed the latest device driver for that particular hardware will usually resolve fatal exception error problems.

CHAPTER SUMMARY

- Windows 2000 combines several advanced technologies to make hardware installation, configuration, and troubleshooting easier than ever before. The four components of hardware management in Windows 2000 work in unison to support the widest possible range of hardware while easing the burden for driver developers and system administrators. The combination of full Plug and Play support and ACPI specification support in Windows 2000 means that most hardware conflicts are a thing of the past, as are the demands on your time and the effort needed to resolve those conflicts. Extensive native support for many new hardware technologies and buses makes Windows 2000 the operating system of the future in many ways. As many large corporations turn their desktop attention to power and system management, Windows 2000's built-in management capabilities make the upgrade decision a snap.

- Microsoft has also spent considerable time and resources building troubleshooting help directly into the operating system. The System Information utility is an invaluable tool for reviewing and documenting your system configuration. Because of Microsoft's meticulous attention to the details of hardware support, Windows 2000 is without a doubt the most mature, well-documented, best-designed, and most extensively supported operating system ever released by the company.

Key Terms

Advanced Configuration and Power Interface (ACPI) specification — Defines Advanced Power Management features and is an integral part of the OnNow system built into Windows 2000. For more information, see the Microsoft Web site: *http://www.microsoft.com/hwdev/onnow/*.

Advanced Power Management (APM) — The legacy specification that implements power management in machine-specific BIOS code.

bus class driver — One of the native Windows 2000 driver layers, which provides all basic driver functionality for bus devices.

bus minidriver — A small device driver that implements manufacturer-specific features not included in the bus class driver. It works in conjunction with the bus class driver.

CardBus — A high-speed bus specification based on the PCMCIA technology found on laptop computers. This hardware interface supports PC Card peripheral technologies.

device class driver — A layer of built-in device support that implements basic support for a class of hardware, such as modems. A device class driver supports all generic or standard features of a particular type of peripheral, thereby easing the development burden for hardware manufacturers.

device driver interfaces (DDIs) — Interfaces that define how device drivers interact with the operating system components, such as OnNow.

Device Manager — An internal Windows 2000 device management routine that handles enumeration, Plug and Play configuration, and device support.

device minidriver — A small device driver that implements manufacturer-specific features not included in the device class driver. It works in conjunction with the device class driver.

driver stack — The entire device driver layer in Windows 2000, including the HAL, bus class and minidrivers, and device class and minidrivers.

enumeration — The process by which Plug and Play adapters are recognized by the operating system and a device tree is built.

hardware devices — Physical hardware, features, and interfaces installed in a PC.

human interface device class — One of the Windows 2000 driver classes devoted to handling input devices such as mice, keyboards, and game controllers.

IEEE 1394 Serial Bus (FireWire) — A high-speed serial bus that supports 63 devices per bus, allows interconnection of 1023 buses, and features automatic device recognition.

legacy virtualization drivers layer — A layer in the driver stack that supports legacy VxD-style device drivers.

MSInfo32 — A system configuration and documentation utility that reports numerous hardware and software settings. Also called the System Information tool.

multiple display support — Native support within Windows 2000 that allows definition and use of as many as nine display monitors.

OnNow system — A Microsoft specification that supports hibernation, "instant-on," and sophisticated power management features. For more information, see the Microsoft Web site: *http://www.microsoft.com/hwdev/onnow/*.

PC Card — Laptop peripheral technology based on the CardBus specification. Similar in design to PCMCIA cards but operating at a higher bus speed.

PCI bus — High-performance personal computer bus that allows component-to-component communication without the need for CPU intervention.

Plug and Play — A hardware specification that allows automatic discovery and configuration of hardware devices.

Plug and Play Manager — The Windows 2000 component that handles operating system recognition of Plug and Play hardware.

power management — The Windows 2000 component that provides operating system power management features and controls hardware power management features.

system buses — The Windows 2000 component that recognizes and controls system buses such as PCI, CardBus, FireWire, and USB.

Universal Serial Bus (USB) — A new high-speed serial bus that supports 127 peripheral devices and automatic device configuration.

Virtual DOS Machine — A software environment within Windows 2000 that supports legacy DOS programs running in a protected environment space.

VxD driver — The legacy device driver model, still supported under Windows 2000, that requires much more development effort than corresponding WDM drivers.

Win32 Driver Model (WDM) — The new Windows driver model that allows simplified device driver development such that one driver can be used on both Windows 2000 and Windows 98 systems.

REVIEW QUESTIONS

1. There are _____ components of hardware management in Windows 2000.
2. What is the acronym for the new Microsoft driver model developed for Windows 2000 and Windows 98?
   a. WfM
   b. DPMI
   c. WDM
   d. DMI
3. The hardware abstraction layer permits applications to directly access system hardware. True or False?
4. Enumeration is the process Windows 2000 uses to do which of the following?
   a. Build the device tree
   b. Perform internal operating system math computations
   c. Perform floating-point calculations
   d. Recognize Plug and Play hardware and resources in use

5. The _____ bus allows high-bandwidth component-to-component communication without CPU intervention.

6. The OnNow system allows a user to immediately do which of the following?

   a. Boot the computer from a hibernation state
   b. Find a missing PC anywhere on the network
   c. Manage the power requirements of a Windows 2000 PC
   d. Trace data flows between system components

7. The device driver stack includes which of the following? (Choose all the correct answers.)

   a. HAL
   b. PCI bus
   c. Device class drivers and minidrivers
   d. System RAM
   e. Bus class drivers and minidrivers
   f. The legacy virtualization drivers layer
   g. External CPU cache

8. APM is the latest development in power management for personal computers. True or False?

9. VxD is the recommended driver model for hardware manufacturers to follow when developing device drivers for use under Windows 2000. True or False?

10. _____ is the high-speed bus that supports PC Cards in laptop computers.

11. You can view and print system hardware and software settings using which of the following utilities? (Choose all correct answers.)

    a. ViewConf
    b. MSInfo32
    c. Device Manager
    d. Services applet in the Control Panel

12. The multiple display support in Windows 2000 supports as many as _____ displays.

13. The IEEE 1394 Serial Bus is also known as which of the following?

    a. FastBus
    b. WireFire
    c. USB
    d. FireWire

14. The ACPI specification includes which of the following features? (Choose all correct answers.)
    a. Advanced operating system-directed power management
    b. The ability to turn peripherals on and off as needed
    c. The ability to manage data flow between system components
    d. The OnNow system
15. USB supports a maximum of how many devices?
    a. 127 devices
    b. 63 devices
    c. 1023 devices
    d. 63 devices per bus and 1023 buses
16. What is the first step in troubleshooting hardware?
    a. Rebooting
    b. Unplugging the PC
    c. Documenting the system configuration
    d. Washing your hands
17. Hardware resource conflicts are most readily visible in the _____ applet in the Control Panel.
18. _____ and _____ is the standard for automatic recognition and resolution of hardware resource conflicts.
19. A device minidriver is a very complex and difficult-to-develop device driver written for use under Windows 2000. True or False?
20. A bus class driver contains generic and standardized features common to all devices that utilize a specific bus. True or False?
21. Device class drivers are provided by device manufacturers, whereas device minidrivers are included in Windows 2000. True or False?
22. The human interface device class controls user ergonomics and screen appearance. True or False?
23. Device drivers developed for use under Win95 work properly under Windows 2000 because of the legacy virtualization drivers layer. True or False?
24. Which of the following buses is supported under Windows 2000? (Choose all correct answers.)
    a. PCI
    b. USB
    c. BART
    d. CardBus
    e. FireWire

25. _____ is the acronym for interfaces that define how device drivers interact with operating system components such as OnNow.
26. The ACPI specification is implemented solely in the system BIOS. True or False?
27. The Virtual DOS Machine support in Windows 2000 supports legacy DOS programs in a protected environment space. True or False?
28. With respect to Windows 2000, what does hibernation refer to?
    a. Suspending operation of a system component or peripheral
    b. Variable-speed CPU support
    c. Variable-bandwidth allocation for network operations
29. What is the best way to avoid fatal exception errors?
    a. Download and install Windows 2000 Service Pack 14
    b. Never turn off the PC without properly shutting it down
    c. Always use the latest device drivers for your installed hardware
30. What is the best way to resolve hardware problems?
    a. Change many parameters at once in an effort to expedite the troubleshooting process
    b. Document your configuration first and change only one parameter at a time whenever possible
    c. Reinstall the operating system
    d. Avoid hardware problems to begin with by upgrading your PC

HANDS-ON PROJECTS

Project 5-1

The most important task you can perform now that will aid you in all future hardware troubleshooting efforts is to document your system setup. Although you can retrieve, view and print system configuration information in several different utilities, you might want to use the MSInfo32 utility to print a complete list of all hardware configurations.

MSInfo32 tallies hardware IRQs in use, memory address usage, I/O ports in use, and software components. You should define a MSInfo32 icon on your desktop to ease the use of this utility and to provide a constant reminder of the importance of system documentation. To create such an icon:

1. Right-click on your desktop and select **New**, **Shortcut** from the menu.
2. Click the **Browse** button and follow the path to **%System_Drive%\Program Files\Common Files\Microsoft Shared\MSInfo**.
3. Click **Msinfo32.exe**, and then click **OK**. See Figure 5-16.

Hands-on Projects 145

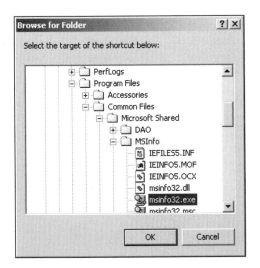

Figure 5-16 Creating a shortcut to Msinfo32.exe

4. Click the **Next** button, then click the **Finish** button. You should now have an MSInfo32 shortcut icon on your desktop.

Project 5-2

Now that you have a shortcut MSInfo32 icon on your desktop, follow these steps to document your system configuration:

1. Double-click the **Msinfo32.exe** icon to launch the Msinfo32 utility. See Figure 5-17.

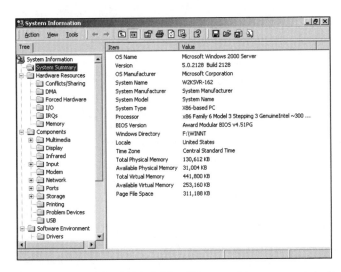

Figure 5-17 The MSInfo32 utility provides a complete list of system information

2. Click the **Action** menu.

3. Select **Print** from the Action menu. You can print to a text file (set up a text file output device in the **Printers** applet) or to one of the attached printers.

4. Select **OK**, and your system configuration will be printed on the selected printer.

Project 5-3

You can also save your system configuration to a file format called a System Information File. If you ever contact Microsoft or a third-party technical support provider, someone might ask you to save your system configuration information to a System Information File and e-mail the file to the company. To save your system configuration to a System Information File:

1. Start the MSInfo32 utility by choosing **Start**, **Programs**, **Administrative Tools**, **Computer Management**, expanding the **System Tools** icon, and selecting **System Information**.

2. From the **Action** menu, select **Save As System Information File**.

3. Enter a descriptive filename—for example, lanwserver, with no file extension (.nfo is automatically appended to the filename).

4. Click **Save**, and wait for the file to be saved.

5. If you need to e-mail the file, you can find the saved configuration file in the **My Documents** folder unless you specify another destination folder as you save the file.

CASE PROJECTS

1. You have just installed a new piece of Plug and Play hardware in your computer. After the hardware installation is complete, you restart the computer. What steps must be taken for Windows 2000 to recognize the newly installed device? Will you have to manually configure resources for the new hardware? If so, how will you configure those resources? If you choose to update the driver for this device in the future, what is the easiest way to do so?

2. Your modem stops working after you install a new serial I/O adapter in your PC. You notice a red X next to your modem device in the Device Manager. How will you discover what resource conflict is causing the malfunction? If you do not know how to resolve the conflict, where can you turn for help? Are there any "gotchas" to be aware of when manually adjusting hardware resources in the Device Manager?

3. You've just been assigned the task of training a new employee who will be helping with hardware support within your organization. Describe the salient points you must communicate to the trainee regarding troubleshooting hardware devices under Windows 2000.

4. Describe the difference between hardware and devices as seen by Windows 2000 and how each are managed or handled under the Windows 2000 operating system.

CHAPTER 6

DATA STORAGE

> **After reading this chapter and completing the exercises, you will be able to:**
> - Explain how physical disks are organized
> - Describe how Windows 2000 reads disks to circumvent the logical limit to partition size
> - Explain how the physical structure of a hard disk relates to its logical organization
> - List the types of volumes supported by Windows 2000
> - Discuss the role of a file system in an operating system
> - Describe the features of each file system supported by Windows 2000
> - Examine the advanced features of NTFS

One of the most important parts of any operating system is its file storage mechanisms. Good file storage provides security from intruders and prevents data loss; bad file storage leaves your organization's data vulnerable to loss. This chapter explains how the Windows 2000 file storage works and discusses the use of volumes and file systems in Windows 2000.

UNDERSTANDING DISK ARCHITECTURE

Let's first consider how hard disks are organized independently of Windows 2000 and how that physical organization relates to the logical storage units. We begin this discussion with an exploration of physical disk structures, then take a look at logical disk structures.

Physical Disk Divisions and Important Files

A hard disk—the metal and plastic contraption inside the computer on which you store data—consists of a set of round, magnetized, metal **platters** organized into a stack. Each side of each platter, called a **surface**, is divided into concentric circles called **tracks** located parallel to one another on each surface of each platter. An electromagnetic read/write **head**, like the needle on a record player, reads the surface of the disk. All heads in the disk move in unison so that they always point to the same track. That is, if head 0 (the first head on the first platter in the disk) is positioned over track 78 on surface 0, then head 4 is positioned over track 78 on surface 4.

Because each track on each surface is parallel to all other tracks with the same number, the tracks are logically combined into a series of nested **cylinders**. The number of tracks and the number of cylinders are the same, so disk manufacturers describe their disks in part by how many cylinders they have.

In addition to the tracks, each platter surface is divided into wedges radiating from the center, thereby dividing each track into units called **sectors**. Sectors are the smallest physical division on a hard disk; by de facto industry standard, sectors are 512 bytes in size. Figure 6-1 shows the disk-level logical divisions of a disk's storage space.

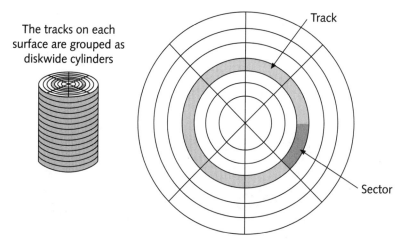

Figure 6-1 Physical disk geometry

The Partition Table

Disk space isn't readable on its own. To make the disk usable, you must logically organize its space into divisions called **partitions**. Each disk has at least one partition and, under normal circumstances, as many as four.

 Windows 2000 includes a type of disk format called dynamic storage that allows you to have more than four partitions on a disk. The later section on volume types discusses this format in more detail.

The first sector on a hard disk stores information that tells the computer how to read that disk. The **partition table** found in this sector is a 64-byte record of each partition (logical division) of the space on a hard disk. Each entry in the partition table is 16 bytes long, so the table may describe a maximum of 4 partitions (64/16 = 4). The entries for each partition include the following information:

- The partition's boot status—bootable or not bootable (8 bits)
- The surface where the partition starts and ends on the disk (8 bits)
- The cylinder where the partition starts and ends on the disk (10 bits)
- The location of the sectors where the partition starts and ends on the disk (6 bits)
- The number of sectors in the partition (32 bits)
- The file system used to format (logically organize) that partition (8 bits)
- If the partition is part of a multidisk volume, the other disks with which the partition works

The size of each field limits the size of the disk that the computer's BIOS (basic input/output system) can "see" without the help of an operating system such as Windows 2000. For example, only 8 bits are available to identify the surface where a partition starts. The entry is written in binary notation, so it can name as many as 2^8 (256) surfaces. No problem—you can just add more cylinders to those surfaces, right? Well, no. Because the entry for the starting and ending cylinders is only 10 bits long, the partition table can identify only disks with a maximum of 1024 (2^{10}) cylinders. And each cylinder can have only 64 (2^6) sectors in it, because the entry for sectors has only 6 bits. (Actually, it's worse than that, because sectors start numbering with 1, not 0 like most computing things do. Thus you have only 63 sectors per cylinder.) You can calculate the total capacity of a disk with the following formula:

```
Disk Capacity = sector size x sectors per track x cylinders
x heads
```

Therefore, the theoretical maximum size of a disk that the BIOS can see is 512 bytes × 63 × 1024 × 256, or 8,455,716,864—approximately 7.8 GB.

If you're looking in confusion at the 10 GB disk inside your computer and wondering how Windows 2000 reads it, fear not. Addressing disks larger than this theoretical limit is a job carried out by the operating system. Once Windows 2000 starts running, it controls the hard disk controller without help from the BIOS (meaning that it's no longer dependent on the BIOS's ability to recognize hard disks). During its operation, Windows 2000 ignores the sections of the partition table that refer to absolute sector and cylinder numbers (which are only 6-bit and 10-bit entries), instead referring to the sections that note the relative sector numbers and the number of sectors (both 32-bit entries). Using these entries allows Windows 2000 to "see" hard disks with 2^32 sectors, or, using the standard 512-byte sector, 2 terabytes.

The Master Boot Record

The partition table is part of a larger structure called the **master boot record (MBR)**. On x86 systems, the MBR contains the partition table for the disk and a small amount of code that can read the partition table into memory and find the system (bootable) partition for that disk if one exists. The MBR then finds the first sector of that system partition on the disk and loads an image of its starting sector—its **boot sector**—into memory. The boot sector finds the files needed to run the operating system controlling that system partition (in the case of Windows 2000, it starts with a file called Ntldr) and loads those files into memory. Thus, the MBR is not operating system-specific, but the boot sector is.

If the disk is not bootable (that is, if it has no operating system installed on it), then the partition table is just loaded into memory where the rest of the computer can access it. (Data on disk is essentially invisible. Only data in memory is usable by any part of the computer or operating system.)

If the MBR or a boot sector isn't working or is missing, the computer cannot identify the system partition and the disk won't boot. A class of viruses called boot viruses target the MBR, because it's a sitting duck. Wipe out the first sector on the hard disk, and you've killed it. To prevent this event from happening, you should use a disk utility to copy the contents of the MBR so that you can restore it if necessary. The Windows 2000 Recovery Console includes a tool called FIXMBR that can create a new MBR on a hard disk, as long as the system disk is bootable. It also contains a tool called FIXBOOT that you can use to replace the boot sector on a partition. Chapter 14 discusses these tools in more detail.

Logical Disk Divisions

Earlier in this chapter, you saw the setup that the partition table uses to identify the system partition on a disk. Although you could use this same system to find files stored on a disk—and early operating systems did—using this technique would be time-consuming and tricky to set up and even trickier to keep updated.

If it's not clear why this technique is so challenging, consider this example: You are working on a spreadsheet. In your no-file-system environment, you have to know which cylinder holds the file, what surface it starts on, what sector it starts on, and how many sectors contain part of the file. Enter all that information, and you can load the spreadsheet. But what happens if you add to the spreadsheet? Even if it's only 512 bytes larger than it used to be, then you must edit the location data to take into account all sectors used by the file. Partition tables work because they deal with small amounts of data that can be updated easily, describing only four elements on the disk. Your computer probably has thousands of files on it. Another problem with this kind of organization is that it's difficult to tell which clusters are used and which are not. Overwriting data can be prevented, but unused space might go to waste because you don't know that it's there.

Rather than attempt to create partition-table-like entries for files, operating systems use **file systems** to organize data on a disk. When you format a partition, you're running a program that evaluates the size of the partition, then, based on that size, groups sectors together into logical units called **clusters**, which are the smallest storage units available to the file system (see Figure 6-2). The number of sectors in a cluster depends both on the size of the partition and on the type of file system being used. Windows 2000 supports three file systems: **FAT (file allocation table)**, **FAT32**, and **NTFS (New Technology File System)**. **FAT16** was designed for backward compatibility with other operating systems; FAT32 is compatible with Windows 98 and more space-efficient than FAT16; and NTFS is designed for Windows NT/2000 and includes advanced features that make it more secure and more flexible than the other two file systems. The details of these file systems and how they organize disk space are discussed later in this chapter.

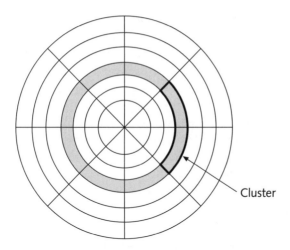

Figure 6-2 When you format a partition, its sectors are logically grouped into clusters

Volume Types

Clusters represent the smallest unit of disk space intelligible to Windows 2000. Those clusters may, in turn, be part of one of several kinds of **volumes** (another term for partitions). The kind of volume depends on the type of disk storage used on those disks. Windows 2000 accommodates two kinds of data storage: basic and dynamic. **Basic storage** supports the partition-oriented disk organization that has been discussed up to this point and is intelligible to all operating systems. **Dynamic storage** supports multidisk volumes. Because dynamic storage is unique to Windows 2000, volumes on dynamic disks—and the dynamic disks themselves—are invisible to any operating systems other than Windows 2000 that are installed on the same computer.

Basic Storage Types A partition is a portion of a hard disk set up to act like a separate physical hard disk. Two kinds of partitions exist: primary and extended. A **primary partition** is a portion of a physical hard disk that the operating system (such as Windows 2000) marks as bootable and assigns a drive letter. Windows 2000 supports a maximum of four partitions per disk, so you could have four operating systems installed on the same physical disk. Only one partition at a time is marked as being active—the one from which you booted. You cannot subdivide primary partitions; once you create them to be a certain size, they will remain that size until they are deleted.

If you want to subdivide a partition, you'll need an **extended partition**. An extended partition can't hold data; it's just a logical division of **unallocated space** (unpartitioned space) on the disk. Once you create an extended partition, you can divide the **free space** in it into **logical drives**, which have drive letters like primary partitions and can hold data once they're formatted. You can have one extended partition on each disk, but may divide that partition into as many logical drives as you like.

Dynamic Storage Types Any volumes that are extended over multiple disks, or that have the capability of becoming so, must be created on dynamic disks. Dynamic disks support several different kinds of storage—some fault-tolerant, and some not.

Chapter 13, "Fault Tolerance," discusses the use of fault-tolerant volumes in detail.

The simplest kinds of dynamic volumes are **simple volumes**. Simple volumes are like primary partitions; they're created from unallocated space, are located on a single disk, are identified by a drive letter, and can be made bootable. Windows 2000, for example, can be installed on a simple volume. **Spanned volumes** are volumes that extend over more than one physical disk, but otherwise work like simple volumes. You can extend simple volumes to become spanned volumes.

Flexibility is the driving force behind simple and spanned volumes. Volume sets are not limited to one physical disk, so with a spanned volume, you can make quite a large volume set out of many small pieces of unallocated space. You can therefore use unallocated space more efficiently than you could if limited to a single disk. It's much easier to fit 300 MB of data into a 350 MB volume set than it is to fit it into two 100 MB logical drives and one 150 MB logical drive. Also, the data will be easier to find once you do fit it in, as it will be stored under one drive letter, not three. Because the data is accessible under a single drive letter rather than many drive letters, it is easier for the system to access the information.

You can increase the size of a volume set by extending it if a physical disk contains more unallocated space, but you cannot make a simple or spanned volume smaller. If you must, then you'll need to delete the volume and create a new one.

Another type of dynamic storage is the stripe set. A **stripe set** is a volume that extends across two or more physical disks. Unlike volumes, which may include areas of unallocated space of any size on the disks, all areas of a stripe set must be the same size on each disk, because of the way in which data are written to a stripe set. When data are written to a volume, a partition or logical drive files are put into the first available clusters, filling up the area from front to back, as it were. Even spanned volumes use only one disk at a time—the second disk is there to handle the overflow when the first one fills up.

In a stripe set, data are written to the areas of the stripe set on each disk in a series of stripes. In other words, not all of your data ends up in one place. Even if one of the areas in the set has enough room for an entire file, the data won't all be written there. The reason for this choice is the attempt to improve read and write times for the volume. Whenever you write data to a disk, a device on the disk called a disk controller is responsible for the process. Using more than one disk means that you can use more than one disk controller, with the result that you reduce disk access time. In other words, all other things being equal, it's faster to read and write data to a stripe set than it is to a primary partition or spanned volume.

It's important to note that volume sets and stripe sets do not protect your data; they merely let you group available drive space efficiently or reduce disk access time. If a hard disk used in a volume set or stripe set stops working, all of the data on it becomes inaccessible, even if the other hard disks in the set are fine. It's true that the more disks you have, the less likely it is that all of them will fail at the same time. The flip side is that the more disks you have, the more likely it is that *one* of them will fail at any given time. In a situation in which one disk failure brings down the entire system, having more disks actually increases your vulnerability to hardware failures. For this reason, it's vital that the data on volume sets and stripe sets be backed up regularly.

Dynamic storage does support two types of **fault-tolerant volumes** (volumes that are arranged in such a way that even if one disk goes bad, your data will still be recoverable): disk mirroring and RAID 5 volumes.

Disk mirroring helps protect your data by storing a copy of it on an identically sized area of free space on another disk—thus a volume of 500 MB needs a mirror of 500 MB. The original and the copy are collectively known as a **mirror set**. If anything happens to one disk in the mirror set, you still have an identical copy of its data on the other disk.

The trouble with mirror sets is that they're not very space-efficient, because every piece of data that you record has an identical twin on the other half of the mirror set. You need exactly twice as much storage space as you have data. Therefore, Windows 2000 supports **stripe sets with parity**, also known as **RAID 5 volumes**. RAID 5 volumes work like the stripe sets mentioned previously, except that, in addition to writing the data in stripes to the disks in the stripe set, the disk controller also writes parity information evenly across the disks in the set. If one disk in the set dies, then the data contained on that disk can be regenerated from the parity information on the other disks in the stripe set. RAID 5 volumes are a little slower when it comes to writing data than other volumes, because of all the parity information that must be written, but they are a more space-efficient option than disk mirroring. Parity information takes up $1/n$ of the total disk space, where n is the number of disks in the set (3–32). Thus, the more disks in the RAID 5 volume, the more space-efficient it is. As shown in Figure 6-3, the Windows 2000 Disk Management tool displays all existing types of volumes and lists the redundancy factor for each.

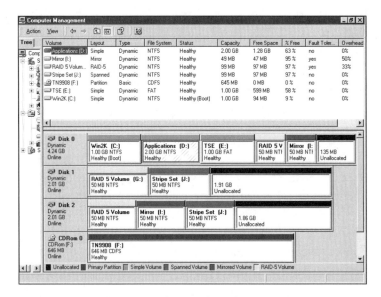

Figure 6-3 Redundant volumes don't have as much room to store data as other volumes do, but are less vulnerable to data loss

RAID 5 volumes get their name from fault-tolerance terminology. A redundant array of independent disks (RAID) is a methodology of keeping data secure by storing the information on multiple disks such that if one disk fails, the data will still be available. Mirror sets are RAID 1 volumes. Windows 2000 calls disk striping with parity "RAID 5" volumes to avoid confusion with the disk striping without parity.

Identifying Partitions and Volumes For you to store data on a drive/volume/partition, that drive/volume/partition must have some identifier so that you can get its attention. Traditionally, in Windows operating systems, this name has been a drive letter—the boot drive, for example, is normally named C:. This method is simple and has the advantage of providing a really short way of leaping to that partition. The disadvantage, of course, is that as long as Windows 2000 insists on using the Roman alphabet, you're limited to a total of 26 letters for all local drives and mapped network connections. If you think you might need more than 26 total connections, you're better off mounting the partition to an empty folder on an NTFS volume.

The basic idea behind **mounting a partition** to a folder is that you redirect all read and write requests sent to that folder to the partition instead. Mount a new partition to G:\My Work Stuff, and every file I/O request you send to G:\My Work stuff will be rerouted to the new partition, even if the real drive G: is located on an entirely different physical disk. You can mount a volume to as many paths as you like; alternatively, you can mount it to both paths and a drive letter to let people access the same storage space from different paths. The only restrictions are that the folders must be empty at the time of mounting and not mapped to any other volumes, and they must be on NTFS volumes on the local computer.

Understanding Windows 2000 File Systems

Whichever kinds of volumes you choose to make, you must format these volumes with a file system before you can store data on them. The role of the file system is to organize the sectors in the disk space so that the instructions to the disk controller, telling it how to read and write data, can be as explicit as possible. As stated earlier, Windows 2000 supports three file systems: FAT16, FAT32, and NTFS. You can distinguish these file systems in three main ways:

- The method used to organize disk space
- The cluster size
- Special features available

FAT16

The FAT file systems were the first Microsoft-compatible file systems. They're simple, not meant for very large disks (when FAT was invented, very large disks didn't exist), and have only a few simple file attributes.

FAT16 and FAT32 use a catalog called the file allocation table to keep track of how clusters are used on the volume. Each cluster is identified as having one of the following states:

- Unused
- Cluster in use by a file
- Bad cluster
- Last cluster in a file

Each folder has a 32-byte entry in the FAT naming the files it holds. A **root folder**—which you see as the root directory on a partition—contains an entry for each folder in the volume. The only difference between the root folder and other folders is that the root folder is at a specified location and has a fixed size of 512 entries (for a hard disk; the number of entries on a floppy disk depends on the size of the disk).

A folder's entry contains the following information:

- Filename
- Attribute byte (8 bits)
- Create time (24 bits)
- Create date (16 bits)
- Last access date (16 bits)
- Last modified time (16 bits)
- Last modified date (16 bits)
- Starting cluster number in the file allocation table (16 bits)
- File size (32 bits)

FAT works like this: Each cluster in the partition has an address. When a file is stored on the volume, it goes into the first available cluster. If the file's too big to fit entirely into a single cluster, then the remaining data go into the next available cluster on the volume and the first cluster gets a pointer to the next cluster holding the file's data. This process continues until the file is completely stored, at which point the final cluster gets an End Of File (EOF) marker. The FAT, stored at the beginning of the volume, records which clusters are chain-linked together and which files are found where.

All operating systems that can read FAT volumes can read the information in the folder. Windows 2000 can store additional time stamps in a FAT folder entry, showing when the file was created or last accessed. These time stamps are used mainly by Portable Operating System Interface for UNIX (POSIX) applications—which is to say, not often.

Because all entries in a folder are the same size, the attribute byte for each entry in a folder describes what kind of entry it is. For example, one bit indicates that the entry is for a sub-folder and another bit marks the entry as a volume label. Typically, only the operating system controls the settings of these bits. The attribute byte includes four bits that can be turned on or off by the user—archive file, system file, hidden file, and read-only file. The **archive attribute** marks a file for backup. The **system attribute** marks the file as a system file. The **hidden attribute** hides a file when turned on. The **read-only attribute** makes a file readable but prevents it from being changed.

The process of reading data from a FAT volume goes something like this:

1. An application attempts to open a file and calls upon the operating system to get the file. This request is passed to the I/O system in the Windows 2000 executive, and from there to the file system driver.

If you're not sure how these parts of the operating system work together, review Chapter 2.

2. The file system driver inspects the FAT at the top of the volume to see whether the file exists.

3. The file system driver notes the location of the first cluster of data as listed in the FAT and retrieves the data.

4. Unless the file is entirely contained within one cluster, the FAT will show a pointer to the next cluster holding data for that file.

5. Step 4 is repeated until the driver finds a data cluster with an EOF notice signaling the end of the file data. The data are then passed to the application that requested the information.

Reading data in this way is a simple process for small volumes and requires little overhead. On large and very fragmented volumes, however, the FAT method of organization can be very slow. FAT also has another problem—it's not very efficient for organizing storage into clusters.

Each cluster in a FAT16 volume has a 16-bit address—hence the name FAT16. Having 16 bits in a binary number means that a FAT16 volume can hold a maximum of 2^{16} (65,536) clusters. This limited cluster size means that big FAT volumes have to use big clusters so as to fit in all of the sectors. Table 6-1 reveals how cluster size increases with partition size in a FAT16 volume.

Table 6-1 Cluster sizes in various sizes of FAT volumes in Windows 2000

Volume Size	Number of Sectors/Cluster	Cluster Size
0 MB–15 MB*	8	4 KB
16 MB–127 MB	4	2 KB
128 MB–255 MB	8	4 KB
256 MB–511 MB	16	8 KB
512 MB–1023 MB	32	16 KB
1024 MB–2048 MB	64	32 KB
2048 MB–4096 MB	128	64 KB
*12-bit FAT.		

As, you can see, really big FAT volumes are so large as to be impractical for storing lots of data. Each cluster can hold only one file's data. Thus, unless you will regularly store only very large files, FAT volumes larger than 2 GB aren't very efficient. You can make clusters smaller by making the volumes smaller, but this option isn't a really great solution, either. To use clusters more efficiently, you need either FAT32 or NTFS.

FAT32

FAT32 is organized essentially the same way as FAT16. The main difference between the two file systems is that FAT32 uses 32-bit addresses for each cluster in a volume, so it can address more clusters within a single partition. As a result, FAT32 clusters can be smaller than FAT16 ones for the same volume—only 4 KB for all volumes from 512 MB to 8 GB.

Although FAT32 in Windows 95-98 supports compression, the version provided with Windows 2000 does not. If you want to compress files, you need to use NTFS.

NTFS

NTFS differs from the FAT file systems in several ways. First, it organizes disk space and data differently. Second, it uses different cluster sizes. Third, it supports many more attributes, providing native support for encryption, file compression, **disk quotas**, and file and folder compression.

Directory Organization

The flat-file database structure that FAT file systems use to organize data is compact and works well on small volumes, but can be slow on larger ones. To speed things up, NTFS uses a treelike hierarchical structure. A catalog located at the beginning of the volume, called the

master file table (MFT), maintains a 2 KB entry for each file in the volume. The MFT contains both entire files (if small enough) and pointers to the locations of those files.

All data files stored on NTFS volumes have the following attributes, arranged as shown in Figure 6-4:

- Header (H)
- Standard information (SI)
- File name (FN)
- Data
- Security descriptor (SD)

Figure 6-4 A simple NTFS file

The file may also include one or more of the system data attributes listed in Table 6-2.

Table 6-2 NTFS file attributes

Attribute	Description	Must Be Resident in Master File Table?
Attribute	Lists the attributes that did not fit into the MFT and their location in the NTFS volume structure.	Yes
Bitmap	Maps the sectors in use on the volume.	No
Data	Contains file data and the file size. A file may have more than one data attribute.	No
Filename	Defines the long and short filenames of the file and the file number of the folder containing the file. If a file appears in more than one folder, there will be a corresponding number of parent directory entries.	Yes
Index allocation	If the index becomes too large to be resident in the MFT, this nonresident attribute can hold the rest of the index.	No
Index root	Used to index files in folders by a given attribute, such as their names or size.	Yes
Object ID	Used to find files linked together in data streams. Files not linked do not have object identifiers.	No
Reparse point	Used to redirect NTFS when reading a path, such as when reading from or writing to a mounted volume.	No

Table 6-2   NTFS file attributes (continued)

Attribute	Description	Must Be Resident in Master File Table?
Security descriptor	Contains the security information for the file, defining who's got what kind of access to it. Also contains an audit field that can hold audit settings (defining which security-related activities associated with this file will be recorded).	No
Standard information attributes	Contain the information that you see when you view a file's property sheet: file creation date, last modification date for file data, last modification date for standard file attributes (read-only, hidden, archive, and system), and the like.	Yes
Volume information	Defines the version of NTFS used.	No
Volume name	Contains the volume label.	No

How does NTFS decide which attributes go into the MFT? As you can see from Table 6-2, some attributes must be **resident**, or stored in the MFT. The arrangement of attributes that don't fit in the MFT depends on just how many attributes are associated with the file.

Files with data attributes of less than 1500 bytes may be resident in their 2 KB entry in the MFT, because that space is generally adequate to store all attributes of such a small file. You can't be sure that small files will indeed be in the MFT (if they have more attributes than expected, they may not fit), but at that level it's possible.

Somewhat larger files won't fit in the MFT. Instead, their 2 KB record contains the attributes that must be resident and a data attribute that points to the true location of the data in the NTFS catalog. This pointer is the virtual cluster number (VCN) for the first cluster of each group of clusters that hold the data, as shown in Figure 6-5.

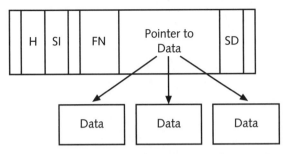

Figure 6-5   Files with data attributes too large to fit in the MFT have a VCN that points to the data's location in the volume

As the entry in the MFT is only 2 KB for each file, the data attribute might not be the only one squeezed out. In that case, very large files with lots of attributes may require a more cascaded structure in the NTFS catalog, as shown in Figure 6-6.

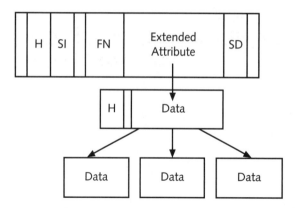

Figure 6-6 The largest files may require several data pointers to point to all their attributes

This tree-shaped database ensures that no file can ever be too large to fit within the NTFS structure. The more complex the file, the longer it will take to retrieve it, but the file will always fit.

Files aren't the only objects that get an entry in the MFT. The folders containing files also need entries, so that NTFS knows which folder contains the files. NTFS organizes folder objects in the same way as it organizes file objects, with one exception: folder objects can contain other objects (files and folders), whereas file objects cannot. The important parts of a directory are its name and its **index**, its list of contained folder and file objects. The name must be resident in the MFT, and the index should be. If the index is too large to fit in the 2 KB permitted for the folder's attributes, then the rest of the index is stored in a nonresident index allocation attribute.

Thus, the process of finding a file under NTFS is as follows:

1. An application attempts to open a file and calls on the operating system to get the file. This request is passed down to the I/O system in the Windows 2000 executive, and from there to the file system driver.

2. The file system driver checks the MFT to see whether such a file exists. If the file is small, then it may be in the MFT. If it is not, the MFT will contain a pointer to the file's attributes.

3. Having found the pointer in the MFT, the file system driver uses the pointer to jump to the file's attributes on the disk. If the file is there, then the driver opens it. If it's just a pointer to more attributes, the driver keeps moving down the directory tree.

This file system can potentially work more quickly on very large volumes, as the scope of the search is limited. Rather than searching the entire MFT, it's necessary to search only the part that points to the requested filename.

Important System Files

Any volume formatted with NTFS contains the following files:

- The MFT records the location and attributes of each file and folder in the volume. For safekeeping, Windows 2000 maintains a backup copy of the MFT on each NTFS volume in case the original is damaged or destroyed.
- A volume file holds the volume name and version.
- An attribute definitions file specifies all system-defined and user-defined attributes in the volume.
- A cluster allocation bitmap maps the storage space on the volume, excluding the cluster at the beginning of the volume. This map helps NTFS find unused space on the volume when it needs to store new files.
- A boot file contains the data that a system volume needs to boot.
- A bad cluster file records the location of all bad clusters (damaged clusters that cannot hold data) on the volume.

If NTFS finds new bad clusters when attempting to write to disk, it records the clusters' locations and tries again to write the data on good clusters, instead of showing the "Error Reading Disk. Abort/Retry/Ignore?" message that you may have seen when attempting to write to a FAT volume with bad clusters.

These NTFS system files may be located anywhere on the volume, rather than having to appear at the beginning of the volume as the FAT does. This flexibility makes NTFS volumes less vulnerable to bad areas of the volume than FAT volumes.

Cluster Sizes

Because NTFS uses 32-bit addressing, it can be more efficient in cluster allocations than FAT16 can. Table 6-3 shows the cluster size relative to partition size on NTFS volumes.

Table 6-3 Cluster sizes in various sizes of NTFS volumes in Windows 2000

Volume Size	Number of Sectors/Cluster	Cluster Size
512 MB or less	1	512 bytes (0.5 KB)
513 MB–1024 MB	2	1 KB
1025 MB–2048 MB	4	2 KB
2048 MB or more	8	4 KB

New NTFS Attributes

NTFS in Windows 2000 includes some attributes not found in either NTFS in previous versions of Windows NT or FAT. These new features make Windows 2000 perform better with large files, keep track of changes to the volume structure, limit the amount of disk space that users' files can occupy, and encrypt their data. Many of these features are explained elsewhere in this book, but the following sections examine the features supported only by the NTFS file system.

Multiple **data stream** attributes allow developers to manage data in different files as a single unit. This feature works a little like mounting—the data files are mounted to a location in the data stream and are therefore linked. Streams can share data between files, but protect file information (such as file size) from being corrupted between files.

Reparse points alter the way that NTFS resolves filenames. For example, under normal circumstances, when you open the file located at C:\WINNT\System32\Example.doc, NTFS finds the C: volume, then finds the boot partition, then the WINNT folder, the System32 folder, and finally the Example.doc file. A reparse point can exist at any point in that path, directing NTFS to search the path differently. For example, when you mount a volume to an NTFS path, you use reparse points to redirect writes sent from one disk to another disk.

NTFS uses the **change journal** to log all changes—additions, deletions, or edits—made to files in the volume. Several volume tools use the change journal to tell when they're supposed to do their jobs: replication managers that copy changed data to a replication partner, the remote storage service that automatically backs up unused data to a tape drive, and incremental backups (which back up only changed files), can all use the change journal.

NTFS now supports the **Encrypted File System (EFS)** to encrypt data on the disk, including temporary files. This encryption prevents anyone from reading data from an operating system other than Windows 2000—it's mostly meant for people using laptops or as protection for removable media.

You may recall from Chapter 4 that when data are read into memory, memory is allocated in a two-stage process: first a process reserves memory that it wants to use, then it allocates that reserved memory by backing it with space in the paging file in case the data need to be paged out of main memory. With very large files, this technique can consume a lot of space in the paging file. That's fine, but some files have a great deal of redundant or nonmeaningful data (for example, long strings of 0s) that takes up space in the paging file. **Sparse files** avoid this problem by marking certain files with an attribute that causes the I/O subsystem to allocate memory only to the file's meaningful data. When a sparse file is read, the allocated data are returned as stored and the nonallocated data are returned as strings of 0s. Basically, the sparse file attribute tells NTFS and the Virtual Memory Manager, "there are nine 0s here," instead of making the Virtual Memory Manager find space in which to put "000000000".

Disk quotas let you restrict the amount of data that users can store on NTFS volumes. If a user tries to write more data than is permitted on that volume, the user will receive an "Access Denied" error.

Finally, NTFS protects itself from volume corruption. Every time you change an NTFS volume (perhaps by adding a new folder), a **transaction log** records the change you wanted to make. When the change has been successfully made, the transaction log notes that the change has been committed. If the disk stops working in the middle of the change to the volume structure, then when Windows 2000 comes up again, NTFS refers to the transaction log for each volume and implements only those changes that have been fully committed. Thus, some changes to the volume structure may be lost, but NTFS volumes are kept from being corrupted by unfinished volume changes.

 The only catch to NTFS for Windows 2000 is that it really works only for Windows 2000. Users with Windows NT Server 4 with Service Pack 4 can read and write to Windows 2000 NTFS volumes, but they can't use any of the special attributes for the volumes if accessing them on the local computer. If you need to support multiple operating systems on the same disk, you must use FAT16, as the most widely supported file system.

Chapter Summary

- Booting the computer from a hard disk isn't the job of the operating system, but rather is the responsibility of a set of instructions in a computer's BIOS. For those who'd like to use that hard disk, however, the operating system is key. An operating system such as Windows 2000 provides instructions that remove the four-partition limit imposed by the partition table; it also supports file systems that make reading and writing data to the disk simple and secure.

- Windows 2000 supports three different operating systems: FAT16, designed for backward compatibility with other operating systems; FAT32, compatible with Windows 98 and more space-efficient than FAT16; and NTFS, designed for Windows NT/2000 and boasting advanced features that make it more secure and more flexible than the other two file systems. The file system you choose will affect how you can use the data storage on your computer—so choose carefully.

Key Terms

archive attribute — A simple attribute that identifies a file as having changed since the last full backup.

basic storage — A hard disk designed to support primary and extended partitions and logical drives. Any operating system can recognize disks set up to use basic storage.

boot sector — An area at the beginning of each partition that names the files to be loaded to run the operating system stored on that partition.

boot virus — Malicious software that targets the master boot record of a disk to make the disk unbootable. Until the advent of macro viruses, boot viruses were the most common virus type.

change journal — A list of all changes made to files in the volume. Some Windows 2000 functions, such as the remote storage service, can refer to the change journal to know when to do their jobs. The change journal is a more efficient way of looking for changes than browsing the volume looking for the desired difference.

cluster — A logical grouping of sectors, with the number of sectors per cluster depending on the size of the partition and the file system being used. A cluster is the smallest storage unit that Windows 2000 file systems can recognize.

cylinder — All of the parallel tracks on all surfaces. For example, Track 10 on all surfaces creates Cylinder 10 for the disk.

data stream — Chunks of data that may be associated with more than one file. Data streaming allows you to deal with several distinct pieces of data as one unit.

disk quotas — A method of preventing users from using more than a predetermined amount of space in a volume. When a user exceeds his or her quota, he or she will be denied write access to the volume until some files have been deleted to go below the quota.

dynamic storage — A new type of storage in Windows 2000 that designs disks to support multidisk volumes. Volumes on dynamic disks may be added, resized, and deleted without rebooting.

Encrypted File System (EFS) — The Windows 2000 native encryption service, which requires Windows 2000 to read files. Intended mainly for people with laptops and for removable storage that's vulnerable to theft.

extended partition — A disk partition on a basic disk that's designed to hold logical drives. Extended partitions can't hold any data on their own—they're just areas of free space in which you can create logical drives. A hard disk may hold one extended partition, but you can make as many logical drives within that partition as you like.

FAT (file allocation table) — A catalog at the beginning of a volume that notes each file and folder in the volume and lists the clusters in which each file is stored.

FAT16 — A file system first used with DOS and supported in Windows 2000 for compatibility reasons—only Windows 2000 can read NTFS volumes, so if you need to support dual-boot machines or write data to floppy disks, you need FAT. FAT16 uses a 16-bit addressing scheme for clusters and can support only fairly small volumes without wasting space from overlarge clusters, but it has little overhead.

FAT32 — A version of FAT that uses a 32-bit addressing scheme, so that it can address more clusters than FAT16.

fault-tolerant volume — Any volume designed to reduce the risk of data loss due to disk failure. Fault-tolerant volumes either keep a copy of data or maintain information from which that data may be regenerated.

file system — A method of logically organizing the physical disk space in a partition for use by the operating system. Different file systems catalog data differently and support different file attributes.

free space — An area of an extended partition not yet made into a logical drive.

head — The read-write mechanism in a disk. Each surface has its own head.

hidden attribute — A simple attribute that hides a file. If the hidden attribute is set, the file will not show up in a DIR listing of the folder's contents, or in Windows Explorer unless hidden files are visible.

index — A list of all files in a folder in an NTFS volume.

logical drive — A formattable division of an extended partition, created from an area of free space. An extended partition may hold as many logical drives as you like.

master boot record (MBR) — A file stored in the first sector of a hard disk. It contains the partition table and links to the boot sectors for all partitions.

master file table (MFT) — A file in each NTFS volume that contains a 2 KB entry for each file and folder in the volume. If the file plus all attributes (including the data attribute) is smaller than 2 KB, then it may be stored in the MFT itself; otherwise, the file's entry in the MFT contains a pointer to the rest of the file's attributes that wouldn't fit.

mirror set — A fault-tolerant volume that exists in two identical, linked volumes on two dynamic disks. When you write data to a mirror set, the information is written to both volumes so that if one disk fails, the data will be recoverable from the other volume.

mounting a partition — Logically linking a volume to an empty folder on another NTFS volume. It means that you can write data to the path on one volume and have that data actually stored on the mounted volume.

NTFS (New Technology File System) — The native file system for Windows NT that is extended in Windows 2000. NTFS has many advanced features that make it more efficient and faster on large drives, supports volume mounting, and offers other features such as disk compression, file quotas, and a native encryption system.

partition — A logical division of disk space. A disk must be partitioned, and the partitions formatted, before it can be used. Disks can have a maximum of four partitions without the help of an operating system.

partition table — A table stored in the first sector of a hard disk, noting the location and size of every partition on the disk and indicating whether those partitions are bootable.

platter — A magnetized metal disk within a hard disk—the actual storage medium.

primary partition — A disk partition on a basic disk that's designed to hold an operating system (although it doesn't have to do so—a primary partition might hold only data). One primary partition is marked active, meaning that the computer will boot from it. A disk may hold a maximum of four primary partitions. Primary partitions may not be subdivided.

RAID 5 volume — A fault-tolerant volume extending over 3–32 disks. It works like a stripe set, except that in addition to writing data in stripes across the disks in the volume, it also writes parity information for the volume. If one disk in the RAID 5 volume fails, then the data on that disk may be regenerated from the parity information on the other disks.

read-only attribute — A simple attribute that makes it impossible to edit a file.

reparse points — NTFS pointers that may be set into a file path to redirect the path from one volume to another. Reparse points make mounted volumes work.

resident — Attributes that are stored in the master file table instead of being pointed to are known as resident attributes. Some attributes are required to be resident.

root folder — The folder in the FAT that lists all folders in the volume and all files in the root directory. A root folder can contain a maximum of 512 entries.

sector — The smallest physical unit of storage on a hard disk.

simple volume — A volume on a dynamic disk that exists on a single disk. Simple volumes may be expanded on the same disk or made into spanned volumes that extend to another physical disk.

spanned volume — A volume that extends over two or more dynamic disks.

sparse files — Files marked with an attribute that says, "Only provide space in the paging file for the parts of this file that actually have data in them, instead of strings of 0s." The data have pointers to the places where the long strings of 0s can be, so that they can be filled in as necessary, but sparse files save room in the paging file and in memory by allocating only the storage that's actually needed.

stripe set — A volume that extends over two or more dynamic disks, but which reduces disk read and write times by writing data to all disks in stripes, instead of filling up the volume from back to front as normal volumes do.

stripe set with parity — See RAID 5 volume.

surface — The side of a disk platter. Each platter has two surfaces.

system attribute — A simple attribute that identifies a file as part of the operating system.

track — A concentric circle traced on the surface of a platter, used to physically divide storage space.

transaction log — A list of changes to the volume structure maintained by NTFS. When changes are complete, they're listed in the transaction log as being committed. If the disk stops working, when it restarts, NTFS rolls back the volume structure to its form at the last committed change. This technique prevents the volume structure from being corrupted by half-made changes.

unallocated space — An area of a physical disk that has not yet been partitioned.

volume — Another name for a partition—a logical division of physical disk space. Most often, volumes refer to areas on dynamic disks, whereas partitions refer to the division of basic disks.

REVIEW QUESTIONS

1. A hard disk has as many heads as it has cylinders. True or False?
2. The smallest physical storage unit on a hard disk is called a(n) _____. By de facto standard, it's _____ in size.
3. Which of the following describes the limit on how many partitions a basic disk may have? (Select all that apply.)
   a. Four primary partitions
   b. Four primary partitions and one extended partition
   c. Four partitions of any kind
   d. A maximum of four extended partitions
4. The _____ is a 64-byte record of each logical division on the disk. It's stored in the first sector on the hard disk.
5. If an operating system must depend on the computer's BIOS to handle hard disk operations, the disk may be as large as _____ in size.

6. Which of the following statements is true?
   a. Windows 2000 can read disks larger than those that the BIOS can read because it refers only to those sections of the partition table that note relative sector numbers and the number of sectors.
   b. Windows 2000 can read disks larger that those that the BIOS can read because it refers only to those sections of the partition table that note the absolute sector numbers and the cylinder numbers.
   c. Windows 2000 uses logical block addressing to read disks larger than 10 GB.
   d. None of the above.
7. Which of the following contains the code that finds the bootable partition for a hard disk?
   a. The partition table
   b. The master file table
   c. The master boot record
   d. The logical block
8. Briefly describe the role of the boot sector.
9. The boot sector and the MBR are required for the disk to be recognized and to boot. True or False?
10. The smallest logical unit of storage in a Windows 2000 file system is the _____.
11. List the file systems that Windows 2000 supports and identify the one designed specifically for use with Windows 2000.
12. _____ storage supports partition-oriented volumes and is visible to any operating system (although the operating system must be able to read the file system to read the drive). _____ storage is designed for use with Windows 2000 only and is required for creating multidisk volumes.
13. How many sectors are in a cluster?
14. How many operating systems could you install on a basic disk?
   a. One
   b. Four
   c. As many as you have extended partitions
   d. One for each logical drive on the disk
15. Which of the following are fault-tolerant volume types?
   a. Spanned volumes
   b. Mirror sets
   c. Simple volumes
   d. Stripe sets
16. _____ are used to improve disk throughput on dynamic disks.

17. How do the two types of fault-tolerant volumes supported by Windows 2000 differ in terms of the amount of space for storing data you get in the volume?
18. Name all the Windows 2000 file systems that support partition mounting.
19. How many clusters does it take to store a 1 MB file under FAT16? Under FAT32? Under NTFS?
20. Both FAT32 and NTFS support file and folder compression. True or False?
21. How large is each file's entry in the master file table?
22. Explain how FAT file systems view data differently from NTFS.
23. NTFS is the only Windows 2000 file system that stores security information with a file's data. True or False?
24. Which of the following features of NTFS is used to make partition mounting work?
    a. Sparse files
    b. Data streaming
    c. Reparse points
    d. Both a and c
25. The _____ attribute in NTFS stores the list of files in a folder.

Hands-on Projects

Project 6-1

When installing Windows 2000, you must create a partition on which to store the operating system. If you make the partition smaller than the entire disk space, you can create another partition (or several) on the disk.

You must have unallocated space on your hard drive to complete this exercise.

To create a 100 MB primary partition on a basic disk:

1. Open the **Computer Management** tool in the **Administrative Tools** folder, and access the **Disk Management** tool (see Figure 6-7).

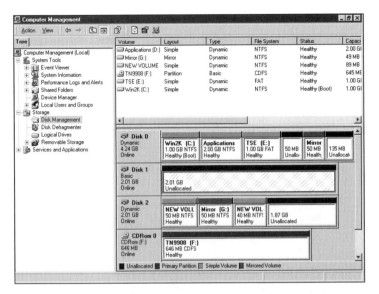

Figure 6-7 Use the Disk Management tool to create, extend, and delete volumes and partitions

2. Right-click on an area of unallocated space on a basic disk, and choose **Create Partition** from the resulting menu.

3. Click through the opening screen of the wizard. From the screen shown in Figure 6-8, choose a partition type. In this case, choose to create a **Primary partition**. Click **Next**.

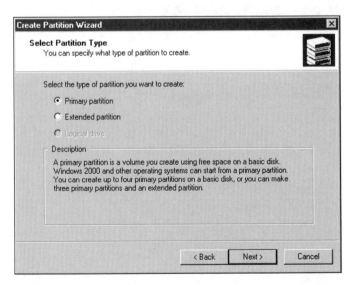

Figure 6-8 Pick a partition type from the options available

4. Make the new partition small enough to leave some room on the volume (see Figure 6-9). In this example, make it **100 MB**. Click **Next**.

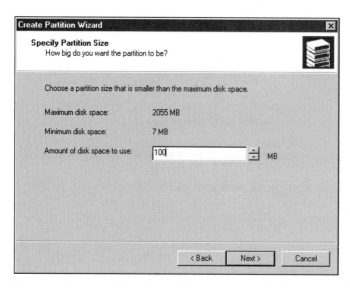

Figure 6-9 A partition doesn't have to use all of the available unallocated space

5. Choose a drive letter for the new primary partition, as shown in Figure 6-10. Name it **Drive X:**, and click **Next**.

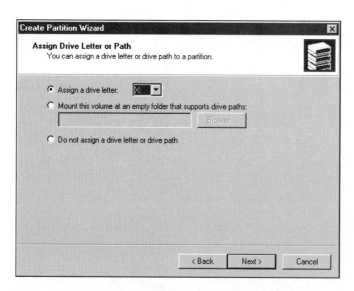

Figure 6-10 You can identify volumes and partitions by drive letter or by mounting them to a volume

6. Choose to format the new partition. For this example, choose **NTFS**, as shown in Figure 6-11. Click **Next**.

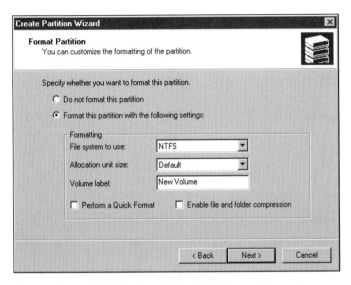

Figure 6-11   NTFS is the default file format for volumes created with the Disk Management tool

7. Review your choices in the final screen of the wizard, then click **Finish** to create the partition. Windows 2000 will take a moment to format the new partition, and then the partition will appear in the Disk Management tool as a segment with a dark blue stripe and labeled "X:".

Project 6-2

You can create only four primary partitions on a basic disk. If you need more logical volumes, you must create an extended partition and then create logical disks from the free space within that extended partition.

To create an extended partition and then create logical disks from the free space within that extended partition:

1. Right-click on an area of unallocated space on a basic disk, and choose **Create Partition** from the resulting menu.
2. Click through the opening screen of the wizard, and choose a partition type. In this case, choose to create an **Extended partition** as shown in Figure 6-12. Click **Next**.

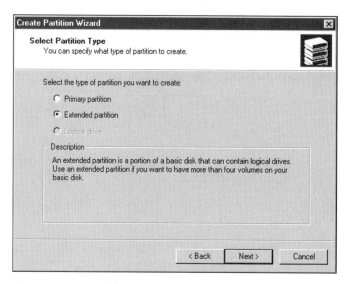

Figure 6-12 Create an extended partition so that you can create logical drives

3. Make the new partition small enough to leave some room on the volume (see Figure 6-13). In this example, make it **100 MB**. Click **Next**.

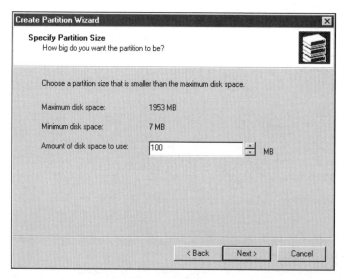

Figure 6-13 Make the extended partition large enough to hold the logical drives

4. In the final screen, review your choices and click the **Finish** button.

The new extended partition will be shown in the Disk Management tool with a thick, green line around it, and its space will have a bright green border and be marked Free Space.

5. Right-click on an area of free space within the extended partition, and choose **Create Logical Drive** from the resulting menu.

6. Click **Next** on the opening screen of the wizard, then choose to create a **Logical drive** (it will be the only option available; if it isn't, then you haven't chosen free space as your starting point). Click **Next**.
7. Pick a size for the logical drive. As shown in Figure 6-14, you can choose any size up to the size of the extended partition. Click **Next**.

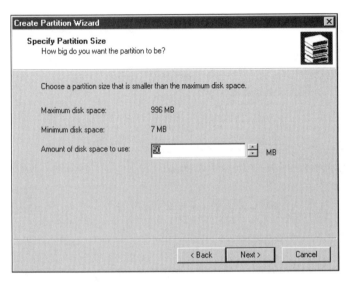

Figure 6-14 Choose a size for the logical drive

8. Assign a drive letter to the logical drive, as shown in Figure 6-15. For this project, choose **I**, and click **Next**.

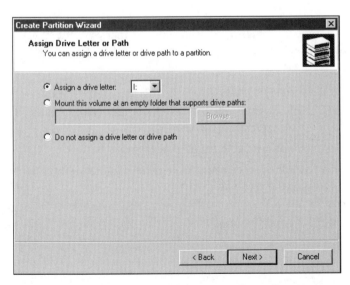

Figure 6-15 Identify the new logical drive with a drive letter

9. Choose to format the new logical drive with **FAT32**, as shown in Figure 6-16. Click **Next**.

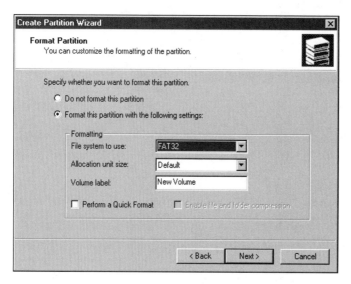

Figure 6-16 Format the new logical drive with FAT32

10. Review your choices in the final screen of the wizard, and click **Finish** to complete the new logical drive.

A new logical drive with a bright blue stripe will appear within the extended partition you created earlier.

Project 6-3

NTFS is the native Windows 2000 file format and supports many advanced features that the other two file systems do not. You don't have to reformat a disk if you want to stop using FAT16 or FAT32—just convert to NTFS.

To convert a FAT or FAT32 volume to NTFS:

1. Find a FAT or FAT32 volume and note its drive letter and volume name, if it has one. In this example, we'll convert **Drive I**.
2. Open the command prompt (available in the **Accessories** folder).
3. From the command prompt, type **convert i: /fs:ntfs**. Enter a volume name if prompted. You'll see output like that in Figure 6-17.

Figure 6-17 Converting a drive to NTFS

 Drive I is now formatted with NTFS. If it doesn't appear in the Disk Management tool as NTFS, right-click the Disk Management folder in the left pane and choose Refresh to refresh the display.

Project 6-4

To create extensible or fault-tolerant volumes on hard disks, you'll need to first upgrade those disks to dynamic disks:

1. Right-click on the gray area of a basic disk (preferably not the one on which your operating system is installed, if you have a choice) and choose **Upgrade to Dynamic Disk** from the resulting menu.

2. In the dialog box that appears (see Figure 6-18), choose all basic disks that you want to upgrade. Click **OK**. You don't necessarily have to upgrade all disks.

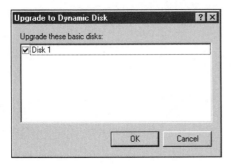

Figure 6-18 Choose disks to upgrade to dynamic disks

3. The Disk Management tool will display the disks you selected. Click **Upgrade**, then **Yes** to confirm the upgrade, and the disks you selected will be upgraded.

176   Chapter 6   Data Storage

Project 6-5

Mounting volumes to drive paths offers several benefits: It permits you to add more space to volumes (such as partitions on basic disks) that couldn't otherwise be made larger; it allows you to make part of a non-fault-tolerant volume become fault-tolerant (if the volume you're mounting is fault-tolerant, that is); and it removes the 26-letter restriction on creating volumes.

To create a simple volume and mount it to a new folder on an NTFS volume:

1. Right-click on an area of unallocated space on the dynamic disk, and choose **Create Volume** from the resulting menu.

2. Click through the opening screen of the wizard. From the next screen, shown in Figure 6-19, choose to create a **Simple volume**. Click **Next**.

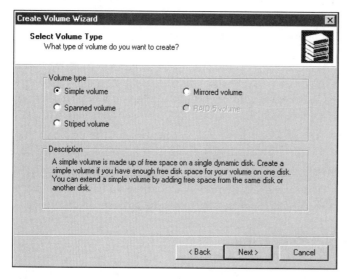

Figure 6-19 Dynamic disks have options different from those of basic disks

The options available in this box will depend on the number of dynamic disks with unallocated space on them that are available. To create a stripe set or mirror set, you'd need two such disks. To create a RAID 5 volume, you'd need at least three such disks.

3. Choose a size for the simple volume, as shown in Figure 6-20.

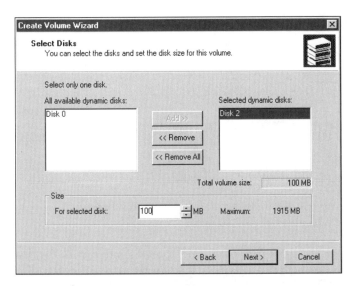

Figure 6-20 Size simple volumes just as you would a partition

4. In the next screen (shown in Figure 6-21), click the option that says to mount the volume and click the **Browse** button.

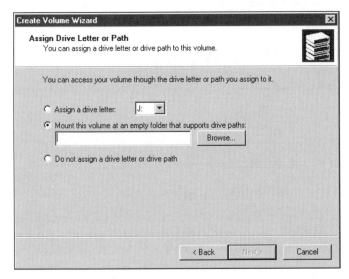

Figure 6-21 Choose to mount the volume, rather than assigning a drive letter

5. Browse for drive **X:**, the NTFS partition you created earlier, from the list shown in Figure 6-22.

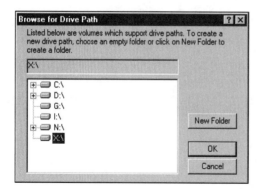

Figure 6-22 Choose drive X: from the list of disks that will support mounted volumes (NTFS volumes)

6. You'll need to create an empty path on drive X: on which to mount the new volume. Click the **New Folder** button, and type a name for the new volume, as shown in Figure 6-23. Click **OK** when you're done; you'll return to the screen where you chose to mount the new volume and the path you selected will be displayed. Click **Next**.

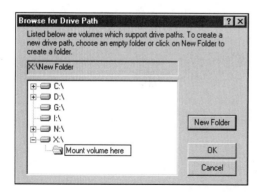

Figure 6-23 You must mount the drive to an empty volume

7. Format the new volume with **NTFS**, and click **Next**.
8. Review your choices in the final screen of the wizard, and click **Finish**. The Disk Management tool will take a moment to create and format the new volume. It will have a mustard-yellow stripe and will not show a path or a drive letter.

Project 6-6

One advantage of dynamic disks is that the NTFS simple or spanned volumes you create can be dynamically resized to make them larger if necessary.

To extend the simple volume that you created earlier to include an area of unallocated space on another dynamic disk:

1. Make sure that at least two dynamic disks with unallocated space are available, and right-click on the simple volume you created. Choose **Extend Volume** from the resulting menu.

2. Click through the opening screen of the wizard, and then choose the disk or disks onto which you want to extend the volume. As shown in Figure 6-24, you can extend the volume onto the same disk or another disk if another dynamic disk with unallocated space is available. Make sure that you choose a different dynamic disk from the one on which you originally created the volume.

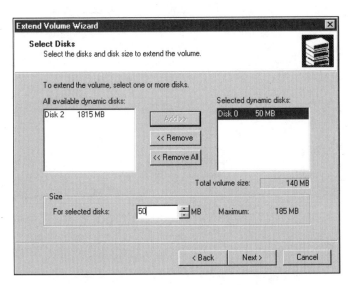

Figure 6-24 Find a dynamic disk with unallocated space available

3. In the same screen, choose the amount of unallocated space you want to add to the volume.

4. In the final screen of the wizard, review your choices and click **Finish**. Windows 2000 will extend the simple volume onto another disk and format the new area with NTFS. The simple volume is now a spanned volume, and has a purple stripe.

CASE PROJECTS

1. You're choosing file systems to use on a couple of computers. One computer is a file server with a 14 GB drive, which will have no other operating systems on it. The other computer is a desktop machine set up to dual-boot with Windows 2000 and Windows 98. Each computer has only one disk. Which file systems should—or could—you use on each computer? What's the basis of your decision?

2. Take the same computers from Case 1 and consider whether you would be well advised to use basic or dynamic storage with each. Would it make a difference if the computers had three disks each instead of one?

3. What would be the result of a virus destroying the master boot record on a hard disk? What would happen if the virus destroyed only the partition table?

4. You've created a terminal server with a complete set of applications and application tweaks that make the applications perform perfectly in a multiuser environment. How could you use the Windows 2000 RAID capabilities to duplicate this server?

CHAPTER 7
STORAGE MANAGEMENT

> **After reading this chapter and completing the exercises, you will be able to:**
> - Create and manage basic and dynamic disks using Windows 2000 disk management tools
> - Understand and create the different Windows 2000 volumes, including simple, spanned, striped, mirrored, and RAID 5 volumes
> - Recover from failed mirrored and RAID 5 volumes in Windows 2000
> - Assign quotas for all users and for individual users
> - Upgrade a basic disk to become a dynamic disk
> - Extend an NTFS volume to include extra disk space

Storage management is a key ingredient in maintaining an operating system. Before you can install any operating system, however, you must create a partition. The operating system will then install its files in this partition (or partitions). Windows 2000 is capable of creating and managing two different types of storage disks: basic and dynamic.

A basic disk uses single partitions with no fault tolerance or increased efficiency. This type of partition is similar to the partitions used in previous versions of Windows, such as Windows 95/98 and Windows NT 4.0, and DOS. A dynamic disk is a new type of storage disk available with Windows 2000. Unlike basic disks, dynamic disks are not limited to the number of partitions that can be created on them.

Organizing Disk Space

Before you can efficiently organize and manage your disk space, you need to understand some of the differences between and features of basic and dynamic disks. It is also important that you become familiar with the Windows 2000 tools that are used to maintain and configure your disks.

When configuring disks in Windows NT 4.0, the Disk Administrator tool was used. This tool no longer exists in its original form in Windows 2000; it has been replaced by the Disk Management tool.

Like many of the administration tools that ship with Windows 2000, the Disk Management tool is simply a Microsoft Management Console (MMC) snap-in. You can either create a custom MMC interface or use the default interface that is available under the Computer Management administration tool. This tool is found under the Administration Tools Start menu option, Computer Management, and is shown in Figure 7-1.

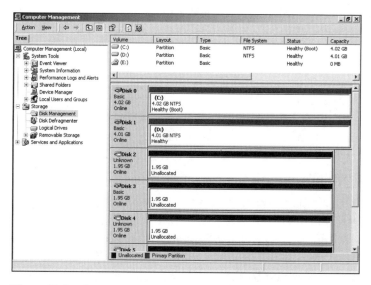

Figure 7-1 Computer Management Administration tool, with Disk Management selected

The next sections discuss the creation and management of basic disks, followed by the creation and management of Windows 2000 dynamic disks.

Basic Disks

If you know how to create and manage disks and partitions in Windows NT 4.0, then you are aware of basic disks. **Basic disks** are simply defined as disks that are compatible with Windows NT 4.0 and earlier Windows operating systems (such as Windows 95/98). When you add a new hard disk to your system, it is first created as a basic disk. You have the option to upgrade it to a dynamic disk later.

A disk can be either basic or dynamic, but not both. You cannot have a single disk that uses both types of storage.

Before Windows 2000 can recognize a new hard disk, it must write a signature to it. Windows 2000 automatically detects any new disks and launches the Write Signature and Upgrade Disk Wizard to write a signature to it. This wizard is shown in Figure 7-2. Any disks that Windows 2000 has not signed yet are listed as unknown (see Figure 7-1). To write a signature to one of these unknown disks, simply right-click the drive and choose the Write Signature option.

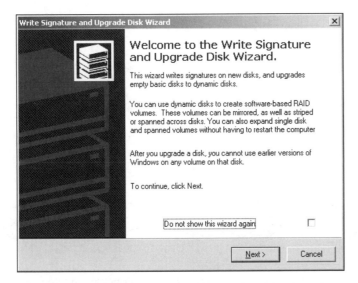

Figure 7-2 Write Signature and Upgrade Disk Wizard

Basic disk drives can have two types of partitions: primary and extended. There is a limit of four partitions on a single physical disk. A primary partition is assigned a drive letter (such as C: or D:), whereas an extended partition can have multiple logical drives created within it. See Figure 7-3.

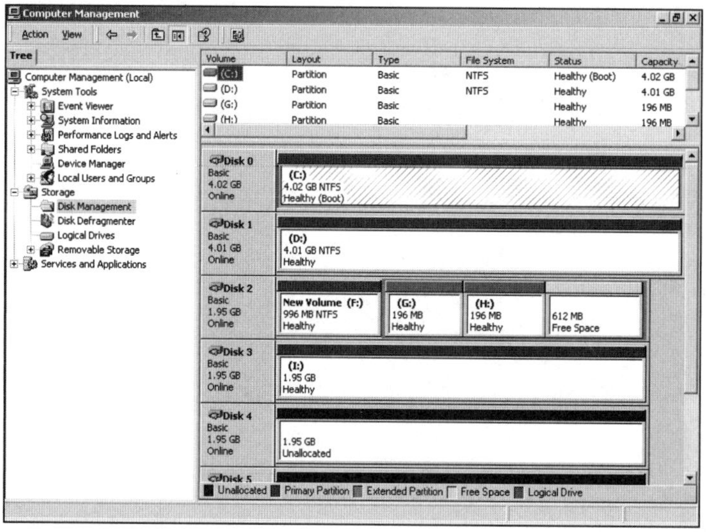

Figure 7-3 A basic disk

In addition to primary and extended partitions, basic disks can contain four types of volumes. Table 7-1 lists the types of volumes with both their Windows NT 4.0 and Windows 2000 names.

Table 7-1 Volume types in Windows NT 4.0 and Windows 2000

Windows NT 4.0	Windows 2000	Description
Volume set	Spanned volume	A way of using the space on different disks as a single volume
Mirror set	Mirrored volume	A way of storing information on two disks at the same time for fault-tolerance purposes
Stripe set	Striped volume	An efficient way of speeding up disk access by using multiple disks that act as a single disk
Stripe set with parity	RAID 5 volume	A fault-tolerant method of using multiple disks to store data

Dynamic Disks

A new feature of Windows 2000 is support for **dynamic disks**. As stated earlier, when new disks are added to your system, they are initially created as basic disks and can be later converted to dynamic disks. Dynamic disks offer some benefits over basic disks, including the following:

- An unlimited number of volumes can be created on a single disk.
- All disk configuration information (including partition sizes and types) is stored on the disk. This setup differs from Windows NT 4.0, where the disk configuration information is stored in the Registry. It allows a disk to be moved from one

system to another without the need to recreate any of the volumes. This convenience is especially notable with mirrored, spanned, or RAID 5 volumes.

- All disk configuration information is replicated to all other dynamic disks in the system. This configuration information can therefore be accessed even if a disk fails. Once the disk is replaced, Windows 2000 can then easily recreate the volume size and type from this configuration information.

- Volumes can be extended by including space available on other disks. The space used does not need to be contiguous. To be extended, a volume must exist on a dynamic disk and be formatted as an NTFS volume.

You can revert from a dynamic disk back to a basic disk only if you remove any volumes that have been created.

An NTFS volume on a basic disk that was upgraded to a dynamic disk cannot be extended. Only volumes created after a disk has been upgraded to a dynamic disk can be extended.

Although you can create an unlimited number of volumes on a single disk, dynamic disks support only five types of volumes:

- A simple volume
- A spanned volume
- A mirrored volume
- A striped volume
- A RAID 5 volume

Two of these volumes are fault-tolerant volumes (mirrored and RAID 5) and are covered in a later section. The remaining three volume types are discussed next.

Simple Volumes

A simple volume is defined as a volume that includes space on a single disk. At first glance, you might think that a simple volume is the same as a partition. There are, however, some distinctions of which you should be aware.

A simple volume does not have the same size restrictions that a partition on a basic disk does. This consideration is extremely important today, because 20 or 60 GB disks are not uncommon. You are also not limited to the number of volumes that you create on a single disk. For example, if you were to partition a 20 GB disk, you would be limited to a maximum of four partitions with only one extended partition. With dynamic disks and simple volumes, you could have as many volumes as needed.

Another advantage of simple volumes is that you can extend them at a later date. If you created a 3 GB simple volume on a 6 GB disk, and later saw that you were about to run out of disk space, you could extend the 3 GB simple volume to the full 6 GB of the disk. Be aware that you can extend the volume only so long as the extra 3 GB has not been allocated to another volume.

A simple volume can be formatted with one of the three file systems supported by Windows 2000: file allocation table (FAT), FAT32, and NTFS. Figure 7-4 shows a simple volume as it appears in the Computer Management administration tool. Hands-on Project 7-6 explains how to create a simple volume.

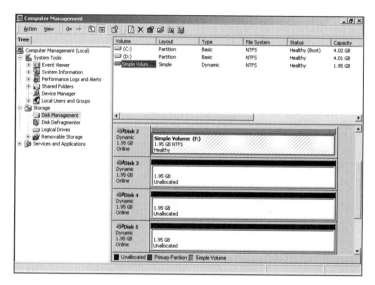

Figure 7-4 A simple volume

 A simple volume may be extended only if it is formatted as an NTFS volume. To extend a FAT or FAT32 volume, you must first convert the volume to NTFS. To convert a FAT or FAT32 volume to NTFS, simply use the CONVERT command. Execute the command using the following format: Convert *driveletter* /FS:NTFS

Spanned Volumes

A spanned volume is a volume that includes space from two or more disks, up to a maximum of 32 disks. Spanned volumes do not give you any fault tolerance or performance improvement over a simple volume; they simply allow you to use space from multiple disks as a single logical disk.

The space on the spanned volume is used in the order that the disks were selected. If, for example, you were to use a 1.1 GB, a 2.0 GB, and a 3.2 GB disk to create a single spanned volume that is 6.3 GB in size, then the 2.0 GB disk will not be written to until the first (1.1 GB) disk is full. Extending a simple volume so that it includes more than one physical disk automatically makes it become a spanned volume. Figure 7-5 depicts a spanned volume. The process involved in creating a spanned volume is covered in Hands-on Project 7-8.

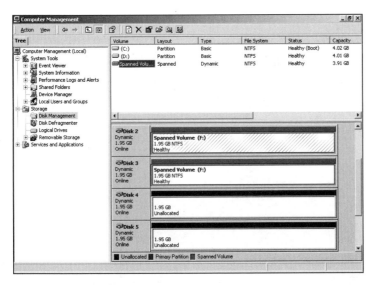

Figure 7-5 A spanned volume

Striped Volumes

Striped volumes are much like spanned volumes, with the only difference being that data are written to all of the disks in the volume in succession. This capability gives a striped volume a performance edge over a spanned volume. The data are written in chunks of 64 KB at a time, called the stripe. This stripe is then written to a disk, the next stripe is written to the next disk, and so on.

Imagine, for example, that you created the striped volume shown in Figure 7-6. The data will be written in 64 KB stripes to disk 2, then disk 3, then disk 4, and then disk 2 again. This process repeats until all data have been written to the disks.

Striped volumes offer a great increase in performance because the controllers can write to multiple disks at the same time. Therefore, instead of writing to disk 2 first, then to disk 3, and then to disk 4, the data are written to disk 2, disk 3, and disk 4 at the same time. You will especially notice a difference in performance on SCSI-based controllers and disks. The process involved in creating a striped volume is outlined in Hands-on Project 7-9.

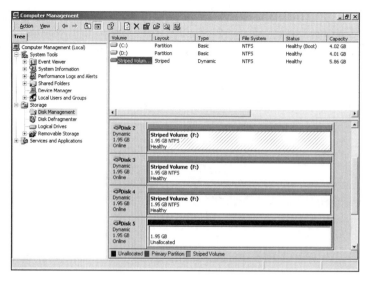

Figure 7-6 A striped volume

Fault-Tolerant Volumes

To most organizations, nothing is more important than their data. Many organizations today would not be able to function without access to their data. Imagine what would happen in your organization if the data stored on the servers suddenly became inaccessible. Unfortunately, not many users would be able to do their job using the pen-and-paper method. For this reason, most servers use some sort of fault tolerance to ensure that their data remain available.

Do not, however, assume that you do not need to back up your data because your data are stored on fault-tolerant volumes. Fault tolerance means just that—tolerant of faults. It is not a guaranteed storage method. No matter how advanced your fault-tolerance system is, do not stop performing regular tape backups on your data.

Most fault-tolerant systems fall under the RAID umbrella. RAID (redundant array of independent disks) is a set of guidelines that defines how disks are used for creating volumes. Each RAID configuration is assigned a level number, usually from 0 to 5 (although other, more advanced RAID levels exist as well). The main RAID levels are as follows:

- *RAID 0*—This sort of spanned volume provides no fault tolerance but is the fastest and most efficient RAID level.

- *RAID 1*—Also known as disk mirroring (or duplexing), this fault-tolerant configuration simply writes data to two different disks at the same time. Thus one of the disks can fail without incurring a loss of data. With disk mirroring, the mirrored disks use the same disk controller; with disk duplexing, the mirrored disks use different disk controllers. Disk duplexing allows for both controller failure and disk failure to occur without data loss.

- *RAID 2*—This scheme uses hamming error correction codes and is intended for use with drives that do not have built-in error detection. All modern SCSI disks have error detection/correction; therefore, this method is rarely used today.

- *RAID 3*—The data are striped between all disks, called a *stripe set*, and the parity is stored on a single-disk. The problem with this method is the amount of overhead required to recreate a failed disk if the parity disk fails. Striping is done at the byte level.

- *RAID 4*—The data are striped between all disks and the parity is stored on a single disk. The problem with this method is the amount of overhead required to recreate a failed disk if the parity disk fails. Striping is done at the block level.

- *RAID 5*—RAID5 is the most popular fault-tolerant system today. All data are striped between all disks and the parity is stored on each disk in succession, called a stripe set with parity. This method balances fault tolerance and performance better than the other RAID levels.

Windows 2000 supports RAID levels 0, 1, and 5 with striped volumes, mirrored volumes, and RAID 5 volumes, respectively. Although Windows NT 2000 are some of the only operating systems that support software RAID 5 (both Windows and NetWare support mirroring and duplexing), most administrators would not use software RAID. The reason for this reluctance is simple: software-based RAID is extremely resource-intensive, and most organizations would rather spend the money on hardware RAID than allow their servers to be negatively affected by performing software RAID.

Mirrored Volumes

Mirroring creates two volumes and writes the same information to both at the same time. If you created a 4 GB mirrored volume, for example, then two 4 GB disks would be needed. One would be the primary disk (such as C:) and the other would be the secondary disk (known as C: prime or C:'). **Mirrored volumes** require two units of storage for every usable unit of storage.

Mirroring disks is the easiest fault-tolerant configuration to set up that is available in Windows 2000. Unfortunately, this technique is also the most expensive method because of lost disk space. To create a mirrored volume, you need two disks with an equal amount of free space available on them (creating a mirrored volume with Windows 2000 is outlined in Hands-on Project 7-10, and recovering from a failed mirrored volume is covered in Hands-on Project 7-12). Figure 7-7 depicts a mirrored volume.

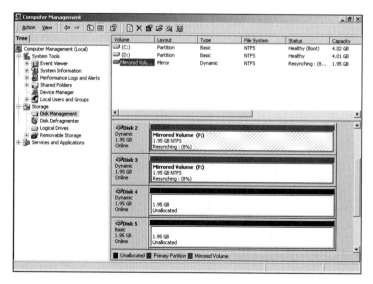

Figure 7-7 A mirrored volume

Another common mirroring technique, known as duplexing, creates a **duplexed volume**. A duplexed volume is essentially the same as a mirrored volume, with the only difference being the controllers to which the disks are connected. In disk mirroring, both mirrored disks are controlled by a single disk controller (either IDE or SCSI). Consequently, with a single disk failure the data would still be available and online. If a controller failure occurs, however, neither mirror disk would be available and the data would be offline. Chances are that the data would still be present on the disks, but you would have no way of accessing that information until you replaced the controller. With disk duplexing, each disk is controlled by its own controller. This technique allows the data to remain online even if a single controller fails.

RAID 5 Volumes

A RAID 5 volume is currently the most popular fault-tolerant method. Under Windows 2000, it consists of 3 to 32 disks. These disks become a single volume. With RAID 5 volumes, the data are divided into stripes, which are then written to the disk in order (disk 1, then disk 2, then disk 3, and so on). What makes this type of volume different from a striped volume, and fault-tolerant, is parity. Parity is simply a mathematical calculation that combines the data on all disks. If one disk fails, the lost data can be recovered from the parity information. For this reason, RAID 5 volumes can survive a single disk failure only. If more than one disk fails, you must replace the failed disks, recreate the volume, and recover the data from a backup. A RAID 5 volume is shown in Figure 7-8 and its creation is outlined in Hands-on Exercise 7-11. Hands-on Project 7-13 explains the steps involved in recovering from a RAID 5 volume failure.

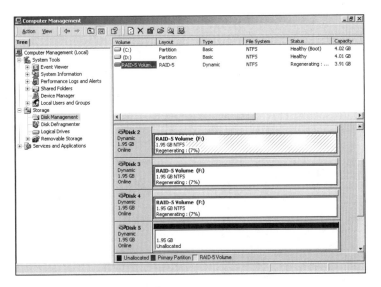

Figure 7-8 A RAID 5 volume

APPLYING USER QUOTAS

One of the features that most network operating systems (such as UNIX and NetWare) have included for years is the ability to limit the amount of disk space on a volume to which a user has access, called a **quota**. Quotas have been lacking in Windows NT since its inception, and Windows NT administrators around the world have been asking for—even demanding—this feature for years. Windows 2000, in addition to providing dynamic disks and NTFS, finally brings this important feature to the Windows world.

Why Use Disk Quotas?

Why would you need disk quotas when disks are so inexpensive? The reasons are simple. You would normally put IDE disks in a desktop system. IDE drives are relatively inexpensive. SCSI disks, especially the high-end ones, remain relatively expensive, however. In small organizations, 30 GB of storage space goes a long way. With large organizations, however, disk space starts to number in the terabytes.

Most users assume that there is no limit when it comes to disk space. Many keep every e-mail, document, and file they've ever received. When the desktop system runs out of disk space, users may resort to copying their data to the server. Once the data are on the server, users assume a problem no longer exists. This practice is problematic for the system administrator, who needs to maintain the server in a stable and efficient manner.

Disk quotas allow you to limit the amount of disk space to which a user has access on a specific volume. They also provide the capability to monitor and control the disk space that these users are using. For disk quotas to be implemented successfully, the partition or volume must be formatted with the NTFS file system under Windows 2000.

A disk or volume that is formatted as NTFS with Windows NT 4.0 will not support quotas, because the version of NTFS that ships with Windows NT is not quota-aware. Windows 2000 NTFS is backward-compatible with Windows NT. For the reverse to be true, you must install Service Pack 4 or higher on your Windows NT 4.0 Servers. Once you have formatted the partition or volume using Windows 2000 NTFS, you can set quotas by accessing the Quota tab of the volume's Properties page, as shown in Figure 7-9. Table 7-2 lists the options and functions on the Quota tab.

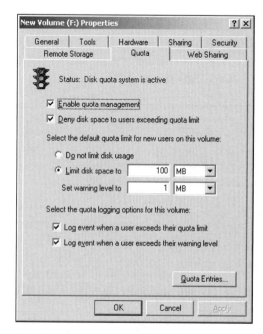

Figure 7-9 Enabling disk quotas

 Any users who have written to a volume before you enable quotas will not have quotas assigned to them unless you manually assign one to them through the Quota Entries application.

Once quotas have been enabled for a specific partition or volume, you can monitor the quota usage by clicking the Quota Entries button on the Quota tab of the partition or volume's Properties dialog box. This action will launch the Quota Entries for New Volume application, as shown in Figure 7-10.

Table 7-2 Options available on the Quota tab and their tasks

Option	Task
Enable quota management	This option turns quota management on for the partition or volume. No quotas are monitored until this option is enabled.
Deny disk space to users exceeding quota limit	Once a user has reached his or her limit, Windows 2000 will not allow the user to write any more information to the volume. The user will receive an error message stating that the user is out of disk space.
Do not limit disk usage	This option tells Windows 2000 not to limit disk usage for users.
Limit disk space to	This amount is the maximum disk space that users are allowed to use on the partition or volume. The user will be denied write access to this volume once he or she has reached this limit if the "Deny disk space to users exceeding quota limit" option is enabled.
Set warning level to	When the user passes this storage level, an event will be logged stating that the user is nearing the limit.
Quota Entries	This button launches the Quota Entries application, which allows you to monitor quota usage for each user and to customize the quotas for individual users.

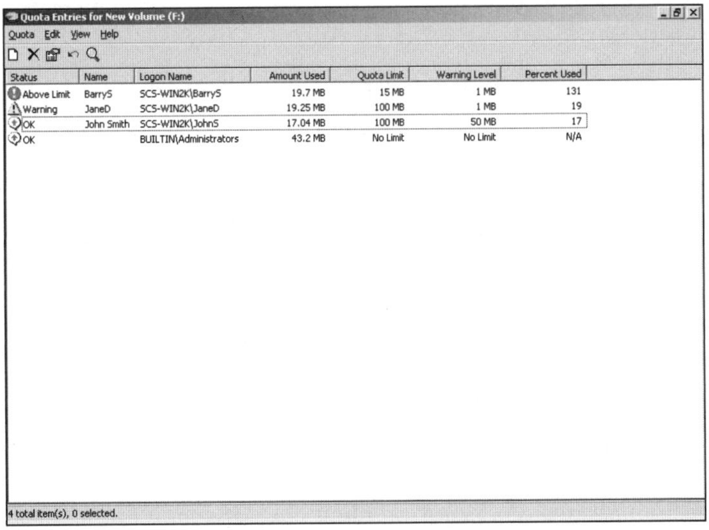

Figure 7-10 Viewing the disk space used by individual users

Once users have accessed and written data to the partition or volume, they will appear in the Quota Entries for New Volume application. Any users who accessed the volume before quotas were enabled will not have any limits assigned to them (see the Administrator user in Figure 7-10).

If you want to change the quota limits assigned to a specific user, you can simply double-click it and reset the quota limits and warning level for that user, as shown in Figure 7-11.

You can also select a number of users by highlighting them and holding down the Ctrl key, and then choosing the Properties option from the Quota menu.

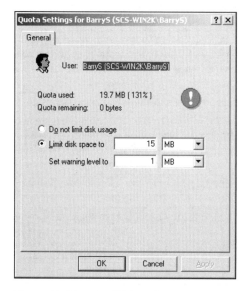

Figure 7-11 Modifying the quota properties for a user

Using this tool, you can also add users who have not accessed the volume via the following method:

1. Choose the New Quota Entry option from the Quota menu.
2. Select the desired user or users in the Select Users dialog box, and click Add.
3. Click OK.
4. Assign the disk limit and warning level for this user or users, and click OK.

ARCHIVING DATA

All of these updated and new features of Windows 2000 should not replace a good, old-fashioned backup. Although the new volumes help in the recovery of lost data, they do not replace the ability to recover a lost copy of a file from a secondary source, such as a tape or remote system.

Four different types of backup exist, as the following list shows. For these backup types to work properly, each file is given an archive bit. The **archive bit** denotes whether the file has been modified, thereby allowing the backup program to determine which files need to be backed up.

- **Copy backup** — A copy backup simply copies all files to the backup media without modifying the state of the archive bit.

- **Differential backup** — A differential backup backs up all information that has been modified since the last full backup. The archive bit is not reset.
- **Full (normal) backup** — A full (normal) backup simply backs up all files on the desired disks and resets the archive bit.
- **Incremental backup** — An incremental backup backs up all information that has been modified since the last backup. The archive bit is reset.

Windows 2000 includes a new version of NTBACKUP, the built-in backup and restore utility, shown in Figure 7-12.

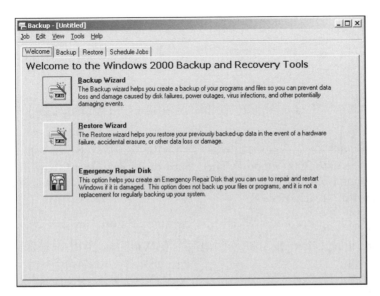

Figure 7-12 The built-in Windows 2000 Backup program

Backup Methods

Three types of backup methods exist: online, offline, and near-line. Each method has its own pros and cons, as described in the following sections.

Online

An **online backup** is simply a method of backing up the data so that the information is available and online at any point in time. Most common online backups copy the data over a network to a remote disk, which resides on a remote server. If the disk on the server fails, you can access the data from the remote system. Although an online backup is a very good way of ensuring that the data are available, it is not a common method for backing up, mostly because of the cost involved in setting up such a system.

Offline

An **offline backup** is the most commonly used method of backing up data. It involves making a copy of the data and placing it on a tape so that it can be recovered at a later date. Most organizations use this method because it is the cheapest and safest way of backing up data. Its main disadvantage is that you must retrieve the tape and restore the data if a failure occurs.

Near-line

A **near-line backup** is becoming increasingly more common with the advent of writable and rewritable CD-ROM drives. The data are still available, albeit on a slower system. This method is very effective for systems that have infrequently used data that must remain accessible at all times.

Chapter Summary

- This chapter discussed the two disk types that are available in Windows 2000: basic and dynamic.

- It also considered the steps involved in maintaining the various types of volumes and partitions that Windows 2000 supports. The Hands-on Projects that follow this chapter, provided you a good introduction to the types of volumes available, as well as the steps for their creation and management.

- Implementing quotas using Windows 2000's new quota feature was also discussed.

- Finally, the chapter explained the methods available in Windows 2000 for backing up data.

Key Terms

archive bit — An attribute that allows the backup program to decide which files have been modified. Any file that has the archive bit set has been modified.

basic disk — A disk that has been partitioned and formatted using Windows NT 4.0. Basic disks can support primary and extended partitions as well as logical disks.

copy backup — A backup method that copies the data to the backup media without changing the archive bit of the files.

differential backup — A backup method that backs up all data added or modified since the last full backup. This method resets the archive bit.

duplexed volume — A volume that uses two disks on two separate controllers. The data are written to both disks at the same time.

dynamic disk — A new type of disk introduced with Windows 2000. It allows for an unlimited number of volumes to be created on a single disk.

full backup — A backup method that completely backs up the data to the backup media and resets the archive bit.

incremental backup — A type of backup that will back up all data added or modified since the last backup without resetting the archive bit.

mirrored volume — A volume on a dynamic disk that uses two disks and writes the same data to both of them.

near-line backup — Data are migrated from the hard disk to a slower, but easily accessible media such as CD-ROMs. This backup technique allows the data to be accessible without using up disk space.

offline backup — A backup method in which data are copied to removable media, such as a tape.

online backup — A backup technique in which a copy of the data is maintained at all times on a separate and remote system.

quota — The amount of disk space to which a user has access on a quota-enabled volume.

striped volume — Same as a stripe set, but for dynamic disks.

REVIEW QUESTIONS

1. What is the maximum number of partitions that can be created on a basic disk?
   a. 1
   b. 2
   c. 3
   d. 4

2. Dynamic disks are created as basic disks and then upgraded. True or False?

3. Once a disk has been upgraded to a dynamic disk, it can no longer become a basic disk. True or False?

4. Which of the following partition types can contain logical disks?
   a. Primary
   b. Secondary
   c. Extended
   d. Logical

5. Any volume or partition that is formatted using NTFS can be extended. True or False?

6. A volume that exists on only a single dynamic disk is known as a:
   a. Simple volume.
   b. Spanned volume.
   c. Striped volume.
   d. Mirrored volume.
   e. RAID 5 volume.

7. A volume that uses striping as well as parity is known as a:
   a. Simple volume.
   b. Spanned volume.
   c. Striped volume.
   d. Mirrored volume.
   e. RAID 5 volume.
8. A volume that uses striping for improved performance but does not include fault tolerance is known as a:
   a. Simple volume.
   b. Spanned volume.
   c. Striped volume.
   d. Mirrored volume.
   e. RAID 5 volume.
9. When data are written to two disks at the same time, the process creates a _____ volume.
10. A volume that includes disk space on more than one physical disk is known as a:
    a. Simple volume.
    b. Spanned volume.
    c. Striped volume.
    d. Mirrored volume.
    e. RAID 5 volume.
11. What is the minimum number of disks in a striped volume?
    a. 1
    b. 2
    c. 3
    d. 4
12. What is the minimum number of disks in a RAID 5 volume?
    a. 1
    b. 2
    c. 3
    d. 4
13. Both basic and dynamic disks can support quotas as long as they are formatted using NTFS and Windows 2000. True or False?
14. "Mirrored volumes" and "duplexed volumes" are interchangeable terms. True or False?
15. You can assign different quotas for each user who accesses an NTFS volume. True or False?

16. Which Windows 2000 administration tool would you use to manage your partitions and volumes?
    a. Disk Administrator
    b. Disk Manager
    c. Volume Manager
    d. Computer Management
17. What is the maximum number of disks that can be supported by striped volumes?
    a. 24
    b. 32
    c. 48
    d. 64
18. What is the maximum number of disks that can be supported by RAID 5 volumes?
    a. 24
    b. 32
    c. 48
    d. 64
19. You can have as many as four extended partitions in a basic disk. True or False?
20. Mirrored volumes can be converted to RAID 5 volumes by adding an extra disk and choosing the Upgrade To RAID 5 option. True or False?

HANDS-ON PROJECTS

Project 7-1

Before Windows 2000 will recognize a new disk, you must allow the operating system to write a signature to the disk.

Note: The disk used in this exercise must be formatted with NTFS.

To write a signature to a new disk:

1. Click **Start**, **Programs**, **Administrative Tools**, **Computer Management**.
2. Highlight the **Disk Management** option in the left pane of the Computer Management tool.
3. Highlight an unallocated basic disk in the lower-right pane and right-click it.
4. Choose the **Write signature** option from the menu.

Project 7-2

When creating a primary partition on a basic disk in Windows 2000, you need to follow the steps described here.

To create a primary partition:

1. Click **Start**, **Programs**, **Administrative Tools**, **Computer Management**.
2. Highlight the **Disk Management** option in the left pane of the Computer Management tool.
3. Highlight an unallocated basic disk in the bottom-right pane and right-click it.
4. Choose the **Create Partition** option from the menu. The Create Partition Wizard will launch. The screen shown in Figure 7-13 appears. Click **Next**.

Figure 7-13 Create Partition Wizard

5. Make sure that **Primary partition** is selected, and click **Next**.
6. Enter the amount of disk space to be used for the partition, as shown in Figure 7-14, and click **Next**.

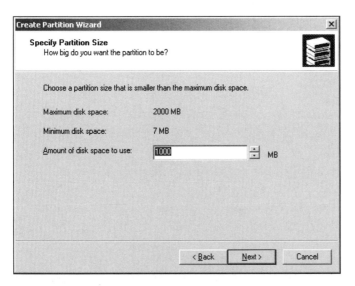

Figure 7-14 Specify Partition Size window

7. Choose either to assign a drive letter to this partition, to mount this volume to a folder that supports drive paths, or to not assign a drive letter, as shown in Figure 7-15, and click **Next**.

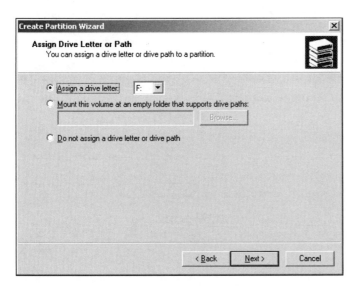

Figure 7-15 Assign Drive Letter or Path window

8. Choose either to leave the partition unformatted or to format it in one of the supported file systems. Refer to Figure 7-16. The file systems supported by primary partitions are FAT, FAT32, and NTFS. Click **Next**.

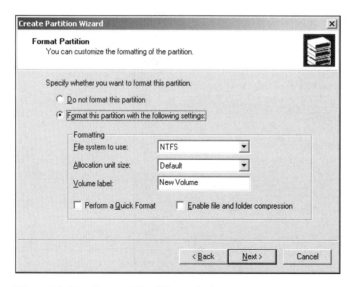

Figure 7-16 Format Partition window

9. Confirm the settings in the wizard, and click **Finish** to create the partition.

Project 7-3

Before logical disks can be created on a basic disk, you must create an extended partition. Only one extended partition is permitted on a single basic disk.

To create an extended partition:

1. Click **Start**, **Programs**, **Administrative Tools**, **Computer Management**.
2. Highlight the **Disk Management** option in the left pane of the Computer Management tool.
3. Highlight an unallocated basic disk in the lower-right pane and right-click it.
4. Choose the **Create Partition** option from the menu. The Create Partition Wizard will launch. Click **Next**.
5. Make sure that **Extended partition** is selected, and click **Next**.
6. Specify the size of the partition. Click **Next**.
7. Click **Finish** to create the extended partition.

Project 7-4

This exercise illustrates the steps involved in creating a logical drive.

To create a logical drive:

1. Highlight the extended partition in the lower-right pane and right-click it.
2. Choose the **Create Logical Drive** option from the drop-down menu. The Create Partition Wizard will launch. Click **Next**.

3. Make sure that **Logical drive** is selected, as shown in Figure 7-17, and click **Next**.

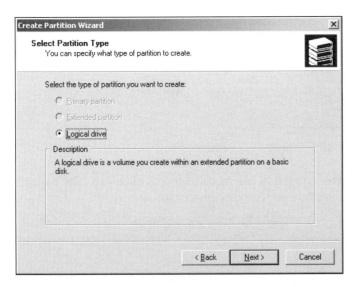

Figure 7-17 Select Partition Type window

4. Enter the amount of disk space to be used for the partition, and click **Next**.
5. Choose either to assign a drive letter to this partition, to mount this volume to a folder that supports drive paths, or to not assign a drive letter, and click **Next**.
6. Choose either to leave the partition unformatted or to format it in one of the supported file systems. The file systems supported by logical disks are FAT, FAT32, and NTFS. Click **Next**.
7. Confirm the settings in the wizard, and click **Finish** to create the partition.

Project 7-5

Before you can use some of the new disk features of Windows 2000, you must upgrade the basic disks to dynamic ones.

To convert a basic disk to a dynamic disk:

1. Click **Start**, **Programs**, **Administrative Tools**, **Computer Management**.
2. Highlight the **Disk Management** option in the left pane of the Computer Management tool.
3. Highlight a basic disk in the lower-right pane and right-click it.
4. Choose the **Upgrade to dynamic disk** option. The window shown in Figure 7-18 will appear.

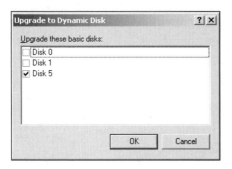

Figure 7-18   Upgrade to Dynamic Disk Wizard

5. Check the disks that you would like to upgrade, and click **OK**. The basic disk will be initialized and will become a dynamic disk shortly.

Note: A dialog box confirming the upgrade may appear. If it does, click OK.

Project 7-6

The most basic volume that can be created on a Windows 2000 dynamic disk is known as a simple volume. A simple volume contains space from only a single disk:

To create a simple volume:

1. Click **Start**, **Programs**, **Administrative Tools**, **Computer Management**.
2. Highlight the **Disk Management** option in the left pane of the Computer Management tool.
3. Highlight an unallocated dynamic disk in the lower-right pane and right-click it.
4. Choose the **Create volume** option from the drop-down menu. The Create Volume Wizard will launch.
5. Click **Next**.
6. Ensure that **Simple volume** is selected, and click **Next**. See Figure 7-19.
7. Choose the amount of disk space to be used in the simple volume, and click **Next**.
8. Choose either to assign a drive letter to this volume, to mount this volume to a folder that supports drive paths, or to not assign a drive letter, and click **Next**.
9. Choose either to leave the volume unformatted or to format it in one of the supported file systems. The file systems supported by simple volumes are FAT, FAT32, and NTFS. Click **Next**.
10. Confirm the settings in the wizard, and click **Finish** to create the volume.

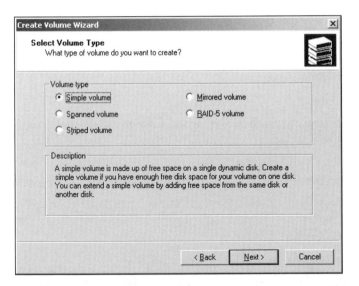

Figure 7-19 Select Volume Type window for dynamic disks

Project 7-7

Once a volume has been created on a dynamic disk and formatted using Windows 2000 NTFS, it can be extended. Extending a volume is the act of increasing the size of the volume by allocating unused free space from the disk to the volume.

To extend a volume:

1. Click **Start**, **Programs**, **Administrative Tools**, **Computer Management**.
2. Highlight the **Disk Management** option in the left pane of the Computer Management tool.
3. Highlight a simple volume in the lower-right pane and right-click it.
4. Choose the **Extend volume** option from the menu. The **Extend Volume Wizard** will launch.
5. Click **Next**.
6. Choose the amount of disk space by which to extend the volume, and click **Next**. Remember, if you extend a simple volume beyond the physical boundaries of a single disk, it will become a spanned volume.
7. Click **Finish** to extend the partition.

Project 7-8

Spanned volumes are similar to simple volumes, but differ in that they contain space from more than one physical disk. There is no limit with dynamic disks as to the number of disks that can be used in the spanned volume.

To create a spanned volume:

1. Click **Start**, **Programs**, **Administrative Tools**, **Computer Management**.
2. Highlight the **Disk Management** option in the left pane of the Computer Management tool.
3. Highlight an unallocated dynamic disk in the lower-right pane and right-click it.
4. Choose the **Create volume** option from the menu. The Create Volume Wizard will launch.
5. Click **Next**.
6. Ensure that **Spanned volume** is selected, and click **Next**.
7. Choose which disks are to be used for the spanned volume and the amount of disk space to be used on each disk, and click **Next**.
8. Choose either to assign a drive letter to this volume, to mount this volume to a folder that supports drive paths, or to not assign a drive letter, and click **Next**.
9. Choose either to leave the volume unformatted or to format it in one of the supported file systems. The file systems supported by spanned volumes are FAT32 and NTFS. Click **Next**.
10. Confirm the settings in the wizard, and click **Finish** to create the volume.

Project 7-9

A striped volume acts in much the same way as a spanned volume does, except that the data are written in stripes to all disks in rapid succession.

To create a striped volume:

1. Click **Start**, **Programs**, **Administrative Tools**, **Computer Management**.
2. Highlight the **Disk Management** option in the left pane of the Computer Management tool.
3. Highlight an unallocated dynamic disk in the lower-right pane and right-click it.
4. Choose the **Create volume** option from the drop-down menu. The Create Volume Wizard will launch.
5. Click **Next**.
6. Ensure that **Striped volume** is selected, and click **Next**.
7. Choose which disks are to be used for the striped volume and the amount of disk space to be used on each disk, and click **Next**.
8. Choose either to assign a drive letter to this volume, to mount this volume to a folder that supports drive paths, or to not assign a drive letter, and click **Next**.

9. Choose either to leave the volume unformatted or to format it in one of the supported file systems. The file systems supported by striped volumes are FAT32 and NTFS. Click **Next**.
10. Confirm the settings in the wizard, and click **Finish** to create the volume.

Project 7-10

Before you create a mirrored volume, you must have two disks with free space on them. The volume size will be limited by the smallest amount of disk space on the two disks.

To create a mirrored volume:

1. Click **Start**, **Programs**, **Administrative Tools**, **Computer Management**.
2. Highlight the **Disk Management** option in the left pane of the Computer Management tool.
3. Highlight an unallocated dynamic disk in the lower-right pane and right-click it.
4. Choose the **Create volume** option from the menu. The Create Volume Wizard will launch.
5. Click **Next**.
6. Ensure that **Mirrored volume** is selected, and click the **Next** button.
7. Choose which disks are to be used for the mirrored volume and the amount of disk space to be used on each disk, and click **Next**.
8. Choose either to assign a drive letter to this volume, to mount this volume to a folder that supports drive paths, or to not assign a drive letter, and click **Next**.
9. Choose either to leave the volume unformatted or to format it in one of the supported file systems. The file systems supported by mirrored volumes are FAT, FAT32, and NTFS. Click **Next**.
10. Confirm the settings in the wizard, and click **Finish** to create the volume.

Project 7-11

At least three disks are required before you can create a RAID 5 volume. These disks must be physically different.

To create a RAID 5 volume:

1. Click **Start**, **Programs**, **Administrative Tools**, **Computer Management**.
2. Highlight the **Disk Management** option in the left pane of the Computer Management tool.
3. Highlight an unallocated dynamic disk in the lower-right pane and right-click it.
4. Choose the **Create volume** option from the menu. The Create Volume Wizard will launch.
5. Click **Next**.
6. Ensure that **RAID 5 volume** is selected, and click **Next**.

7. Choose which disks are to be used for the RAID 5 volume (with a minimum of three) and the amount of disk space to be used on each disk, and click **Next**.
8. Choose either to assign a drive letter to this volume, to mount this volume to a folder that supports drive paths, or to not assign a drive letter, and click **Next**.
9. Choose either to leave the volume unformatted or to format it in one of the supported file systems. The file systems supported by RAID 5 volumes are FAT, FAT32, and NTFS. Click **Next**.
10. Confirm the settings in the wizard, and click **Finish** to create the volume.

Project 7-12

This exercise illustrates the steps involved in recovering from a failed mirrored disk.

To repair a failed mirrored volume:

1. When a disk in a mirrored volume fails, the error message shown in Figure 7-20 will be displayed. The Disk Management administration tool will notify you as to which disk has failed. You will need to replace this disk before continuing. See Figure 7-21.

Figure 7-20 A failed disk error message

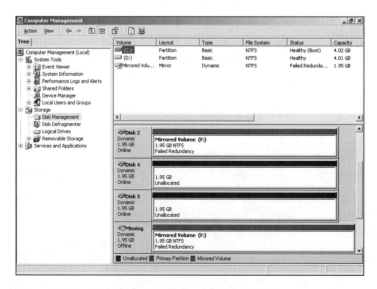

Figure 7-21 A failed mirrored volume member

If your disk array supports hot-swappable disks, then you can replace the failed disk without rebooting the system. Otherwise, a reboot is required before the failed mirrored volume is regenerated.

2. After the disk has been replaced, Windows 2000 will continue to see it as being offline. You will need to reactivate it. To do so, right-click the disk and choose the **Reactivate disk** option from the menu.

3. Windows 2000 will bring the new disk online and automatically regenerate the failed mirrored volume, if possible. If the volume is not automatically regenerated, right-click the failed volume in the upper-right pane and choose either the **Repair Volume**, **Resynchronize volume**, or **Reactivate volume** option.

Project 7-13

This exercise illustrates the steps involved in recovering from a failed RAID 5 disk.

To repair a failed RAID 5 volume:

1. When a disk in a RAID 5 volume fails, an error message will be displayed to notify you of the failure. The Disk Management administration tool will notify you as to which disk has failed. You will need to replace this disk before continuing. See Figure 7-22.

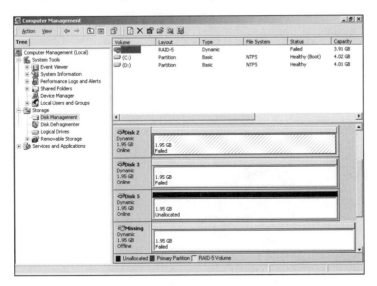

Figure 7-22 A failed RAID 5 volume member

If your disk array supports hot-swappable disks, then you can replace the failed disk without rebooting the system. Otherwise, a reboot is required before the failed mirrored volume is regenerated.

2. After the disk has been replaced, Windows 2000 will continue to see it as being offline. You will need to reactivate it. To do so, right-click the disk and choose the **Reactivate disk** option from the menu.
3. Windows 2000 will bring the new disk online and automatically regenerate the failed RAID 5 volume, if possible. If the volume is not automatically regenerated, right-click the failed volume in the top-right pane and choose either the **Repair Volume** or **Reactivate volume** option.

CASE PROJECTS

1. You are adding a drive array to an existing Windows 2000 system. You would like to maximize the performance of these new disks while maintaining a single volume. You do not require any fault tolerance. Which volume type would you create?
2. You are installing Windows 2000 on a system that has five disks available to it. You would like to create a fault-tolerant system that will give you the largest amount of free space possible. Which volume type would you create?
3. You are trying to extend an existing volume that is formatted with the FAT file system on your Windows 2000 system, but your attempt is unsuccessful. Why?
4. You would like to protect your Windows 2000 system from a single disk or disk controller failure. Which volume type would you implement?

CHAPTER 8

NETWORKING BASICS

> **After reading this chapter and completing the exercises, you will be able to:**
> - List and describe the seven layers of the OSI model
> - Understand the role of protocols and services in networks
> - Explain the differences between a normal operating system and a network operating system
> - List the differences between client and server roles

The advent of networks is one of the best (or debatably, the worst) things to happen to computers. Networks open up options that did not exist a relatively short time ago. This chapter looks at some of the networking basics, as well as the Open Systems Interconnection (OSI) model for networking. The OSI model is a set of guidelines for making all operating systems and system components work together in an open infrastructure. The chapter also covers the role of protocols and services in Windows 2000 Server.

Principles of Networking

What is a **network**? In its most rudimentary form, a network consists of two or more computers connected so that data can be transferred between them. Most of the networks that you encounter will, however, be much more complex than this model.

In the past, the first networks to which most businesses were exposed were known as "sneaker-nets." Transferring data from one computer to another in a sneaker-net network was a simple matter of placing the required data on a floppy disk, walking over to the receiving computer, and copying the data from the floppy disk to the second computer's hard drive. Setting up these networks was easy, expanding them was easier, and failures were almost unknown. Since the time of sneaker-nets, networks have grown by leaps and bounds. The following sections cover the basic types of modern networks.

LANs, WANs, and MANs

There are basically three types of networks: **local area networks (lans)**, **wide area networks (wans)**, and **metropolitan area networks (mans)**.

A LAN is a network that is confined to a single location, such as an office, a floor in a building, or an entire office building. LANs usually use high-speed connections between the different systems—for example, 10 or 100 Mbps Ethernet, Asynchronous Transfer Mode (ATM), or Fiber Distributed Data Interface (FDDI). The actual physical connection is usually owned by the organization that uses the network.

WANs are networks that are connected over great distances, such as across a state, throughout a country, or between countries and continents. WANs are connected using slower connections that usually rely on telecommunications companies for the physical medium.

The third network type, a MAN, is similar to a WAN except that it connects locations within a city rather than between cities. This term is rarely used today, as most organizations use the term "WAN" to describe both intracity and intercity networks.

OSI Reference Model

As businesses around the world began to embrace the idea of networks, it became apparent that some sort of standard or guideline was necessary to allow separate and heterogeneous networks to communicate efficiently. In 1977, the International Organization for Standardization (ISO), a committee representing a wide range of organizations, developed a new standard for networking. This standard is the Open Systems Interconnection (OSI) reference model. The OSI model is nothing more than a set of guidelines for companies to use when developing network products (including network cards, routers, hubs, and **protocols**).

The OSI model consists of seven distinct levels, also called layers; each layer describes how its part in the communication scheme should function. In addition, each layer is also assigned a number from 1 to 7. Table 8-1 lists the seven layers and their associated numbers.

Table 8-1 OSI model layers

Layer name	Layer number
Application layer	Layer 7
Presentation layer	Layer 6
Session layer	Layer 5
Transport layer	Layer 4
Network layer	Layer 3
Data Link layer	Layer 2
Physical Layer	Layer 1

The OSI model allows software manufacturers to develop products that work and communicate at one or more layers within the model, with the assurance that those products will function with products developed by other vendors that conform to the model. For example, a network card manufacturer that develops an Ethernet card knows that the TCP/IP protocol written to conform to the OSI model in Windows 2000 will function after the appropriate driver is installed on the system.

In the following sections, we look at each of the OSI layers and examine its role and functions in the OSI model.

An easy way to remember the name of the layers in the OSI model is to use the anagram: **P**lease **D**o **N**ot **T**hrow **S**ausage **P**izza **A**way.

Application Layer

Most people initially assume that the **Application layer** refers to a user application, such as Microsoft PowerPoint or Word. In fact, this interpretation is not the case. The Application layer is responsible for the actual communication between a program that runs on the system and the network resources that the program accesses (for example, loading a Microsoft PowerPoint file from a shared location on a remote server).

Presentation Layer

The **Presentation layer** is responsible for determining the format of the data that are sent on the network. The remote system might exist in a different country and use a different character set, so a standard format that all systems understand is needed. The sending computer translates the format of its Application layer into this standard format, and the receiving computer translates the standard format into a format that is understood by its Application layer.

The most commonly used component that resides at this level is a **redirector**. A redirector simply captures the input or output of an application and redirects it to a different location.

This ability allows you to save a file to the G: drive when it is actually a mapped drive to a share on a remote server's hard drive, for example. The Presentation layer is also responsible for data compression, encryption, and decryption, as well as protocol and character set conversion.

Session Layer

The **Session layer** is responsible for establishing and maintaining connections between communicating systems. This layer ensures that all data are transferred to the correct application and the correct system when multiple communication streams are active. You can compare the Session layer to making a phone call. The telecommunications company that supplies you with your phone service has a switch that connects you to the correct number when you dial it. The company's equipment must then maintain that connection until you or the person at the other end of the line disconnects. Telephone companies manage thousands of simultaneous connections, and, depending on the size of your network, the Session layer may have to do the same.

Transport Layer

Under most circumstances, the data you send over the network are larger than a single **frame**, also called a data packet. The **Transport layer** is responsible for breaking the data up into smaller sections so that the pieces can be sent in individual frames. To ensure that the receiving computer's Transport layer can reassemble the data, the sending computer's Transport layer assigns a sequence number to each frame. The receiving computer's Transport layer makes sure that the frames are reassembled into the data stream in the correct order. A **cyclic redundancy check (CRC)** is also performed on the frames to ensure that they have been received error-free.

Network Layer

The **Network layer** controls the way that data are routed from one system to another. A routable protocol needs to have an addressing scheme that specifies not only its local address, but also its global address. You can compare this addressing scheme to telephone area codes. Several locations (networks) may have the same phone number (local address), but what distinguishes the same number (local address) in city A (network A) from that in city B (network B) is the area code (global address) that precedes the number. This layer also figures out the best path that the data should traverse to get from the sending system to the receiving system.

Data Link Layer

The **Data Link layer** is responsible for connecting the physical media of the layer below it (the copper and electrical pulses from the Physical layer) and the data of the layers above it.

It is at this layer that **hardware addresses** are used. Hardware addresses are also known as **Media Access Control (MAC) addresses**.

 MAC addresses consist of six hexadecimal bytes (ranging from 00 to FF). These bytes are usually written with either a dash (-) or a colon (:) separating them—or example, 12:34:56:78:90:AB (or AB-CD-EF-12-34-56). The first three octets represent a unique number that is assigned to each company that produces network cards and devices and are known as the official Institute of Electrical and Electronic Engineers (IEEE) Organizationally Unique Identifier (OUI). Each organization must assign a unique value to each device that it produces. That value must use the last three bytes. For more information on the currently assigned company prefixes and the process of applying for one, visit the IEEE's OUI Web page at *http://standards.ieee.org/regauth/oui/index.html*.

Physical Layer

The **Physical layer** defines an actual physical network device, which can include the type of connectors, the type of media (copper and fiber), and electrical voltage. In effect, the Physical layer takes the signal, amplifies it, and sends it down the "wire." The components at the Physical layer do not look at the data within each of the frames; they do not care what the data include or where the information might be heading.

PUTTING IT ALL TOGETHER

Each layer in the OSI model describes how its part in the communication scheme should function. It is important to understand that communication can take place only between layers that are in direct contact with each other (that is, directly above or below each other). For example, the Application layer can talk only to the Presentation layer, the Presentation layer can talk to either the Application or the Session layer, the Session layer can talk to either the Presentation or the Transport layer, and so on. Layers on different systems can also communicate—for example, the Session layer on system A can communicate with the Session layer on system B. This communication must "flow" through the OSI model on both systems—except in the Physical layer; only the Physical layers on separate networks can communicate with each other directly (see Figure 8-1).

To envision the data flow between the OSI model layers, imagine that there are two adjacent seven-story buildings (building A and building B) both owned by the company where you work as a mail clerk. The departments on each floor of each building correspond to one another. That is, the names of the departments (listed in Table 8-2) on each floor of both buildings are the same.

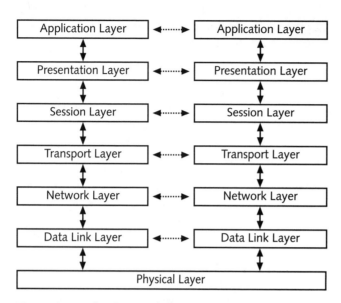

Figure 8-1 The OSI model

Table 8-2 Department names for buildings A and B

Floor	Department
7	Accounting
6	Purchasing
5	Sales
4	Telecommunication
3	Personnel
2	Lobby
1	Parking Garage

Every morning you start your rounds in building A on the 7th floor in the Accounting department. You pick up all Accounting department mail and then descend to the Purchasing department on the 6th floor, where you pick up all of that department's mail. This pattern continues until you finally reach the parking garage (which connects the two buildings). You walk over to building B and repeat the process in reverse, starting in the lobby and working your way up to the Accounting department on the 7th floor. Company policy states that mail can be transferred only from one department to its sister department in the other building (Accounting A to Accounting B, Purchasing A to Purchasing B, and so on).

The OSI model works in much the same way. The information you send (that is, the data) is analogous to the mail cart that you use to carry the mail. As the data pass by each layer (department), that layer (department) attaches a component to the data (puts its mail in the cart) and passes it down. At the receiving end, each layer (department) strips the component (mail) placed on the data (cart) by its sister layer and passes it up the layers until the Application layer passes only the data to the user programs running on the computer.

ROLE OF PROTOCOLS AND SERVICES

Before computers can communicate with one another over a network, they need to "speak" the same language. This common language is known as a protocol. The protocol is charged with answering following questions:

- Will communications use data compression? If so, what type of compression?
- How do computers on different networks communicate?
- How does the receiving computer know that all of the data has been sent?
- How does the receiving computer notify the sending computer that it has received all of the data?
- Will communications use error correction?
- How many frames should a computer receive before acknowledging them?

The protocol that you use on your network really depends on the network's infrastructure. Protocols can be classified into two types: local and remote. A local protocol is one that can be used only in a single network environment and is known as a **nonroutable protocol**. A remote protocol, also known as a **routable protocol**, functions in local environments and can communicate with remote networks. Nonroutable protocols tend to be faster. In a single network environment, there is no need to worry about duplicate addresses, maintenance of a list of routes from one network to another, and name-to-address translations.

Currently, three main protocols are used on networks: **NetBIOS Enhanced User Interface (NetBEUI)**, **Internetwork Packet Exchange/Sequenced Packet Exchange (IPX/SPX)**, and **Transmission Control Protocol/Internet Protocol (TCP/IP)**. NetBEUI is a nonroutable protocol, and IPX/SPX and TCP/IP are routable protocols. Microsoft designed Windows 2000 so that it depends on one of these protocols—TCP/IP. Each of these protocols is discussed in the following sections.

NetBEUI

NetBEUI is actually an acronym within an acronym: It stands for NetBIOS Enhanced (or Extended) User Interface, and NetBIOS in turn stands for Network Basic Input/Output System. IBM developed this protocol in the early 1980s, and Novell and Microsoft later adopted it. Currently, it is most commonly found in small, single-network, Microsoft-based environments. NetBEUI cannot be used in a WAN environment because it is nonroutable; for the same reason, however, it is also extremely easy to set up and very fast. In fact, it is the fastest of the three protocols.

 Do not confuse NetBEUI and NetBIOS. NetBEUI is a transport protocol, whereas NetBIOS is an API.

IPX/SPX

IPX/SPX is Novell's networking protocol. Until the release of Novell's NetWare 5, all NetWare environments required IPX/SPX. (NetWare 5 also supports TCP/IP.) Microsoft's operating systems use a version of this protocol called NWLink, which is an IPX/SPX-compatible protocol. IPX/SPX is actually a suite of protocols. In this suite, SPX is a Transport layer protocol that runs on top of IPX (a Network layer protocol).

IPX/SPX uses the MAC address of each system on the network as its network address. Another address is also given to the entire network. This scheme allows IPX/SPX to be routed. IPX/SPX is used only on internal networks, however, because most Internet routers do not support it.

TCP/IP

The Internet uses the TCP/IP protocol exclusively, leading to the last part of the expansion of the acronym—Internet Protocol. TCP/IP is often referred to as the TCP/IP protocol suite, because most systems support both the TCP/IP protocol and the applications that go with it. Without this particular protocol, the Internet would not exist in its present, familiar form.

Understanding TCP/IP is a must when dealing with Windows 2000 systems, because most Windows 2000 features rely on it to work. TCP/IP domains have replaced Windows NT domains, which allows the close integration of Windows 2000 networks with the Internet and permits the networks to interact fully with all Internet technologies.

Although TCP/IP is the most widely used protocol today, it is also the slowest of the three protocols mentioned in this section. TCP/IP was originally designed as a protocol that would allow a network developed by the U.S. military to recover from catastrophic failures. That network eventually evolved into the Internet. The original idea behind the Internet was the creation of a network that would enable military installations to communicate even if one or more of these sites became destroyed in a war. Because the TCP/IP protocol was designed to ensure that devices (now known as routers) could decide on the best path to send the data so that the information was received, it needed flexible addressing schemes and error correction. These addressing schemes and error correction add overhead to devices using the protocol, making TCP/IP very slow, but also highly robust.

Services

Services are server-based applications that run on a server. They tend to run in the background and give the operating system its functionality. Windows 2000 includes services for logon and authentication, computer naming, addressing, and Web and File Transfer Protocol (FTP), as well as many others. In previous versions of Windows NT, services were accessed through the Control Panel; in Windows 2000, you access the services using the Component Services application. To access these services, follow these steps:

1. Click on Start, Programs, Administrative Tools, Component Services.

2. Select the Services (local) option in the left pane. The services installed on the system will appear in the right pane, as shown in Figure 8-2.

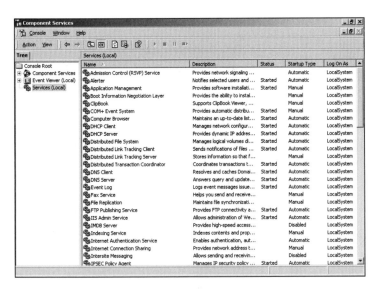

Figure 8-2 The Component Services administrative tool

To configure a service's properties, you double-click the service name in the right pane of the Component Services application. You can also access the service's properties by choosing the Properties option from the Action menu. A service's properties are classified into four categories:

- General settings
- Logon preferences
- Recovery options
- Service dependencies

In the following sections, we discuss each of these service configuration properties.

General Settings

The General tab of the service properties allows you to modify the default display name (the name by which the service is referred to in the Component Services application) and the service's description. (Figure 8-3 shows the General tab of the DNS Server service properties.) It allows you to customize the look and feel of your service administration tool. Notice that the path to the service is listed on this tab as well, which helps you to troubleshoot your services. If a service executable becomes corrupted, you can find the executable file for the service, note its creation date and size, and copy the file from another installation of Windows 2000 that uses the same file information.

The next two sections in the General properties tab are Startup type and Service status. The startup type defines how (or if) Windows starts the service during its initialization procedure.

- *Startup type:* Three service startup types exist: automatic, manual, and disabled. When a service is given an automatic startup type, it starts when Windows 2000

Server initializes and starts the services. Under the manual startup type, the service does not start during the Windows 2000 initialization procedure, but can be started by either a dependent service or a user. With the disabled startup type, the service cannot be started by Windows 2000 initialization, a dependent service, or a user. This last option is useful when a service is temporarily not required and disabling it will free up system resources that would normally be assigned to this particular service.

- *Service status:* This item indicates the current status of a service. The service can be in one of three states: started, stopped, or paused. A started service has been executed and is currently running on the system. A stopped service is not running and does not respond to any requests. A paused service does not accept any new connections unless the user attempting the connection is a member of either the Administrator or Server Operators group. You must click the Resume button if a service is paused to enable users to connect to the service again.

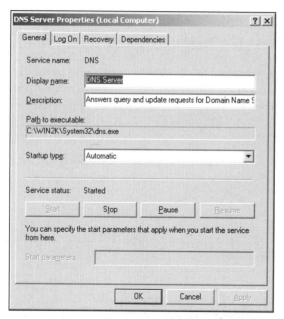

Figure 8-3 Services properties window

Log On Preferences

Most services use the local system account to access the operating system. That is, when the service needs to request or send information to the operating system, it uses the authentication properties of an internal account. This account cannot be modified and is recognized by the operating system as having the appropriate permissions to perform most system tasks. In some instances, you might want to create a dedicated account for the service to use in performing its tasks. Usually, the applications that require the service must be aware of the account name and the password before they can run successfully. An example of such an application is Microsoft Exchange. Exchange uses an account called the Exchange Service Account to log into the system and obtain information about users. If you change the user name or password for this service without notifying the Exchange Administrator program, Exchange will fail when it tries to access the system.

Windows 2000 also offers the ability to control which services are started for a specific profile. In the past, with Windows NT, users could control which devices and device drivers were started and used with a specific profile, but they lacked an easy way to control individual services. The ability to control which services are started for a specific profile is useful when testing a system or dealing with a system that is used as a backup. To understand how this ability works, consider the following scenario: Your organization is running a Windows 2000 Server as a domain controller. You need to bring it down occasionally for servicing, but your company cannot afford to purchase a second system to act as a backup. You can install Windows 2000 Server on a desktop system and create a secondary profile that starts the server as a domain controller. When you need to service the server, you simply reboot the system and choose the secondary profile. Although the system might not run as efficiently as the server would, it will run.

Figure 8-4 shows the Log On tab.

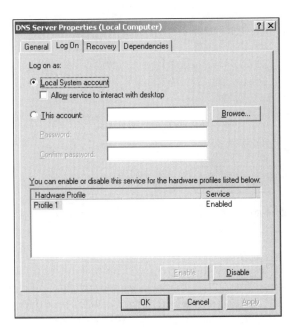

Figure 8-4 Service Properties, Log On tab

Recovery Options

Another Windows 2000 Server feature is the ability to dynamically respond to service failures. By default, if a service fails, Windows 2000 Server will not react. You can, however, configure services so that they will perform tasks that you specify in the event of a failure. This type of definition can be made for all services or for only selected ones. As shown in Figure 8-5, you have three levels of failure: first, second, and subsequent failures. When choosing which action Windows 2000 Server will take if a service fails, you can opt to take no action (the default option on all failures), to restart the service, to run a file, or to reboot the computer. All of these actions are fairly self-explanatory, except perhaps for the "run a file" option. With this option, you can have Windows 2000 Server execute an external file that sends an e-mail or pages an administrator, notifying him or her of the error.

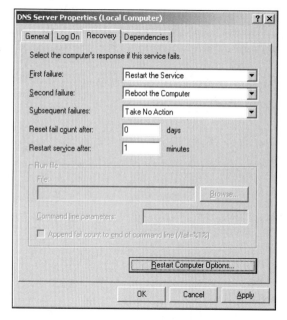

Figure 8-5 Recovery options for a service

Service Dependencies

The last tab in the service properties is Dependencies (see Figure 8-6). This tab is strictly informational and cannot be modified. The services on which the selected service depends are listed in the top window (if any), whereas the services that depend on the selected service appear in the bottom window (if any). When service A depends on service B, service B must be running before service A can start. If service B is set to either an automatic or manual startup type, either the operating system or service A will start it before starting itself.

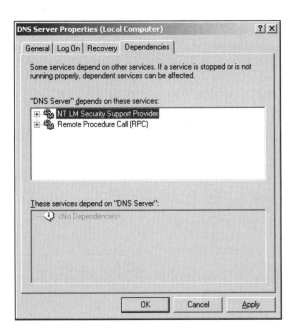

Figure 8-6 Service dependencies window

NORMAL AND NETWORK OPERATING SYSTEM BASICS

On the surface, it may appear as if many network operating systems are not much different from their desktop counterparts. In reality, nothing could be further from the truth. Although the Windows 2000 Server interface looks like the Windows 95/98 interface, the operating system is not the same. Both Windows NT and Windows 2000 Server are 32-bit operating systems that were written for networking from the ground up. As a result, they do not have some of the limitations of the Windows 95/98 operating systems. Most of today's operating systems have the ability to share printers and files as well as to run FTP or Web services. Consequently, it is important to understand the differences between a normal operating system and a network operating system (NOS).

A network operating system is designed to work with network services first and desktop applications second, whereas the opposite is true for a traditional (normal) operating system. Although most network operating systems can run applications such as word processor or spreadsheet programs, some (for example, Novell's NetWare) do not. Network operating systems are written to serve information to clients first and run applications second. In contrast, normal operating systems focus on running applications locally.

You can configure Windows 2000 Server to allocate a portion of system resources to background applications (such as services) and another portion to foreground applications. To access this configuration option, follow these steps:

1. Right-click My Computer and choose Properties from the drop-down menu.
2. Click the Advanced tab in the System Properties dialog box.

3. Click the Performance Options button. A window similar to the one shown in Figure 8-7 appears. At this point, you can choose the Applications radio button to optimize Windows 2000 Server to run foreground applications or the Background Services radio button to optimize it to run the services. The latter is the default configuration when you install Windows 2000 Server.
4. Click OK to close the Performance Options dialog box.
5. Close the System Properties dialog box.

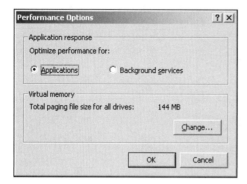

Figure 8-7 Windows 2000 Server performance configuration

In general, network operating systems support more high-end hardware configurations, such as symmetric multiprocessing (the ability to use multiple processors in a single system), extremely large hard disk support, and fault-tolerant storage systems (such as SCSI and fiber-channel solutions). You will also find that a network operating system gives you better control over network security.

WINDOWS 2000 NETWORKING MODEL

The best way to describe the Windows 2000 networking model is to explain how it corresponds to the OSI model (starting from the Application layer at the top). At the Application layer, Windows has *providers*. These providers create a way for the applications running on the system to communicate with the network.

The line between the Application and Presentation layers in the OSI model corresponds to the one between the User mode and the Kernel mode in the Windows model. All executive services run in the Presentation layer.

Redirectors exist at the Session layer. These redirect any requests for information from a physical device to a logical one. For example, when an application saves a file to a network drive rather than a physical one, the redirector sends the information to the correct location.

At the Transport and Network layers, you will find the Transport protocols, or the languages that are used to communicate on the network. Connecting these protocols to the redirectors is the **Transport Driver Interface (TDI)**. This layer allows the protocols to remain independent of the redirectors.

At the Data Link layer, the network interface card drivers exist. These drivers allow the system to communicate with the physical network cards. The NDIS interface appears between these drivers and the Transport protocols. Like the TDI, this interface allows the drivers to communicate with the transport protocols above without the need to rewrite any code.

ROUTING AND REMOTE ACCESS

A major strength of the TCP/IP protocol is its ability to address a huge number of addresses and networks. The process of transferring or forwarding packets of data from one network to another is known as **routing**. If your network spans a single location, then you probably will not encounter routing. If your network spans more than a single location or needs to communicate with a WAN or the Internet, however, then routing becomes an essential component of the network.

IP Routing

As stated earlier, routing is simply the transferring of packets from one network to another. When a computer attempts to route a packet between two networks, it checks its **routing table**. The routing table lists the available networks and the network interfaces over which the system must communicate to contact the remote network. Figure 8-8 depicts a routing table. Two types of routing exist: **static routing** and **dynamic routing**.

Figure 8-8 A routing table

Static Routes

With a static route, the administrator is responsible for manually configuring all paths (or routes) from one network to another. If the route changes, the router will not notify other routers of the change—it is up to an administrator to manually modify the route. This method of configuring routes is good only for small networks or for devices that do not have the ability to broadcast their location (such as some print servers) and whose addresses do not change regularly.

Windows 2000 offers several ways to create and modify static routes. One new option in Windows 2000 for adding static routes is the Static Route dialog box. You can execute this dialog box from the Routing and Remote Access console (as seen in Figure 8-9).

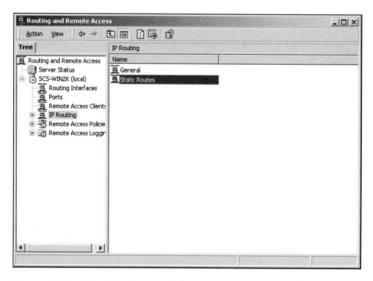

Figure 8-9 The Routing and Remote Access console

Two command prompt commands are available to you for configuring static routes: *route* and *ipkern*. The route command has been around for a while; you would issue a route add command to add a route. The ipkern command is new in Windows 2000; it is the command-prompt version of the Static Route dialog box (see Figure 8-10).

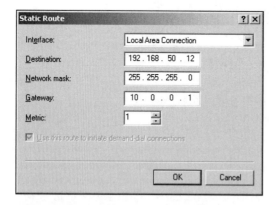

Figure 8-10 Static Route dialog box

 A static route can overwrite a dynamic route.

Dynamic Routes

With dynamic routing, all routing information is shared between the routers. When a router learns of a route to a network, it will pass that information along to the routers with which it communicates. The routers can therefore "learn" about the networks with which they communicate. This technique is the most common way of routing packets today. Windows 2000 supports two TCP/IP routing protocols: **Routing Information Protocol for Internet Protocol (RIP for IP)** and **Open Shortest Path First (OSPF)**.

Remote Access

Remote access allows you to connect remote clients to your network using a multitude of hardware devices. When a client connects to the remote access server, it becomes part of the network. It can browse files and folders, print to network printers, collaborate with other network users, and run applications. In Windows 2000, you use the Routing and Remote Access management console to configure remote access on a server (see Figure 8-11).

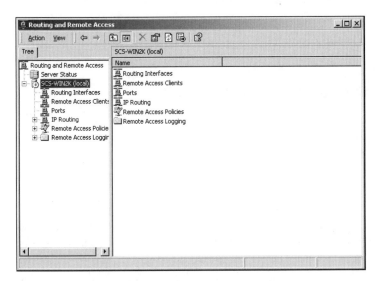

Figure 8-11 Routing and Remote Access console

Remote access includes two components, the client and the server. The client connects to the network, whereas the server acts as the gateway between the network and the remote client. To permit this type of communication, they need to share some protocols. Windows 2000 supports the following protocols for remote access:

- TCP/IP
- NetBEUI
- **AppleTalk Remote Access Protocol (ARAP)**
- NWLink IPX/SPX-compatible protocol

Windows 2000 also supports **virtual private networks (VPNs)**. VPNs add a second secure protocol to allow the client to use the Internet to connect to the network. With the regular remote access protocols, the client connects directly to the Windows 2000 Server. With a VPN, however, the client first connects to the Internet using its preferred Internet service provider. The client would then create a second session (also known as a **tunnel**) to a remote access server on the LAN, thereby producing an encrypted channel between the client and the server. The client can then participate on the network as if it were physically connected to the LAN.

VPNs can use either of two protocols to create these secure connections: **Point-to-Point Tunneling Protocol (PPTP)** and **Layer Two Tunneling Protocol (L2TP)**. PPTP is a technology that existed in Windows NT 4.0; L2TP is a protocol that is new to Windows 2000.

PPTP will encrypt all data that are sent between the client and the server. Secondary TCP/IP addresses are assigned to both the client and the server, and all data are routed using these "private" addresses. Anyone who captures the data stream between the two systems will have to decrypt the information to make it readable and useful.

L2TP resembles PPTP, except that it provides only the tunneling capability, not the encryption. All encryption is handled by a second method, such as IP Security (IPSec).

SERVER VERSUS CLIENT ROLES

It is important that you understand some of the different roles that a Windows 2000 server can play. A server typically can switch between client and server roles. As a rule, a *server role* can be defined as any task that is performed by the system for the benefit of another system (the client). A *client role* is defined as any task that the system requests from another, remote system.

Servers can play several client roles; from logging into the network, to printing to a network printer, to accessing files and applications on servers. The service that supports this flexibility is the Workstation Service. When this service is active, the server acts as a workstation. If you disable the Workstation Service, the system would no longer be able to connect to network resources.

In much the same way, servers use the Server Service to share files, printers, and other resources to clients. By disabling the Server Service, you effectively deny any client access to the network. This feature is a good way to stop clients from connecting to the network, if you need to make a modification to the server. Another common practice is to pause this service, rather than to stop it. Pausing the service maintains all existing connections to the server, while denying any new connections from being forged.

All Windows 2000 systems include both the Workstation and Server services. The Workstation Service on one system communicates with the Server Service on the other, and vice versa.

Chapter Summary

- A network can be defined as a collection of computers that use a common language (protocol) to communicate. Networks allow you to share data, printers, and applications between users.

- The OSI model was developed to enable developers to create modular components that will "fit" together without having to rewrite all of the components for each device. Without such a standard, the entire networking suite would have to be replaced for any new application, network card, or protocol that was introduced.

- The seven distinct layers of the OSI model (Application, Presentation, Session, Transport, Network, Data Link, and Physical) and network protocols are basic to an understanding of computer networking. The three main protocols employed are NetBEUI, IPX/SPX, and TCP/IP. Protocols are the common languages that systems use to communicate. If one system uses a protocol that is different from that of another system, the two systems will not be able to communicate, even though they may be physically on the same network.

- Services are applications that run on servers and that allow components to run when no users are logged into the server. If services did not exist, applications would have to be executed while a user is logged in. These applications would be terminated if the user is logged out of the system.

- Network operating systems differ from desktop operating systems in that they are tuned to run on the "back end." As a result, they are better suited to running applications and services for other systems than running applications locally. For example, Microsoft Word would run considerably better on a Windows 2000 Professional system than on a Windows 2000 Server system, because the Professional system is designed to run Word, whereas the Server system is not.

- Routing allows Windows 2000 to connect two or more networks. Using some of the built-in services in Windows 2000, you can effectively convert a server into a router. The server will then transfer information between the networks.

- Remote access allows clients that are not connected directly to the LAN to connect to a Windows 2000 Server and participate on the network as if they were physically connected to it. This feature gives remote users access to network resources, such as printers, applications, and files.

- Servers tend to run both server and client components. Server components are geared toward servicing the requests of clients, whereas workstation components request information from a server.

Key Terms

AppleTalk Remote Access Protocol (ARAP) — A protocol that allows Apple Macintosh computers to connect to a remote access server.

Application layer — The layer of the OSI model that allows access to networking services.

cyclic redundancy check (CRC) — A mathematical recipe that generates a specific value, called a checksum, based on the contents of a data frame. The CRC is calculated before a data frame is transmitted and then is included with the frame; on receipt, the CRC is recalculated and compared with the sent value. If the two agree, the data frame is assumed to have been delivered intact; if they disagree, the data frame must be retransmitted.

Data Link layer — The layer of the OSI model that uses the hardware address of the system to communicate.

dynamic routing — The process used by routers to dynamically learn about the routes that they can take to connect to remote networks.

frame — The basic package of bits that represents a protocol data unit (PDU) sent from one computer to another across a network. In addition to its contents, a frame includes the sender's and receiver's network addresses as well as control information at the head and a CRC at the tail.

hardware address — See *Media Access Control (MAC) address*.

Internetwork Packet Exchange/Sequenced Packet Exchange (IPX/SPX) — A protocol developed by Novell for its NetWare operating system. It may be used in routed environments.

Layer Two Tunneling Protocol (L2TP) — A protocol that relies on other encryption methods (such as IPSec) for communication. It creates the secure connection, but other methods of encryption must be used.

local area network (LAN) — A group of computers that are connected to form a network within a small area, such as a floor or a building.

Media Access Control (MAC) address — A unique number that is assigned to each network device. It ensures that no two devices exist with the same addressing information.

metropolitan area network (MAN) — A network of computers that exist within the same metropolitan area, such as a city.

NetBIOS Enhanced User Interface (NetBEUI) — A protocol that can be used in small, nonrouted environments.

network — Two or more computers connected so that they can transfer information.

Network layer — The layer of the OSI model that addresses the messages for delivery.

nonroutable protocol — A network protocol that cannot be used in a routed network environment.

Open Shortest Path First (OSPF) — A protocol used by routers to learn about different routes to remote networks.

Organizationally Unique Identifier (OUI) — A unique number that is assigned to each network device vendor to ensure that hardware addresses do not overlap.

Physical layer — The layer of the OSI model that defines the physical structure of the network (copper, fiber, and so on).

Point-to-Point Tunneling Protocol (PPTP) — A protocol that is used to encrypt data between a server and a client.

Presentation layer — The layer of the OSI model that translates data from a format understood by the application into a generic format that can be understood by other systems.

protocol — A common language that allows heterogeneous systems to communicate and share information on a network.

redirector — An Application layer software component that captures application output and redirects it to a different location.

routable protocol — A network protocol that can be used in a routed environment to communicate with remote networks.

routing — The process of transferring packets of information from one network to another network.

Routing Information Protocol for Internet Protocol (RIP for IP) — A protocol used by routers to learn about different routes to remote networks.

routing table — A list of available networks and interfaces over which a system must communicate to contact a remote system.

service — A software component that exists on servers that run in the background so as to perform normal server operations, such as file and print sharing, Web and FTP services, and DNS services.

Session layer — The layer of the OSI model that initiates and maintains the communication between different systems on the network.

static routing — A system in which the network administrator must manually configure all paths from one network to another.

Transmission Control Protocol/Internet Protocol (TCP/IP) — The protocol for the Internet. It allows for the connection of large networks in different geographical locations.

Transport Driver Interface (TDI) — The specification to which all transport protocols must be written so that they can be used by higher-layer services, such as programming interfaces, file systems, and interprocess communication mechanisms.

Transport layer — The layer of the OSI model that is responsible for ensuring error-free transmission and reception of data.

tunnel — A communication mechanism used by VPNs to establish a second, secure session between a client and remote server.

virtual private network (VPN) — A secure connection between a client and a private network over the Internet.

wide area network (WAN) — A group of computers that are networked over great distances, such as between cities.

Review Questions

1. The OSI model is a set of rules and standards that vendors must follow. True or False?
2. Only the Physical layer of the OSI model communicates directly with the Physical layer on another network. True or False?
3. At which OSI layer is error checking added?
   a. Physical layer
   b. Data Link layer
   c. Network layer
   d. Transport layer
   e. Session layer
   f. Presentation layer
   g. Application layer
4. At which OSI layer does compression take place?
   a. Physical layer
   b. Data Link layer
   c. Network layer
   d. Transport layer
   e. Session layer
   f. Presentation layer
   g. Application layer
5. At which OSI layer is the actual configuration of the networking media defined?
   a. Physical layer
   b. Data Link layer
   c. Network layer
   d. Transport layer
   e. Session layer
   f. Presentation layer
   g. Application layer
6. At which OSI layer is network redirection completed?
   a. Physical layer
   b. Data Link layer
   c. Network layer
   d. Transport layer

    e. Session layer

    f. Presentation layer

    g. Application layer

7. At which OSI layer are physical addresses used to send data?

    a. Physical layer

    b. Data Link layer

    c. Network layer

    d. Transport layer

    e. Session layer

    f. Presentation layer

    g. Application layer

8. At which OSI layer is ongoing communication controlled?

    a. Physical layer

    b. Data Link layer

    c. Network layer

    d. Transport layer

    e. Session layer

    f. Presentation layer

    g. Application layer

9. At which OSI layer are TCP/IP addresses used?

    a. Physical layer

    b. Data Link layer

    c. Network layer

    d. Transport layer

    e. Session layer

    f. Presentation layer

    g. Application layer

10. All network operating systems allow you to run applications such as word processors on them. True or False?

11. When one layer communicates with its counterpoint on another system, it does so directly. True or False?

12. Which of the following is *not* a startup type for Windows 2000 Server services?

    a. Automatic

    b. Manual

    c. Dependent

    d. Disabled

13. Once a service has been disabled, which user group(s) can still connect to the service?
    a. Administrators and Account Operators
    b. Administrators and Service Operators
    c. Administrators only
    d. Administrators and Server Operators
14. Changing the background services optimization to application optimization does not require rebooting the server. True or False?
15. You access the Windows 2000 Server service configuration options through the Services Control Panel. True or False?
16. Of the three main Windows 2000 Server-supported protocols, only _____ and _____ are routable.
17. Of the three main Windows 2000 Server-supported protocols, _____ is the fastest and easiest to configure.
18. Windows 2000 Server domains and Windows NT domains are the same. True or False?
19. All operating systems support symmetric multiprocessing. True or False?
20. NetBEUI is one of the routable protocols supported by Windows 2000 Server. True or False?

Hands-on Projects

Project 8-1

This exercise demonstrates the steps involved in modifying the startup type of a service.

To change the startup type of a service:

1. Click **Start**, **Programs**, **Administrative Tools**, **Component Services**.
2. Highlight the **Services (Local)** option in the left pane (refer to Figure 8-2 earlier in the chapter).
3. Double-click the **DNS Server** service.
4. From the Startup type drop-down menu, choose the **Manual** option (see Figure 8-12).
5. Click the **Apply** button to implement the changes.
6. Click **OK** to close the DNS Server Properties dialog box.
7. Close the **Component Services** window.

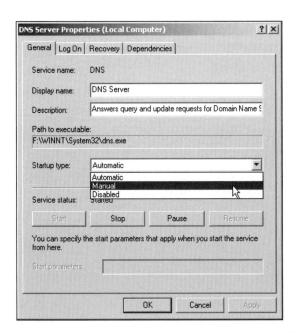

Figure 8-12 Setting the Startup type for the DNS Server service

Project 8-2

This exercise demonstrates the steps involved in stopping and restarting a service.

To stop and start a service:

1. Click **Start**, **Programs**, **Administrative Tools**, **Component Services**.
2. Highlight the **Services (local)** option in the left pane.
3. Double-click the **DNS Server** service.
4. Click the **Stop** button (see Figure 8-13). The DNS Server service is now stopped.
5. Click the **Start** button to restart the service.
6. Click **OK** to close the DNS Server Properties dialog box.
7. Close the **Component Services** window.

Project 8-3

This exercise demonstrates the steps involved in pausing and restarting a service.

To pause and restart a service:

1. Click **Start**, **Programs**, **Administrative Tools**, **Component Services**.
2. Highlight the **Services (Local)** option in the left pane.
3. Double-click the **DNS Server** service.
4. Click the **Pause** button. The DNS Server service is now paused.

5. Click the **Resume** button. The DNS Server service begins running again.
6. Click **OK** to close the DNS Server Properties dialog box.
7. Close the **Component Services** window.

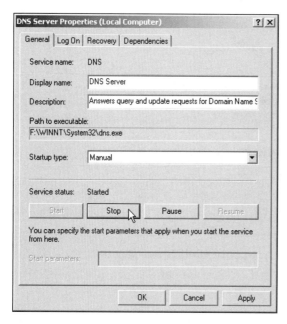

Figure 8-13 Stopping the DNS Server service

Project 8-4

This exercise demonstrates the steps involved in modifying the logon account used by a service.

To change the logon account of a service:

1. Click **Start**, **Programs**, **Administrative Tools**, **Component Services**.
2. Highlight the **Services (Local)** option in the left pane.
3. Double-click the **DNS Server** service.
4. Click the **Logon** tab.
5. Click the **This account** radio button (see Figure 8-14).
6. Click the **Browse** button and select the desired user account, by either highlighting the user's name in the list, or typing it in the Name field (see Figure 8-15).

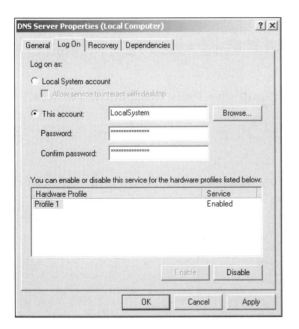

Figure 8-14 Changing the logon account for the DNS Server service

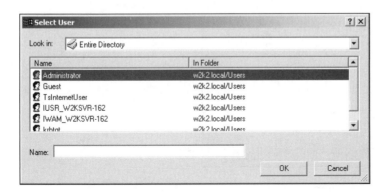

Figure 8-15 Selecting the user to log on to a service

7. Enter the password for the user.
8. Reenter the password for confirmation.
9. Click the **Apply** button to implement the changes.
10. Click **OK** when the confirmation dialog box appears.
11. Click **OK** when the system informs you that the computer must be restarted for the changes to take effect.
12. Click **OK** to close the DNS Server Properties dialog box.
13. Close the **Component Services** window.

Project 8-5

This exercise demonstrates the steps involved in disabling a service in a specific profile.

To disable a service:

1. Click **Start**, **Programs**, **Administrative Tools**, **Component Services**.
2. Highlight the **Services (local)** option in the left pane.
3. Double-click the **DNS Server** service.
4. Click the **Logon** tab.
5. In the lower part of the window, highlight the profile in which you would like this service disabled (see Figure 8-16).

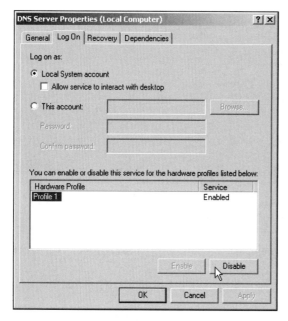

Figure 8-16 Disabling a service

6. Click the **Disable** button.
7. Click the **Apply** button to implement the changes.

Project 8-6

This exercise demonstrates the steps involved in configuring the recovery options of a service. At the first failure, we attempt to restart the service. After the second failure, we execute a program to page an administrator. (This choice assumes that a modem is connected and configured on the server, and that the paging software is installed in the C:\Pager folder.)

To change the recovery options of a service:

1. Click **Start**, **Programs**, **Administrative Tools**, **Component Services**.

2. Highlight the **Services (local)** option in the left pane.
3. Double-click the **DNS Server** service.
4. Click the **Recovery** tab.
5. From the First failure: drop-down menu, choose the **Restart the service** option.
6. From the Second Failure: drop-down menu, choose the **Run a File** option.
7. Browse to the C:\Pager\Page.exe program.
8. Enter any required information for the Page.exe program (such as the pager phone number).
9. From the **Subsequent failures** drop-down menu, choose the **Reboot the Computer** option (see Figure 8-17).
10. Click on the **Restart Computer Options** button and enter the time before system shutdown and an optional message to send to connected users to notify them of the shutdown.
11. Click on the **Apply** button to set the changes.
12. Click **OK** to close the DNS Server Properties dialog box.
13. Close the **Component Services** window.

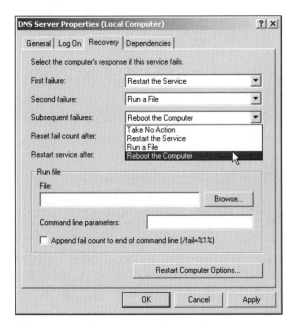

Figure 8-17 Configuring the recovery options of a service

CASE PROJECTS

1. Your organization is looking for a protocol that will allow it to connect its multiple offices. Each of the offices will also be connected to the Internet. Which protocol would you recommend?

2. Your current network uses NetBEUI as its only protocol. Your organization has merged with a second company in another location in the city. Will this protocol work? If not, then which ones will?

3. You have been asked to install a small network for one of your clients. It will run a peer-to-peer network and your client would like to become connected in the least painful and fastest way. Which protocol would you recommend?

4. A client has multiple sites and wants to connect them via Frame Relay connections. Which protocols can be used to accomplish this goal? Which would you recommend and why?

CHAPTER 9

NETWORK IDENTIFICATION

After reading this chapter and completing the exercises, you will be able to:

- Explain the naming protocols used in Windows 2000 Server
- Configure the Microsoft Domain Name Service for Windows 2000 Server
- Install and manage the Microsoft Windows Internet Name Service for Windows 2000 Server
- Assign TCP/IP addressing information to clients dynamically using the Microsoft Dynamic Host Configuration Protocol service for Windows 2000 Server
- Create DHCP scopes, superscopes, and multicast scopes
- Understand the basic concepts underlying TCP/IP subnets and domains

This chapter discusses the components that allow Windows 2000 Server to resolve names and TCP/IP addresses. Three main services in Windows 2000 Server take care of this task: **Domain Naming Service (DNS)**, **Windows Internet Naming Service (WINS)**, and **Dynamic Host Configuration Protocol (DHCP)**. DNS resolves TCP/IP addresses to Internet names, WINS resolves TCP/IP addresses to NetBIOS names, and DHCP assigns TCP/IP addresses to clients dynamically.

User Identification Versus Computer Identification

It is important to understand the differences in how systems recognize users and other computers. In the following sections, you will see why it is necessary to differentiate between them and how Windows 2000 networks handle the different names.

Users

A user is simply a name and password combination that is assigned to a specific person. After a person receives a user name, he or she is considered a user and you can assign permissions and attributes to that user. For example, you can assign the user the rights to print to specific printers or to access certain resources.

NetBIOS Names

NetBIOS names are names that are assigned to computers in a Windows NT or 95/98 network. For backward compatibility, Windows 2000 must also use NetBIOS names. A NetBIOS name can have a maximum length of 15 characters, but may have a hidden sixteenth character, which is used to identify the service that will be accessed on the server.

Machine Identification and Name Resolution

Computers communicate with one another using their hardware and protocol addresses. People find it difficult to remember long strings of numbers (and letters in the case of hardware addresses). Consequently, computers usually have two names for things: the names the computers understand, and the names humans understand. As a result, a method is needed for converting between these names and their addresses. This process is known as **name resolution**.

Domain Name Service

Windows 2000 Server relies heavily on Internet technologies and, therefore, on Internet naming conventions, known as domains. It is important to differentiate between a Windows 2000 domain and an Internet domain. The distinction is covered in detail in the "Domains" section later in this chapter. For now, simply remember that we are dealing with Internet domains.

Like most Windows 2000 Server services, DNS requires that the server be configured with a static IP address. By default, Windows 2000 Server configures itself as a client. You must assign it a unique, static IP address. You also need to give it a host name and a domain name.

When Active Directory is installed on a Windows 2000 Server computer, you are prompted either to have the Active Directory installation wizard configure your DNS or to manually configure DNS. Hands-on Project 9-1 details how to install DNS manually.

Zones

Microsoft DNS divides domain namespaces into **zones**. A zone is simply a logical group of addresses. For example, Microsoft.com is a zone, as is Seattle.Microsoft.com. All zone information is stored in a **zone database file**, which is a simple text file (assuming that you configure the zone as a standard zone, as described next) that is used by DNS to resolve TCP/IP names and addresses.

Windows 2000 Server DNS allows you to configure one of three zone types. These zone types, as shown in Figure 9-1, are:

- **Active Directory-integrated zone.** This zone type integrates all host and TCP/IP address information for this zone into the Active Directory. This option gives you the security and flexibility of Active Directory, while allowing Active Directory replication to update all zone information between servers. Creating an Active Directory-integrated zone is covered in Hands-on Project 9-4.

- **Standard primary zone.** This zone type, also known as a **master zone**, stores the original information for the zone. It is referred to as the authority for the zone or the domain, because it is in charge of all changes to the zone. Each zone can have a single standard primary zone. All zone information is stored in a text file, which is located in the *%systemroot%*\system32\dns directory. Creating a standard primary zone is covered in Hands-on Project 9-2.

- **Standard secondary zone.** This zone type stores a copy, or replica, of the standard primary zone information. The information is stored in a read-only format and is used for fault tolerance if the primary zone is not available. Multiple standard secondary zones can be configured on a network. As with standard primary zones, all secondary zone information is stored in a text file, which is located in the *%systemroot%*\system32\dns directory. Creating a standard secondary zone is covered in Hands-on Project 9-3.

Primary and secondary zones do not need to reside on the same physical network. Instead, they can exist in different companies, cities, states, or countries.

As noted earlier, zone information is stored in a zone database file. This file contains the name resolution information for the zone, known as **resources**. Several resource types exist in the Windows 2000 Server implementation of DNS. Some of the most common ones are listed in Table 9-1. By default, the zone database file carries a .dns extension.

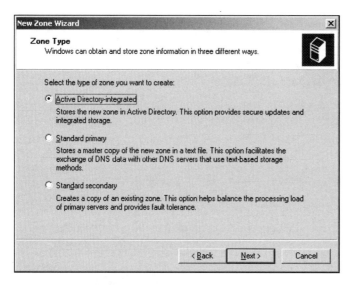

Figure 9-1 Windows 2000 Server zone types

Table 9-1 Domain Name Service resource types

Resource Record Type	Abbreviation	Definition
Start of Authority	SOA	Affects how a zone transfer takes place.
Name Server	NS	Defines one or more name servers as servers that will resolve names and IP addresses for this domain.
Mail Exchanger	MX	Identifies the server on the domain that is to receive e-mail messages for the domain.
Address	A	Used to resolve a TCP/IP host name to a TCP/IP address. Also known as a forward lookup.
Pointer	PTR	Used to resolve a TCP/IP address to a TCP/IP host name. Also known as a reverse lookup.
Canonical Name	CNAME	Defines aliases (if any) assigned to a TCP/IP host. A single host can have an unlimited number of aliases (or "nicknames").
Service Location	SRV	Defines a remote server that hosts a specific service, such as Kerberos, FTP, LDAP, or HTTP.
Windows Internet Name Service	WINS	Defines a server used to resolve Windows NT NetBIOS names (covered later in this chapter).

The configuration of most of these resource records is self-explanatory (and Windows 2000 Server automates most of the configuration).

SOA

One resource record that should be explored in some detail is the **Start of Authority (SOA)**, which affects how a zone transfer takes place (covered later in this chapter). Five numerical values make up the SOA. These values and their functions are as follows:

- *Serial Number.* A number used to track changes in the zone database file. Every time a change is made to the database, this variable is incremented by 1. It ensures that all changes are transferred to secondary zones. It is common to use a serial number in the form, *YYYYMMDD##* (for example, 1999090901 for the first change on September 9, 1999). This number not only tracks the changes, but also allows you to monitor when changes last took place.

- *Refresh Interval.* The amount of time (in seconds) that a secondary server waits before refreshing its zone database (assuming that changes exist) with the primary server.

- *Retry Interval.* The amount of time (in seconds) that the secondary server waits if it fails to contact the primary server for a zone database refresh. This value is used only if the primary database cannot be contacted.

- *Expire Interval.* The amount of time (in seconds) that the secondary server maintains a zone database, assuming that it cannot contact the primary database for updates. After this interval is reached, the secondary server stops resolving names and addresses.

- *Minimum Time-to-Live (TTL).* The amount of time (in seconds) that the query response remains valid. After the TTL reaches zero, the query response is no longer valid and the DNS server must be requeried. This method ensures that any changes to the databases will eventually reach all systems on the network or Internet.

Zones are most commonly used in one of two ways: as **forward lookup zones** or as **reverse lookup zones**. These two ways are basically mirror images of one another. One is used to find the other. Creating a reverse lookup zone is detailed in Hands-on Project 9-5.

A forward lookup zone can contain any of the resource types (except a PTR record). The most common type of record that is stored in a forward lookup zone is the **Address (A) resource record**. Given a fully qualified domain name (FQDN), such as www.sprockets.com, this zone file is used to resolve it to the FQDN's TCP/IP address. In other words, when the DNS server is queried for the FQDN, it returns the IP address to the client. An example of a forward lookup file follows:

```
;  Database file sales.sprockets.com.dns for sales.
sprockets.com zone.
;    Zone version:   1
;
```

Chapter 9 Network Identification

```
@                       IN      SOA dns1.sprockets.com.  administrator.
sprockets.com. (
                                1               ; serial number
                                900             ; refresh
                                600             ; retry
                                86400           ; expire
                                3600            ) ; minimum TTL
;
;   Zone NS records
;
@                       NS      dns1.sprockets.com.
@                       NS      dns.provider.net.

;
;   Zone records
;
gateway         IN      A       10.0.0.1
www             IN      A       10.0.0.2
ftp             IN      A       10.0.0.3
mail            IN      A       10.0.0.4
dns1            IN      A       10.0.0.5
pop             IN      CNAME           mail.sprockets.com.
smtp            IN      CNAME           mail.sprockets.com.

mail            IN      MX      10      mail.sprockets.com.
```

Reverse lookup zones usually contain only PTR records. These records are used when a client system queries the server for the FQDN of a system given its TCP/IP address. Many Internet sites today will not grant access to information (such as downloads) unless their system can perform a reverse lookup on the TCP/IP address. An example of a reverse lookup zone file follows:

```
;   Database file 0.0.10.in-addr.arpa.dns for 0.0.10.in-
addr.arpa zone.
;       Zone version:   1
;

@                       IN      SOA dns1.sprockets.com.  administrator.
sprockets.com. (
                                1               ; serial number
                                900             ; refresh
                                600             ; retry
                                86400           ; expire
                                3600            ) ; minimum TTL

;
;   Zone NS records
;
```

```
        @               NS      dns1.sprockets.com.
;
;       Zone records
;
        1               IN      PTR     gateway.sprockets.com.
        2               IN      PTR     www.sprockets.com.
        3               IN      PTR     ftp.sprockets.com.
        4               IN      PTR     mail.sprockets.com.
        5               IN      PTR     dns1.sprockets.com.
```

Zone Transfers

The process of transferring information between standard primary and standard secondary servers is known as **zone transfer**. A zone transfer occurs when one of three events takes place:

- The primary server notifies a secondary server(s) of any changes within its databases.
- A secondary server contacts the primary server for any changes during the DNS service start-up.
- The refresh interval ends (as listed in the SOA record).

Two types of zone transfers exist: **Full Zone Transfer (AXFR)** and **Incremental Zone Transfer (IXFR)**.

The AXFR technique is the most commonly used method of transferring information between zones. It is compatible with most current implementations of DNS (independent of operating system). After the refresh interval on the secondary name server expires, this server contacts the primary name server and requests the SOA record. It then compares the serial number of this SOA record with the one stored in its configuration of the zone. If the serial numbers are the same, no zone transfer takes place. If the serial numbers are different, the secondary server assumes that its database information is outdated, and it copies the entire zone database from the primary server to its own database.

IXFR is a new method of updating zone information found in Windows 2000 Server. As with AXFR, the secondary server requests the SOA record from the primary server after its refresh interval expires. If the serial numbers match, no zone transfer takes place. If the serial numbers do not match, however, the secondary server requests only the changed records. This zone transfer method greatly increases performance between the primary and secondary servers, while minimizing network traffic, especially in environments with a large number of hosts in their DNS databases.

Windows Internet Name Service

Before Windows 2000 Server became available, Windows 95/98/NT relied on the NetBIOS protocol. Windows 2000 Server will not run in a true NetBIOS environment. If only one non-Windows 2000 system is installed on your network, however, NetBIOS becomes a necessity. For this reason, Windows 2000 Server ships with WINS. WINS is to NetBIOS names as DNS is to

TCP/IP names. That is, it simply allows for a dynamic conversion between a NetBIOS name and its TCP/IP address. WINS installation is detailed in Hands-on Project 9-6.

Four forms of communication between the WINS client and the WINS server are possible:

- Name registration
- Name query
- Name release
- Name renewal

You can configure primary and secondary WINS servers for each client. The client will attempt to contact the primary WINS server three times. If the primary WINS server does not respond, the client contacts the secondary WINS server.

If the primary server cannot resolve an address query, the secondary server is not contacted. A secondary server is contacted only if the primary server is not available. Each of these tasks is covered in detail in the following sections.

Name Registration

Every client that is configured to communicate with the WINS server contacts the server every time it boots and is initialized. The client sends a name registration request message to the WINS server that contains the following information:

- Its TCP/IP address (source)
- The WINS server's address (destination)
- The name to register (its NetBIOS name)

After the WINS server receives the registration request, it checks its database to see whether the name has already been registered. If it has, the WINS server attempts to contact the system that originally registered the name (it makes this attempt three times). If the original system responds, the requesting system is sent a negative name registration and the client is notified of the name conflict.

If the original registrant cannot be contacted, the WINS server drops it from its database and creates a new entry for the requesting system consisting of its NetBIOS name and TCP/IP address. The server responds to the client with the following information:

- Its TCP/IP address (source)
- The client's destination address
- The name that was registered
- A TTL that is assigned to the name

If the client cannot contact the primary WINS server, it attempts to contact the secondary WINS server. If that server does not respond, the client attempts to broadcast a registration request. It then becomes the responsibility of the individual clients to inform the requesting client of any name conflicts on the network.

Name Query

After the client has registered its name and address with the WINS server, it can query the server for the addresses of any computers that it may need to contact. It does not, however, contact the WINS server first. Instead, it follows these steps:

1. The client system checks its NetBIOS cache to see whether it still has a record of the remote system's address.

2. If the cache does not contain the desired information, the client queries the primary WINS server for the remote system's address.

3. If neither WINS server can be contacted or the queried name does not exist in the WINS database, the client broadcasts its request. The system that has the broadcasted name will respond with its TCP/IP address.

 Note You can view the current NetBIOS cache by issuing the *nbtstat -c* command from an MS-DOS prompt. To review nbtstat parameters, type *nbtstat ?* at the command prompt (see Figure 9-2).

Figure 9-2 nbstat parameters

Name Release

When a system no longer requires that its NetBIOS name be registered in the WINS server database, it sends a request to have the entry removed. This operation usually occurs when either the system name changes or the system is shut down (or rebooted). The client sends the following information with its name release request:

- Its TCP/IP address (source)
- The WINS server's TCP/IP address (destination)
- The name to release

After the WINS server receives the name release request, it queries its database for the information. If it does not find the name of the requesting computer, it sends a negative name release message back to the client. If the WINS server finds the client's name in its database, it responds with the following information:

- The WINS server's TCP/IP address
- The client's TCP/IP address
- The name that was originally leased
- A TTL set to zero

After the client receives a name with the TTL set to zero, it releases its name and continues with either its shutdown process or its renaming process. The WINS server is not contacted again until the system is restarted or the client attempts to register the new name.

Name Renewal

WINS clients are configured to renew their registrations at set intervals. A WINS client attempts to contact its WINS server using the following criteria:

1. The client attempts to contact the primary WINS server at one-eighth of the TTL.
2. If no response is returned, the client attempts to renew its name registration every two minutes until one-half of the TTL has expired.
3. If the primary WINS server does not respond after one-half of the TTL has expired, the client sends a name registration renewal request to the secondary WINS server. At this point, the client treats the request as the first request.
4. The client sends a request every one-eighth of the TTL until one-half of the TTL has expired.
5. The client attempts to contact the primary WINS server again.
6. After a client has renewed its registration the first time, it attempts to contact the WINS server (to renew its registration) at one-half of the TTL.

Dynamic Host Configuration Protocol

DHCP is a protocol in the TCP/IP suite that is designed to ease a network administrator's job. The Windows 2000 DHCP service automatically assigns TCP/IP configuration information to your workstations. This scheme ensures that most TCP/IP addressing network problems are eliminated. It is accomplished by having the server running the DHCP service lease addresses and other TCP/IP information to client systems. Installation of the DHCP service is detailed in Hands-on Project 9-7.

By default, Windows 2000 systems are configured as DHCP clients. When the client starts, it requests a TCP/IP address from a DHCP server. The **DHCP lease** consists of three mandatory values and several optional ones. At the least, the server must assign clients their own unique TCP/IP address, as well as a subnet mask and a TTL for the lease. Optional parameters include the following:

- A default gateway address
- The domain name
- The TCP/IP address of one or more DNS servers
- The TCP/IP address of one or more WINS servers
- The TCP/IP address of one or more Simple Mail Transfer Protocol (SMTP) servers

The DHCP server responds to any DHCP client request by offering it a TCP/IP address. This process is known as DHCP lease generation.

The DHCP Lease

The DHCP lease is a four-phase process. These four phases are as follows:

- DHCPDISCOVER
- DHCPOFFER
- DHCPREQUEST
- DHCPACK

DHCPDISCOVER As you can imagine, when a DHCP client is first initialized, it knows nothing about the network. It does not know its TCP/IP address, subnet mask, or even the address of the DHCP server. To discover this information, it "yells"—stated in more technical terms, it sends a broadcast, which is known as a DHCPDISCOVER message.

Because the client does not have its own dedicated TCP/IP address, it sends its IP address as 0.0.0.0, transmitting this message to the TCP/IP address 255.255.255.255 (producing a complete broadcast). Every computer on the local network hears this message, but only systems that are configured as DHCP servers respond. The DHCP server (or servers) may receive a large number of requests simultaneously; as a consequence, the client includes its hardware address (or MAC address) and its computer name.

DHCPOFFER All DHCP servers "hear" the broadcast and the ones with TCP/IP addresses available to lease to the client respond. Because the client still does not have a unique

TCP/IP address configured, the DCHP server broadcasts the information. Broadcasting the DHCPOFFER message performs two important tasks:

- It notifies the DHCP client that a TCP/IP address is being offered to it.
- It notifies any other DHCP servers on the network that an offer has been made. It is important to remember that all DHCP servers with available TCP/IP address leases will offer one. The DHCPOFFER message just lets all of the servers know that other options exist for the client.

After the DHCP server offers a TCP/IP address to the client, it reserves that address so that it will not be offered to another client. The DHCP offer includes the following information:

- The client's hardware address (it is the only way to distinguish between different DHCP clients requesting TCP/IP addresses)
- The offered TCP/IP address
- The offered subnet mask
- The TCP/IP address of the DHCP server making the offer
- The length of the DHCP lease

DHCPREQUEST The DHCP client is not picky about which DHCP lease it accepts. It simply accepts the first one that it receives. After it has received the offer, it broadcasts a DHCPREQUEST message. Although the DHCP client has the required TCP/IP addressing information (although limited), it nevertheless broadcasts the DHCPREQUEST message. This message notifies any and all DHCP servers that made an offer that an offer has been accepted. After a DHCP server receives a DHCPREQUEST that is directed at a DHCP server other than itself, it retracts its TCP/IP offer and frees that address for another client. For this process to take place successfully, the client must include the TCP/IP address of the DHCP server from which it is accepting an offer.

DHCPACK The DHCP server that made the original offer sends a final message to the DHCP client in which it acknowledges the lease. The client is now notified (via a broadcast message) of the valid lease, and any other configuration information, such as **default gateway** or DNS servers, is sent to the client.

The DHCP client initializes the TCP/IP protocol stack and binds the protocol to any suitable network cards. At this point, the client can communicate with the network, because it now has a unique TCP/IP address on the network.

 Because the client does not have its own unique TCP/IP address until all four of the previously mentioned messages are transferred, all communications between the client and the DHCP server are sent as broadcast messages.

The DHCP Lease Renewal

At some point, the DHCP lease expires. A lease can be renewed in two ways: by using the automatic lease renewal method, or by using the manual lease renewal method. Automatic lease renewal occurs based on some specific rules, which are covered in the following section. Manual renewal allows an administrator or user to renew the lease at any time. The manual lease renewal is also employed when changing from one DHCP server to another.

Automatic DHCP Renewal   As with WINS, in DHCP the client renegotiates its lease with the DHCP server at set intervals. By default, the DHCP client attempts to renew the lease at 50 percent of the lease. For example, if the lease is set to 72 hours (3 days), the client attempts to renew the lease when 36 hours have passed (1.5 days). To accomplish this goal, it sends a directed DHCPREQUEST message (that is, it does not broadcast the message but it uses the TCP/IP address of the DHCP server). If the DHCP server is online, it responds to the message with a DHCPACK message. This message contains the length of the lease and any configuration information that needs to be updated. The client then updates its configuration to match the new information (if any) received from the server.

If the DHCP server that assigned the address to the client is not available, the client maintains its current TCP/IP configuration as originally assigned by the DHCP server. It attempts to contact the server again with a DHCPREQUEST message when seven-eighths (87.5 percent) of the lease has expired. Although the original DHCP server can respond with a DHCPACK message, any DHCP server can respond to the DHCPREQUEST message with a DHCPNACK. This response forces the client to drop its DHCP lease and attempt to lease a different one.

Manual DHCP Lease Renewal   You may find a need to release the DHCP-assigned address from a client, such as during a DHCP reservation or when moving a system from one network to another. In such situations, you can manually release and/or renew the DHCP addresses. To accomplish this task, you need to run the IPCONFIG application from a command prompt (see Figure 9-3).

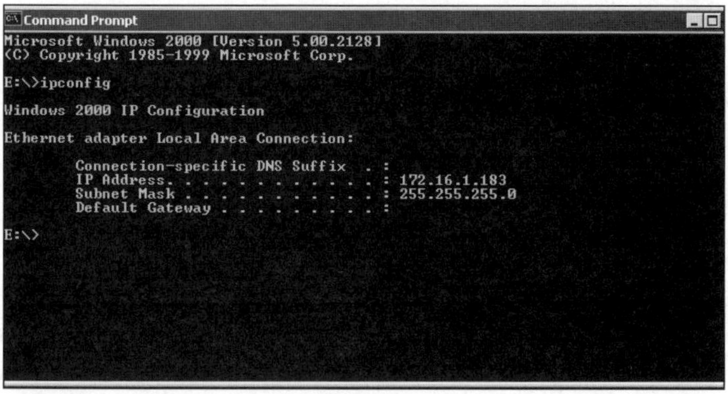

Figure 9-3   Output from ipconfig

To renew the DHCP-assigned address, you can issue the IPCONFIG /RENEW command. This command sends a DHCPREQUEST message to the DHCP server that originally assigned it the TCP/IP address. In most cases, it does not change the TCP/IP address, but simply updates any configuration changes from the server. If you configured a reservation, that reserved TCP/IP address is assigned.

In some situations, you may want the client to receive a new TCP/IP address either from the same DHCP server that assigned the previous address or from a new DHCP server. In such cases, you issue the IPCONFIG /RELEASE command, which forces the DHCP client to drop its entire DHCP configuration. At this point, the client is no longer able to communicate on the network. You must issue the IPCONFIG /RENEW command to restart the entire lease request process.

DHCP and Active Directory

To allow for greater control over DHCP in Windows 2000 Server, you must authorize all DHCP servers in Active Directory. A DHCP service will start only if it has been authorized. If no authorization has been issued, the service will fail.

When a DHCP server attempts to start, it broadcasts a change status message to Active Directory. If any changes in the authorization are detected, the DHCP server responds accordingly. This scheme allows you to deauthorize a server without having to visit the actual system on which the DHCP service is running. You would simply remove the authorization, and the DHCP service would stop the next time it detects the change.

DHCP Scopes

After the DHCP service is installed and running (and authorized in Active Directory), you need to configure a **DHCP scope**. A scope is simply a logical boundary that is assigned to TCP/IP addresses. That is, the scope is the "pool" of addresses from which the server is allowed to pull to lease to clients. When configuring the scope, you need to supply the following information:

- The name for the scope
- A description for the scope (optional)
- An address range
- A subnet mask
- A list of excluded addresses (optional)
- The length of the lease

In the New Scope Wizard (shown in Figure 9-4), you have the chance of configuring some DHCP options that may be sent to all DHCP clients. As stated previously, these options include the default gateway, host name, and DNS server addresses. Creating a DHCP scope is detailed in Hands-on Project 9-8.

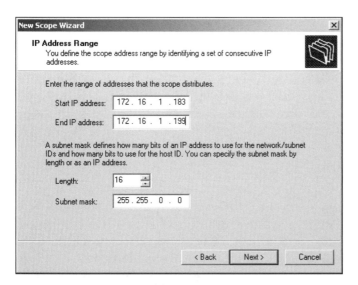

Figure 9-4 New Scope Wizard.

Windows 2000 Server also supports two other types of scopes: **superscopes** and **multicast scopes**. Superscopes are simply an administrative way to combine two or more scopes into a single administrative unit. They are most commonly used when a network grows beyond its original boundaries, requiring more than one scope to define it. Multicast scopes are designed for collaborative applications, such as streaming multimedia or conferencing. This type of scope allows you to send information to a single directed address and have the entire multicast group receive and process the information. Before multicast scopes existed, the only way to configure a multicast group was to manually assign addresses to the clients that were to participate. Hands-on Project 9-9 details how to create a superscope; the creation of a multicast scope is discussed in Hands-on Project 9-10.

NETWORK ORGANIZATION

Windows 2000 Server uses the TCP/IP networking and domain models as its network model. The next two sections define and examine subnets and gateways, as well as Internet (and Windows 2000) domains.

Subnets and Gateways

A **subnet** is a logical boundary on your network. A computer uses the subnet mask to determine whether a system it is trying to contact is local or remote. Anything that exists within the same network is "local." Likewise, any systems outside the subnet are "remote."

You can think of a subnet as being analogous to a city. Any mail sent within the city is local; therefore, it can be delivered directly to the recipient. When you need to send a package to a resident in the city, you simply put enough local postage on it and drop it off at the post office. The post office then delivers the package to its destination.

When the package is destined for a remote location (such as another city or state), the post office recognizes that fact and sends the package to that site. It then becomes the responsibility of the remote site to deliver the package. For that remote site, the package becomes local.

With TCP/IP networks, the data are sent to the default gateway. Simply put, a default gateway is a device (a multihomed computer or a router) that can communicate between two networks. Any information that is destined to a remote system is passed to the default gateway and eventually sent to its destination.

Domains

Computers use TCP/IP and MAC addresses to find and contact each other. People do not have the ability to remember the TCP/IP addresses of systems. For example, if you were asked to give Microsoft's Web site address, you would answer *www.microsoft.com*. If you were asked to give Microsoft's TCP/IP or MAC address, however, you would most likely need to look up that information. To simplify the naming conventions, domains were created.

Domains are analogous to the root system for a tree (see Figure 9-5). At the top of the tree, you find the root. The root is usually shown as a period (.), although this period is assumed and not usually written. Directly below the root are the top-level domains. They include .com, .org, .mil, .edu, and .net, as well as the various country codes (for example, .us, .ca, .uk).

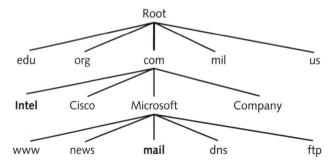

Figure 9-5 Domain structure

Below the top-level domains are the second-level domains, which are controlled by individual organizations. For example, Microsoft controls the Microsoft.com domain, and no other company can make changes to it. In contrast, no one really owns the top-level domains. They are controlled by InterNIC, the company that controls the registration of domain names.

CHAPTER SUMMARY

- Users are the people who access resources on the network. At a minimum, a user is granted a user name and a password. Users are also granted permissions to access and modify resources on the network.

- Three protocols exist in Windows 2000 to assist with name resolution and address assignment. DNS bridges the gap between TCP/IP addresses and Internet names, whereas WINS resolves TCP/IP addresses and NetBIOS names. DHCP is a protocol that is used to dynamically assign TCP/IP addresses and other network-related values—such as the default gateway, DNS server, or WINS server—to computers.

- A Windows 2000 network is made up of subnets. Subnets are simply logical boundaries that are set on networks. For networks to communicate with each other between subnets, a device (either a router or a default gateway) must be present that passes information between the networks.

KEY TERMS

Active Directory-integrated zone — A zone that allows for Active Directory security to control replication of the database information.

Address (A) resource record — An address resolution from a regular name to a TCP/IP address.

Canonical Name — An alias that can be assigned to a TCP/IP host.

default gateway — A device (a multihomed computer or a router) that can communicate between two different networks.

DHCP lease — An IP address, subnet mask, and optional parameters that are given to a DHCP client for a configured amount of time.

DHCP scope — A logical grouping of TCP/IP addresses that can be assigned to DHCP clients by the server.

Domain Name Service (DNS) — A dynamic method for resolving TCP/IP addresses to Internet names, and vice versa.

Dynamic Host Configuration Protocol (DHCP) — A protocol that allows for the automatic configuration of TCP/IP properties for clients.

forward lookup zone — The zone in charge of Internet name to TCP/IP address resolution.

Full Zone Transfer (AXFR) — A complete transfer of all zone information from the primary site to the secondary sites.

Incremental Zone Transfer (IXFR) — A partial transfer of modified zone information between the primary and secondary sites.

Mail Exchanger — A DNS record used to resolve which server in the domain takes charge of e-mail.

master zone — See *standard primary zone*.

multicast scope — A scope that is used to send collaborative information to a group of computers without the need to manually configure the clients.

name resolution — The method of converting between human-readable names and computer names and addresses.

Name Server — A DNS record that defines which server in the domain acts as the name server.

Pointer — A DNS record that resolves a TCP/IP address to its Internet name.

resources — Name resolution information for a zone.

reverse lookup zone — A zone that maintains the pointer records and resolves IP addresses to names.

Service Location — Allows you to configure services that are located on remote systems.

standard primary zone — The authority for the zone. It is in charge of all changes to the domains.

standard secondary zone — A read-only copy of the standard primary zone database. It is used for fault tolerance and load balancing.

Start of Authority (SOA) — A DNS record that defines the different timeout and TTL values for the domain.

subnet — A logical boundary on a network.

superscope — A process of combining two or more scopes to group them into a single administrative unit.

Windows Internet Name Service (WINS) — A service that resolves NetBIOS names (or computer names) to TCP/IP addresses.

WINS — A DNS record that defines the TCP/IP address of one or more WINS servers on the network.

zone — A logical group of addresses.

zone database file — A simple text file in a standard zone that is used by DNS to resolve TCP/IP names and addresses.

zone transfer — The process of transferring information between standard primary and standard secondary servers.

Review Questions

1. Which of the following DHCP options is not a required value?

    a. Default gateway

    b. TCP/IP address

    c. Subnet mask

    d. Lease length

2. Windows 2000 Server domains and Internet domains are one and the same. True or False?

3. Which of the following is not a DHCP message?
    a. DHCPDISCOVER
    b. DHCPOFFER
    c. DHCPREQUEST
    d. DHCPACCEPT
4. A DHCP gateway must be authorized in the Active Directory before it can assign TCP/IP addresses. True or False?
5. A DHCP server can have a DHCP-assigned IP address. True or False?
6. After a scope is created, the subnet mask cannot be changed without deleting and recreating the scope. True or False?
7. Which of the following is not a zone type in Windows 2000 Server DNS?
    a. Active Directory-integrated
    b. Active Directory-authorized
    c. Standard primary
    d. Standard secondary
8. A Windows 2000 network does not require NetBEUI names to operate, so it does not require WINS. True or False?
9. A DHCP client will attempt to renew its lease at _____ percent of the lease time.
10. If a DHCP client cannot renew its lease at the amount of time specified in Question 9, it will attempt again at _____ percent of the lease time.
11. If the primary DNS server cannot resolve a name, the secondary server will attempt to resolve it. True or False?
12. Static mappings can be created with WINS. True or False?
13. What is a default gateway used for?
    a. Communication with local networks
    b. Communication with remote networks
    c. Name resolution for TCP/IP names
    d. Name resolution for NetBIOS names
14. Windows 2000 Server running DNS cannot act as a standard secondary zone to a Windows NT 4.0 Server. True or False?
15. DHCP is a Microsoft standard rather than an industry standard. True or False?

HANDS-ON PROJECTS

Project 9-1

To install the Domain Name Service:

1. Click **Start** and choose **Programs, Administrative Tools, Configure Your Server**.
2. Click the **Advanced** option in the left pane of the window and choose **Optional Components**.
3. Click **Start** in the right pane to start the Windows Component Wizard.
4. Highlight the **Networking Services** option and click **Details**.
5. Select the **Domain Name System (DNS)** option (as shown in Figure 9-6), and click **OK**.
6. Back in the Windows Component Wizard, click **Next** and complete the steps as prompted.

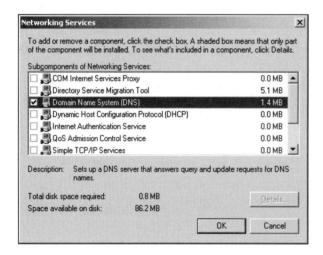

Figure 9-6 Setting up Domain Name Service

Project 9-2

To create a standard primary zone:

1. Click **Start** and choose **Programs, Administrative Tools, DNS**. (See Figure 9-7.)
2. Highlight the server in which you want to create the zone.
3. Click the **Action** menu and choose **New Zone**. The New Zone Wizard starts.
4. Click **Next**. Figure 9-8 is displayed and prompts you to choose the zone type.

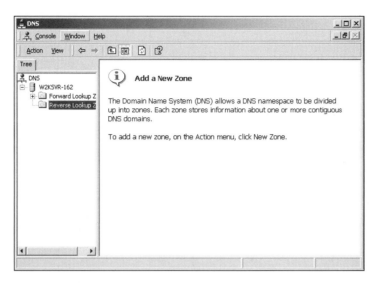

Figure 9-7 The DNS configuration tool

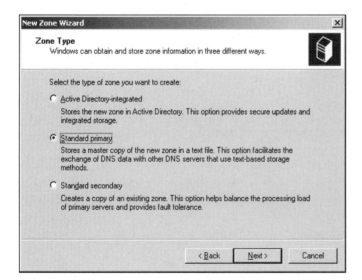

Figure 9-8 Configuring a standard primary zone

5. Select **Standard primary** and click **Next**.
6. In the **Name** field, enter a name to be assigned to this zone (it will usually be the domain name for which this DNS server is being configured). Click **Next**.
7. Choose either to create a new database file or to use an existing one. Notice that the filename is automatically created as the name assigned in Step 5 with the *.dns* extension added. Click **Next**.
8. Click **Finish** to complete the primary zone creation.

Project 9-3

To create a standard secondary zone:

1. Click **Start** and choose **Programs**, **Administrative Tools**, **DNS**.
2. Highlight the server in which you want to create the zone.
3. Click the **Action** menu and choose **New Zone**. The New Zone Wizard starts.
4. Click **Next**.
5. Select the **Standard secondary** option, and click **Next** (see Figure 9-9).

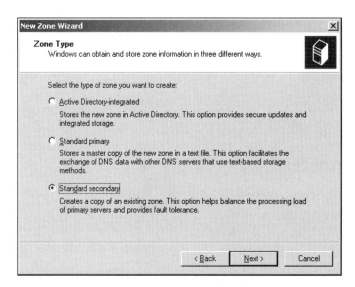

Figure 9-9 Configuring a standard secondary zone

6. In the **Name** field, enter a name to be assigned to this zone (it will usually be the domain name for which this DNS server is being configured). Click **Next**.
7. Enter the TCP/IP address of the primary zone server in the **IP Address** field, and click **Add**. Click **Next**.
8. Click **Finish** to complete the zone creation.

Project 9-4

To create a Active Directory-integrated zone:

1. Click **Start** and choose **Programs**, **Administrative Tools**, **DNS**.
2. Highlight the server in which you want to create the zone.
3. Click the **Action** menu and choose **New Zone**. The New Zone Wizard starts.
4. Click **Next**.
5. Ensure that the **Active Directory-integrated** option is selected, and click **Next** (see Figure 9-10).

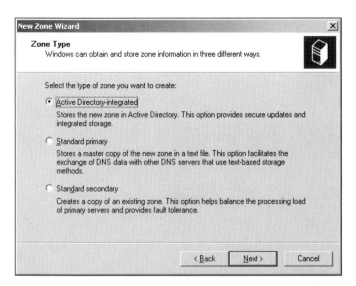

Figure 9-10 Configuring an Active Directory-integrated zone

6. In the **Name** field, enter a name to be assigned to this zone (it will usually be the domain name for which this DNS server is being configured). Click **Next**.

7. Click **Finish** to complete the zone creation.

Project 9-5

To create a reverse lookup zone:

1. Click **Start** and choose **Programs**, **Administrative Tools**, **DNS**.

2. Highlight the **Reverse Lookup Zones** option in the left pane. Click the **Action** menu and choose **New Zone**. The New Zone Wizard starts.

3. Click **Next**.

4. Choose the zone option that you would like to configure (**Active Directory-integrated**, **Standard primary**, or **Standard secondary**), and click **Next**.

5. Enter the **Network ID** (see Figure 9-11) or specify that you will manually create the reverse lookup zone. Click **Next**.

6. Choose either to create a new database file or to use an existing one (again, this file will have the *.dns* extension), and click **Next**.

7. Click **Finish**.

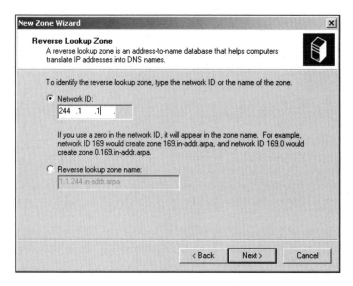

Figure 9-11 Configuring a reverse lookup zone

Project 9-6

To install the Windows Internet Name Service:

1. Click **Start** and choose **Programs**, **Administrative Tools**, **Configure Your Server**.
2. Click the **Advanced** option in the left pane of the window.
3. Choose the **Optional Components** selection from the left pane.
4. Click **Start** in the right pane to start the Windows Component Wizard.
5. Highlight the **Networking Services** option, and click the **Details** button.
6. Select the **Windows Internet Name Service (WINS)** option (as shown in Figure 9-12), and click **OK**.
7. In the Windows Components Wizard, click **Next**, then click **Finish**.

Project 9-7

To install the Dynamic Host Configuration Protocol service:

1. Click **Start** and choose **Programs**, **Administrative Tools**, **Configure Your Server**.
2. Click the **Advanced** option in the left pane of the window, and choose **Optional Components**.
3. Click **Start** in the right pane to start the Windows Component Wizard.
4. Highlight the **Networking Services** option, and click the **Details** button.
5. Select the **Dynamic Host Configuration Protocol (DHCP)** option (as shown in Figure 9-13), and click **OK**.
6. In the Windows Components Wizard, click **Next**, then click **Finish**.

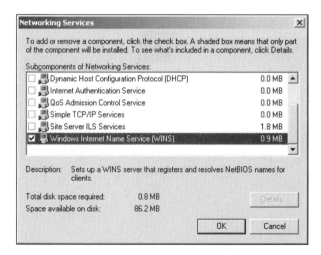

Figure 9-12 Setting up Windows Internet Naming Service

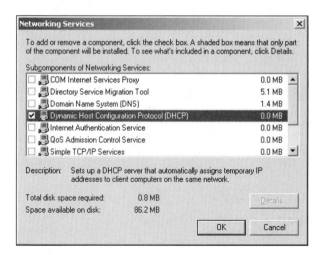

Figure 9-13 Setting up Dynamic Host Configuration Protocol

Project 9-8

To create a new DHCP scope:

1. Click **Start** and choose **Programs**, **Administrative Tools**, **DHCP**.
2. Select the server to configure, then, from the **Action** menu, choose the **New Scope** option. The New Scope Wizard starts.
3. Click **Next**.
4. Enter a name for the scope and an optional description, and click the **Next** button.
5. Enter the starting and ending TCP/IP addresses that will define this scope, as well as the subnet mask (see Figure 9-14). Click **Next**.

266 Chapter 9 Network Identification

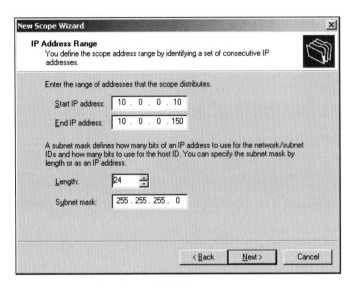

Figure 9-14 Creating a DHCP scope

6. Enter any TCP/IP address exclusions (these include TCP/IP addresses of static systems such as servers), as shown in Figure 9-15. Click **Next**.

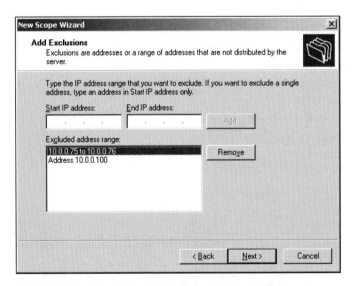

Figure 9-15 Excluding addresses within a DHCP scope

 If you need to exclude a single TCP/IP address, simply enter the address for both the start and end address and click Add.

7. Enter the lease duration, and click **Next**.

8. You are now asked if you want to configure the optional settings now or later. If you choose to configure them now, you see three screens (Figures 9-16 through 9-18): Router (Default Gateway), Domain Name and DNS Servers, and WINS Servers, respectively.

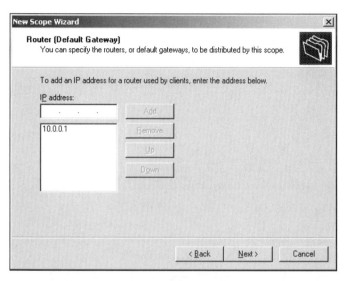

Figure 9-16 Configuring an optional default gateway with DHCP

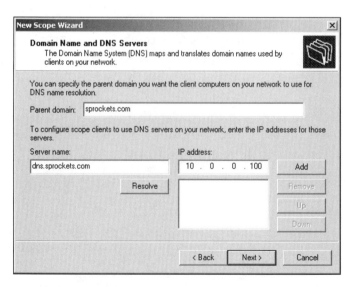

Figure 9-17 Configuring an optional DNS server with DHCP

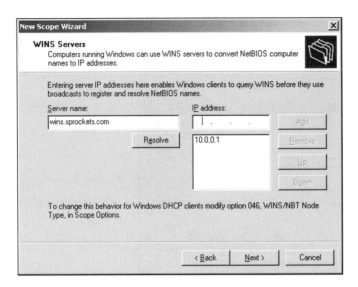

Figure 9-18 Configuring an optional WINS server with DHCP

9. Choose whether you will activate the scope. By activating the scope, you allow the DHCP server to start assigning IP addresses. Click **Next**.
10. Click **Finish**.

Project 9-9

To complete this project, please repeat Hands-on Project 9-8 and create a different scope so that two scopes are available to create the superscope.

To configure a superscope:

1. Click **Start** and choose **Programs**, **Administrative Tools**, **DHCP**.
2. From the **Action** menu, choose the **New Superscope** option. The New Superscope Wizard starts.
3. Click **Next**.
4. Enter a name for the superscope, and click **Next**.
5. Select two (or more) scopes to include in the superscope (see Figure 9-19), and click **Next**.

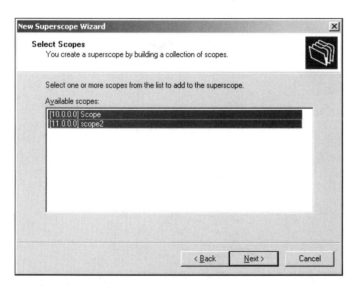

Figure 9-19 Setting up a superscope

6. Click **Finish**.

Project 9-10

To configure a multicast scope:

1. Click **Start** and choose **Programs**, **Administrative Tools**, **DHCP**.
2. From the **Action** menu, choose the **New Multicast Scope** option. The New Multicast Scope Wizard starts.
3. Click **Next**.
4. Enter a name and an optional description for the multicast scope, and click the **Next** button.
5. Enter a valid TCP/IP range (from 224.1.1.1 to 224.1.1.254), and click the **Next** button, as shown in Figure 9-20.
6. Add any address exclusions for this scope, and click **Next**.
7. Enter a value for the term of the lease (the default is 30 days), and click **Next**.
8. Choose whether to activate this multicast scope, and click **Next**.
9. Click **Finish**.

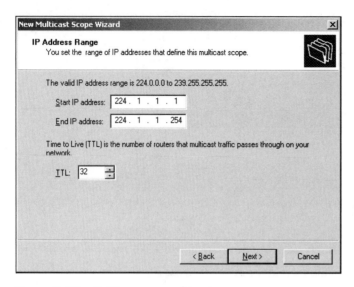

Figure 9-20 Setting up a multicast scope

CASE PROJECTS

1. You upgrade your network to a Windows 2000 network. You still have some Windows 95/98 systems on the network. Do you continue to require WINS to resolve names?

2. Your organization would like to connect to the Internet and control all of its Internet names and domains. Which Windows 2000 service would you need to implement?

3. As an administrator, you have been asked to implement a TCP/IP-based network. One task that you would like to avoid is the manual assignment of TCP/IP addresses to each of your network's workstations. Which Windows 2000 service would you install?

4. You currently have a Windows NT 4.0 network installed. You would like to upgrade your network to a Windows 2000 network with Active Directory. Do you have to upgrade the DNS servers to Windows 2000 dynamic DNS at the first step or the last? Why or why not?

CHAPTER 10

ORGANIZING NETWORK RESOURCES

> **After reading this chapter and completing the exercises, you will be able to:**
> - Understand the differences between an Active Directory domain and a Windows NT domain
> - Explore Active Directory organizational units, domains, trees, and forests
> - Maintain and control the Active Directory
> - Understand how Active Directory maintains its files and logs
> - Complete a backup of the Active Directory
> - Recover and restore the Active Directory in case of failure

A major drawback of Windows NT was its flat directory structure. In the Windows NT networking world, there were really only two types of users: administrators and regular users. Administrators were all-powerful, whereas regular users really had no permissions to handle any management functions. In small organizations with one or two administrators, this structure was not really an issue because administrators could easily communicate any changes that they wanted to perform on the network. In large enterprise environments with many administrators, however, different levels of administrators are needed. For example, there might be a need for an administrator to control all users and groups in a specific department without that administrator having the power to modify users and groups in any other department. The only way to accomplish this task in Windows NT was to create multiple domains, which is not the most efficient way of designing a Microsoft Windows NT network.

With Windows 2000, Microsoft introduces a new way of looking at directory objects, such as users and groups. This new method is known as the Microsoft **Active Directory**. With Active Directory, Windows 2000 offers a way to create users with different permissions. Instead of giving a user the permission to modify all users and groups (as is the case in Windows NT), Windows 2000 allows you to give them the permission to modify only certain users and groups.

This chapter discusses the Microsoft Active Directory, and how you should prepare, design, maintain, and recover it. You will also learn the differences between a Windows NT domain and a Windows 2000 Active Directory domain.

USER AND RESOURCE IDENTIFICATION

Before you can truly understand what Active Directory means for your organization, you need to be clear on the differences between an Active Directory domain and a Windows NT domain. The best way to understand these differences is to compare the logical structures of the two types of domains. In the following sections, you will learn the components that make up both of these directories.

Active Directory consists of as many as five components:

- Object
- Organizational unit
- Domain
- Tree
- Forest

The subsequent sections detail each of these components and describe how they fit into the Active Directory scheme.

Object

An **object** is the smallest unit within the Active Directory. The role of the Active Directory is to control all of these objects. Objects can include computers, contacts, groups, printers, shared folders, and users.

Objects can be further divided into their **object attributes**. The object attributes define the configuration of each object. For example, a user object can contain several attributes, including first name, middle initial, last name, logon name, password, and description. Some of these attributes are mandatory, such as a name (either the first name, last name, or initials) and a logon name (see Figure 10-1). Other attributes are optional, such as a password and description.

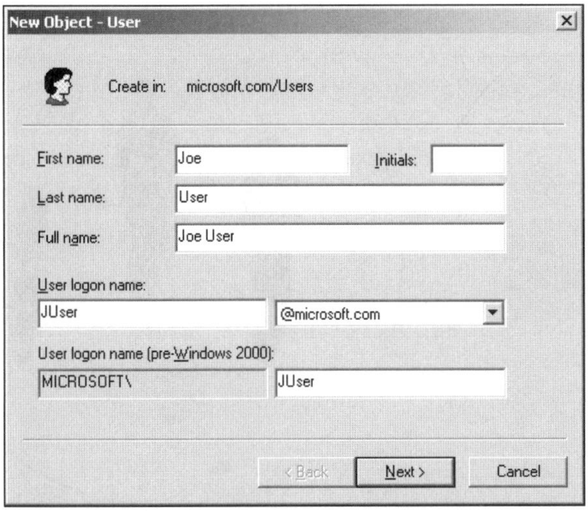

Figure 10-1 Active Directory object attributes

Microsoft has designed Active Directory so that you can extend it and modify it as you see fit. To do so, you need to create definitions for new objects, or **object classes**. The definitions for all object classes within the Active Directory are stored within the **schema**. The schema is the way in which the Active Directory recognizes different objects. You can modify the schema to add information, such as a user's picture.

Organizational Unit

An **organizational unit (OU)** is a container that organizes objects within a domain into a single administrative unit. You can then assign permissions or administrative roles to these organizational units. Organizational units can also be used to separate departments (such as Accounting, Research and Development, and Human Resources) and maintain all of their resources in one place. For example, you may want to configure an Accounting OU to contain all users, groups, computers, and printers that belong to the Accounting department. A single administrator could then be assigned to this OU who would manage this OU and no others. Figure 10-2 shows an example of an organizational unit. In the figure, the Human Resource OU contains a document that can be sent to the printer located in the Accounting OU.

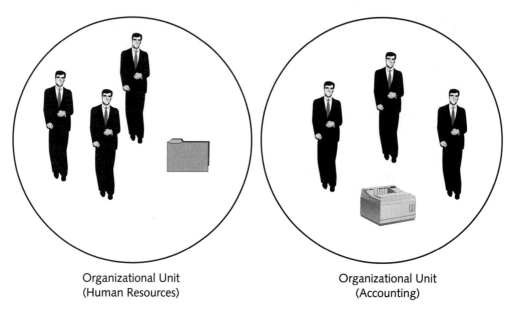

Organizational Unit (Human Resources)   Organizational Unit (Accounting)

Figure 10-2 Organizational unit

Domain

It is important to understand the differences between a Windows 2000 Active Directory domain and a Windows NT 4.0 domain. In essence, an **Active Directory domain** is the same as an Internet domain, whereas a **Windows NT domain** is a logical collection of computers that share the same security information and user database.

A domain is a security context that is assigned to multiple computers and users. Domains are logical, meaning that computers in the domain do not need to be physically close to one another. In fact, two computers connected to the same Ethernet hub may reside in different domains. Each will have the security set to it by the domain controllers. All objects within a domain share the same administration configuration, security context, and directory replication.

A Windows 2000 domain differs from a Windows NT domain in the way in which the domain controllers are configured and maintained. First, you will learn how Windows NT domains operate. You will then find a definition of how Windows 2000 domains differ.

In Windows NT, a single domain will have a single **primary domain controller (PDC)** and, optionally, one or more **backup domain controllers (BDCs)**. The PDC maintains the only version of the directory database that can be directly updated. All changes to the database are performed on the PDC and then replicated to the BDCs. If the PDC goes offline, no changes to the domain may be made, including modification of user properties or computer memberships in the domain, until a BDC is promoted to become a PDC.

During this promotion stage, information that has not been replicated from the PDC to the BDC may be lost.

Windows 2000 uses the **multimaster replication** method. With this method, each **domain controller** stores and maintains a writable, or read-write, version of the portion of the Active Directory database that belongs to its domain, or its domain's partition. When any changes are made to the databases of any of the domain controllers, they are replicated to all members of that domain. Because all domain controllers maintain the same read-write Active Directory database, the entire Active Directory partition is available to any domain controller at any time. If a domain controller fails, the other domain controllers within the domain will automatically take over its role until it comes back into the network. Figure 10-3 depicts an Active Directory domain.

 The read-write portion of the Active Directory database is also known as a **replica**.

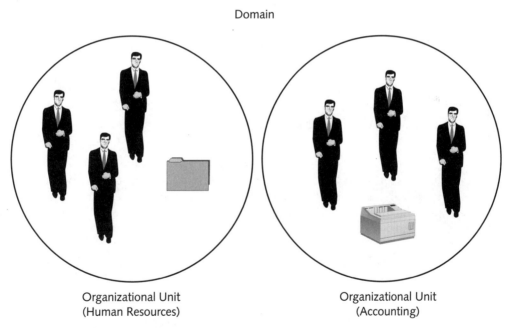

Figure 10-3 Active Directory domain

Tree

When multiple domains are connected so that they share a common schema, a **tree** is created. Domains within a tree are linked together by using **trust relationships**. Unlike with Windows NT, Windows 2000 trust relationships are based on the Kerberos protocol. Previously, trust relationships were not secured by a protocol.

 Unlike in Windows NT, trust relationships are transitive in Windows 2000. That is, if you have three domains in your organization (Accounting, Human Resources, and R&D), and Accounting trusts Human Resources and Human Resources trusts R&D, then Accounting will automatically trust R&D.

All domains within a tree share a common root domain name (for example, Lanw.com). Figure 10-4 shows an example of a Windows 2000 tree.

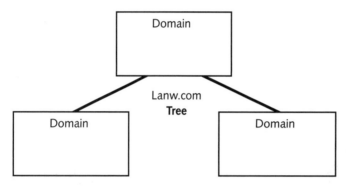

Figure 10-4 Active Directory tree

Forest

When one or more trees do not share the same root domain name but maintain the same schema and configuration, they are said to be part of a **forest** (see Figure 10-5). All trees within the forest trust each other using automatic transitive trusts. If your organization has multiple forests in it, explicit trusts must be configured.

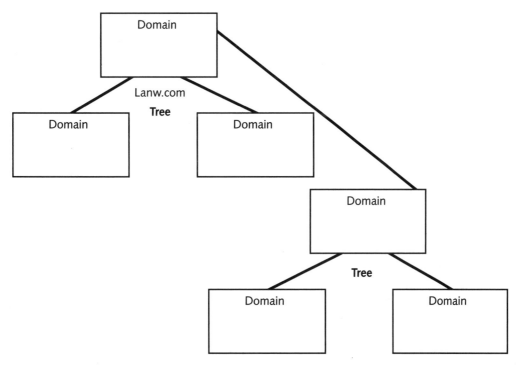

Figure 10-5 Active Directory forest

PREPARING FOR ACTIVE DIRECTORY

Microsoft's Active Directory is an extremely complex system. Although you may not fully understand all of its inner workings, you must be aware of how to prepare for Active Directory. Two scenarios for installing Windows 2000 with Active Directory exist: upgrading an existing Windows NT network and installing a new Windows 2000 network. The next two sections will detail some of the prerequisites and criteria that must be met before installing Active Directory.

Upgrading an Existing Windows NT Network

Remember that Windows 2000 Active Directory is based on the Internet domain structure and therefore requires you to install and configure TCP/IP and DNS. Active Directory installation is covered in Hands-on Project 10-1.

When your organization decides to upgrade its existing network to a Windows 2000 network, you may have to deal with some basic issues. Windows 2000 can run in one of two modes: **mixed mode** or **native mode**. Any time that at least one domain controller is still running Windows NT, the network is said to be running in mixed mode.

Mixed Mode

Mixed mode is necessary because of the way in which Windows NT and Windows 2000 differ. In a Windows NT network (one that is configured with domains), a single domain controller acts as the PDC. That system maintains the directory database and is the only system that can modify this database. In a Windows 2000 network, every domain controller maintains a read-write copy of the database. Modifications take place on the local domain controller, with the updated information being replicated to all of the members within the domain. If you were to configure a network with both Windows NT and Windows 2000 domain controllers, you would have an obvious problem: The Windows 2000 domain controllers would attempt to modify the database on their own, without notifying the PDC.

To support the Windows NT networking model, each Windows 2000 domain can designate a single domain controller to act as a PDC. This domain controller is known as the **PDC emulator**. It is the first domain controller that is upgraded in the Active Directory domain that assumes this role. As far as the Windows NT BDCs are concerned, this domain controller becomes the PDC and therefore controls all changes to the domain. Any new Windows 2000 domain controller that is added will maintain a read-write copy of the database (as per the Windows 2000 multimaster replication model). It then simply acts as a gateway between the Windows 2000 and the Windows NT networks. Because the Windows 2000 PDC emulator appears to be a Windows NT PDC to the rest of the Windows NT network, no changes need to be made on the clients. They will still see the network as though nothing has changed.

Once all domain controllers in the domain have been upgraded to Windows 2000, the network will continue to run in mixed mode. To change the way in which the network operates, you would have to manually reconfigure the network into native mode.

Native Mode

As the name implies, native mode is the way in which Windows 2000 systems communicate with other Windows 2000 systems. For this mode to work, you need to upgrade all of your domain controllers to Windows 2000. Table 10-1 highlights the differences between a Windows 2000 network running in mixed mode and one that is running in native mode.

Table 10-1 Mixed mode versus native mode

Mixed Mode	Native Mode
Multimaster replication	Multimaster replication
Nontransitive trusts	Transitive trusts
Only global and local groups exist because Windows NT does not support other group types	All Windows 2000 groups are supported, including domain local, local, global, and universal
No nested security groups	Nested security groups

The easiest way to upgrade an existing Windows NT network to Windows 2000 is to perform an **in-place upgrade**.

In this type of upgrade, all current domain configurations are maintained. Before you complete an upgrade, however, Microsoft recommends that you perform the following steps:

- Back up your current system, especially the domain controllers.
- Verify that the backups were completed and the data on the tapes are valid.
- Synchronize the entire domain. This step ensures that all domain controllers have the most up-to-date information.
- Remove one BDC from the network. This BDC will be used for two tasks. First, it will be used to check the backup of the domain. Second, it will be maintained as a backup during and after the upgrade (for one or two weeks). Once this BDC is removed from the domain, promote it to a PDC and make sure that no directory data have been corrupted. Restore the backup and again verify that no directory data have been corrupted.

Once you have tested the backup for the Windows NT domain, you can upgrade the PDC to Windows 2000. Once the upgrade is complete and stable, you can upgrade each of the remaining BDCs.

Installing a New Windows 2000 Network

The simplest way to install Windows 2000 Active Directory is by installing a fresh copy of the operating system on all servers. This tactic may not be feasible for most organizations, but it is the cleanest way to install the system. One problem with such an installation is that all users, groups, and applications must be reinstalled on the domain.

When installing Active Directory on a Windows 2000 Server, you use the Active Directory Installation Wizard. This wizard introduces a new feature into Windows 2000 that has been lacking from the Windows NT networking world since its initial release: the ability to upgrade and downgrade regular servers to domain controllers. In Windows NT, you had the option to configure the server as either a PDC, a BDC, or a stand-alone server. Once this choice was made, the only way to make a domain controller become a stand-alone server or a stand-alone server become a domain controller was to reinstall the operating system. Today, third-party tools and nonsupported methods of moving a domain controller from one domain to another are available, but there is no way to install or uninstall the domain controller components. The Active Directory Installation Wizard (see Figure 10-6), called **Dcpromo.exe**, is found in the WINNT\System32 directory. It allows you to install your server as a domain controller or to remove it as one. Note that doing so requires you to reboot the server.

Figure 10-6 Active Directory Installation Wizard

When running the Active Directory Installation Wizard, your server must have an NTFS partition that is formatted in NTFS version 5. The installation will fail if no such partition exists.

The installation wizard gives you the choice either to configure DNS yourself or to have the wizard do it for you.

Remember that Windows 2000 depends on TCP/IP and especially on DNS. Without DNS, Active Directory will not function properly. If your organization has registered its Internet domain with an Internet registrar (such as Network Systems), then you can use that domain name for the Active Directory domain name (for example, sprockets.com).

DESIGNING DIRECTORY STRUCTURES

No set rules dictate how you must design and name your Active Directory structure. Every organization will take a different tack. These differences could reflect the inherent way in which the organization is structured (a small local organization versus a large, multinational one). Nevertheless, one configuration item must exist and must follow a set of rules: the root domain.

The first domain that you install and configure in Active Directory is known as the **root domain**. When you choose a root domain, you must follow certain guidelines:

- Choose a name that will not change. Although some name changes are unavoidable, such as those caused by a corporate restructuring or a merger, you should nevertheless try to stick with a name that is static.

- Make sure that the name matches your organization's Internet name. This choice will ensure connectivity between Active Directory and the Internet. For example, everyone knows that Microsoft's domain is *microsoft.com*.

The levels within the Active Directory tree will depend on the organization in which Active Directory is being installed. Some organizations will choose to name the child and grandchild domains based on geographical locations, whereas others will use department names (for example, *seattle.microsoft.com* and *sales.microsoft.com*). It does not matter which method your organization decides to use—just make sure to adhere to this standard. Nothing is more confusing than a domain that uses both of these methods at the same level. (For example, using both at the same time would introduce the question for Microsoft: Where is the sales team in relation to the Seattle office? Or, is there no sales department in Seattle?) You can, however, use both methods effectively, such as in the following example:

sales.seattle.microsoft.com and *sales.newyork.microsoft.com*.

Once your organization has determined its preferred domain structure, you can start to design the organizational unit structure. Remember that OUs are containers used to collect information about objects and to set properties about them, such as applications, computers, groups, policies, printers, shares, and users.

One of the main strengths of creating and implementing organizational units is that they permit delegation of administration. A new feature in Windows 2000, **delegation of administration** allows you to implement users having different permissions. For example, you can create a marketing organization unit and assign an administrator to it. That administrator will have the right to modify the objects within the marketing organizational unit, but not in organizational units that exist above it.

TROUBLESHOOTING ACTIVE DIRECTORY

Before you can successfully troubleshoot and recover your network's Active Directory, you should understand how the Windows 2000 Active Directory stores data. The following sections will look at the files that are used to store the Active Directory database information, then examine the backup and recovery of that data.

Active Directory uses a transaction-based system for storing its information. The Active Directory is descended from the Microsoft Exchange Directory. In fact, Microsoft used some of the developers of the Exchange Directory to develop the Active Directory for Windows 2000. All modifications to the Active Directory database are carried out as transactions. This method allows for the design of highly recoverable databases. If some of the data becomes corrupted, Active Directory can rebuild the lost data from the transaction log files.

The following four steps follow the process involved in modifying the Active Directory:

1. An administrator makes a change to the Active Directory, such as modifying a group membership, and Active Directory creates a corresponding transaction.
2. The transaction is written to a log file on the disk.
3. The transaction is committed to the Active Directory database stored in memory.
4. The transaction is written to the database stored on disk. This task is normally completed at shutdown and at system idle times.

Active Directory Files

The Active Directory files can be separated into two categories: the database file and the log files. The database file stores all of the Active Directory information, whereas the log files store the transactions before they are committed to the database and maintain these transactions. The following log files exist in Active Directory:

- Transaction log files
- Checkpoint file
- Reserved log files

Database File

The database file is stored in the WINNT\NTDS directory (see Figure 10-7) and is called Ntds.dit. This file stores all Active Directory components (such as users and groups), the relationships between objects (these users are members of these groups), and the schema information (the objects that exist within the Active Directory).

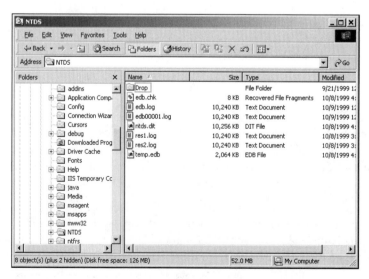

Figure 10-7 The Active Directory database and log files

Transaction Log Files

The transaction log files store all of the transactions before they are committed to the database. Notice that there is usually more than one log file and that each log file is approximately 10 MB in size. The current log file is called Edb.log. The log files are automatically set to 10 MB by the Active Directory as a placeholder, even if they contain little or no information. Once a log file is filled, it is renamed using the following naming convention:

EDBxxxxx.log

These log files are deleted when a backup is completed, as you will see in the next section. Microsoft Active Directory can log transactions in one of two ways:

- Circular logging disabled
- Circular logging enabled

With **circular logging**, the older log files are overwritten when the current log file is filled to capacity. When this option is enabled, data recovery is greatly minimized, because not all transactions may be available during the recovery process. By default, circular logging is disabled.

Checkpoint File

The checkpoint file (Edb.chk) is simply a pointer to the committed transactions. Once transactions are committed to the database, the checkpoint file is modified to reflect the noncommitted transactions. This process ensures that transactions are committed in sequence and only once.

Reserved Log Files

Active Directory automatically creates reserved log files (Res1.log and Res2.log). These log files are 10 MB in size and serve as an emergency storage location. When the transaction log file is full and Active Directory attempts to create a new one, if no more disk space exists, the transactions will be written to these two reserved log files. In this event, Active Directory will shut itself down and report an out-of-disk-space error in the event log.

Backing Up the Active Directory

Luckily for Windows 2000 administrators, the Windows 2000 new backup utility is aware of the Active Directory and will back it up properly. When you back up your system, you will notice that a new entry exists that you can select, called **System State**. Within the System State, you can choose which components to back up, such as the Active Directory, the boot files, and the Registry (see Figure 10-8). When this option is selected, all Active Directory information will be backed up.

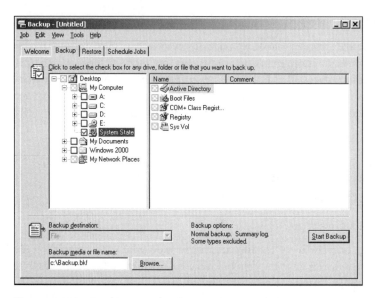

Figure 10-8 Backing up the System State

Recovering and Restoring the Active Directory

Recovering the Active Directory is somewhat more complex, because Windows 2000 will not let you restore the Active Directory while the service is running. To complete a recovery, you must reboot your server and choose the Directory Services Restore Mode option (see Hands-on Project 10-6). Once the system is restarted using this method, you can choose the System State\Active Directory option from the Restore tab of the backup program. This choice will restore your Active Directory database. You would then need to restart the system to restart the Active Directory.

CHAPTER SUMMARY

- Windows 2000 introduces a new way of organizing directory objects, called the Active Directory, which provides a way to create users with only the permissions they need.

- This chapter explored the Microsoft Active Directory and showed you how to prepare, design, maintain, and recover the Active Directory.

- It also discussed the differences between a Windows NT domain and Windows 2000 Active Directory domains.

- Finally, it explored how to back up and restore Active Directory.

Key Terms

Active Directory — A hierarchical directory database used in Windows 2000 to store all object information, including information about users, groups, and computers.

Active Directory domain — A logical domain of Windows 2000 computers that share the same security and user information.

backup domain controller (BDC) — A Windows NT Server that maintains a read-only version of the directory database to authenticate users.

circular logging — A process by which older log files are overwritten as the current log file fills to capacity. When this option is enabled, data recovery is greatly minimized.

Dcpromo.exe — The Active Directory Installation Wizard, which is found in the WINNT\System32 directory. This wizard allows you to install your server as a domain controller or to remove it as one.

delegation of administration — A Windows 2000 feature that allows you to implement users having different permissions. For example, you can create an organizational unit and assign an administrator who will have the right to modify the objects within that organizational unit, but not in organizational units that exist above it.

domain controller — A Windows 2000 Server that authenticates users in a Windows 2000 network.

forest — A collection of two or more trees with noncontiguous namespace.

in-place upgrade — An upgrade to Windows 2000 in which all current domain configurations are maintained.

mixed mode — A mode in which Windows 2000 runs so as to maintain backward compatibility with Windows NT domains.

multimaster replication — A situation in which all domain controllers maintain a read-write copy of the database that they replicate to all other domain controllers.

native mode — The way in which Windows 2000 systems communicate with other Windows 2000 systems.

object — A component of the Active Directory, such as a user, group, computer, or application.

object attributes — Configuration variables for objects.

object classes — The definitions for new objects and for object classes within the Active Directory, which are stored within the schema.

organizational unit (OU) — A way to maintain a set security model for several objects within a domain. Similar to Windows NT domains.

PDC emulator — A service that runs on a Windows 2000 system that emulates the single-master replication method used in Windows NT. This service is used until all servers have been upgraded to Windows 2000.

primary domain controller (PDC) — The Windows NT Server that maintains the master copy of the security database.

replica — A copy of part of the directory.

root domain — The top-level domain in Active Directory (for example, microsoft.com).

schema — The way in which the Active Directory recognizes different objects. You can modify the schema to add information, such as a user's picture.

System State — An option that allows you to choose which components to back up, such as the Active Directory, the boot files, and the Registry.

transitive trust — A relationship that states that if domain A trusts domain B, and domain B trusts domain C, then domain A will automatically trust domain C.

tree — A collection of domains that use the same contiguous namespace.

trust relationship — A relationship that is set up between domains so that one domain can trust resources from another domain.

Windows NT domain — A logical collection of Windows NT computers that share the same user database and security models.

REVIEW QUESTIONS

1. Active Directory is a flat database file system. True or False?
2. Windows 2000 Active Directory uses a(n) _____ replication model.
3. In a Windows 2000 network running Active Directory, every domain controller maintains a read-write version of the database. True or False?
4. Which of the following log files is used to store database transactions?
   a. Edb.log
   b. Edb00001.log
   c. Res1.log
   d. Edb.chk
5. Which of the following log files is used to store old transactions?
   a. Edb.log
   b. Edb00001.log
   c. Res1.log
   d. Edb.chk
6. Which of the following log files is used to determine which transactions have already been committed to the database?
   a. Edb.log
   b. Edb00001.log
   c. Res1.log
   d. Edb.chk

7. Which of the following log files is used in case the system runs out of disk space?
   a. Edb.log
   b. Edb00001.log
   c. Res1.log
   d. Edb.chk
8. For maximum recoverability, the log files and the database files should reside on the same partition. True or False?
9. Once a Windows 2000 Server is installed as a domain controller, it cannot be demoted to a non-domain-controller role. True or False?
10. Windows 2000 domain controllers cannot be moved from one domain to another. True or False?
11. When you want to add objects to the Active Directory Database, you would modify the _____.
12. When two or more domains share the same namespace, they are said to be in the same _____.
13. When two or more domains do not share the same namespace, they are said to be in a(n) _____.
14. Organizational units are used to group objects that require the same security rights. True or False?
15. DNS is a requirement of Active Directory. True or False?
16. Select the _____ _____ option to automatically back up certain system components, such as the Active Directory, the boot files, and the Registry.
17. With _____ _____, older log files are overwritten as the current log file fills to capacity.
18. Name the five components that make up the Active Directory.
19. What new feature in Windows 2000 allows you to implement users of different permissions?
20. What defines the configuration of each object in Windows 2000?

HANDS-ON PROJECTS

Project 10-1

To install Active Directory in a new domain:

1. Click **Start**, **Run**.
2. In the **Open** field, type **dcpromo** and then click **OK**.
3. The Active Directory Installation Wizard will appear (see Figure 10-6 earlier in the chapter). Click **Next**.

4. Choose the **Domain controller for a new domain** option, and then click **Next** (see Figure 10-9).

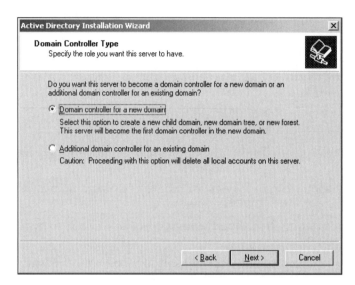

Figure 10-9 Choosing to install a new domain

5. Choose the **Create a new domain tree** option, and then click **Next** (see Figure 10-10).

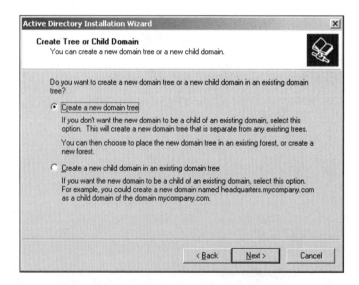

Figure 10-10 Choosing to create a new tree

6. Choose the **Create a new forest of domain trees** option, and then click **Next** (see Figure 10-11).

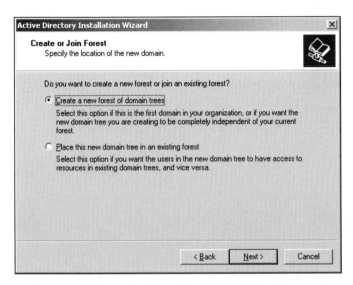

Figure 10-11 Choosing to create a new forest

7. Enter the full domain name of the desired domain, and then click **Next** (see Figure 10-12). The wizard will now check whether that domain name is already in use.

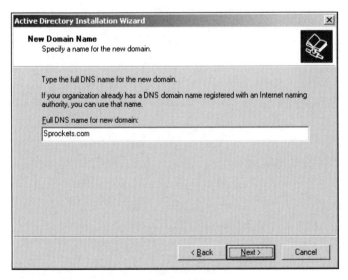

Figure 10-12 Entering the domain name

290   Chapter 10   Organizing Network Resources

8. Enter a NetBIOS domain name for backward compatibility with Windows NT systems, and then click **Next** (see Figure 10-13).

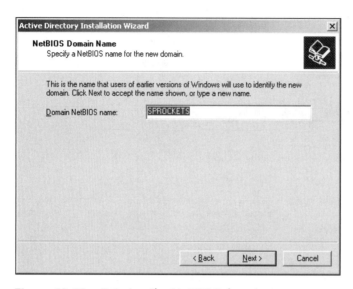

Figure 10-13   Entering the NetBIOS domain name

9. Choose a location for the Active Directory database and log files, and then click **Next** (see Figure 10-14).

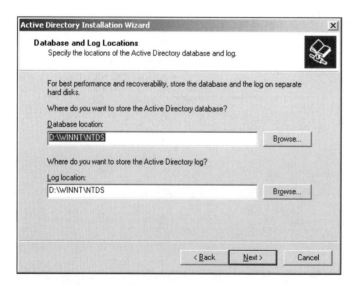

Figure 10-14   Active Directory file locations

Hands-on Projects 291

 For maximum recoverability, store the database file and the log files on two (physically different) hard drives.

10. Enter a location for the Sysvol folder (see Figure 10-15). This information will be replicated to all other domain controllers in the domain (this folder must reside on an NTFS version 5 volume).

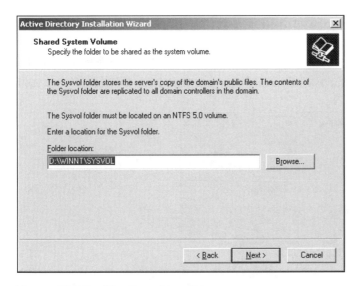

Figure 10-15 The Sysvol location

11. Choose whether to allow the wizard to automatically configure DNS for you, and then click **Next**.
12. Choose the permission compatibility for users and groups, and then click **Next**.
13. Enter a user name and password for an administrative account with the correct permissions to complete the installation, and then click **Next**.
14. Click **Next** to complete the installation. Windows 2000 will now install Active Directory.
15. Click **Finish**, and then reboot your system.

Project 10-2

To add a domain controller to an existing domain:

1. Click **Start**, **Run**.
2. In the **open** field, type **dcpromo**, and then click **OK**.

3. The Active Directory Installation Wizard will appear. Click **Next**.
4. Choose the **Additional domain controller for an existing domain** option, and then click **Next**.
5. You will be asked to authenticate the user and choose the domain.

Project 10-3

To create an organizational unit:

1. Click **Start**, **Programs**, **Administrative Tools**, **Active Directory Users and Computers**.
2. In the left pane, right-click the domain and choose **New**, **Organizational Unit**.
3. Enter a name for the organizational unit, and then click **OK** (see Figure 10-16).

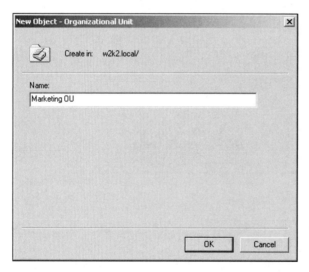

Figure 10-16 Creating a new organizational unit

Project 10-4

To enable circular logging:

1. Click **Start**, **Run**.
2. In the **open** field, type **regedt32**, and then click **OK**.
3. Browse to the **HKEY_LOCAL_MACHINE\SYSTEM\CurrentControlSet\ Services\NTDS\Parameters** key (see Figure 10-17).

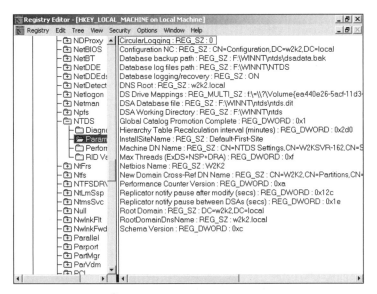

Figure 10-17 Editing the HKEY_LOCAL_MACHINE\SYSTEM\CurrentControlSet\Services\NTDS\Parameters key in regedt32

4. To enable circular logging, select **Add Value** from the **Edit** menu and name it **CircularLogging** (See Figure 10-18). Click **OK**.

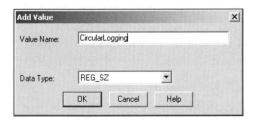

Figure 10-18 Adding a circular logging value RegEdt32

5. The String Editor dialog box appears. If you set the string to equal **1**, then circular logging will be enabled. Setting it to **0** will disable circular logging.
6. Close the Registry Editor by clicking the **Close** button at the top right of the screen.

Project 10-5

To back up Active Directory:

1. Click **Start**, **Run** and type **Ntbackup**.
2. Choose the **Backup** tab.
3. At the very least, select the **System State** option in the left pane (refer to Figure 10-8).

4. Click **Start Backup**.
5. Click **Start Backup** on the Backup Job Info dialog box.

Project 10-6

To restore Active Directory:

1. Reboot your server.
2. In the boot menu, press the **F8** key.
3. Choose the **Directory Services Restore Mode** option, and press the **Enter** key.
4. When the system restarts, log in and run the backup program.
5. Choose the **Restore** tab, select the **System State** option, and click **Start Restore**.
6. Confirm the Restore process when prompted.

CASE PROJECTS

1. Your organization is running Windows 2000 and merges with another company that is running a Windows NT domain model. How would you connect the two networks?
2. Your Active Directory server has failed. You have a good backup system, but when you run the restoration operation, it fails. Why?
3. When logging transactions, Active Directory shuts itself down and reports an out of disk space error. Why?
4. You attempt to enable your Windows NT domain controllers and Windows 2000 controllers to run in native mode, but it is not functioning properly. Why?

CHAPTER
11
SHARING NETWORK RESOURCES

> **After reading this chapter and completing the exercises, you will be able to:**
> - Understand resource sharing and the steps necessary to share resources, files, folders, and printers on a Windows 2000 Server
> - Discuss IntelliMirror and the software installation and maintenance features
> - Install and configure Internet Information Services for sharing Web resources
> - Install and configure Windows 2000 Terminal Server

Perhaps the single biggest reason for installing a network is to share resources such as files and printers. This chapter explores the areas of resource sharing. In addition, it discusses three advanced Windows 2000 features: IntelliMirror, Internet Information Server (IIS), and Terminal Server.

Resource Sharing Basics

An encounter with the topic of resource sharing poses an important initial question: What is a resource and how can it be shared? Quite simply, a resource on a Windows 2000 network is anything to which users would like access. It includes everything from disk space on the file server's hard drives to networked printers to modem pools. The principle of sharing resources inspired the development of the first networks, and it remains the foundation of Microsoft's networking model. In later sections of this chapter, we'll discuss file and printer sharing.

When a resource is connected directly to a computer on the network, the user of that computer has access to the resource. For example, before many networks were installed, each computer in a company had its own printer. If a particular user required multiple types of printers, the user had direct connections to those printers in the immediate area. As you can imagine, this approach could get rather expensive, particularly because everyone wanted laser printers sitting on their desks. In addition, if one user needed to access files that were located on another user's computer, the user had to transport the files via "sneakernet"—that is, put them on a floppy disk or tape and walk them to their destination.

With the advent of networks, this picture changed rather dramatically. Now, resources such as printers can be shared over the network to allow users who are not directly connected to the physical devices to use them. To accomplish this goal, the computer that manages the device need only be configured to allow remote users to access the resource. We'll get into the nitty gritty of how this operation is performed with particular resources in later sections of this chapter.

Finding Resources

When a resource is configured to be shared over the network, it makes this information known through a series of **broadcasts**. To find a resource on the network, the Windows-based client computers monitor the broadcasts. Windows 2000 computers keep a list of the available resources and display them when the **My Network Places** icon is accessed. Figure 11-1 shows the My Network Places dialog box for a Windows 2000 Server connected to a small network.

Although this dialog box serves a purpose similar to that of Network Neighborhood in Windows 95/98 and NT 4.0, Microsoft has expanded its functionality quite a bit. My Network Places is designed to be the location for shortcuts to your most-used shared network folders. You can create these shortcuts by using the Add Network Place applet, which is accessed by double-clicking the Add Network Place icon from within the My Network Places applet. When you select this option, you are prompted to provide the location of the **Network Place**, or you can utilize the Browse button to find the folder on the network. The LANWrights folder shown in Figure 11-1 is a shortcut to a folder on another computer on the network.

Also in the My Network Places dialog box are the Entire Network and Computers Near Me icons. Clicking the Entire Network icon displays all domains and workgroups on the network; you can browse through these items to find network resources.

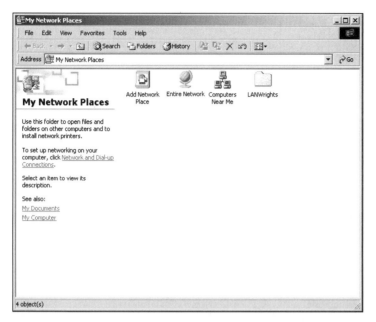

Figure 11-1 My Network Places dialog box on a Windows 2000 Server

Clicking the Computers Near Me icon displays the computers and other network resources that reside in the same domain or workgroup as the local computer. For example, if computers JOHNSYS1, AUSSERV, and MAMAPUTER are in the domain AUSTEX, and computers ANDERCOMP, DALSERV, and MARYSYS are in the domain MAINOFFICE, the Computers Near Me dialog box on JOHNSYS1 would include only JOHNSYS1, AUSSERV, and MAMAPUTER, as shown in Figure 11-2.

Because many clients that will be connecting to Windows 2000 Servers will not also run Windows 2000, it's important to note the similarities between Windows 2000 applications and applications in other Microsoft operating systems. As mentioned earlier, Network Neighborhood is the Windows 95/98 and NT 4.0 utility that is used to locate network resources. Like the Computers Near Me dialog box, Network Neighborhood lists computers in the same domain or workgroup. The Entire Network icon performs the same function in earlier versions of Windows as it does in Windows 2000—displaying all domains and workgroups on the network.

 Unfortunately for those clients using earlier versions of Windows, no quick method exists for adding shortcuts like the Add Network Place icon.

Figure 11-2 The members of the AUSTEX domain

Connecting to Resources from the Client

From a client computer on the network, connecting to shared resources is as easy as a double-click. Once the user finds a resource through the My Network Places dialog box, he or she can access it by double-clicking its icon. If the user that is logged into the client computer has been granted permission to use the resource, access will be given immediately. If the user is not on the list of users permitted access, however, an Access Denied dialog box will be displayed. You'll learn more about granting access permissions to users and groups in Chapter 12. For now, be aware that network resources can be secured from unauthorized access by using the Windows 2000 security features.

If a user is granted access to the resource, he or she can create a shortcut to the resource or use the Map Network Drive feature in Windows Explorer to create a permanent path to the object. Mapping a network drive assigns a drive letter to the remote resource so that the local operating system sees the remote drive as if it were directly attached. For example, most computer systems include multiple drives. A user may choose to connect to the network and map a drive to the location of the e-mail program used by the company. He or she might decide to use the M: drive to indicate the mail directory (although users may choose any drive letter that is not already in use). In this example, the user's Windows Explorer window will contain four drive letters, A:, C:, D:, and M:. This mapping decreases the complexity of repeatedly finding frequently used network resources and ensures that the user is always able to find the e-mail program. Many companies use this method for locating departmental folders on the network's servers as well as applications such as e-mail.

DEVICE SHARING

As mentioned earlier, for devices to be accessed by other computers on the network, they must be shared on a local computer. This statement holds true for both Windows 2000 Server and Windows 2000 Professional systems, as well as for Windows 95, 98, or NT. Like accessing shared resources, the act of sharing the device is fairly straightforward. The various permissions available for each device can, however, make it a challenge.

Using Windows Explorer and My Network Places

The first step in sharing a device is performed through Windows Explorer or My Network Places. By default, no devices are shared in Windows 2000. Each device to be accessed by remote users must be shared manually. Figure 11-3 shows the My Computer window on a basic Windows 2000 Advanced Server computer. To share the CD-ROM on this computer, you would right-click the SBE97CD2 (E:) icon and select Sharing . . . from the menu that appears. Note that you would reach the same configuration window by selecting Properties from the File menu and selecting the Sharing tab. After you make a selection, the Properties dialog box appears.

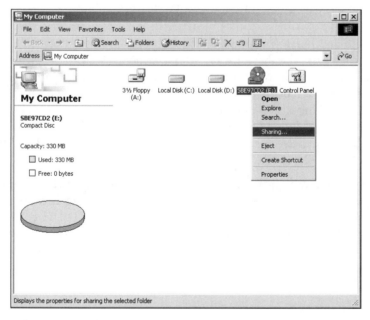

Figure 11-3 Sharing the CD-ROM on a Windows 2000 Advanced Server computer

As shown in Figure 11-4, the Do not share this folder option is selected by default. To share the device, select the Share this folder radio button. The Sharing tab of this dialog box is the same regardless of the resource being shared.

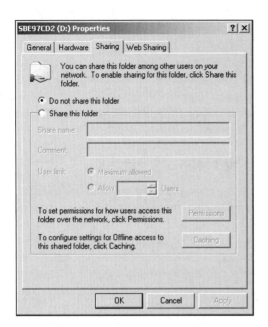

Figure 11-4 Properties dialog box for the CD-ROM device

After selecting Share this folder, you are presented with options for naming the share (share name), a comment, and the number of users who will be allowed to access the resource simultaneously. By default, the share name is the same as the device name. In the case of the CD-ROM device on the Windows 2000 Server, it is E. It is usually a good idea to change the share name to something that is easily understood by all users on the network. Imagine a network with 300 servers, all of whose E: drives were shared with the device name E. Such a network would be completely unusable. In this case, our server's name is AUSSERV, so we will call our share AUSSERV CDROM.

Comments that are added during the sharing process are displayed on client computers in Windows Explorer when the device is accessed if Windows Explorer is set to the Detail view. For the purpose of this example, we'll include the comment "CD Drive on the Austin Server." Figure 11-5 shows how this information is displayed through Windows Explorer on a client computer.

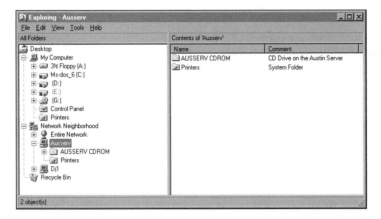

Figure 11-5 Share comments displayed on a client computer

Also on the Sharing tab of the Properties dialog box are settings for the number of users who can simultaneously be connected to the shared device, a Permissions button, a Caching button, and a New Share button. If more than one share exists for a particular device, a Remove Share button is available.

By default, the Maximum allowed radio button is selected when a share is created. It allows all users who are logged into the system to access the share. The maximum number allowed is determined by the version of Windows 2000 that is running and the operating system license. For example, Windows 2000 Professional allows only 10 active remote connections. Therefore, only 10 users could possibly access a share on a Windows 2000 Professional system at any one time. In contrast, Windows 2000 Advanced Server does not limit the number of remote connections in the same way; selecting the Maximum allowed button means that many users might be accessing the share at the same time. This point is often not an issue with hard disk devices, but may become a performance issue when accessing devices such as CD-ROM drives. For this reason, you can also establish a set number of simultaneous connections by selecting the radio button next to Allow and specifying the number of users in the coinciding list box. In Figure 11-6, we have limited the number of users accessing the CD-ROM to 7.

Clicking the Permissions button opens the Permissions dialog box for the share. Permissions are described in greater detail in Chapter 12, but we will discuss the basics now. The dialog box is divided into two sections: the Name window and the Permissions window. The Name window lists the users, computers, and groups that have been granted permission to access the share. Clicking the Add button allows you to add new users, computers, or groups to the permissions list. As you might expect, clicking the Remove button deletes the selected object from the permissions list.

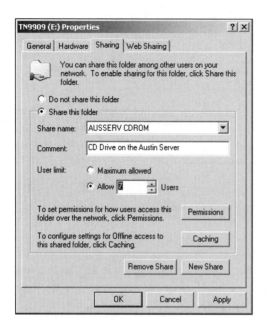

Figure 11-6 Limiting the number of users who can connect to a shared device

The Permissions window of the dialog box displays the access rights that the user, computer, or group is granted to the shared resource. As you work with Windows 2000, you'll run into this dialog box often. The same dialog box applies when sharing drives, folders, or files. For example, as shown in Figure 11-7, users can be granted or denied three types of access to a CD-ROM drive: Full Control, Change, and Read. The permissions shown in Figure 11-7 are granted by default when a share is created. The group Everyone is granted all access rights to the share. To restrict access to the resource, you can either uncheck the Allow box for the specific permission, or check the Deny box for the permission.

 Because the default permissions for all new shares grant Full Control to the Everyone group, be sure to review these permissions anytime you create a new share to avoid any possible security breaches for sensitive information.

The Caching dialog box, which is accessed by clicking the Caching button on the Properties dialog box, is used to specify whether shared files can be accessed offline. When this option is enabled, the **Offline Files and Folders** feature allows mobile Windows 2000 users to access shared files and folders even when they are not connected to the network. To facilitate this access, Offline Files and Folders stores a copy of the files in the cache on the mobile computer. By default, the cache size is set to 10 percent of the available drive space and stored in the root directory of the hard disk.

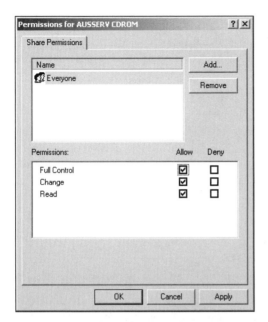

Figure 11-7 Permissions dialog box for the AUSSERV CDROM device

When sharing a resource, you have three options for caching files for offline access: **Manual Caching for Documents**, **Automatic Caching for Programs**, and **Automatic Caching for Documents**. By default, all shared resources are set to Manual Caching for Documents. With this setting, the user who seeks to access the shared files must manually configure them for offline access. Microsoft recommends this setting for shared folders containing files that can be accessed by several people.

The Automatic Caching for Programs option is the best configuration for folders containing files that do not change. When a user accesses the shared folder, Offline Files and Folders automatically copies the contents of the folder to the local cache. This option can be used to reduce network traffic, because the files are accessed from the cache rather than across the network. In turn, this strategy increases the speed with which the applications can be used. It is important when using this option to restrict the files in the shared folder to read-only access.

The last option, Automatic Caching for Documents, automatically loads the files that a user accesses into his or her local cache. Unlike with Automatic Caching for Programs, only those files that are opened by the user are copied to the cache; all files are not accessible offline.

FILE AND FOLDER SHARING

The principles behind sharing are the same regardless of whether a device, file, or folder is being shared. As you learned in Chapter 6, Windows 2000 supports two file systems: FAT32 and NTFS. The file system being used has an effect on your ability to share files and folders. The FAT32 file system does not include the detailed security information provided by

NTFS. For this reason, disks formatted as FAT32 can be shared only down to the folder level. If a FAT32 folder is shared, all files within the folder are accessible to remote users. NTFS partitions allow you to limit the access that users have to files in a folder, providing a higher level of security.

The process used for sharing folders, either on FAT32 or NTFS partitions, is basically the same as that used for sharing devices. Through Windows Explorer or My Computer, locate the folder to be shared. Right-click the folder name, and select Sharing from the menu. The folder's Properties dialog box, Sharing tab, will be displayed. The available options (Share Name, Comment, User Limit, Permissions, and Caching) are identical and perform the same functions.

Distributed File System

A new feature with Windows 2000 is the Distributed File System (DFS). DFS allows administrators to present a logical view of shares on multiple servers across the network. For example, before the advent of DFS, users had to know the Universal Naming Convention (UNC) path to each shared folder to which they needed access.

As networks grew and more servers were added, it became increasingly difficult for users to find the files and folders needed to perform their jobs. Using DFS, however, administrators can create logical views of the servers to facilitate browsing and file location. For example, an administrator can set up a DFS volume called MARKETING that includes shared folders on six servers on the network. From the user's point of view, all files are located on the MARKETING volume.

Managing DFS

DFS is managed through the Distributed File System tool, located in the Programs, Administrative Tools entry in the Start menu. A **DFS root** is the local server share that acts as the starting point for users to access the resources in the DFS share. To initiate a DFS root, select New DFS Root from the Action menu in the Distributed File System application, as shown in Figure 11-8. This selection initiates the New DFS Root Wizard, which steps you through the creation of a DFS root.

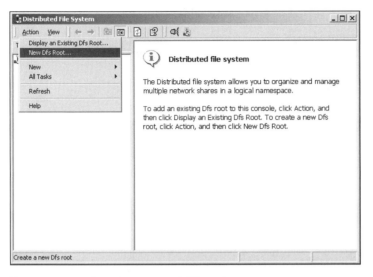

Figure 11-8 Creating a new DFS root

Creating a DFS Root

The first option with which you are presented when creating a new DFS root is whether to create a domain DFS root or a stand-alone DFS root. Domain DFS roots use Active Directory to store the DFS configuration and support DNS naming and automatic replication. Stand-alone DFS roots do not utilize Active Directory. After selecting the type of DFS root desired, you will be asked which server will host the DFS root. Most likely, it will be the server on which you are currently creating the root. If it is not, select the desired server by using the Browse button. Once the server has been located, click Next. You will then be asked to supply the name of the share that will act as the DFS root. As shown in Figure 11-9, you can use an existing share or create a new share in a specified location. After clicking Next, you can add comments to the DFS share. The final step is to confirm the configuration and click Finish in the New DFS Root Wizard.

Once the DFS root has been created, you can create **DFS links** to additional shares by choosing the New DFS Link option from the Actions menu. The Create New DFS Link dialog box enables you to name the link, locate the shared folder that is the basis of the link, and provide comments. Figure 11-10 shows the new LANW DFS root with additional links added on various computers on the network. On network client computers, all folders within the DFS root appear as if they were folders of the original share.

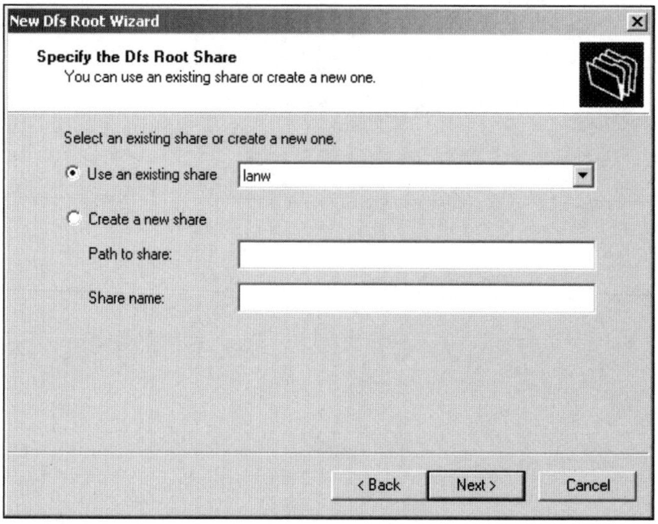

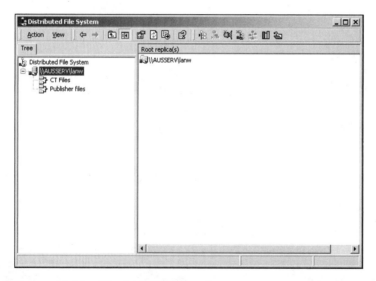

Figure 11-9 Selecting the new DFS root share

Figure 11-10 The LANW DFS root

PRINTER SHARING

The Windows 2000 environment allows you to share printing resources across an entire network and administer printing functions from a single location. The Windows printing system provides easy access for all Windows-based clients and can also be configured to support other client types, such as NetWare and Macintosh.

Like many things in the Microsoft environment, printing is handled in a special manner. More specifically, the terminology used in Microsoft printing may not always be what you expect. For example, most people think of a printer as a physical device that sits on the end of your desk and periodically produces printed output. In the Windows printing environment, it is called a **print device**, whereas a **printer** is actually a software interface between the operating system and the physical device. The printer configuration specifies where the document will be sent to reach the print device (that is, through a local port or across the network) and other variables such as when the job will be printed and how it will be handled by the operating system.

Two types of print devices exist in the Windows 2000 environment: the **local print device** and the **network-interface print device**. A local print device is directly connected to a port on the computer, such as the LPT port. This configuration is the one with which most people are familiar. As network computing has evolved, however, many companies have developed printing interfaces that allow printers to be directly connected to the network cabling, without the interference of a computer. An example of this type of device is the Hewlett-Packard JetDirect, which acts as a network interface for the printers to which it is attached. It provides for more efficient network configuration and speedier printing. A print device attached to this type of device is called a network-interface print device.

A **print server** is a computer that is configured to manage the printing activities of one or more print devices. Print servers receive print jobs from clients on the network and store them until the print devices are able to complete the jobs. Network printers are shared on print servers.

A **print driver** is a software component that is used to translate jobs into the language used by a printer, such as PCL or PostScript. Drivers are written for specific printers and usually cannot be interchanged. For example, the printer driver for a Hewlett-Packard LaserJet 6L cannot be used to send print jobs to an Epson Stylus 760C. It is important, then, that the appropriate drivers be loaded on the print server to ensure that documents print correctly.

Printing in Windows 2000

To print in a Windows 2000 environment, at least one computer must act as the print server. In most cases, you will want to use a Windows 2000 Server computer as the print server. For purposes of our examples here, we'll use a Windows 2000 Advanced Server computer with a Hewlett-Packard Laser Jet 6L directly attached to the LPT port as the print server.

Before beginning the installation process, be sure that you are logged in as the Administrator.

Creating a Printer

On the server, start the Printers applet by selecting Start, Settings, Printers, or double-click the Printers icon in the Control Panel. The Printers dialog box will open. The first icon available in the dialog box is the Add Printer icon. Double-click Add Printer to start the Add Printer Wizard. After the wizard has started, click Next. The next dialog box asks you to select whether the printer will be a local or network printer. Because our printer is directly attached to the computer, we'll select Local printer, as shown in Figure 11-11. For a local printer, Windows 2000 can detect and install the necessary drivers for Plug and Play devices. For this exercise, however, we'll uncheck this box and select the printer manually. Click Next.

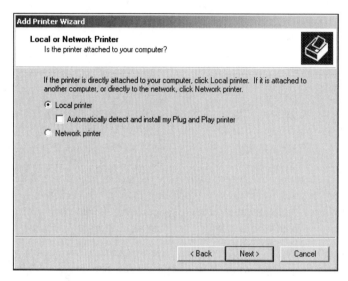

Figure 11-11 Selecting Local or Network printer

Next, select the port to which the printer is attached. In this case, the printer is attached to LPT1. An option in this dialog box also allows you to create a new port to which you can connect the printer. In most cases, you will not need to utilize this function for directly attached printers, but it may be necessary when connecting to a TCP/IP-enabled network-interface print device. To bring up the list of available printers for which Windows 2000 has included drivers, select LPT1 from the list of available ports and click Next. Drivers for many of the printers currently on the market are included with Windows 2000, including the Hewlett-Packard model we are using. If you are installing a printer that is not listed, click the Have Disk button and enter the path for the printer drivers. For our purposes, we'll select HP (for Hewlett-Packard) from the left side of the dialog box and HP LaserJet 6L, as shown in Figure 11-12. Click Next to continue.

Now you are prompted to provide a name for your printer. As when you are naming shares, the name for the printer should be unique and readily identify the printer and its location. If this device is not the first printer attached to the computer, the dialog box asks whether it should specify the new printer as the default printer for all Windows-based programs. Name the new printer Austin HP 6, and click Next to continue.

The next dialog box asks whether you want to share this printer on the network. In most cases, you will select "Share as" and provide a name for the share printer. We will cover sharing existing printers in the next section, so we'll select "Do not share this printer" here. Click Next to continue.

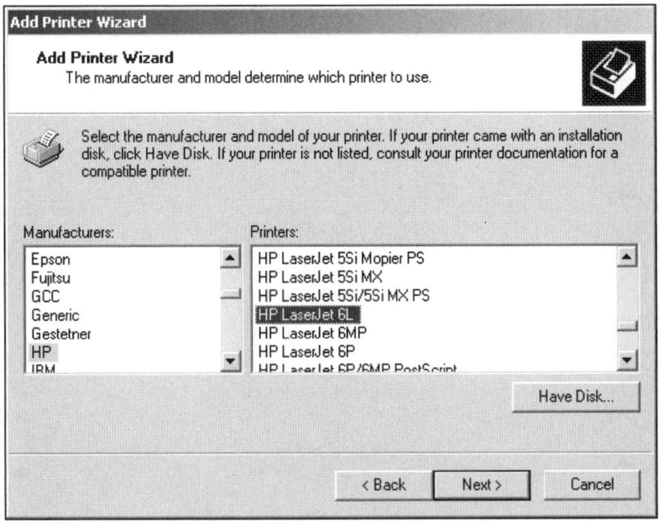

Printer Sharing 309

Figure 11-12 Selecting the printer driver

Finally, you are asked to print a test page. This test is always a good idea to ensure that the printer is connected and functioning properly. Select Yes and click Next to proceed to the end of the Add Printer Wizard. Clicking Finish, as shown in Figure 11-13, will print the test page and complete the installation of the new printer. After clicking Finish, the system will copy the necessary files from the Windows 2000 CD and print the test page as selected. Once the installation is complete, a dialog box will ask whether the test page printed correctly. Click OK if the page printed; otherwise, click Troubleshoot to utilize the Windows 2000 Help features to determine the cause of the error.

Figure 11-13 Finishing the new printer installation

Sharing Existing Windows 2000 Printers

As mentioned in the previous section, the process for adding a new printer on a Windows 2000 Server computer includes a step in which you can share the printer as it is created. On some occasions, however, printers that were not previously shared *must* be configured to be shared. As with other shared devices, this reconfiguration is a straightforward process. To begin sharing an existing print device, open the Printers dialog box through Start, Settings, Printers. Select the printer, and right-click its icon. Select Sharing from the displayed menu to open the printer's Properties dialog box, as shown in Figure 11-14. To share the printer, simply select the radio button next to Shared as: and provide a share name for the printer.

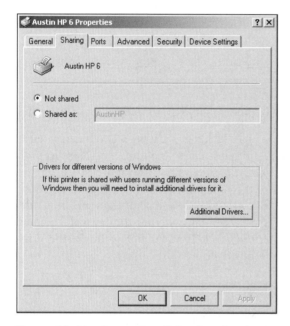

Figure 11-14 Properties dialog box for the Austin HP 6 printer

 Unlike when sharing other devices, an Additional Drivers button appears on the printer's Properties dialog box, Sharing tab. This feature allows you to load the drivers for different Windows operating systems on the server so that any Windows client can print to the printer. The operating systems accommodated include Windows 95/98, Windows NT 3.51 and 4.0 on the Alpha computer, Intel, MIPS, and PowerPC platforms.

The various resources on Windows 2000 computers are shared in much the same way. In the next section, we'll explore sharing applications in a distributed manner by using the Windows 2000 new IntelliMirror features.

INTELLIMIRROR FOR APPLICATION DISTRIBUTION

With Windows 2000, Microsoft has introduced IntelliMirror, which is actually a combination of utilities that provide advanced control over computers on the network. IntelliMirror actually comprises three features: User Data Management, Software Installation and Maintenance, and User Settings Management. In this chapter, we'll look at the Software Installation and Maintenance feature of IntelliMirror.

For more information on the other IntelliMirror features, refer to the Windows 2000 Resource Kit or Microsoft TechNet.

The Windows 2000 Software Installation and Maintenance feature allows for policy-based deployment and software management. As upgrades become available, software can be configured to be automatically updated based on the policies in use on the Windows 2000 systems. The Software Installation and Maintenance feature uses just-in-time software installation and automatic repair of applications to provide seamless access to software, regardless of which computer the user utilizes to connect to the network. Once a user's profile has been created, the same applications and configuration will automatically follow the user to any computer on the network. The policies that govern the Software Installation service are defined on the basis of sites, domains, and organizational units in the Active Directory environment. (Active Directory was covered in detail in Chapter 10.)

Applications that use the Windows Installer service must be written to take advantage of its features. A prime example of this type of application is Windows 2000 itself. It can be configured to use the Windows Installer to remotely install and maintain the Windows 2000 operating system on computers on the network.

Administrators can use the Installer service to either publish or assign software to groups of users and computers. **Published software** is made available to users on an as-needed basis. That is, Administrators specify the software made available to users based on the business, technical, or geographic requirements of the groups. The users can select from a list of published software through the Add/Remove Programs applet in the Control Panel. In addition, if a user opens a document that requires a published application, the required software will be installed automatically and the application will start.

Assigned software is installed automatically, without user choice or intervention. When new software is assigned to a computer, it is installed the next time that the computer is restarted. This type of configuration can be used to deploy service packs or driver updates to all computers on the network.

IIS for Web Serving

Microsoft's **Internet Information Service (IIS) 5.0** is included as part of Windows 2000 and used to provide Web services for clients on the network. Like many other Windows 2000 components, IIS is a feature-rich and detailed environment. Here we'll discuss the basic functions of IIS, installing IIS, and configuring folders for access over the World Wide Web.

In the previous versions, IIS was expanded as Internet Information Server. However, the version included with Windows 2000 is called Internet Information Services.

IIS has been included with Windows NT products, in one form or another, since version 3.51. The implementation included with Windows 2000 is much more robust than that provided in earlier versions of Windows NT and encompasses the complete set of components necessary to support a commercial Web site. Features of IIS include the following:

- *HTTP 1.1 support:* IIS supports version 1.1 of the HyperText Transfer Protocol (HTTP), which is used to transmit information on the Internet. HTTP 1.1 extends the capabilities of HTTP to include pipelining (which allows clients to send many requests before receiving a response from a server), persistent connections (which ensures that clients maintain connections with Internet servers by using keep-alives), and transfer chunk encoding for Active Server Pages.

- *Support for SMTP mail:* The Simple Mail Transfer Protocol (SMTP) was developed to facilitate sending specific types of e-mail messages, such as the confirmation messages generated by registering for a Web service.

- *NNTP support:* IIS includes support for the Network News Transfer Protocol (NNTP), which is used by applications to enable users to take part in local news discussion groups. Note, however, that the NNTP version included with Windows 2000 does not support full news feeds from the Internet. To obtain this functionality, you must purchase Microsoft Exchange Server.

- *Web application development tools:* IIS includes a number of tools and applications that can be used to design Web-based applications more effectively. They include support for transactional Active Server Pages, process isolation, message queuing, and an updated Java Virtual Machine.

IIS can be installed when the Windows 2000 operating system is installed by selecting the Internet Information Services box. If IIS was not installed at that time, it is easy to install all or some of the IIS components after the fact. IIS installation is detailed in Hands-on Project 11-5. The following components are available when installing the Windows 2000 version of IIS:

- *File Transfer Protocol (FTP) Server:* This component provides file transfer and management services for clients using the FTP protocol. FTP servers are often used in situations where clients need only to transfer files to their local systems, not view or change the files. An example of an FTP server would be an Internet site containing drivers for sound cards.

- *FrontPage 2000 Server Extensions:* Microsoft's Web page development application is FrontPage. The IIS installation provides special extensions that can be used on FrontPage 2000-generated Web pages.

- *Internet Information Services Snap-In:* This component is the MMC snap-in for the IIS services.

- *Internet Services Manager (HTML):* In addition to the MMC, IIS can be managed through a Web interface if these components are installed. This feature allows for easy remote management of IIS servers regardless of their physical location.

- *NNTP Service:* As mentioned earlier, Windows 2000 IIS supports a localized NNTP news service if this application is installed.

- *SMTP Service:* This component supports SMTP mail messages such as those automatically generated by the IIS server.

- *Visual InterDev RAD Remote Deployment Support:* Visual InterDev is used to create interactive Web applications. The RAD Deployment Support module enables the remote deployment of InterDev applications on the Web server.

- *World Wide Web Server:* This component provides support for serving HTML documents to clients either on a local intranet or on the Internet.

Configuring Folders for IIS Access

Once IIS is installed, it must be configured to serve files in particular folders to Web clients. This configuration can be performed in one of two ways: through the **Internet Services Manager (ISM)**, or through the Properties dialog box for the folder. ISM is used to administer all IIS services and is accessed through the Administrative Tools group in the Start menu. It displays the information for the configured server and the services running on that server, as shown in Figure 11-15.

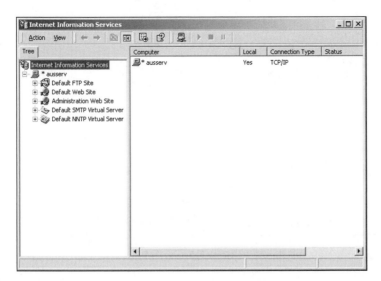

Figure 11-15 IIS running on a typical Web server

IIS can support multiple Web sites on a single server. In Figure 11-15, the Default Web Site is displayed along with the Default FTP Site, the Administration Web Site, the Default SMTP Virtual Server, and the Default NNTP Virtual Server. Folders that are served by the Web service are called **virtual directories**. To enable a folder to be accessed by the Web service, select New from the Action menu, then select Virtual Directory. The Virtual Directory Creation Wizard will then open.

When the initial screen of the dialog box appears, click Next. You are next prompted to provide an alias for the virtual directory. When selecting this alias, the same naming conventions used when naming another folder or directory apply. For example, if this folder provides Human Resources data to the company's intranet, you might name the alias HR Data. Click Next to proceed with the Virtual Directory creation.

Now you will be asked to specify the folder that will hold the shared content. Click Browse to locate the directory on the server, click OK, then click Next. Note that the content folder does not have to be shared before it provides data to the Web. Creating the virtual directory will share the folder and its contents to the Web service for distribution on the Web.

The next screen shown in Figure 11-16 asks you to specify the access permissions for the virtual directory. The options are Read, Run scripts (such as ASP), Execute (such as ISAPI applications or CGI), Write, and Browse. The default permissions, Read and Run, are sufficient for most Web sites. Execute should be enabled only if special applications or scripts are used on the Web site. Write should not be enabled for most Web sites, because it gives any user the ability to place files in the virtual directory. The Browse permission provides very limited access to the virtual directory and is not sufficient on its own to support a Web site. Click Next, then Finish to complete creation of the virtual directory. The files in the folder are now available for distribution by the Web service.

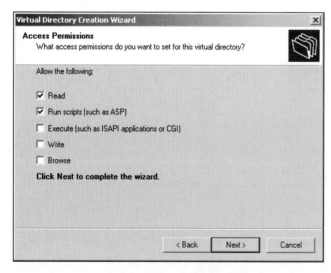

Figure 11-16 Available virtual directory permissions

Sharing Folders

As mentioned, you can also share a folder for Web access through the folder's Properties dialog box. To begin, use Windows Explorer to locate the folder that will be accessed from the Web. Right-click the folder name, and select Properties from the displayed menu. Click the Web Sharing tab, shown in Figure 11-17, to configure the folder for use by IIS. Select the Web site to which to share the folder from the Share on: drop-down list.

This method can be used only for existing Web sites. To share a folder to a new Web site, you must use ISM.

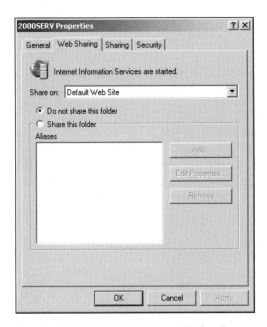

Figure 11-17 Web Sharing tab for the 2000SERV folder

Clicking the radio button next to Share this folder invokes the Edit Alias dialog box. Through this dialog box, you specify the name of the alias and the access permissions for the virtual directory. The access permissions displayed differ somewhat from those seen in the ISM. The Access permissions section of the dialog box lets you select or deselect Read, Write, Script source access, and Directory browsing. The Application permissions area lets you select whether no applications can be run (None), only scripts will be run (Scripts), or all applications can be run (Execute). By default, the Read and Scripts selections are used, which equate to the Read and Run permissions as configured through the ISM. Once these configurations are set, IIS will provide Web services for the files in the specified folders.

Terminal Services

Windows 2000 **Terminal Services** provide Windows emulation to disparate hardware platforms in a heterogeneous network environment. Through terminal emulation, you can deploy 32-bit Windows "thin client" solutions to a full range of client computers on your network, regardless of their current Windows operating system. This ability provides a mainframe-like environment in which low-cost terminals can be spread throughout the network, but managed from a central location.

Windows 2000 Terminal Services consists of four components: the Terminal Server, the Remote Display Protocol, the Terminal Server Client, and the Administration Tools.

The Terminal Server is a multiuser server module capable of hosting multiple client sessions on a Windows 2000 Server. It can directly host multiple client desktop environments running on both Windows- and non-Windows-based hardware. If applications are properly written to support Terminal Services, multiple users should be able to utilize the applications simultaneously. In addition, the standard Windows 2000 management utilities can be used to manage the client desktops.

The **Remote Display Protocol (RDP)** has been developed to facilitate client communication with the Terminal Server on the network. It is based on the International Telecommunications Union's T.120 standard protocol, which supports encryption and is tuned for high-bandwidth enterprise environments. The Terminal Server Client software presents the familiar Windows user interface on a wide variety of client computers.

The Terminal Server Client software can be loaded on personal computers running Windows for Workgroups 3.11, Windows 95/Windows 98, Windows NT 3.51 and 4.0, and Windows 2000 Professional. In addition, new terminal devices can be created that embed the Terminal Services Client software on the device to realize true "thin client" configurations.

The Terminal Services also offer set of Administration Tools that follow the standard Windows 2000 administration look and feel. These tools include the Terminal Services License Manager, the Terminal Server Client Creator, the Terminal Services Configuration Snap-In for the MMC, and Terminal Server Administration tools for managing client sessions. Additional Performance Monitor objects (Session and User) are available to provide monitoring and tuning for the unique Terminal Services environment.

Setting Up Terminal Services

Establishing a Terminal Services environment involves two steps: installing Terminal Services on the Windows 2000 Server, and installing the client software on the client computers on the network. Installing Terminal Services on a Windows 2000 Server is accomplished in the same way as you would install other Windows 2000 components. Terminal Services installation is detailed in Hands-on Project 11-4.

In most cases, you will want to license Terminal Services only to your domain or workgroup. Ensure that this option is selected and click Next; this action will begin installing the software from the Windows 2000 CD. Click Finish to complete the installation. Click Yes when prompted to restart the computer. The Windows 2000 Terminal Services will then be installed on the server and ready to accept connections from clients.

The first step in connecting a client computer to the Terminal Server is to create the installation disks necessary for the client. This goal is accomplished by using the Terminal Services Client Creator application, located in Start/Programs/Administrative Tools. Selecting this program starts the Client Creator application, as shown in Figure 11-18. Three types of installation disks can be created: Terminal Services for 16-bit windows, Terminal Services for 32-bit x86 windows, and Terminal Services for 32-bit Alpha windows. You can also choose the floppy drive to which the files will be copied and whether to format the disks before creation.

Figure 11-18 Terminal Services Client Creator application

The number of disks required depends on the client type being created. Terminal Services for 16-bit windows requires four disks, whereas both 32-bit versions require only two disks.

After selecting the client type, click OK to continue. You are asked to insert the disk that will be Installation Disk 1 into the drive and click OK to continue. A final confirmation dialog box states that this process will erase all data on the disk. Click Yes to continue. When prompted, insert Disk 2, click OK, then confirm by clicking Yes.

Once the installation disks are created, you can install the Terminal Client software on the client computers. Regardless of the client type, this installation consists of loading Disk 1 into the floppy drive and running the a:\setup program. You will be prompted to supply a destination directory for the software. No additional configuration options are available for this software. Once the software is installed, you can connect to the Terminal Server by starting the Terminal Services Client software. On a Windows 95 computer, for example, you would select Start, Programs, Terminal Services Client, then click the Terminal Services Client application. When the application starts, you will be asked to specify the server to which you want to connect and the screen area to be used for the Terminal window. Select the server and click Connect. When prompted, log on to the server. After successfully logging in, you will be able to run any applications loaded on the server as if you were sitting at the server's console.

Administration Tools

When Terminal Services is installed on a Windows 2000 Server, two other administration tools are installed as well. The Administration Tool is used to manage Terminal Server processes, sessions, and users connected to the Terminal Server. For example, it is used to send a message to a session or user, reset a session, display session connection information, disconnect a session or user, display client information, and manage Terminal Server processes. The Terminal Server Configuration tool is used to manage Terminal Server sessions and session sets. For example, it handles configuring a new connection, managing permissions for a connection, managing Terminal Server users and groups, and managing disconnect and timeout settings. Each of these tools is available in the Administrative Tools group of the Start menu.

CHAPTER SUMMARY

- The need to share resources is perhaps the single biggest reason for installing networks. Users are granted direct access to resources directly connected to their computers, but they must be specifically granted access to resources reached through the network.

- Windows 2000 computers display shared resources in the My Network Places dialog box, which is similar to Network Neighborhood on other Windows versions. When a client using the My Network Places dialog box double-clicks a specific resource, the user is granted access based on his or her permissions for that resource. If the user is not allowed to access a resource, an "Access denied" message appears.

- Windows 2000 printers are added through the Add Printer Wizard in the Printers applet of the Control Panel. Existing printers are shared via the Sharing tab of a printer's properties. Additional drivers can be loaded on the print server to support other types of clients, such as Windows 95/98.

- With Windows 2000, Microsoft introduced IntelliMirror, which is a combination of utilities that provide advanced control over computers on the network. Three utilities make up IntelliMirror: User Data Management, Software Installation and Maintenance, and User Settings Management. Administrators can either publish or assign software in the IntelliMirror environment. Published software is made available to users on an as-needed basis depending on their business, technical, or geographic requirements. Assigned software is installed automatically, without user intervention, the next time that the computer restarts. Software assignment is used to ensure that all network users have the same version of software and is often applied to service packs and driver updates.

- Internet Information Services 5.0 provides Web services in Windows 2000. It supports HTTP 1.1, SMTP, NNTP, and advanced Web application development tools, such as Active Server Pages. The IIS installation is part of the Windows 2000 component installation.

- Windows 2000 also supports virtual terminal access through Terminal Services, which allows Windows-based clients to access applications loaded on the Terminal Server as if the user were sitting directly at the server console. This capability allows for thin client compatibility in a mainframe-like environment.

Key Terms

assigned software — Software that is installed automatically when a user reboots his or her computer. The feature is often used for software patches and service packs.

Automatic Caching for Documents — The caching option that automatically caches only those files that are accessed by the user. This setting does not cache the entire contents of the directory, nor does it require user intervention.

Automatic Caching for Programs — The caching option that automatically copies the entire contents of the folder to the user's local cache.

broadcast — The signal sent across the network by a resource to notify users of its availability.

DFS link — A pointer to an additional share included in the DFS configuration.

DFS root — The local server share that acts as the starting point for users to access resources on the DFS share.

Internet Information Services (IIS) — Microsoft's Web services software that is included with Windows 2000 and is used to make information available on the World Wide Web.

Internet Services Manager (ISM) — The application used to manage and maintain IIS applications.

local print device — A printing device directly connected to the computer.

Manual Caching for Documents — The caching setting that requires users to manually transfer files to be used offline from the server to their local computer; this is the default setting for shares.

My Network Places — The starting point for accessing network resources on a Windows 2000 computer.

network-interface print device — A printing device attached to a special network interface card that does not require a direct computer connection.

Network Place — A resource on the network, generally accessed through a shortcut from the My Network Places dialog box.

Offline Files and Folders — The Windows 2000 feature that allows users to cache files on their local drives for access when they are not connected to the network.

print device — A physical printing device.

print driver — A software component that is used to translate print jobs into the language used by the print device.

printer — A software interface between the operating system and the physical printing device.

print server — A computer configured to manage the printing activities of one or more print devices.

published software — Software made available to users on an as-needed basis. Users can select from the list of published software to determine whether they want to install available applications.

Remote Display Protocol (RDP) — The specialized protocol developed for Terminal Services that facilitates communication between the client and the server.

Terminal Services — The Windows 2000 component that provides access to the Windows 2000 console for many types of clients. Similar to terminal functions in a mainframe environment.

virtual directories — Folders used by the Web service to provide content to the Internet.

REVIEW QUESTIONS

1. Which of the following protocols is used by Terminal Services for communication between the client and the server?

    a. FTP

    b. NNTP

    c. RDP

    d. SMTP

2. If a user attempts to connect to a network resource to which he or she has not previously been granted access, the Windows 2000 security system will prompt the user to provide a valid user name and password for the resource. True or False?

3. In Windows 2000, _____ is similar to Network Neighborhood in Windows 95/98.

4. By default, a share's name is the same as the device's name. True or False?

5. Which of the following software types is automatically downloaded to a user's computer without the user's intervention?

    a. Requested

    b. Assigned

    c. Mandated

    d. Published

6. A(n) _____ is a software interface between the operating system and a physical print device.

7. The _____ caching method copies only those files that are opened by the user to the cache.

8. Which of the following access types can be granted or denied for a shared CD-ROM drive? (Choose all that apply.)

    a. Modify

    b. Read

    c. Change

    d. Full Control

9. The NNTP server included with Windows 2000 IIS does not support full news feeds from the Internet. True or False?

10. Which of the following must be installed to administer an IIS server from a Web interface?
    a. Internet Services Manager (HTML)
    b. Internet Information Services snap-in
    c. World Wide Web server
    d. FrontPage 2000 Server Extensions
11. Both file systems supported by Windows 2000 provide the same level of security. True or False?
12. The Windows 2000 _____ feature allows files to be accessed by a mobile user even when the user is not connected to the network.
13. Which of the following is displayed when the Computers Near Me dialog box is opened?
    a. All computers on the network
    b. Only computers with the same IP address
    c. All computers to which a certain user is logged on
    d. Only computers in the same domain or workgroup
14. By default, _____ users are allowed to connect to a newly created share.
15. Virtual directories can be established only through the Internet Services Manager. True or False?
16. To easily connect to frequently accessed shared network resources, use the _____ to create a _____.
17. Which of the following DFS root types uses Active Directory to store the DFS configuration?
    a. Active root
    b. Domain root
    c. Standalone root
    d. Primary root
18. To print in a Windows 2000 environment, it is not necessary for a computer to act as a print server. True or False?
19. Which of the following can be used to configure a shared folder for use by IIS? (Choose all that apply.)
    a. The ISM
    b. The System applet in Control Panel
    c. The Properties dialog box for the folder
    d. The Server applet in Control Panel
20. The Terminal Services client software is designed to operate on all versions of Windows since version 3.11. True or False?

HANDS-ON PROJECTS

Project 11-1

To add a network shortcut in the My Network Places dialog box:

1. Log on to a Windows 2000 computer.
2. Double-click **My Network Places** on the desktop.
3. Double-click **Add Network Place** to open the Add Network Place Wizard.
4. To locate the folder to which you would like to create the shortcut, click **Browse**. A diagram of the network will appear, like that shown in Figure 11-19.

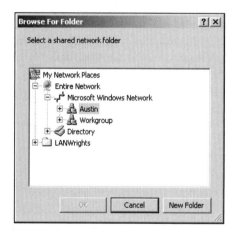

Figure 11-19 Browse For Folder dialog box

5. Navigate through the network to locate the shared folder to which you want to connect, highlight it, and then click **OK**.
6. Click **Next** to proceed with the Add Network Place Wizard.
7. Provide a descriptive name for the shortcut you're creating, and then click **Finish** to complete the process. The folder to which you connected will open to ensure that you have connected to the correct location. Close the window and review the My Network Places dialog box. It should now include the newly created shortcut.

Project 11-2

To share a device or folder:

1. If you are not currently logged on, log on to a Windows 2000 computer.
2. Double-click **My Computer** and select the **CD-ROM** drive in your system. If your system does not include a CD-ROM drive, double-click a hard drive and select a folder.
3. Right-click the selected device, and then choose **Sharing** from the menu.
4. The Properties dialog box for the device will open to the Sharing tab.

5. Select **Share this folder** (refer to Figure 11-4).
6. Enter a name for the shared device. Remember that the share name should be readily understood by others on the network and should describe the location and function of the resource.
7. Add a comment to further describe the shared device.
8. Specify that only five users will be allowed to access the device simultaneously by clicking the radio button next to **Allow** and using the scroll buttons to change the value to **5** (refer to Figure 11-6).
9. Click **OK** to complete sharing the device. After the device is shared, a hand appears on the icon for the device. It indicates that the device is shared and can be accessed from the network.

Project 11-3

You will not need a physical printer device attached to the system to complete this project.

To create printer on a Windows 2000 computer:

1. If you are not already logged on to a Windows 2000 computer, do so as an **Administrator**.
2. Open the Printers dialog box by selecting **Start**, **Settings**, **Printers**.
3. Double-click the **Add Printer** icon.
4. On the first screen of the Add Printer Wizard dialog box, click **Next**.
5. For this exercise, you will be connecting a local printer. Ensure that the **Local printer** option is selected (refer to Figure 11-11).
6. Uncheck the box next to **Automatically detect and install my Plug and Play printer**, if necessary. Because you may not have a printer connected to your machine, you do not want to take this step.
7. Click **Next**.
8. Select the port to which the printer is connected. For the purpose of this exercise, select **LPT1** (unless this port is already assigned to a printer, otherwise select LPT2) in the **Use the following port area** of the dialog box (see Figure 11-20).
9. Click **Next**.
10. From the list of available printers, select **Epson** from the left window.
11. Scroll through the list of printers in the right window, and select **Epson Stylus COLOR 740 ESC/P 2**.
12. Click **Next**.
13. Enter a descriptive name for the printer. Ensure that it accurately describes the type of printer and its location.

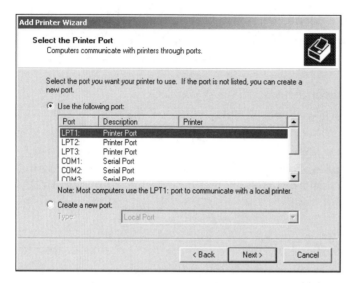

Figure 11-20 Selecting a port for the printer

14. Select the **Yes** radio button to ensure that Windows-based programs will use the new printer as the default (see Figure 11-21).

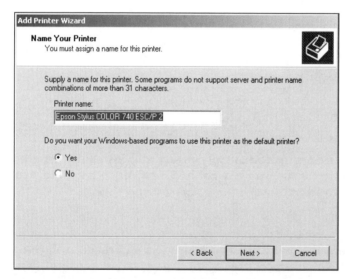

Figure 11-21 Naming the new printer and setting it as the default

15. Click **Next**.
16. Ensure that the radio button next to **Do not share this printer** is selected, and click **Next**.
17. Select **No** when asked if you want to print a test page.

18. Click **Next**.
19. Figure 11-22 shows the final dialog box of the Add New Printer Wizard as it should appear on your screen. Click **Finish** to complete the installation.

Figure 11-22 Final dialog box of the Add New Printer Wizard

Project 11-4

To install Terminal Services:

1. Open the Control Panel (**Start**, **Settings**, **Control Panel**).
2. Double-click **Add/Remove Programs**.
3. Select **Add/Remove Windows Components**, select the **Terminal Services and Terminal Services Licensing** check boxes (see Figure 11-23) from the list of available components, and then click **Next**.

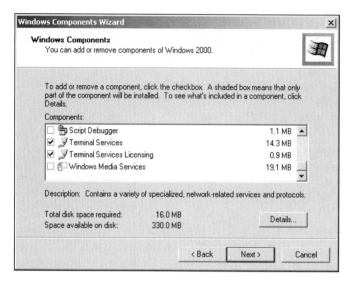

Figure 11-23 Adding Terminal Services and Terminal Services Licensing

4. You will be asked whether this server will operate in Remote administration mode or Application server mode. Select **Remote administration mode**, (see Figure 11-24) and click **Next**.

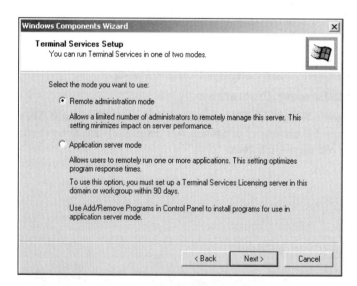

Figure 11-24 Selecting Remote administration mode

5. Specify to whom Terminal Services will be licensed—either the entire enterprise or just your domain or workgroup.
6. Click **Next**, then click Finish, and then click **Yes** to reboot the computer.

Project 11-5

To install IIS:

1. Launch the **Control Panel** and select **Add/Remove Programs**.
2. Click the **Add/Remove Windows Components** button. A list of all Windows 2000 components will be displayed, with those that are currently installed indicated by check marks.
3. You can check the check box next to the Internet Information Services (IIS) option to load all IIS components. To select only certain components, click the **Details** button.
4. Once you have selected the desired components, click **OK** to return to the Windows Components Wizard dialog box, shown in Figure 11-25.

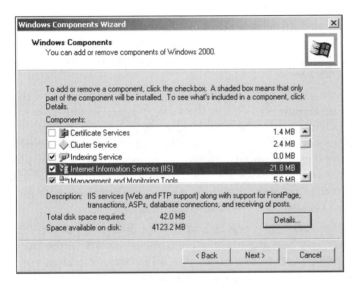

Figure 11-25 Windows Component Wizard

5. Click **Next** to continue installing the IIS components selected.
6. In the next dialog box, select **Remote Administration mode** or **Application server**. Click **Next** to copy the files from the Windows 2000 CD-ROM. Once the installation is complete, IIS is ready for operation.

CASE PROJECTS

1. As the administrator for an enterprise network, you have been struggling with training issues with regard to users understanding the layout of the network and where their data and applications reside. While attending a conference in Las Vegas, you learned that Windows 2000 supports DFS and you feel that it will help you reduce users' confusion. Your network encompasses more than 300 servers, but 16 servers are reserved for the Engineering department, its applications, and its data. Develop a test plan for implementing a Windows 2000 Server and DFS for use in the Engineering department. Include information on the DFS roots and DFS links, their configuration, and their maintenance.

2. You have begun implementing an intranet for information specific to your company. You realize that the default folders available in IIS are not sufficient to support the various Web sites needed. Develop a plan for adding virtual directories to the current Web site to include human resources, information technology, and marketing information. Each department has its own server on the network from which the information should be read.

3. In trying to convince your boss to upgrade to Windows 2000, you noted the increased application support provided by the new operating system. Your initial plan was to upgrade all client computers on your network to support Windows 2000 Professional. Budgets being what they are, your boss approved only the purchase of the new server and its applications. Your network consists of 130 Windows for Workgroups systems and 55 Windows 95 systems that you were planning to upgrade. Develop an implementation plan for providing all client computers with access to the applications that are available on the Windows 2000 Server.

4. At inception, your small company was able to allocate dedicated printers to all employees. However, you have experienced phenomenal growth in the last year, increasing from 23 employees to more than 100. It has become evident that the old way of doing things will no longer work. Your company is divided into six divisions, each of which requires shared printing access. You have 20 printers to share among the various departments in the company. Develop a plan to share the printers effectively and outline the steps required to implement the plan.

CHAPTER

12

SECURING NETWORK RESOURCES

> **After reading this chapter and completing the exercises, you will be able to:**
> - Explain how an operating system and applications are licensed
> - Explain how to edit the rights and permissions associated with groups and create your own groups with special rights
> - Explain the various methods of user authentication available in Windows 2000
> - Distinguish between policies and profiles and explain how both are used in Windows 2000
> - Discuss the encryption methods employed by Windows 2000

The point of a network operating system is to share resources with the other people using the network. Sometimes, however, you don't want everyone using the network to have access to every available resource. Perhaps they haven't paid for access to the resource, or perhaps you'd rather not allow a certain person or group to use a particular resource.

This chapter outlines the ways in which you can use an operating system to control access to network resources. We explain how an operating system and applications are licensed, and how to edit the rights and permissions associated with groups, or create your own groups with special rights. We also distinguish policies and profiles and explain how each are used in Windows 2000. Then, we explain the various methods of user authentication available in Windows 2000 and discuss the encryption methods employed by Windows 2000.

Application and Client Licensing

When you purchase an operating system or an application, you don't so much purchase the software as the right to use that software. This is an important distinction. Buy a server operating system, for example, and you might get 10 **client access licenses (CALs)** with it, which means that up to 10 people are allowed to connect to the server running that operating system. If more than 10 people want to connect to the server, you need to buy more CALs. Applications work the same way. For example, when you buy a copy of any application, you purchase a license to use the application under certain conditions outlined within the software. You don't have the right to make that software available to additional users or to install it on as many computers as you like. The exact conditions of the license—the number of people who can use the software and under what conditions—depend on the wording of the application's **End User License Agreement (EULA)**.

Per-Seat Versus Per-User Licensing

Two basic categories (or modes) of licenses are available: per-session (also called per-user) and per-seat.

Per-session licenses allow a certain number of simultaneous connections (sessions) to the licensed operating system or application. That is, if your operating system comes with 10 per-user licenses, 10 people can log onto the server at once. If an eleventh person wants a connection, either he or she must wait for someone to log off the server or you must buy another user license.

Per-seat licenses work a little differently. These types of licenses apply to computers, rather than users. That is, a certain computer is given the right to access the licensed operating system or application. As many people as you like may use that computer for access, but only the computers with the licenses may be used. Therefore, if computers Alpha, Beta, Gamma, and Delta all have per-seat licenses to WordCruncher running on an application server, Jane can sit at any one of those computers to run WordCruncher. She cannot run WordCruncher from computer Epsilon, however, because that computer is not licensed. When access to an application or operating system is governed by a per-seat license, any computer that connects to that application or operating system needs a valid access license—even if it uses the application once only once per year.

 Specific types of licenses are available that can be either per-seat or per-session, as you will see in the next section, "Types of Licenses Required."

The two main classes of licenses each have their own advantages, but you can't choose the class of license that best fits your needs on the basis of its advantages or disadvantages. Licenses are sold on an "as-is" basis; that is, an application or operating system is licensed on a per-seat or per-session basis by its creator. You can't pick which kind of license you'd like to have.

Occasionally, you may encounter an application or operating system that gives you an option of licensing by seat or by session. After you make the choice, you must stick with it, and you can't buy some licenses of one class and the rest of the other.

Types of Licenses Required

To access a Windows 2000 operating system, you might need any or all of four types of licenses: a console license, a client access license, a terminal server license, or an application license. All of these types of licenses may be either per-session or per-seat licenses, depending on the software involved.

Console License

The **console license** comes with an operating system and represents permission to install the operating system on a single computer and log onto it. Console licenses are by their nature per-seat; they allow you to install an operating system once and work with it at that computer. They do not allow you to install the software on as many computers as you like so long as you're the only person using the operating system.

Client Access Licenses

A **client access license** allows the bearer to access a server—in this case, a Windows 2000 Server. That access includes some use of the server's functionality; for example, Domain Name System (DNS) name resolution, the lease of an Internet Protocol (IP) address from a Dynamic Host Configuration Protocol (DHCP) server, or the ability to reach shared devices and resources on the network. Basically, a client access license permits you to use the core functionality of the Windows 2000 Server. If you plan to log onto a Windows 2000 Server from the network, you need a valid client access license.

Windows 2000 includes a licensing tool that you can use to monitor the licenses available to the Windows 2000 and Windows NT Servers in the local or trusted **domains** on the network. Using this tool (shown in Figure 12-1), you can see the number of licenses available on each server in the network and the number that are currently in use. You can also keep records of purchasing licenses.

Terminal Server Licenses

Anyone accessing terminal server sessions (described in Chapter 11) needs one of two types of **terminal server client access license (TSCAL)**. People who are members of the Windows 2000 domain need a standard TSCAL to run a terminal services session, as well as a client access license to access the server in the first place. TSCALs are given on a per-seat basis, meaning that before people start logging onto the terminal server, you need to determine who has that right and who doesn't.

 Windows 2000 Professional comes with a TSCAL, so you can log onto a terminal server from this operating system without having to use one of the Windows 2000 server terminal server licenses. Other operating systems need an extra TSCAL.

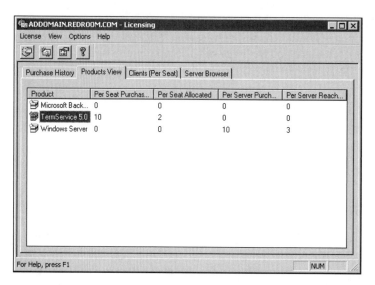

Figure 12-1 The Windows 2000 Licensing tool

People accessing the terminal server from the Internet who are not members of the Windows 2000 domain can pay for access to the terminal server with a per-session **Internet client license (ICL)**. Only anonymous users are allowed to log onto the terminal server via the ICL—not people with domain accounts. ICLs are intended for people accessing **application service providers (ASPs)**, companies that license applications via the Web for a fee. ICLs are really useless for any other purpose. For example, they cannot be used by companies to allow employees to access the terminal server from their homes via the Web.

To keep track of how TSCAL and ICLs are used, Windows 2000 supports a Terminal Services Licensing service and a related tool that you can use to monitor the license usage on each server running a licensing service (other than the regular Windows 2000 licensing). This tool is available from the Administrative Tools section of the Programs menu, as shown in Figure 12-2. The server running this service does not have to be running the Terminal Services software.

Application Licenses

Client access licenses and TSCALs apply only to operating system use. To use an application from that operating system, you need an **application license** that allows you to run the software. The way that the license works depends on the type of application involved. Single-user applications, such as word processors or spreadsheets, come with single licenses; applications that are used by several people at once, such as e-mail servers, come with a group license. These multiuser applications are sometimes called **groupware**.

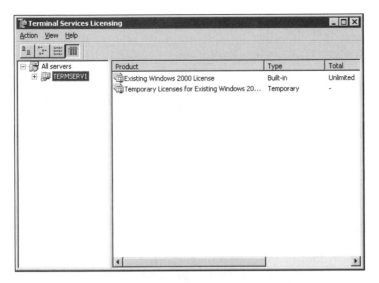

Figure 12-2 The Terminal Services Licensing tool

USER AND GROUP RIGHTS AND PERMISSIONS

After you have all of the licenses required to access the resources on the network, obtaining the actual access still depends on the rights and permissions you have on the network. Those rights and permissions are controlled by the security management part of the operating system. In Windows 2000, they are governed by the Security Manager in the Windows 2000 executive.

Server Accounts Versus Domain Accounts

Everyone using network resources needs an account to log onto the network. This account can be either a server account or a domain account. Server accounts allow you to log onto a specific server, but do not grant access to any other network resources. The user account is located in a user account database stored on the server.

Domain accounts grant you access (or, more precisely, potential access) to the resources shared by all servers in the domain, which is the group of computers that rely on a centralized account database to secure resources. This centralized account database, which is stored on a server called a **domain controller**, is responsible for checking the credentials of anyone who attempts to log onto the domain. When the domain controller confirms that a user has an account on the domain, the user can browse the network resources on the domain. The user may or may not be able to use all resources on the computer; the user's access depends on the rights and permissions associated with his or her user account.

A domain can have more than one domain controller, which reduces the stress on the domain controllers when many people attempt to log onto the domain simultaneously. The presence of multiple domain controllers also prevents the domain from becoming inaccessible if one domain controller crashes and is unable to authenticate anyone. If you're running a mixed domain of Windows 2000 and other computers, the domain controller is responsible for authenticating your access to any network resources.

> A server account does not necessarily give you access to all shared resources on that server, nor does a domain account automatically ensure access to all shared resources on the domain. The kind of access that a user actually obtains depends on the rights and permissions attached to the user account and whether those rights are sufficient to access the objects in the domain.

USER AUTHENTICATION METHODS

Access to resources in Windows 2000 is based on **authentication**, which is the process of determining that you are who you say you are. When you type your user name and password to log onto a particular domain, WinLogon intercepts the information and passes it to the **Local Security Authority (LSA)**. If you're logging onto a single server with its own security database, the LSA checks whether you have an account on the local computer. If you're logging onto either the local domain or a trusted domain, the LSA communicates with that domain's domain controller to see whether you have an account in the domain controller's security database. If the LSA is able to confirm your identity (that is, if you have a valid user account), you are assigned a set of rights and permissions on the server or domain. If you don't have a valid account on the server or domain, you are denied access and not permitted to log on. Windows 2000 demands that you log on before you can use even the local computer; the security system does not allow you to bypass the LSA and just use local resources. The act of sitting at the keyboard and typing your name and password is called an **interactive logon**.

The LSA's job is not necessarily finished when an interactive logon is complete. At that point, you are authenticated at the computer you have logged into and are permitted to browse the network. If you attempt to connect to a resource on the domain, however, the LSA intercepts the request again and passes your credentials to the remote server to show that you're allowed to connect to that server.

As you can see, a lot of chatter takes place on the network as the LSA on your computer authenticates you at the other servers you want to access. The protocol used for this chatter in a LAN environment containing at least one pre-Windows 2000 operating system (including Windows NT 4, Windows 95/98, and Windows 3.1) is **NT LAN Manager (NTLM)**. Otherwise, the network uses **Kerberos**, which is the native Windows 2000 authentication protocol. The only exception occurs when you're being authenticated to a single computer—in other words, when you're logging onto a server, rather than a domain. In that case, NTLM is used even if you're logging onto a Windows 2000 server from a Windows 2000 Professional workstation. All computers on the network must use the same authentication protocol for remote communications, so if the network contains a single pre-Windows 2000 computer, then all computers must use NTLM authentication.

NTLM

NTLM is the default authentication protocol used in Windows NT 4. Basically, it makes sure that the client requesting a resource or service has permission to use that resource or service by communicating with a domain controller. Every time a client tries to access a server, the LSA consults the domain controller to verify that the client is permitted access. If access is permitted, the LSA grants access; if it is not, the client is denied access to the resource. The domain controller plays a part in all such transactions.

This method has some limitations. First, servers know that the clients are who they say they are, but the clients don't have similar knowledge about the servers. A rogue computer or service could impersonate a server and intercept requests from the client. Second, the domain controller must authenticate every communication between client and server, which leads to a lot of network traffic and can put unnecessary strain on the domain controller. For these reasons, Kerberos is a more secure and potentially faster authentication protocol.

Kerberos

Kerberos is the native Windows 2000 user authentication protocol that is designed for networks assumed to be insecure. Before any communication can take place between a client and a server—that is, between the computer requesting the resource and the computer that's got it—the identity of both client and server must be authenticated. Once a connection is established, the server and client can continue to use it until the client disconnects. If the client disconnects from the domain and then reconnects, the client and server must re-authenticate themselves.

Kerberos relies on a model of shared secrets. The idea is that if only two people (or computers, in this case) know a secret, they can use that secret to prove their identities to one another. For example, if Computer A wants to communicate with Computer B, Computer A must show Computer B that it knows the shared secret. Computer B then knows that it really is Computer A initiating the communication.

One way to communicate the secret is to include the secret in the network transmission. This technique, however, admits the possibility of a third computer listening on the same network, intercepting the message, and learning the secret. Thus, there must be way to use the secret without ever actually saying it.

Kerberos solves this problem by means of a cryptographic key known to both computers. Computer A demonstrates that it knows this key by encrypting the communication with it. Computer B demonstrates that it knows the key by decrypting the data and sending a receipt back to Computer A. If Computer B can't decrypt the data with the right key, it knows that the message wasn't really from Computer A. If Computer A receives a receipt, it knows that the message successfully reached the real Computer B. Because only the data encrypted with the key—not the key itself—actually goes on the network, a third party cannot intercept the key and use it. This process is called **secret key communication**.

Secret key communication raises some questions, however: For example:

- How did Computer A and Computer B obtain the shared cryptographic key in the first place?
- If Computer A needs to communicate with many servers and Computer B needs to communicate with many clients, how do they organize the keys that they need for each type of communication?
- How are the keys protected if every Windows 2000 machine needs to store these shared secrets locally?

The answer to these questions lies in the fact that Kerberos authentication is dependent not only on communication between client and server, but also on a third party: the **Key Distribution Center (KDC)**. The KDC is a Windows 2000 service that runs on a physically secure server. It maintains a database of all **security principals**—Windows 2000 computers—in its realm. The KDC maintains a key with each of its security principals to secure its communications. This key is generated from the password of the person or service using the security principal, and by requests from the client-side Kerberos client, immediately after someone logs onto the Windows 2000 computer.

When one security principal needs to communicate with another security principal, the first security principal contacts the KDC and asks for a key for that communication. The KDC generates such a key and sends it to the client computer—Computer A, to return to our earlier example. Computer A's copy of the key is encrypted with the long-term key that it shares with the KDC. Computer B's copy of the key is embedded in a data structure, called a **ticket**, which also includes authentication information for Computer A. The ticket is encrypted with the key shared by the KDC shares with Computer B. It doesn't matter that Computer A can't read the ticket because it doesn't know the key shared by the KDC and Computer B. Instead, Computer A simply stores the ticket in memory and passes it to Computer B when Computer A wants to start the communication. Computer B decrypts the communication with the key that it shares with the KDC and now has a shared key with Computer A.

Certificates

Certificates represent a portable method of authentication for a user or service. Basically, a certificate says, "I am what I say I am." Although certificates don't guarantee anything else about the person or service that they're identifying (for instance, a service with a certificate could potentially have a damaging effect on your computer), they assure you (or, more precisely, Windows 2000) that the identity of the user or service is known. Because certificates are such a trusted source of identification, you must have an equally trusted **certificate authority** to assign them. (A certificate authority is a server entrusted with the task of creating certificates for users and services.)

User Profiles and Group Policies

When using a modern operating system, people expect to be able to customize the interface. Users want to be able to modify environment settings, and network administrators want to be able to control the appearance and settings available to each user so as to better manage what users can and can't do on their computers. In Windows 2000, **user profiles** and **group policies** are the mechanisms that make this kind of control possible.

User Profiles

You can specify the custom settings defining the user environment and have Windows 2000 save those settings to a file, called a user profile. A user profile in Windows 2000 includes the following information:

- Screen colors
- Program items
- Network and printer connections
- Mouse settings
- Window size and position
- Redirected folders

Three kinds of user profiles exist: local, roaming, and mandatory. A **local user profile** is created the first time a user logs onto a computer and is stored on the computer's hard disk. The profile is then loaded and defines the user environment whenever that particular user logs onto that computer. If the user changes the profile, the modifications are saved when the user logs off. Users with local user profiles may have different environment settings for each computer they log into.

Roaming user profiles are set up by the system administrator and stored on a network server. When a user logs on, the profile server downloads the profile to the user's computer. As with local profiles, any changes that the user makes to the profile are saved when the user logs off. Users with roaming user profiles always have the same environment settings, no matter where they log into the network.

Mandatory user profiles are roaming user profiles that the user cannot edit. Only the system administrator can edit a mandatory user profile.

A local user profile is the simplest to create—it is created when the user logs onto a computer and then logs off. Roaming and mandatory profiles are a bit more complicated to create, because the system administrator must edit the profile settings for that user account (as shown in Figure 12-3) to point to the directory path from which the profile should be loaded. To assign a roaming profile, you type the network path to the profile's location, followed by the user's logon name, like this: \\servername\profilesfoldername\username. The roaming profile doesn't have to exist at the location you specify, because the user creates it automatically at logon in a folder with the same name as the user's logon name.

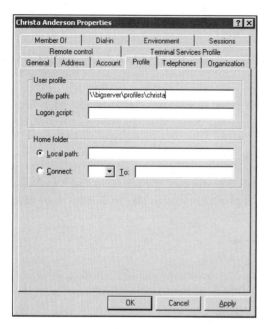

Figure 12-3 Configuring the location of a user profile

To assign a mandatory profile, you must create a profile and then point to it. To create a mandatory profile, open the System applet and access the user Profiles tab. Select an existing profile with the desired settings (see Figure 12-4) and copy it to the profiles folder. Once the file exists there, rename it with a .man (for mandatory) extension. Next, return to the Profiles tab of the property sheet for the user account. Type the network path to the profile's location and specify the name of the mandatory user profile, like this: \\servername\profilesfoldername\filename. You don't need to include the file's .man extension unless the domain includes Windows NT 3.x computers.

You can also create mandatory profiles for various groups. For example, the mandatory profile for people in the Users group could be Users.man; the mandatory profile for people in the Account Operators group could be Ao.man.

 A user can have different user profiles for ordinary network sessions and for terminal sessions. For example, a user might have a roaming network profile, but a mandatory terminal services profile. Configure network client profiles from the Profiles tab of a user's property sheet; configure terminal session profiles from the Terminal Services Profile tab.

Group Policies

Group policies control the security settings for computers and users in the domain. Almost any kind of control you might apply to a user account, user group, or computer in the domain can be set in the group policies.

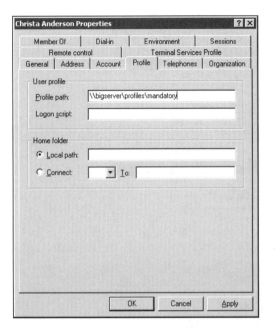

Figure 12-4 Mandatory profiles are based on existing profiles

Types of Group Policies

Group policies for users and computers are classified into three broad categories: software settings, Windows settings, and administrative templates. The exact contents of each policy depend on whether you are talking about a policy applied to a computer or to a user.

- Software settings control how software is installed and performs on the computer or for the user to whom the policy applies.

- Windows settings for users and computers control which logon and logoff scripts are run; they also configure security settings for the policy. For group profiles, the Windows settings control Internet Explorer settings and choice options for the Remote Installation Services, which permit users to install applications over the network. The Windows settings in some group policies might also include a Folder Redirection policy (see Figure 12-5). You can use this policy to point program folders to a new location, either using the same location for all users within that part of the Active Directory or pointing users in different groups to different folders customized to the needs of those group members. For example, you can use this setting to customize the Start menu for each group.

The Administrative Templates section, found in both user and computer group policies, is a comprehensive collection of settings that allow you to manage every part of the user environment that's controlled in the Registry.

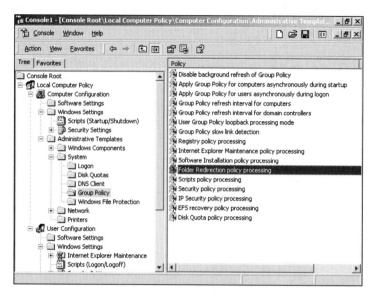

Figure 12-5 The Folder Redirection policy

The default setting for all group policy options is not configured; in fact, group policies are not applied until you explicitly apply them. You can either enable or disable a group policy, depending on the wording of the policy itself as displayed in the Microsoft Management Console (MMC). For example, to disable the Registry editing tools in a particular user policy, you would enable the policy that said to disable the tools. Disabling the policy not only makes those tools available, but can prevent another policy from making the tools available.

Applying Group Policies

In Windows 2000, group policies are normally applied at some level of the Active Directory structure; from there, they are inherited by the parts of the Active Directory that fall beneath them. For example, the domain might have one group policy, while each of the domain's organizational units (OUs) has another policy. When a user logs onto the domain, the group policy applied to that session depends on the OU of which the computer is part and the OU to which the account belongs. If more than one group policy is associated with a particular OU, site, or domain, the group policy with the highest precedence takes control. Precedence is set from the Group Policy tab of the Properties sheet of the part of Active Directory for which you're establishing a group policy.

Group policies are an extremely complex part of security in Windows 2000. Their characteristics can be summarized as follows:

- Group policies control security and Registry settings for domain use.
- Group policies may be set for either users or computers, or both.
- Group policies are set for each part of a domain. If two policies conflict, the least restrictive policy normally takes control. The only time when this statement doesn't hold true is when policy inheritance is disabled.

Data Encryption

One method of protecting data involves encrypting it. **Encryption** is a blanket term for any method of systematically garbling text into a form called **ciphertext** to conceal its meaning. To read it, you must apply an algorithm called a **key** that reverses the logic used to encrypt the text. When you apply the key to the ciphertext, you turn it back to its readable form, called **plaintext**. Only the people who have the key can decrypt the ciphertext. The encryption method may be simple, such as substituting each letter for the one that occurs three letters later in the alphabet, or it may be very complex. The more complex the encryption algorithm, the longer it takes to encrypt and decrypt data, even with the key. Very complicated keys are left to computers, which can quickly perform the calculations required to apply the algorithm.

Two main types of encryption exist: **symmetric encryption** and asymmetric (or **public key**) encryption key. These types of encryption are discussed in the following sections.

Symmetric Encryption

Symmetric encryption uses the same algorithm to encrypt and decrypt text. Kerberos uses symmetric encryption, because clients and servers share a cryptographic key. For files to be used and accessible only to a single person, symmetric encryption is adequate because only a single person needs to know the key. If several people must share a file, however, the situation becomes more complicated. The person doing the encrypting needs to tell the person planning to decrypt the file what the key is, without compromising the key's security. For example, Susan can encrypt data for Fred, but Fred will need the key to decrypt the data and read it. If Susan works in Texas and Fred is located in Wisconsin, getting the key to Fred securely is tricky. Letters, telephone calls, or e-mail can all be intercepted, thereby compromising the key. One solution is to maintain a book that indicates which keys to use under which circumstances. As both sides found out during the course of World War I, such books of this type may be lost.

Another issue with symmetric encryption is the problem of ascertaining who encrypted a file. For example, someone passes an encrypted file to George, indicating that the file came from Susan. The key George has works on the file, so he knows that Susan could have encrypted it. Because Susan shares files with other people, however, Fred could have just as easily created the file while trying to pass it off as Susan's.

Public Key Encryption

Because of the shortcomings of symmetric encryption, public key encryption has emerged as the de facto standard for encrypting data intended for computer transmission. This encryption method uses two user-specific keys to encrypt and decrypt data: one public and one private. To encrypt data, you must encrypt it with the recipient's public key. The recipient applies that **private key** to decrypt the text. Public keys can be distributed, but private keys are reserved for their owners; there's no such thing as a generic private key. If you want to encrypt data for David, you must use David's public key to do it.

Data Encryption in Windows 2000

Support for encrypted text is not new to Windows. Many encryption tools are available on the Web that you can use with any operating system to secure your data, such as Elgamal, RSA (Rivest, Shamir, and Adelman), Diffie-Hellman, and DSA (Digital Signature Algorithm). Windows 2000 is unique among Windows operating systems, however, in that native encryption is built into its NTFS file system. This feature allows you to secure your documents so that only you—or the people to whom you give the private key—can view the documents. As a result, you can even keep shared documents private or secure files on a computer, such as a laptop, that might easily be stolen. The files are visible to anyone with access to the directories in which they're stored. When someone attempts to open an encrypted file, however, Windows 2000 checks whether the user has a key to that file. If so, the file opens normally. If not, the user is forbidden access to the file. The denial isn't application-dependent. For example, although it's possible to open .doc files in either Microsoft Word or WordPad (the word processor that comes with Windows 2000), you can't open an encrypted .doc file in either application. Without the key to that file, you don't have permission to open it.

Although Windows 2000 supports three file systems (FAT16, FAT32, and NTFS), you can encrypt only files stored on NTFS volumes. This restriction applies because encryption is an NTFS **attribute**, which is a characteristic of a file. FAT file systems under Windows 2000 do not include an encryption attribute, just as they do not include attributes for many of the other advanced features of the NTFS file system, such as file compression and local file security.

When you encrypt data for the first time, you generate a request for a new security certificate that identifies you to Windows 2000. A cryptographic service provider (CSP) generates two 56-bit unrelated keys: a public key, used for encrypting data destined for you, and a private key, used for decrypting that data. The CSP passes the security certificate to the certificate authority, which uses it to create a public key for you. The certificate and public key are stored in the Personal, Certificates folder located in the Certificates add-in to the MMC (see Figure 12-6).

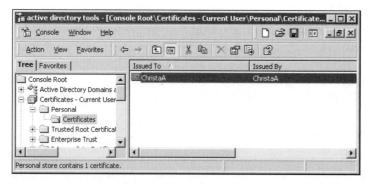

Figure 12-6 Personal encryption certificates are visible from the Certificates add-in

Encryption Tools in Windows 2000

The process of encrypting data in Windows 2000 is very simple. Open Windows Explorer (Start, Programs, Accessories, Windows Explorer). Right-click a file or folder stored in an NTFS directory, and then choose Properties from the context menu. Select the General tab, and click the Advanced button to open the dialog box shown in Figure 12-7. (If you don't see an Advanced button, the file you selected isn't stored in an NTFS volume.)

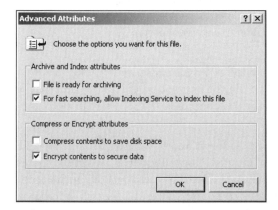

Figure 12-7 Setting encryption attributes for a file

As you can see, two advanced NTFS attributes are available: encryption and compression. The two are mutually exclusive: a file cannot be both encrypted and compressed with NTFS attributes. Check the box that says "Encrypt contents to secure data," and click OK. Click OK again to exit the property sheet. Check the option you want, and click OK. If the folder containing the file is not encrypted, you will be warned of this fact before you close the property sheet and prompted to encrypt both the folder and the file. Because new files inherit the encryption attributes of the folder in which they're stored, it is a good idea to store only encrypted files in encrypted folders. Otherwise, if the file changes in a way that makes Windows 2000 perceive it as new, the file will lose its encryption attribute.

Moving and copying files between encrypted and plaintext directories introduces some problems. If you copy or move an unencrypted file to an encrypted NTFS folder, the file becomes encrypted. If you copy or move an encrypted file to an unencrypted NTFS folder, the file remains encrypted. If you copy or move an encrypted file to a FAT or FAT32 folder, the file is no longer encrypted (because encryption is an NTFS attribute). As a security measure, Windows 2000 does not allow you to copy an encrypted file to an unencrypted folder unless you have the private key needed to decrypt the file.

Windows 2000 users can encrypt data across the network, but the certificate always remains on the Windows 2000 machine where the ciphertext is stored. The private key is stored in the Registry of the computer holding the ciphertext.

Windows 2000 also supports a command-line encryption utility called CIPHER. To encrypt a single folder in the current directory, type **cipher /e** *foldername*, where "foldername" is the name of the folder you want to encrypt and "/e" stands for "encrypt." To decrypt the same folder, replace the /e switch with /d, like this: **cipher /d** *foldername*. The command will report whether the operation succeeded. Because compressed data can't be encrypted, if you try to encrypt a compressed file or folder from the command line, you will receive an Access Denied error. You must uncompress the file or folder before Windows 2000 can apply the encryption attribute to the file object.

Windows 2000 can't encrypt or decrypt a folder's contents if they're in use (or even displayed in a Windows Explorer window), so make sure that no one is using files that you are attempting to encrypt or decrypt.

Windows 2000 makes the process of decrypting a file transparent to the person who uses the file. Whenever you attempt to open the file, the encryption file system checks whether a private key belonging to you is stored on the computer. If it is, you can open the file. If it is not, you are denied access.

Removing the encryption attribute altogether is another matter. To decrypt a file or folder to allow anyone to read it, right-click the file, choose Properties, select the General tab, and click the Advanced button. In the Advanced Attributes dialog box, uncheck the "Encrypt contents to secure data" check box (refer to Figure 12-7). The file will then be open to anyone with the permission to access it.

Enforcing Encryption

Encrypted files don't have any obvious differences alerting people to their off-limits status. Indeed, the contents of an encrypted folder are displayed like any other shared or locally available data. The only way you can tell that you have attempted to open an encrypted file is that you won't be able to open it. If you try, the server will chug away for a moment or two while Windows 2000 looks for a private key that matches your certificate, then the system will deny access when it doesn't find one. Not even administrators can open or decrypt files that someone else has encrypted. In addition, file ownership is not relevant to decryption—if a person takes ownership of someone else's encrypted file, the new owner will not be able to open it.

Protecting Encryption Keys

Microsoft implemented the Windows 2000 encryption services especially for the benefit of laptop users who wanted to keep their data secure even if their laptops were stolen. This security plan has a major hole, however. If someone steals a laptop and you haven't protected your account, the thief can read your encrypted files. To avoid this problem, Microsoft recommends exporting each user's certificate with the private key and saving it to disk, then deleting the certificate on the computer. That way, even if intruders log onto the computer with your account, they won't be able to read the encrypted files stored there.

CHAPTER SUMMARY

- To secure your network, you need to know how you can use the operating system to control access to network resources. Two main modes of licensing exist: per-seat and per-user. Different types of licenses are also available: console license, client access license, terminal server license, and application license.

- After your licenses are in place, you need to assign user and group permissions, which you do via server or domain accounts and various methods of authentication, such as NTLM and Kerberos. You can also control security by managing your user profiles and group policies and by using certificates and data encryption. Two types of encryption exist: symmetric and public key. You can manage encryption in Windows 2000 via Windows Explorer or through the CIPHER command-line utility.

KEY TERMS

application license — A license that allows you to run a particular application.

application service provider (ASP) — A service running applications from a terminal server and making them available to anonymous users via the Internet for a fee.

attribute — A characteristic associated with a file object (file or folder). Different file systems have different attributes.

authentication — The process that a computer undertakes to determine that you are who you say you are.

certificate — A portable method of authentication that demonstrates the identity of a user or service. Certificates are files that may be imported or exported, so you can move or copy them if necessary.

certificate authority — A server entrusted with the task of creating certificates for users and services.

ciphertext — Encrypted data.

client access license — A type of license that permits the holder to access a server from the network.

console license — A type of license that comes with an operating system and represents permission to install the operating system on a single machine and use it from that machine.

domain — A group of computers that shares a centralized security database.

domain controller — The computer that stores the domain's security database. A domain can have more than one domain controller to ease the burden of authenticating users.

encryption — A blanket term for any method of systematically obscuring the meaning of data by applying an encryption key to it.

End User License Agreement (EULA) — Paper or software text accompanying software that defines the conditions under which the licensee may use the software.

group policies — Policies that control the security settings for computers and users in the domain.

groupware — Multiuser applications that come with a group license and are used by several people simultaneously, such as e-mail servers.

interactive logon — The act of typing your name and password into the login screen of a Windows 2000 computer.

Internet client license (ICL) — A type of license that permits an anonymous user to log onto a terminal server via the Internet. ICLs are restricted for anonymous use; people with domain accounts can't use them.

Kerberos — The native Windows 2000 authentication protocol. Kerberos relies on a system of shared secrets for mutual authentication of client and server.

key — An algorithm used to encrypt or decrypt data. Sometimes, the same key may do both; at other times, the encryption key may be different from the decryption key.

Key Distribution Center (KDC) — A secure server in a Windows 2000 domain that's responsible for generating the cryptographic keys and tickets that are the basis of Kerberos security.

Local Security Authority (LSA) — The component that checks whether a user logging on has an account on a local or a trusted domain. When you are logging onto another domain, the LSA must communicate with that domain's domain controller to see whether the domain controller has an account for you in its security database.

local user profile — A user profile stored on the local computer; the default setting for all user profiles. Local user profiles exist on a per-computer basis, so a user may have different environment settings depending on which computer he or she logs onto. Changes to the profile are saved to the local computer when the user logs off.

mandatory user profile — A roaming user profile that is not user-definable. If the user changes the environment settings, those changes are not saved at logoff. A mandatory user profile has a .man extension.

NT LAN Manager (NTLM) — The default authentication protocol used in Windows NT 4.

per-seat license — A type of license that permits a predefined number of computer connections to the operating system or application being licensed.

per-session license — A type of license that permits a predefined number of simultaneous user connections to the operating system or application being licensed.

plaintext — Unencrypted data.

private key — A key devoted to decrypting data for a particular person. Private keys should be kept secure.

public key — A key devoted to encrypting data for a particular person. A public key only encrypts; it does not decrypt.

roaming user profile — A user profile stored on a network server and downloaded to whichever computer a user is currently logged into. Changes to the profile are saved to the network server when the user logs off.

secret key communication — The method of authentication on which Kerberos is based, where a client and server must both know and use the same cryptographic key to protect the network.

security principal — A Windows 2000 computer in a domain using Kerberos.

symmetric encryption — A method of data encryption that uses the same algorithm to encrypt and decrypt plaintext.

terminal server client access license (TSCAL) — A type of license that permits the computer to which it's assigned to run a session from a terminal server.

ticket — A data structure generated by the KDC when a client computer asks the KDC for a secret key. The server's half of the secret key is embedded in the ticket and encrypted with the key that the KDC and the server have in common.

user profile — A file containing environment settings, which is loaded when a person logs onto a computer or domain. User profiles may be stored on the local computer or on a server, and may be either user-definable or locked down.

REVIEW QUESTIONS

1. What is the Windows 2000 file system that supports native encryption?
   a. FAT32
   b. NTFS
   c. FAT
   d. Kernel

2. _____ licenses permit a certain number of simultaneous connections to the operating system or application being licensed.

3. Per-seat licenses are assigned to users. True or False?

4. You're running one instance of WordCruncher on your local computer (running Windows 98) and one in a terminal session on the same computer. WordCruncher is licensed on a per-seat basis. You need one application license. True or False?

5. Does your answer to question 4 change if your computer is running Windows 2000 Professional? Why or why not?

6. Which of the following describes the interactive logon process?
   a. When you type your name and password, the Local Security Authority passes the information to WinLogon, which then communicates with the domain controller to see whether you have a valid account.
   b. When you type your name and password, the domain controller generates a certificate that authenticates you on the domain.
   c. When you type your name and password, the Local Security Authority generates a secure key from the password and passes that key to the domain controller to secure communications.
   d. When you type your name and password, WinLogon accepts the information and passes it to the Local Security Authority, which compares the information with the contents of the domain security database.

7. Which authentication protocols for LANs does Windows 2000 support? (Choose all that apply.)
   a. TCP/IP
   b. Kerberos
   c. IPX/SPX
   d. NTLM
8. The native Windows 2000 authentication protocol works with a system of shared secrets. Both the client and the server know the same cryptographic key, and must prove their identities by sending the key across the network before any communication can begin. True or False?
9. Which of the following is part of the native Windows 2000 authentication process? (Choose all that apply.)
   a. Clients
   b. Protocols
   c. KDC
   d. Server
10. _____ can define the contents of your Documents folder; _____ can define whether you have a Documents folder and redirect it to a new location.
11. By default, what are the per-user environment settings?
    a. Stored on the local computer
    b. Stored on the domain controller
    c. Stored in the Active Directory
    d. None of the above
12. Kerberos uses symmetric encryption. True or False?
13. If you take ownership of someone else's encrypted file, can you read the file? Why or why not?
14. To access a Windows 2000 terminal server from Windows 2000 Professional, what do you need?
    a. A CAL
    b. A TSCAL
    c. A groupware license
    d. All of the above
15. Which of the following is not a reason to have multiple domain controllers in the domain? (Choose all that apply.)
    a. Having multiple domain controllers reduces network traffic.
    b. Having multiple domain controllers may make user authentications faster.

c. Having multiple domain controllers reduces the amount of time required for Kerberos authentication.

d. Having multiple domain controllers reduces the stress on the main domain controller.

16. Which of the following statements about the Local Security Authority are true?

    a. You don't need it in a Windows 2000-only network because Kerberos fulfills the same function.

    b. It authenticates you both at the computer you log onto and when you access a network resource in a mixed network.

    c. Both a and b

    d. Neither a nor b

17. Which of the following operating systems support Kerberos?

    a. Windows NT and Windows 2000

    b. Windows NT Server Enterprise Edition and Windows 2000

    c. Windows 2000 Server

    d. Windows 2000

18. Which of the following describes Kerberos?

    a. Kerberos requires a central server.

    b. Kerberos does not require you to be reauthenticated on the network each time you access a new resource.

    c. Kerberos uses private key encryption to prove client and server identities.

    d. To make Kerberos work, you need a central server to pass out tickets.

19. Which of the following cannot be set with a mandatory user profile?

    a. Window size and position

    b. Program items

    c. Network and printer connections

    d. None of the above

20. Group policies may be applied on many different levels of the Active Directory structure. If policy settings for a particular person conflict, which policy takes precedence?

    a. The domain level

    b. The user level

    c. The group level

    d. The least restrictive policy controls

Hands-on Projects

Project 12-1

To copy a profile to a new location and make it a mandatory profile:

1. Open the **System applet** in the **Control Panel** and select the **User Profiles** tab, as shown in Figure 12-8. Select a profile not currently in use.

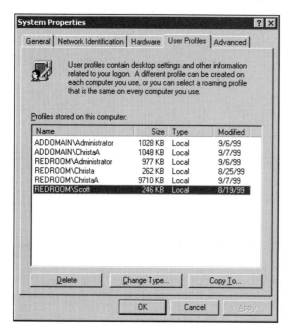

Figure 12-8 The User Profiles tab displays all user profiles stored on the local computer

2. Click the **Copy To** button to open the dialog box shown in Figure 12-9.

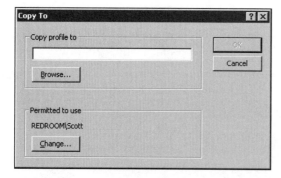

Figure 12-9 Choose a shared folder in which to store the profile

3. Click the **Browse** button and choose a shared folder in which to put the profile. To keep things simple, it is best to name this folder "Profiles."
4. Click **OK**, then click **Yes** to confirm the copy operation. Finally, click **OK** to exit the system applet.
5. In Windows Explorer, browse to the folder where you copied the file. Set the view so that you can see hidden files. Look for a file named Ntuser.dat (see Figure 12-10) and rename it with a .man extension.

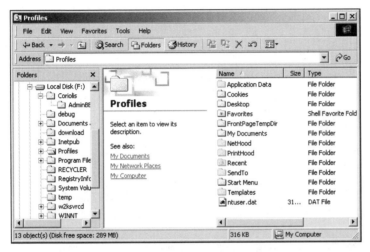

Figure 12-10 Rename a profile file with a .man extension to make it mandatory

Project 12-2

To export a certificate and private key from one Windows 2000 computer and import it to another computer:

1. In the MMC (**Start**, **Run**, **MMC**), add the **Certificates snap-in** (be sure to select the **My User Account** option).
2. In the **Personal** folder, open the **Certificates** folder. The per-user certificates on the computer are displayed in the right pane. Right-click the certificate that you want to export as a file, and choose **Export** from the **All Tasks** menu. The Certificate Export Wizard opens.
3. Click past the opening screen to the first screen (Figure 12-11), which asks whether you would like to export the private key along with the certificate. You need the private key to decrypt data, so select it.

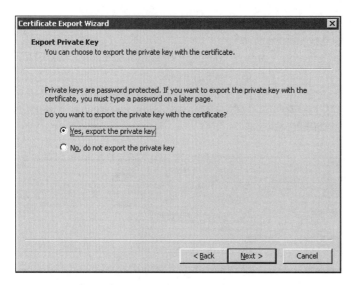

Figure 12-11 Export the private key with the certificate

4. In the next screen, shown in Figure 12-12, choose the export options, including the file type, the strength of encryption, and action to take with the local key if the export works.

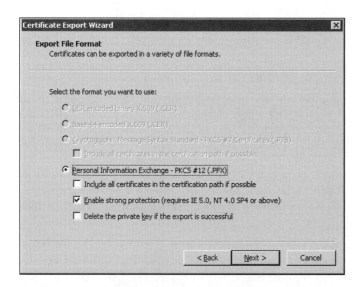

Figure 12-12 Set certificate export options

5. In the next screen of the wizard, supply a password to import the certificate and private key. Choose this password carefully.
6. Choose a filename for the key, by either typing a path or browsing for it. Although you can save the file on any volume, NTFS volumes are generally a more secure storage

location if you don't need the flexibility of a floppy disk. Save the certificate on a floppy disk or, better yet, in a safe network location where it can be backed up, then delete it from the computer. You'll be able to open encrypted files, but the certificate will no longer reside on the machine.

7. The final screen of the wizard displays your choices. Review them carefully, then click **Finish** to export the keys. If the export operation worked, Windows 2000 displays a message box to tell you so (see Figure 12-13).

Figure 12-13 Successful certificate export confirmation

Project 12-3

To import a certificate to a new computer:

1. To import the certificate to another computer or replace it on the same one, open the **Personal** folder, right-click the **Certificates** folder, and choose **Import** from the **All Tasks** list. The Certificate Import Wizard opens.

2. Click **Next** on the opening screen, then browse for the file you saved in Hands-on Project 12-2.

3. If the certificate you're importing includes the private key, you need to supply the password assigned when the key was exported. Type it as shown in Figure 12-14, and choose the degree of control you want over the private key.

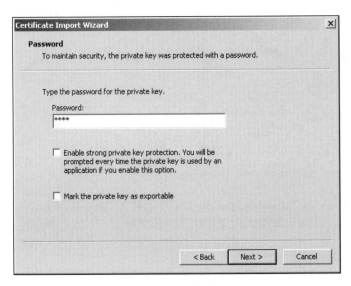

Figure 12-14 Provide the password to the private key and choose the degree of control

4. Specify where the new key should go. For user keys, the Personal folder should be fine.

5. Review the importing options, then click the **Finish** button to import the key. Windows 2000 will tell you whether the importing action succeeded.

Project 12-4

To edit a group policy setting:

1. In the MMC (**Start**, **Run**, **MMC**), add the **Group Policy snap-in** for the local computer. You should see an icon for the Group Policy snap-in.

2. Click **Local Computer Policy** in the left pane of the MMC to reveal the User Configuration and Computer Configuration objects within it. Double-click the **User Configuration** object to show its contents.

3. Open the **Administrative Templates** folder, the **Control Panel** folder, and then the **Display** folder.

4. Double-click **Disable changing wallpaper** to open the property sheet shown in Figure 12-15. Click the **Explain** tab to see an explanation of this policy.

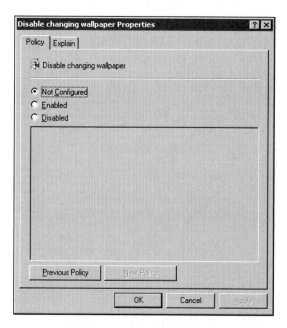

Figure 12-15 View the properties for a group policy

5. From the **Policy** tab, click **Enable**, and then click **OK**. Users to whom this policy applies will not be able to change their system wallpaper.

Project 12-5

To encrypt a folder from Windows Explorer:

1. Right-click a folder stored in an NTFS directory, and then choose **Properties** from the context menu to open the folder's property sheet.
2. On the **General** tab, click the **Advanced** button to open the dialog box shown in Figure 12-16. (If you don't see an Advanced button, the file you selected isn't stored in an NTFS volume.)

Figure 12-16 Encrypting a folder

3. Two advanced NTFS attributes appear here: encryption and compression. The two are mutually exclusive; a file cannot be both encrypted and compressed with NTFS attributes. Click the box next to **Encrypt contents to secure data**, and then click **OK**.
4. Click **OK** again to exit the property sheet. Click **OK** again to confirm the attribute change. The file is now encrypted.

Project 12-6

To specify a new path for a roaming user profile:

1. From the **Active Directory Users and Computers** snap-in to the MMC, open the **Users** folder as shown in Figure 12-17.

356   **Chapter 12**   **Securing Network Resources**

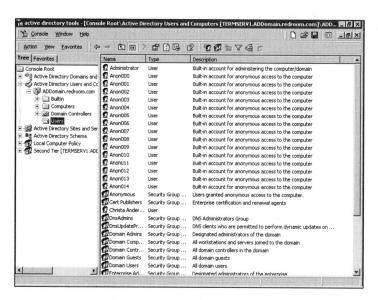

Figure 12-17   Edit user settings from the Management Console

2. Right-click one of the anonymous accounts and choose **Properties** from its context menu. Select the **Profile** tab, as shown in Figure 12-18.

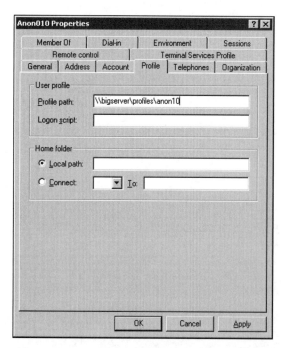

Figure 12-18   Manipulating user account properties

3. Type the path to the shared profiles directory, ending the path with the name of the account. For example, for Anon10, the path might look like this: \\bigserver\profiles\anon10. Do not refer to the profile location with a drive letter name, because that technique works only if the shared folder is always mapped to the same drive letter on all computers.

4. Click **OK** to save the change. Anon10 now stores his user profile in the location you specified.

CASE PROJECTS

1. You have set up a domain using all Windows 2000 Servers for domain controllers. All network servers are running Windows 2000. The clients are running Windows NT Workstation. Which authentication protocol will you use, and why?

2. You're logging onto a Windows 2000 terminal server from a Windows 98 computer. How many licenses must you purchase to make this setup legal? How does the answer change if you're running the terminal session from a Windows 2000 computer?

3. Describe briefly how Windows 2000 applies group policies if a user logs into an OU with one group policy but that OU is part of a domain with another group policy, and the policies conflict in some way. Which policy will maintain control?

4. Describe how you would encrypt data for someone—and how that person would decrypt it—in a public key encryption system.

CHAPTER 13
FAULT TOLERANCE

> **After reading this chapter and completing the exercises, you will be able to:**
> - Define the parts of an operating system that make it fault-tolerant
> - Explain how the various backup operations work
> - List the backup media supported by Windows 2000
> - Explain what RAID is and how the various forms of RAID supported by Windows 2000 contribute to its fault tolerance
> - Define clustering and explain how it works

A key component of any operating system is availability. That is, you shouldn't have to wonder whether your data will be available for use. To ensure that your data remain available to users at all times, you must implement some form of **fault tolerance**.

To provide this high availability, the operating system you're using should be fault-tolerant. Fault-tolerant systems protect user and system configuration data and make sure that the computer itself remains available. In the course of this chapter, you will learn about the methods that an operating system can employ to be fault-tolerant, such as backups, fault-tolerant disk arrays, and (for Windows 2000 Advanced Server and Windows 2000 Datacenter) **clustering**.

Backing Up and Restoring Data

All computers fail sooner or later—hard disks stop working, drive controllers fail, power glitches zap motherboards, and so forth. Although you can take prophylactic measures to keep this failure from affecting production too badly, you can't prevent a computer from ever failing. All you can do is make sure that the computer is as easily replaceable as possible if it does fail.

The first line of defense for making a computer replaceable is having a current and reliable backup. If you have a reliable backup of your data and your computer stops working, you can load the data somewhere else. After all, the important part of the computer is not the computer itself, but rather the files you create and store on it. In addition to backing up the files on your computer, you should back up your system configuration data; you can then re-create the behavior of your system as well as the data it contained. You will especially want to take this step if your computer has a complicated configuration or you have done much fine-tuning to get your computer exactly the way you like it. For example, if you have backed up your system and application configuration data, you can reinstall WordCruncher on the new machine and then restore all of the special settings you made for this program, such as file locations, locations and contents of toolbars, new templates, and the like. You can always rebuild application configuration information, but it is a long and tedious process.

Backing up system configuration data—called **system state data** in Windows 2000—is even more important than backing up application configuration data. This importance stems from the fact that some data structures are identified to the operating system not by the names you give them, but by their **security identification (SID) numbers**. You cannot manually edit these SID numbers from the Windows 2000 tools. For example, imagine that you have a domain called ALPHA that has a single domain controller named ROVER. One day, the domain controller fails. You buy a new computer, reinstall Windows 2000, create a domain named ALPHA, and name the domain controller ROVER. You may think everything is fixed, but it is not. No one will be able to log onto the domain, because the domain to which everyone else belonged had a different SID number than the one you just created. To remedy this problem, all the computers must rejoin the ALPHA domain.

On a similar note, imagine that you configured security auditing for certain people to allow them to monitor their network activity. If you have to rebuild the account database (a long and tedious process, because you must re-create all user rights associated with those accounts), you also need to reconfigure the audit trail. To Windows 2000, the rebuilt accounts look like new accounts because their SID numbers are different from the ones that auditing was previously set up to configure. Windows 2000 doesn't pay attention to the names that you assign users, groups, or domains; it pays attention to the SID numbers.

System state data for a Windows 2000 Server computer include all of the following:

- The system Registry
- The COM+ class registration database of file associations
- The boot files for the computer
- The certificate services database (for a certificate server)
- The Active Directory structure (for a domain controller)
- The SYSVOL directory (for a domain controller)

You can't pick and choose certain parts of the system state data to back up—backing up is an all-or-nothing proposition in this case. System state data tend to be large (hundreds of megabytes, at least, and perhaps more depending on the complexity of the Active Directory structure)—keep that fact in mind when you choose a backup destination (for example, on another computer's hard drive or a tape backup).

Unless you want to take the chance that you will have to rebuild your servers and domain controllers from the ground up when computers fail, you need to back up. Read on to learn about the tools that Windows 2000 provides for this endeavor and the ways in which you can use them to easily and effectively protect your data.

Backup Tools

The mechanics behind a backup are simple. During the backup process, the backup application reads the directories and files you select and decides which files are eligible for backup by using the criteria you established when you set up the backup operation. Backing up is simply a file copy operation like the one you do when you use the COPY or XCOPY command. Files are copied from a source folder to a destination folder. To the backup tool, the source folder consists of the folder where you normally store the files, and the destination folder consists of the backup media. Restoring data from backup media works in the same way, only in reverse.

Windows 2000 comes with two tools that you can use to back up and restore user data and system configuration information: the graphical backup tool located in the System Tools section of the Accessories program group (see Figure 13-1), and a command-line tool called **NTBACKUP**. The two are similar in function, but not identical.

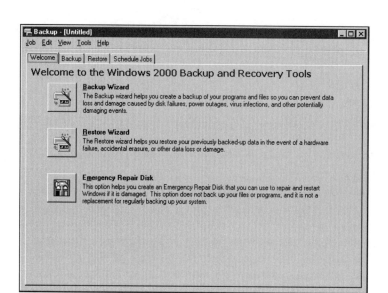

Figure 13-1 Backup tool in Windows 2000

Whichever tool you use, in the course of setting up a backup operation, you will configure some or all of the following options:

- *Backup or restore?* The backup tools can both back up and restore data.

- *Copy system state data?* Specifies that all system state data should be backed up and sets the backup type to normal or copy. This option is available only if you are backing up the local computer—for security reasons, you can't back up system configuration information over the network.

- *Name of backup file?* Backups are stored in a special file called a **selection information file** that has a .bks extension. More than one backup job can go into the same selection information file. You must create this file from the GUI before referencing it from the command line.

- *Name of the backup job?* You must assign a name to the backup job. NTBACKUP stores this job in a selection information file with a .bks extension.

- *Where will the selection information file be stored?* You can identify the backup location for each job you schedule. This backup location may be a media pool (a logical grouping of removable media, such as a tape library), a tape, a removable drive, a floppy disk, or a file on the hard disk.

- *Description of the backup job?* In addition to naming a backup job for identification purposes, you can give it a description to further delineate it.

- *Append or replace?* When backing up to a specific physical location (as opposed to backing up to a media pool), you can choose to either append the new backup to the existing data or wipe the old data out and write only the new data.

- *Verify the backup job?* Verifying a backup—that is, making sure that the final product of the backup matches the data on the original media—adds some time to the backup process but is a good way to ensure that the data were written correctly.

- *Who gets to use the backup media?* You can specify whether anyone can restore the backup or whether that privilege is restricted to only members of the Administrators group and the person who created the backup. Limiting the number of people authorized to restore a backup may make it a little more inconvenient to restore data, but it prevents unauthorized people from stealing information from backup tapes.

- *What kind of backup logging do you want to do?* A backup log is a text file that shows the process of the backup and lists any errors that occurred during the backup. The Windows 2000 backup applications support three options for backup logging: full (lists every file copied to the backup media), summary (logs only errors and important events such as the start and end of the backup), and none (which doesn't log errors at all). Generally, the summary option—the default—is the best choice because it provides you with the information you need to know. Use a full log only if you need a record of every file that was included in the backup, perhaps for auditing purposes.

- *What type of backup should be performed?* As discussed in the next section, the Windows 2000 backup applications support several backup types: normal, differential, incremental, copy, and daily. A particular backup job can perform only one of these types of backups.

- *Back up removable storage database?* Windows 2000 supports hierarchical storage management, which is a system of moving rarely used files to removable storage but maintaining a pointer to these files on the hard disk. When you access a file that's been moved, it appears as if you are opening a file stored on disk; in reality, the file is opened from tape. If you don't back up the removable storage database that records the locations of archived files, you cannot retrieve moved files because no record exists of where the files were stored.

- *Use hardware compression?* If you're backing up to a tape drive that supports hardware compression (most do), you have the option of using this compression. Go ahead and use hardware compression if it's available, because it allows you to get more use out of your tapes.

Backup Schemes

Windows 2000 supports several types of backup schemes that you can combine to back up your data quickly and thoroughly. Most backup types are dependent on a file attribute called the **archive bit** that is turned on (set) when a file is edited (or added—all new files carry the archive bit) and turned off when the backup program turns it off (resets it). Depending on the backup scheme employed by the backup program, the archive bit signals whether a file should be backed up.

Normal Backups

A **normal backup** copies every selected file to the backup media and resets the archive bit to show that the files have been backed up. Normal backups are the cornerstone of any backup program, because they are the only backup method that ensures that you get a complete copy of your file set. A network administrator's backup scheme typically calls for a normal backup at least once per week.

Backing up once per week isn't enough, however. Think about all the work you did over the past seven days. If your computer crashed, could you re-create all of it? How about those crucial insights that aren't written anywhere else, or the complex CAD drawings you did? If you had hard copies, you might be able to re-create the data, but it would be a laborious process and waste a great deal of time. Think of how long it would take an entire company to re-create a week's worth of data—while probably needing to use those data simultaneously—and you can see that backing up once weekly is not enough. Performing a normal backup every night would be another option, but backing up gigabytes of files takes a long time and requires gigabytes of storage space. Although tape storage is less expensive than disk storage, storing a complete backup for every night would add up—both in terms of buying tapes and in terms of finding storage space for those tapes. In addition, you would face the problem of finding the time to back up gigabytes of data every day. Because the Windows 2000 backup programs do not back up open files, you need a decent chunk of time when no one is using any data files to perform the backup. That may not be possible every night, especially when more people are working at home on at least a part-time basis, and communicating with the network via a dial-up connection or terminal services. Backups need to be complete, but they also need to happen as quickly as possible.

To make it easier for companies to perform fast and complete backups, the Windows 2000 backup programs include two kinds of partial backups (incremental and differential backups) that copy only a certain set of files to the backup media. You can use these types of backups to supplement your normal backups, perhaps running an incremental or daily backup every day and a normal backup once each week.

Incremental Backups

An **incremental backup** copies every file that has the archive bit set (meaning that the file is new or has been edited since the last full backup) and resets the archive bit to show that the file has been backed up. If you perform an incremental backup every day, you have a day-to-day record of which files were changed. In addition, backing up takes only as long as copying the changed files, rather than copying every file.

To restore incremental backups to a server, you must collect all of the incremental backups performed since the previous normal backup and restore them. This process ensures that the most recent files appear on the server. Incremental backups take little time to perform because the collection of the files that change each day (or however often you back up) is bound to be small. Restoring the files may take some time, however, because you must restore each backup set separately. On the other hand, incremental backups make it easy for you to preserve multiple copies of files, in case you need to restore a version that is not necessarily the most recent. For example, if a virus was introduced to the system on Wednesday, you would want to back up from files saved before then.

Differential Backups

A **differential backup** copies every file that has the archive bit set, but does not reset the archive bit. Therefore, each time you back up, the backup set becomes larger because the previously backed up files are included in the backup set even if they haven't changed. To restore a server, you simply restore the last normal backup, then restore the most recent differential backup.

Although differential backups allow you to restore a server with ease, they are apt to take longer to perform than incremental backups, because you must first run the last normal backup, then perform the differential backup. They're also a little less flexible when it comes to finding a specific version of a file, because you can't easily tell which files changed on a specific day.

Creating a Backup Scheme

Most often, you won't use a single backup type. Instead, you will combine several types in some way to create a comprehensive backup plan that guarantees the following:

- A complete and updated set of data for the server
- A previous copy of data, in case the current backups are corrupted
- Maximum availability for the network—meaning that the backup system itself cannot interfere with the operation of the network

A backup can interfere with the network in several ways. As mentioned earlier, the Windows 2000 backup tools don't let you copy open files; therefore, to back up a server, you must shut down all server connections to ensure that all files are closed. Also, if you are backing up over the main network, the stream of data uses up a lot of available bandwidth. For this reason, many people implementing network backup solutions create a dedicated backup network that does not interfere with the main network.

A core part of the backup plan is the backup schedule. Microsoft suggests two possible schedule types: **Grandfather/Father/Son (GFS)** and the **Tower of Hanoi (ToH)**, named after a math puzzle.

In the GFS backup scheme, the "grandfather" is a monthly full backup, the "father" is a weekly full backup, and the "son" is a daily incremental or differential backup. GFS uses a total of 12 tapes (depending on the capacity of your tapes) or other backup media to keep a three-month record of the backup data—long enough to restore even rarely used files that someone accidentally erased two months ago. You could, of course, keep two series of the GFS scheme to create an even larger archive.

ToH is more complicated than GFS, but keeps a longer record of server data—32 weeks instead of 12 weeks. In ToH, you use five tapes labeled A–E in the following order: A B A C A B A D A B A C A B A E, and you perform a full backup on each tape. Tape A is reused every 2 weeks, tape B every 4 weeks, tape C every 8 weeks, tape D every 16 weeks, and tape E every

32 weeks. Because all of these operations are normal backups, it is a good idea to supplement ToH with a daily incremental or differential backup.

Table 13-1 shows a simple backup schedule based on the GFS backup scheme, having started with full backup tape 1 and assuming that no one works weekends.

Table 13-1 A sample backup schedule

Week	Day	Backup Type and Tape Used
Week 1	Monday	Differential tape A
	Tuesday	Differential tape B
	Wednesday	Differential tape C
	Thursday	Differential tape D
	Friday	Full backup tape 2
Week 2	Monday	Differential tape E
	Tuesday	Differential tape F
	Wednesday	Differential tape G
	Thursday	Differential tape H
	Friday	Full backup tape 3
Week 3	Monday	Differential tape A (overwrite)
	Tuesday	Differential tape B (overwrite)
	Wednesday	Differential tape C (overwrite)
	Thursday	Differential tape D (overwrite)
	Friday	Full backup tape 4
Week 4	Monday	Differential tape E (overwrite)
	Tuesday	Differential tape F overwrite)
	Wednesday	Differential tape G (overwrite)
	Thursday	Differential tape H (overwrite)
	Friday	Full backup tape 5

Other Backup Types

The Windows 2000 backup applications also include some other backup types (copy and daily backups) that are not really intended for backups, but rather more for file archiving or copying currently used files to other media. A **copy backup** works like a normal backup in that it copies all selected files to the backup media, regardless of whether the archive bit is set. It does not reset the archive bit, however. Copy backups are a good way to make a complete copy of data without interfering with the regular backup schedule—for example, if you want to make a copy of the server's data.

A **daily backup** is intended more for the itinerant worker. If you are going on a trip and need to take along the files on which you are currently working, a daily backup provides a quick and simple way of copying all of the files that were changed recently. This type of backup copies only those files that have changed on the day of the backup.

On the other hand, if you need files that were modified before the day of the backup, the daily backup cannot help you.

A Quick Tour of Backup Media Supported in Windows 2000

Unlike the Windows NT backup programs, which worked with tape drives only, the Windows 2000 backup applications recognize any form of storage. You can back up files to floppy disks, to removable drives, to a network drive, to a CD-R device, or even to the local computer's hard disk. The only requirements are that the media be compatible with Windows 2000 and have a name (either a drive letter or a path to which to mount). To verify that the media are compatible with Windows 2000, check the Microsoft Hardware Compatibility List (HCL), which includes all devices supported by the various Microsoft operating systems. The most recent HCL can be found at *www.microsoft.com/hwtest/hcl*.

USING FAULT-TOLERANT DISK CONFIGURATIONS

Backups are an important part of fault tolerance, but they have one problem: they're useless until you restore them, and restoring files takes time. This time lag might be acceptable if you are restoring a client workstation (because it inconveniences only one person). If a server goes down, however, you need to get it back up and running as quickly as possible so that everyone who depends on that server can go to work. Even better, the server should *remain* up and running so that no interruption of service occurs.

One way to ensure that a server remains running is to use a fault-tolerant disk configuration. Although disks are not the only parts of a computer that can fail, they are nevertheless the parts that are most likely to do so. Unlike many of the other computer components, disks have moving parts. Any device with moving parts is more prone to failure than a solid-state device, because the former is at risk for mechanical failures as well as electrical ones. If you power-protect memory and keep the inside of the computer cool, the disk should keep working; unfortunately, however, hard disks can fail even if they're power-protected. Hard disks are extremely vulnerable to contaminants such as smoke, pollen, hair, and dust. Consequently, it is in your best interest to make sure that the failure of a single disk does not affect your operations.

To accomplish this goal, you can group disks logically so that Windows 2000 sees the set as a single unit of storage and maintains parity information for the data stored on the **group**. If one disk in the logical group fails, another disk can take over for the one that failed—even if it died in the middle of a read or write operation. The technique of using multiple disks in this way is called **Redundant Array of Independent Disks (RAID)**. It is based on the idea that the more disks you have, the less likely it is that all of your disk space will fail at once—that's where the "redundancy" part arises.

The process of communicating with fault-tolerant disk volumes (or multidisk volumes that are not fault-tolerant) is a little different from that of communicating with simple disk volumes on basic disks. To a point, the process remains as we described in Chapter 2:

1. An application accepts an open file request from a user.
2. The application passes the request to the environmental subsystem.
3. The environmental subsystem passes the request to the file system driver.
4. The file system driver passes the read request to the disk management subsystem.

This point is where things change. The two kinds of requests now branch off. Disk read (or write) requests sent to logical drives or partitions on basic disks are handled by the fault-tolerant disk driver, which is used in Windows 2000 to communicate with basic disks and in Windows NT to communicate with fault-tolerant volumes. Disk access requests going to any volumes on a dynamic disk are handled by the logical disk manager, a driver that is unique to Windows 2000. The practical upshot of this setup is that fault-tolerant volumes in Windows 2000, which can be located only on dynamic disks, are only locally available to Windows 2000 because other operating systems don't have logical disk managers.

Fault-tolerant volumes are unavailable to locally installed operating systems other than Windows 2000. If these operating systems are accessing a volume on the dynamic disk from across the network, then no problem arises. Network access to a hard disk goes through the network card driver, which can then pass the connection to the file system drivers.

RAID Levels Supported in Windows 2000

A number of different kinds of RAID exists that combine physical disks in various ways to provide data security. Until a few years ago, Windows operating systems needed to support RAID with hardware disk arrays. The introduction of Windows NT incorporated software support into the base operating system. Windows NT—and now Windows 2000—support the RAID 1 and RAID 5 fault-tolerant disk configurations.

Disk Mirroring

RAID 1's full name is **disk mirroring**. In disk mirroring, partitions of the same size and on different physical disks are logically linked into a group called a **mirror set**. The operating system treats the mirror set as a single drive, and it is identified by a drive letter (or mounted to an empty path on a NTFS drive, as discussed in Chapter 7). An exact copy of the data is kept on both halves of the mirror set; therefore, if a disk in the set stops working, the data remain accessible. The data are not considered fault-tolerant until you replace the failed disk and remake the mirror set, but you can nevertheless read and write to the logical drive defined by the mirror set.

As an example, consider the following setup: A mirror set consisting of identical partitions on physical disks 0 and 1 has the drive letter H. When you save a document to drive H, the Windows 2000 disk controller writes the document to the partition on disk 0 and the partition on disk 1, as shown in Figure 13-2. When you open that document again, the disk controller pulls its data from both disks, shortening the time required to transfer the document into memory. If disk 0 fails, drive H will still be available, even though the drive controller will now write data only to the partition on disk 1.

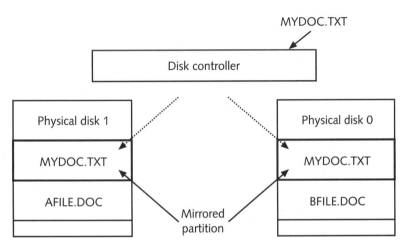

Figure 13-2 How disk mirroring works

 When you mirror partitions on two disks attached to different disk controllers, you are using **disk duplexing**. Disk duplexing is even more secure than disk mirroring, because it protects you from controller failures as well as disk failures.

You can create a mirror set at the time that you create a logical partition, or you can mirror an existing partition onto an unallocated piece of space on another disk. When you create the mirror set from an existing partition, any data already on the original partition will be regenerated to the new partition in the mirror set. This strategy is therefore fault-tolerant for all data, not just data stored since you established the mirror set.

Because it requires only two physical disks, disk mirroring is an inexpensive way to make disks fault-tolerant; mirrored disks are very inefficient, however, in terms of storage space. Only half the space in a mirror set is available for storing original data—the other half is reserved for an exact copy of the data. That's a lot of overhead. No matter how large the mirror set, the proportion of overhead to actual data always remains 1:1. For this reason, most people prefer to use the other form of fault-tolerant RAID supported by Windows 2000: RAID 5.

Disk Striping

RAID 5's full name is **disk striping with parity**. Like mirror sets, stripe sets are composed of partitions of the same size and located on different physical disks, yet treated by Windows 2000 as a single logical disk. When you write data to the stripe set, the data are distributed over the partitions in the stripe set in stripes, even if the partition on the first disk has more than enough room. For example, you save Myfile.doc to a stripe set. The beginning of Myfile.doc is written to stripe 1 of member 1, more data are recorded on stripe 2 of member 2, and the rest appears on stripe 3 of member 3.

Windows 2000 supports RAID 0, a type of disk striping that works in this way. RAID 0 volumes are not fault-tolerant, however. In fact, RAID 0 is actually more prone to failure than saving data to a single disk. The reason is simple: The more disks you have, the more likely that one of those disks will stop working at any given time. If Myfile.doc is stored on three disks, one of which stops working, you cannot load Myfile.doc again, because part of its contents are no longer available. This weakness doesn't make disk striping useless by any means. In fact, it improves disk access time by allowing a disk controller to pull data from several disks at once. It does mean, however, that backing up disk stripes regularly is crucial.

The fault-tolerant form of disk striping is disk striping with parity (RAID 5). Disk striping with parity works much like disk striping, except that in addition to writing data across the partitions in the stripe set, it writes parity information for that data. This parity information is not a copy of the original data, but instead contains the instructions that allow Windows 2000 to reconstruct the data if one of the disks in the **RAID 5 volume** stops working. Figure 13-3 illustrates the distribution of data in a RAID 5 volume.

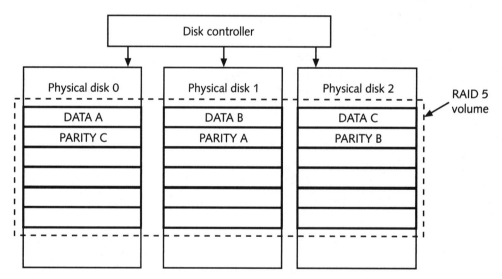

Figure 13-3 How RAID 5 volumes work

The proportion of parity data relative to user data in a RAID 5 volume is given by $1/n$, where n is the number of physical disks supporting the volume. Therefore, the more disks included in a RAID 5 volume, the more space-efficient the volume is. Sadly, you cannot add more disks to a RAID 5 volume after you have created it, nor can you make the partitions supporting it any larger. The created size is the size it will stay.

Each time that you save a file to the RAID 5 volume, the parity information for that file must be updated to reflect its current status (new time stamp, new data, or some other change). If this information is not updated regularly, the RAID 5 volume maintains backup parity information for every file on the volume, which is not only a big waste of space, but also a security breach. When you delete a file from a volume, you want it to disappear—not to be reconstructible from parity information left behind. (If you really need the file, you should drag out the backups discussed earlier in this chapter. You still don't want someone to be able to reconstruct files that you intended to remove from the volume.)

A RAID 5 volume can update the parity information in one of two ways, both of which are dependent on an XOR calculation. On a very basic level, **exclusive OR (XOR) arithmetic** is a function that compares two 1-bit inputs and produces a single-bit output that shows the result of the comparison. If the two bits are the same, the output is 0. If the two bits are different, the output is 1. Therefore:

```
0 XOR 0 = 0
1 XOR 0 = 1
0 XOR 1 = 1
1 XOR 1 = 0
```

When you perform an XOR calculation on two numbers with more than one bit, just match the bits and calculate them individually. For example, 1101010 XOR 0101000 equals 1000010. (For numbers that are not the same number of bits, you just add more 0s to the left side of the number. For example, 1101010 and 0001101010 are the same number.) The result produced by function is the parity information, from which the original data can be recalculated by applying the parity information to whatever data remain. If you know that the result of 1101010 XOR something is 1000010, you can easily figure out which collection of 1s and 0s would produce that XOR.

One way to calculate the new parity information would be to recalculate the XOR to obtain the parity information each time that data are written to the RAID 5 volume. This approach would obviously be slow, because the disk controller would have to read the entire contents of the RAID 5 volume and perform the algorithm. A better approach—and the one that Windows 2000 uses—is to read the old data that are supposed to be overwritten and XOR it with the new data to determine the differences between the two. This calculation produces a **bit mask** that has a 1 in the position of every changed bit. (Remember that a 1 means that the two bits don't match.) After Windows 2000 has this bit mask, it can XOR it with the old parity information to compare those two numbers. This calculation yields the new parity information for the file. Although the process probably seems a little convoluted, it requires only two file reads and two XOR calculations on a small amount of data—rather than a single large file read and an XOR calculation on all data on the volume. It is much faster and less prone to error because you are dealing with a relatively small amount of data.

Faster or not, recalculating the XOR every time you change a file in a RAID 5 volume partly explains why RAID 5 volumes take longer to read data than mirrored volumes, which maintain an exact copy of a volume's data on a second volume. Although RAID 5 volumes are much more space-efficient than mirrored volumes, because of the time it takes to read the data, they are not the best choice in an environment where speed and CPU cycles are crucial. Terminal servers, in particular, should not be made fault-tolerant with RAID 5 volumes.

Creating Fault-Tolerant Volumes with the Disk Management Tool

To create fault-tolerant volumes, you need to use the Disk Management tool introduced in Chapter 7. Creating a fault-tolerant volume works like creating any other volume on a dynamic disk, with the following caveats:

- To build a mirror set, you must have two areas of unallocated space on two separate physical disks available.

- You can also mirror an existing simple volume on a dynamic disk. Other types of volumes (and volumes on basic disks) cannot be mirrored.

- To build a RAID 5 volume, you must have at least 3 and a maximum of 32 areas of unallocated space on the same number of physical disks.

The Hands-on Projects at the end of this chapter walk you through the mechanics of creating fault-tolerant volumes.

If you do not want to maintain redundant information, or if you need to mirror the data in a different place (perhaps because the other half of the mirror set has stopped working), you need to get rid of the mirror set. How you discard it depends largely on what you are trying to do. You have three options:

- Discard the data in the mirror set and remove the volume (**deleting the mirror set**).

- Keep the data in half of the mirror set (either half) but make it no longer fault-tolerant (**removing the mirror set**).

- Keep both sets of the data but make the halves independent so that you can modify the data on one without affecting the other (**breaking the mirror set**).

To destroy all data in a mirror set and convert the volume back into unallocated space, right-click the mirrored volume and choose Delete Volume from the resulting menu. The Disk Management tool will ask you to confirm your choice. Click Yes to continue deleting the mirror. Only do so if you have backed up the mirror set, because deleting the mirror set destroys the data that it contained.

A more likely scenario is that one of the disks supporting the mirror set fails. The data on the remaining disk will still be available, but no longer fault-tolerant. When this situation arises, the mirror set appears in the Disk Management tool with a Failed note on it.

To protect the data again, you need to remirror the volume. You cannot, however, remirror a volume—even if one of the disks in the mirror set has failed, the mirror set remains valid. Therefore, you need to remove the mirror set. Right-click the failed mirror set, and choose Remove Mirror from the resulting menu. You will see a dialog box showing the two halves of the mirror. Pick the half you don't want to keep and click Remove Mirror. When asked to confirm your choice, click Yes to continue. The half of the mirror set you selected returns to unallocated space, and the remaining half of the mirror set becomes a simple volume.

If both halves of the disk are still working but you don't want to mirror the data anymore, you can break the mirror set, thereby making the two volumes act like simple volumes again.

Right-click a mirror set that is still functioning (if the mirrored volume has failed, you have to remove the mirror, not break it), and choose Break Mirror from the resulting menu. You will see a message asking you to confirm your choice and warning you that your data will no longer be fault-tolerant. Click Yes to continue. Once broken, the two halves of the mirrored volume become separate simple volumes. One half retains the drive letter that had belonged to the mirrored volume; the other half gets the next available drive letter.

SERVER CLUSTERING

Server clustering takes logical disk grouping a step further. Rather than using disk arrays to provide fault tolerance and improve performance, clustering employs server arrays of two or more computers to achieve this goal. More specifically, clustering is designed to:

- Improve resource availability by keeping resources available even in case of hardware or software failure

- Improve system scalability by enabling you to add more resources to the network without making it obvious that you are doing so

- Improve server manageability by making it possible to administer a collection of servers from a single interface

Clustering Terminology

Before getting into a detailed discussion of how clustering in Windows 2000 Advanced Server and Windows 2000 Datacenter works (Windows 2000 Server does not support clustering on its own), you need to understand the terminology involved.

How Clusters Perceive Servers and Applications

The servers in a cluster are individually known as **nodes**. From the client's perspective, each node in a cluster looks like a single server, called a **virtual server**. Each virtual server is identified by a single network name and IP address (see Figure 13-4). That is, when a client machine addresses a cluster, the client initiates a connection to BIGCLUSTER, not to Node Alpha of BIGCLUSTER. The node in the cluster that actually takes over the connection depends on which server is available for client requests. To the client, however, it does not matter whether Alpha or Beta takes the request. Similarly, when a client accesses a cluster resource, that resource is identified as part of the virtual server, rather than being associated with a particular node.

374 Chapter 13 Fault Tolerance

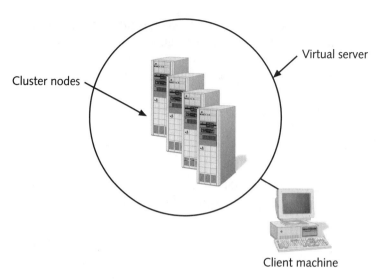

Figure 13-4 How clients perceive cluster nodes

The **cluster service** running on these nodes manages all cluster-specific activity, such as replication of Registry information between nodes and failover. The hardware and software that the cluster service manages are collectively known as **resources**. These resources can include devices such as network cards or physical disks, or logical items such as IP addresses, logical disk volumes, applications, and databases. When a resource provides its service on its node, it is considered to be **online**. A collection of resources of the same type, such as the physical disks in a cluster, is by the cluster service as a group and as a resource type. A resource can be owned by only a single node at one time, although the cluster service can handle multiple resources of the same type if the resource itself may be duplicated.

One special kind of resource, called a **quorum resource**, is used as a tiebreaker when a cluster is being booted. The node in the cluster that controls the quorum resource (often a physical disk, though it doesn't have to be) forms the cluster, and every other node in the cluster must follow its lead. The node does not necessarily keep the quorum resource while the cluster is online; if necessary, the resource can be moved to another node during failover or for some other reason.

The cluster service manages resources as a collection of dynamic link libraries (DLLs). The Windows 2000 clustering product includes DLLs for the following resource types:

- Physical disks
- Logical volumes consisting of one or more physical disks
- File and print shares
- Network addresses and names
- Services and applications (a generic DLL)
- Internet server service (a DLL specific to IIS)

Microsoft also provides a software developer's kit (SDK) that developers can use to create more DLLs for resources that should fail over from one node to another. For example, imagine that you want to cluster database servers and make sure that a specific database remains available. You could use the generic application DLL to define the database application as a resource. If you did so, however, the entire database application (and all databases associated with that application) would have to fail over to the secondary server at failover time. The more data you have to fail over, the longer it takes. Consequently, this scheme is not the best way to run things. If you defined a resource for a specific database, you could fail over just that database, without having to move everything.

Parts of the Cluster Service

The cluster service in Windows 2000 (Clussvc.exe) that runs on each node consists of a service such as the Internet Information Server or Terminal Service. It includes the following components:

- *Node Manager* Keeps track of cluster membership (that is, which nodes are part of the cluster) and monitors the health of the cluster.
- *Configuration Database Manager* Maintains the cluster configuration database that shows how resources are organized.
- *Resource Manager/Failover Manager* Is responsible for all management decisions pertaining to resources and groups and initiates failover to move those groups to the node where they should be in case of failover.
- *Event Processor* Holds together the components of the cluster service, handling common operations and initializing the cluster service.
- *Communications Manager* Handles communication between nodes of the cluster, via remote procedure calls (RPCs).
- *Global Update Manager* Updates cluster-wide information about the status of the cluster service components running on each node.
- *Time Service* Keeps the nodes in the cluster synchronized so that they can communicate. The time service is actually a resource, rather than part of the cluster service.
- *Resource Monitor* Supports the cluster service, but is not part of it. Instead, it runs in a separate process from the cluster service and monitors the status of each resource in the cluster.

That is fault tolerance in a nutshell. As you have seen, fault tolerance means keeping both your data and your network resources available.

Cluster Types

In terms of function, three main types of clusters exist:

- Active/active
- Active/standby
- Fault-tolerant

All types of clusters are fault-tolerant to some degree, by virtue of providing redundancy. The degree to which they are fault-tolerant and the speed with which one node can take over for another, however, depends on the type of cluster involved.

 To keep the descriptions simple, the clusters in our examples have only two nodes: a primary node and a secondary node. You can, however, have more than two nodes in a cluster with some clustering packages, and you may want to add more servers to a cluster as time goes by to improve cluster responsiveness.

In an **active/active cluster** (used by Windows 2000 Advanced Server and Windows 2000 Datacenter), all of the nodes in the cluster are functioning and supporting user requests all the time. If one node fails, then it fails over to the other node, sending its workload there. The failover time can take as long as 90 seconds. At the end of the failover, the remaining server is supporting all client requests. Figure 13-5 shows how this type of clustering works.

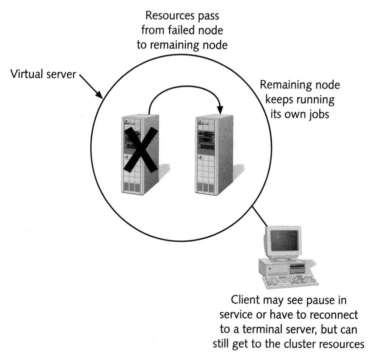

Figure 13-5 How active/active clusters fail over

In an **active/standby cluster** (see Figure 13-6), only the primary node actually handles client requests. The secondary node waits for the main server to fail (it may be doing something else, but it is always "on call" in case the primary node cannot fulfill a client request). If the active node fails, it passes its workload to the standby node. Failover time in this case takes 15 to 90 seconds. If the standby node was doing something before the failover, all of those operations stop and only the operations that had been running on the failed server are carried out.

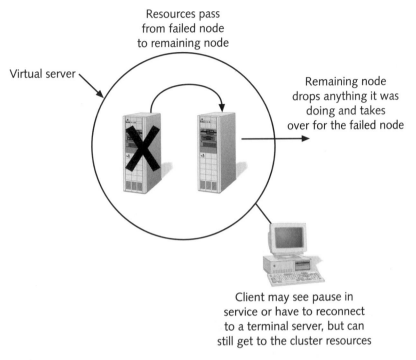

Figure 13-6 How active/standby clusters fail over

In these cluster types, the nodes in the cluster don't have to be doing the same thing. In an active/active cluster, the secondary node that takes over for the failed primary server adds the failed node's jobs to its own. In an active/standby cluster, the secondary node drops what it was doing and replaces its workload with that of the failed primary node. In neither case does the node hardware have to be identical. That is, the two devices must be identical in function—capable of storing the same data in the same place or running the same applications (clustered e-mail servers obviously must have e-mail server software installed)—but they don't have to be physically identical.

In both the active/active and active/standby cluster types, any client connections to the failed primary node are terminated when the server fails. Any services running on the primary server also stop.

In a **fault-tolerant cluster**, the setup is a little different. In this case, all of the nodes in the cluster are identical and operate in tandem, so all nodes in the cluster are always performing the same operations all the time. If one node fails, another node can take over for it nearly instantaneously, with less than one second required for the failover. Like disk mirroring, fault-tolerant clustering is inefficient in space because it provides 100% redundancy of data and function; like mirroring, it also is an excellent way of keeping data available with no downtime. Windows 2000 clustering is not really fault-tolerant in this sense.

The physical connection may also vary depending on the clustering package implemented. Today, clustered servers typically communicate via a high-speed SCSI connection, or via a fiber channel fabric that provides network connectivity at local-access speeds.

How Clustering Works

To create a new cluster, you run a cluster installation tool on a server that will be part of the new cluster and name the new cluster. This server becomes the first node of the new cluster. You can then use the administration tools to configure the parts of the server that should become resources.

To add more nodes to the cluster, you run the installation service on each server in turn, filling in the name of the cluster (it is like a workgroup, in a way) when prompted. As each node joins the cluster, the cluster service of the node manager on the first node sends the new node a copy of the existing cluster database that is maintained by the configuration database manager.

Thereafter, whenever a node in the cluster boots up, the cluster service starts automatically and broadcasts messages to find the cluster that it joined earlier. If the cluster answers and the node supplies the correct password to join the cluster, it is in. If the node can't find its cluster or its password is refused, the node attempts to form its own cluster. To form a resource, it must get access to a quorum resource.

When you power down a node, it sends a message to the other cluster members that it is leaving the cluster. Although the node doesn't wait for any acknowledgment of its departure, this message means that all other nodes in the cluster are immediately aware of the changed membership of the cluster (maintained by the node manager) and don't have to go through the discovery process again to discover that the node is gone.

Client–Cluster Communications

As mentioned earlier, the nodes in a Windows 2000 cluster are exposed to the client as a single virtual server. This server is identified to the outside world with a single network name and network IP address. (Windows 2000 clustering requires the use of TCP/IP as the network protocol; IPX/SPX and NetBEUI don't work with clustering.)

Each node in the cluster is set up to perform the same job and share a common disk array; therefore, if one server fails or an application stops working, the cluster service can fail over the resources from the failed node, and another node can take its place. If a node or an application on a node stops responding, the clustering software restarts the application on another server in the cluster or redistributes the work of the failed server to another server in the cluster. The person using the server should see only a slight pause in service during the failover. For example, you might cluster two e-mail servers. Then, even if one server fails, network users can still pick up their e-mail. Clustering the e-mail servers could also provide high availability by **load balancing**, or distributing the client requests among the nodes in the cluster. Because load balancing always gives new jobs to the least busy node, it improves availability by reducing server response time.

Although nodes in a cluster can be load balanced, not all load-balanced servers are clustered. For example, software can load-balance identical terminal servers so that the least busy terminal server always services a new client request. These load-balanced servers are not necessarily clustered, however. In fact, it is rare that terminal servers are clustered, because the added cost of clustering is greater than the benefits derived from making the servers fault-tolerant. If a terminal server fails, any users running terminal sessions must reconnect to another terminal server to continue working, and they lose any data still in RAM and not saved to a file server. That said, an active/active cluster (like the one supported by the Windows 2000 cluster service) would lose this information anyway. Although most resources can be restarted gracefully after failover, any current operations will be lost. For example, any current print jobs will be aborted and must be restarted, and any database queries will be lost and must be reissued.

Requirements for Clustered Applications

Not all applications work in a clustered environment. In fact, many don't use clustering at all. For an application to support clustering, all of the following must be true:

- The application must use TCP/IP for communications, not NetBEUI or IPX/SPX.

- The client-side applications and operating system must not crash or hang if a cluster must fail over a client to another client. If a server or application on a server fails, the client must be able to automatically or manually retry the connection to the virtual server until the failover is complete and the other server can take the connection.

- You must be able to configure server applications so that they store only data on the disk array common to all servers in the cluster.

- Applications should not store large data structures in the Registry. The cluster service logs any changes to the Registry in servers in the physical cluster. When a server application fails over to another node, the cluster service checks the log for changes to the Registry on the failed server and then replicates those changes to the secondary server; hence the same settings become available to the application when it restarts on the secondary server. Putting large amounts of data in the system Registry stresses the network by increasing the amount of data that must be replicated, thereby increasing failover time.

- The applications must be able to restart on the secondary server even if the primary server fails suddenly.

- Applications must refer to the virtual server name and IP address, not the server name and IP address of a physical computer. Otherwise, when the application fails over to the secondary server, the application won't work because it won't be able to find the physical server on which it was installed.

- A server application must be installed on all servers in the cluster. Thus, if one sever fails, the secondary server can take over. The server application must be configurable as a **cluster resource**, an object that can be moved between servers in the cluster. The cluster service then starts and stops the application by taking the cluster resource representing the application online and offline.

Chapter Summary

- Fault tolerance is a matter of keeping available the tools you need. To keep data available, you can (and should) use backups. To keep data available without having to restore data to a server, you can use fault-tolerant disk configurations. Finally, to keep data available even if an entire server goes down, you can cluster servers. In each case, the name of the game is redundancy—whether redundancy of data, redundancy of disk space, or redundancy of servers.

- Sometimes, even fault tolerance can't do everything. That situation is addressed in Chapter 14, which details the Windows 2000 disaster recovery tools.

Key Terms

active/active cluster — A type of cluster found in Windows 2000 Advanced Server and Windows 2000 Datacenter in which both nodes in the cluster are serving client requests all the time. If one node fails, the cluster service moves its resources to the other node and the second node manages both workloads. The two nodes do not have to be identical.

active/standby cluster — A type of cluster in which one node is serving client requests and the other is dormant, or doing work that may be discarded. When the active node fails, the cluster service moves its resources to the standby node, and the standby node drops whatever it had been doing and takes over the active server's workload. The two nodes do not have to be physically identical.

archive bit — An attribute that is set (turned on) when a file is created or edited, and turned off when the file is backed up.

bit mask — The result of an XOR function. The bit mask contains a 1 for every mismatch between numbers and a 0 for every match.

breaking the mirror set — Reverting both halves of a mirror set to independent simple volumes.

clustering — A technique that involves logically combining two or more servers for redundancy.

cluster resource — An object that can be moved between servers in the cluster.

cluster service — A Windows 2000 service running on all nodes of a cluster, facilitating communication and failover between nodes.

copy backup — A type of backup that works like a normal backup in that it copies all selected files to the backup media, regardless of whether the archive bit is set. A copy backup does not reset the archive bit.

daily backup — A type of backup that copies only those files that have changed on the day of the backup.

deleting the mirror set — Removing the mirror set volume and thus discarding all of its data.

differential backup — A type of backup that copies to the backup media every selected file that has the archive bit set, but does not reset the archive bit.

disk duplexing — A mirror set that incorporates two disks attached to different disk controllers, so they are not affected by controller failure.

disk mirroring — A RAID type that combines space on two physical disks to create a mirror image; that is, when data are written to one disk, the same information is written to the other disk.

disk striping with parity — See *RAID 5 volume*.

exclusive OR (XOR) arithmetic — The function that RAID 5 volumes use to calculate the parity information for their data. When calculating the XOR for two binary numbers, you compare them side by side. The result will have a 0 in every place where the numbers match and a 1 in every place where they do not.

fault tolerance — An aspect of an operating system that ensures high availability of both user and system data and of the computing resources.

fault-tolerant cluster — A cluster type in which two physically identical nodes operate in tandem, performing the same functions. If one node fails, the other takes over for it almost instantly because no resource transfer is needed.

Grandfather/Father/Son (GFS) — A backup scheme that uses a monthly normal backup, a weekly normal backup, and a daily incremental or differential backup to create a three-month record of server data.

group — A collection of like cluster resources that the cluster service can manage as a single logical unit.

incremental backup — A type of backup that copies to the backup media every selected file that has the archive bit set and then resets the archive bit to show that the file has been backed up.

load balancing — Distributing client requests among grouped (but not necessarily clustered) servers so that the least busy server always services the next client request.

mirror set — The name for the combined disk space that is turned into a disk mirror.

nodes — Individual servers in a cluster.

normal backup — A type of backup that copies every selected file to the backup media and resets the archive bit on the original files. This backup type is the core of a backup strategy.

NTBACKUP — The backup program that comes with Windows 2000. It is accessed by selecting Start, Run, and typing NTBACKUP.

online — In terms of fault tolerance, when a resource provides its service on its node.

quorum resource — A cluster resource that is used as a tiebreaker when two servers are trying to form a cluster at once. The one with control of the quorum resource controls the cluster.

RAID 5 volume — An elaboration of disk striping in which parity information for the data written to the volume is also written to the volume. If one disk in a RAID 5 volume fails, the data that it contained may be reconstructed from the parity information on the remaining disks.

Redundant Array of Independent Disks (RAID) — The technique of logically combining physical disks to make fault-tolerant disk volumes. If one disk in a RAID array fails, the other disk or disks can take over until the broken disk can be replaced.

removing the mirror set — Discarding one half of a mirror set's data (converting the volume to unallocated space) and reverting the other half to a simple volume.

resources — Part of a cluster (hardware or software) that the cluster software manages. The cluster service includes DLLs that represent some common potential resources, and developers can build their own.

security identification (SID) number — A unique number assigned by Windows 2000 to each user account.

selection information file — The file in which backups are stored. This file has a .bks extension.

system state data — The Windows 2000 name for system configuration information. System state data include the Registry, the boot files, the class registration database, and, if applicable, the certificate services database, Active Directory structure, and SYSVOL.

Tower of Hanoi (ToH) — A backup scheme that uses five tapes in rotation to create a 32-week record of normal backups. Because this backup scheme does not include differential or incremental backups, it should not be used as the sole backup plan.

virtual server — The name by which the nodes in a cluster are collectively known. Clients connect to the virtual server, not to the individual nodes within the server.

REVIEW QUESTIONS

1. Which of the following is *not* a resource for which the Windows 2000 cluster server already has a DLL?
   a. Print shares
   b. Applications
   c. Databases
   d. None of the above

2. One of the disks in your mirror set has stopped working. To make the data in the mirror set fault-tolerant again, what do you need to do first?
   a. Back up the volume.
   b. Delete the mirror set.
   c. Break the mirror set.
   d. Remove the mirror set.

3. What is the minimum number of disks that you need to make a RAID 5 volume? A mirror set?

4. The _____ in a cluster are logically combined to create a virtual server.

5. Briefly describe the role of a quorum resource in a cluster.

6. Which node(s) in a cluster does the cluster service run on?
   a. The lead node
   b. The node controlling the quorum resource

c. All nodes in the cluster

d. The node maintaining the cluster configuration database

7. Which of the following is *not* part of the system state data for a Windows 2000 member server?

   a. The COM+ class registration database of file associations

   b. The boot files for the computer

   c. The Active Directory structure

   d. None of the above

8. List the parts of the system state data that are part of a domain controller but not part of a member server.

9. You've set up a RAID 5 volume on five disks ranging in size from 100 MB to 5 GB. Each partition in the volume is 100 MB in size. How much of the RAID 5 volume will be used to store user data and how much will be used to store parity information?

   a. 100 MB

   b. 50 MB

   c. 500 MB

   d. 250 MB

10. You have two 2 GB dynamic disks that you want to support a mirror set. One of the disks has 250 MB of unallocated space; the other has 450 MB of unallocated space. How large a mirror set could you create from these two disks?

11. Taking the same disk configuration in question 10, assume that you made the largest mirror set possible. If the mirror set was full, how much disk space would be taken up with redundant data? How much with user data?

12. The backup tool in Windows 2000 is located in the Administrative Tools folder. True or False?

13. What is a selection information file?

    a. The file in which Windows 2000 backup jobs are stored

    b. The file on a disk that tells you which partitions are fault-tolerant

    c. A record of changes to the volume structure of an NTFS partition

    d. The record of which nodes are in a cluster

14. To back up data with Windows 2000, you need a tape drive. True or False?

15. You want to automatically generate a complete list of all files that were backed up during a single backup procedure. How would you accomplish this task?

16. Which of the following are fault-tolerant disk configurations that Windows 2000 supports in software? (Choose all that apply.)

    a. Disk striping

    b. RAID 5 volumes

    c. Mirror sets

    d. All of the above

17. How does the logical disk manager fit into Windows 2000 fault tolerance?
18. Which backup media can use hardware compression?

    a. Removable disks

    b. Floppy disks

    c. Tape drives

    d. All of the above

19. Which fault-tolerant disk configuration would you want to use to protect a compute-bound server?
20. Which backup type will back up only those files with the archive bit set and then reset the archive bit?

    a. Normal

    b. Differential

    c. Incremental

    d. Copy

21. It is simpler to completely restore a server's data from a week's worth of differential backups than from a week's worth of incremental backups. True or False?
22. Briefly explain how normal backups and copy backups differ.
23. You want to protect the data on your server, but need to keep initial costs as low as possible. Which Windows 2000 fault-tolerant disk configuration would you choose, and why?
24. What does 10001011 XOR 10101001 equal?

    a. 00100010

    b. 10101011

    c. 00110101

    d. 00101011

25. You want to take the data in a mirror set and insert it in a new computer without affecting the original data in any way. Before you remove the disk and put it in the new computer, what do you need to do to the mirror set?

    a. Break it.

    b. Delete it.

    c. Remove it.

    d. Copy it.

HANDS-ON PROJECTS

Project 13-1

To create a mirror set and format it with FAT32:

1. Start the Computer Management tool by selecting **Start**, **Programs**, **Administrative Tools**, **Computer Management**.
2. Expand the **Storage** section and select the **Disk Management** tool in the right pane. Make sure that at least two dynamic disks with unallocated space are available.
3. In the right pane, right-click an area of unallocated space on one of the dynamic disks, or right-click the gray disk label to the left. From the context menu that appears, choose **Add Volume** to start the Create Volume Wizard.
4. Click past the opening screen, then choose **Mirrored Volume** in the **Select Volume Type** page (see Figure 13-7). Click **Next**.

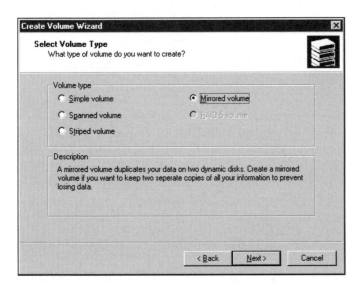

Figure 13-7 Choose to create a mirror set

5. From the Select Disks screen shown in Figure 13-8, choose the disks that you want to be in the mirror set. The disk from which you started the process will already be selected. Choose another disk from the ones listed in the column on the left.

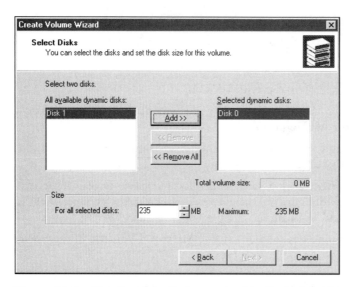

Figure 13-8 Pick the disks that you want to form the mirror set

 If you have three or more dynamic disks available from which to create the mirror set, you can deselect the current disk and select two others from the list of available disks.

6. While still in the Select Disks screen, type a size for the mirror set, ranging from 1 MB to the maximum possible size. The size you choose should reflect the total storage area available. Click **Next**.

 Because the two areas of unallocated space must be the same size, the maximum possible size for the mirror set depends on the amount of unallocated space on which you build the disks. Pick and choose the disks you want to include to see how the maximum size of the mirror set changes accordingly.

7. In the Assign Drive Letter or Path screen shown in Figure 13-9, assign a drive letter to the mirror set or mount it to an empty volume on an NTFS partition as described in Chapter 7, and then click **Next**.

 You create a partition with the Disk Management tool, which is accessed by selecting Start, Programs, Administrative Tools, Computer Management. From within Disk Management, select to create a primary partition.

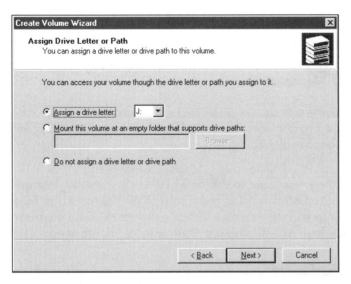

Figure 13-9 Label the volume in some way so that you can access it

8. In the Format Volume screen (see Figure 13-10), choose **FAT32** from the list of available disk formats. Click **Next** when you are done.

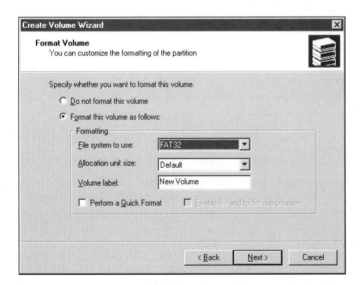

Figure 13-10 Format the new mirror volume with FAT32

9. Review your choices, and click **Finish** to start building the mirror set. The Disk Management tool chugs away for a few minutes to create the volumes and set them up to communicate. The mirror set will be available right away—you don't need to reboot.

Project 13-2

To mirror an existing simple volume:

1. Start the Computer Management tool by selecting **Start**, **Programs**, **Administrative Tools**, **Computer Management**.

Only dynamic disks with areas of unallocated space large enough to mirror the selected volume are listed. If no area of unallocated space is large enough, you won't have the option of mirroring the volume.

2. Right-click the volume you want to mirror, and then choose **Add Mirror** from the resulting menu. An Add Mirror dialog box similar to the one shown in Figure 13-11 appears, asking you to select the disk on which you want to create the mirror. Click the disk so that it is highlighted—this operation won't work otherwise.

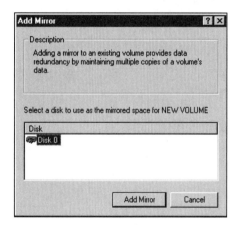

Figure 13-11 Choose a dynamic disk with unallocated space on which to mirror the simple volume

3. Click the **Add Mirror** button. In the unallocated space, the Disk Management tool will create a partition that is the same size and format as the simple volume that you are mirroring. The redundant data are regenerated onto the new partition. (Depending on the size of the volume you're mirroring, this step may take a while. It is not a fast process on large volumes.)

4. The new partition will have the same drive letter or mounted path as the one you mirrored and will be available as soon as all of the data are regenerated—no reboot is required.

Project 13-3

To use the Windows 2000 graphical backup tool to create an incremental backup job that backs up the contents of the My Documents folder to a network location and then verifies the data after it's backed up:

1. Choose **Start**, **Programs**, **Accessories**, **System Tools**, **Backup**.
2. Click the **Backup Wizard** button on the Backup utility (see Figure 13-12).

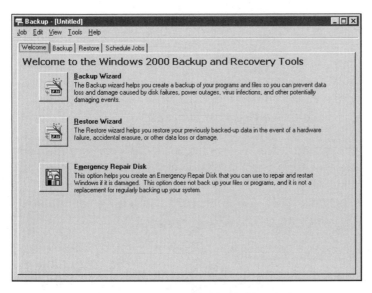

Figure 13-12 Opening screen of the Backup tool

3. Click past the opening screen of the wizard, and in the What to Back Up screen choose **Back up Selected files, drives, or network data**. Click **Next**.
4. In the Items to Back Up screen, choose **My Documents**. When the folder is selected, it will have a blue check mark in the box next to the folder's icon. Click **Next**.
5. In the Where to Store the Backup screen shown in Figure 13-13, provide a name and location for the backup's selection information file. Click **Next**.

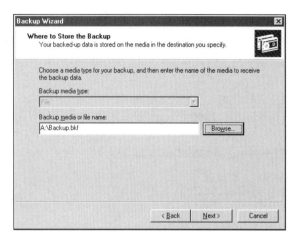

Figure 13-13 Choose a destination location for the backup

6. Review the options displayed in the Completing the Backup Wizard screen. In this example, the Verify setting is currently off and it is a normal backup. To turn the Verify setting on, you'll need to use the Advanced options. Click the **Advanced** button.

7. In the Type of Backup screen shown in Figure 13-14, choose **Incremental** from the drop-down list. Click **Next**.

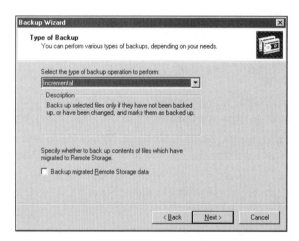

Figure 13-14 Choose to create an incremental backup

8. In the How to Back Up screen of the wizard, choose **Verify data after backup**. Click **Next**.

9. Review the rest of the options in the Advanced Backup Wizard, noting that you can choose to append or replace data, specify a new backup label and job name (perhaps "Incremental copy of the My Documents folder"), and choose to schedule the backup for a later time. When you reach the end of the wizard, click the **Finish** button to start the backup.

Project 13-4

To create a new RAID 5 volume and mount it to an empty new folder on a NTFS volume:

1. Make sure that at least three dynamic disks are installed in the server and start the Computer Management tool by selecting **Start**, **Programs**, **Administrative Tools**, **Computer Management**.

2. Right-click any area of unallocated space on any dynamic physical disk. From the resulting menu, choose **Create Volume**.

3. Click **Next** in the opening screen of the Create Volume Wizard. On the Select Volume Type page shown in earlier in Figure 13-7, select **RAID-5 Volume** and then click **Next**.

4. In the Select Disks screen shown in Figure 13-15, choose at least three disks that you want to be involved in the stripe set. The disk with which you started (the one with the area of unallocated space) will appear in the right column of disks to use; the other dynamic disks with unallocated space will appear on the left side. To remove a disk from the volume, select it in the list of selected dynamic disks and click the **Remove** button.

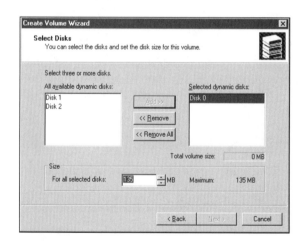

Figure 13-15 Pick the disks that you want to be part of the RAID 5 volume and choose a size for the volume

5. In this same screen, pick the size of the stripe set. In the Size box, the Disk Management tool displays the maximum size of the stripes based on the unallocated space on the chosen drives. The value in Total Volume Size reflects the total amount of room available for data, not the total space in the stripe set. Click **Next**.

Because $1/n$ of the space in a RAID 5 volume (where n is the number of disks in the set) is used for parity information, the more disks you have, the larger percentage of data storage the volume will have.

6. In the Assign Drive Letter or Path screen, choose **Mount This Volume** and click the **Browse** button.

7. In the Browse for Drive Path dialog box that appears (see Figure 13-16), you'll see all of the logical drives formatted with NTFS. Select one (in our example, we chose D) and click the **New Folder** button. Type a name for the new folder in the space provided, and then click **OK** to return to the original screen.

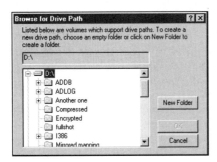

Figure 13-16 Find the local NTFS volume to which you want to mount the RAID 5 volume

8. In the Format Volume screen, choose whether to format the new volume immediately and, if so, the disk format you want to use (NTFS, FAT32, or FAT).

9. Review your choices, backing up to change any of them or clicking **Finish** to create the RAID 5 volume. Windows 2000 will grind away for a few minutes, setting up the new stripe set. When it's done, the RAID 5 volume will be immediately ready to use—no reboot is required.

Project 13-5

To use the command-line NTBACKUP utility to perform a differential backup of C:\MYFILES and label it accordingly:

1. Choose **Start**, **Programs**, **Accessories**, **Command Prompt**.

2. In the Command Prompt window, type **ntbackup /?** to get a complete list of all NTBACKUP switches that control the backup options. It is a long list, but the options you'll be looking at for this exercise are the /m, /f, and /j switches.

3. Type the following command and then press **Enter**:

   ntbackup c:\myfiles\ /m differential /f d:\system1.bkf /j "Differential backup of MYFILES folder"

Project 13-6

To break the mirror set you created earlier so that the two halves are separate but retain their data:

1. Start the Computer Management tool by selecting **Start**, **Programs**, **Administrative Tools**, **Computer Management**.

2. Right-click a mirror set and choose **Break Mirror** from the menu that appears. You'll see a dialog box like the one in Figure 13-17, warning you that breaking the mirror set will make it no longer fault-tolerant.

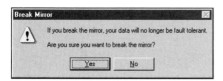

Figure 13-17 Confirm that you want to break the mirror

3. Click **Yes**, and the two halves will become separate simple volumes. One half will retain the drive letter that you assigned the mirror set, and the other will take the next drive letter available. Both halves will retain any volume label that the mirror set had.

CASE PROJECTS

1. You have four disks in a server. To retain dual-boot capabilities with an alternative operating system, you want to keep one of them a basic disk. Which fault-tolerant disk configurations are available if you use only the Windows 2000 RAID software? Which option would you choose if you were most concerned about the speed of disk writes? What if you were concerned about getting as much storage space out of the fault-tolerant array as possible?

2. Which Windows 2000 backup types would you use to back up a server so that you always have a daily record, can restore the backups in as few steps as possible, and have an archive of old backups?

CHAPTER 14

DISASTER RECOVERY MECHANISMS

> **After reading this chapter and completing the exercises, you will be able to:**
> - Understand the differences between an Active Directory domain and a Windows NT domain
> - Describe what happens during the Windows 2000 boot process
> - Explain how the tools in the Advanced Options menu work to repair a damaged operating system
> - Explain how the Emergency Repair Disk and the Recovery Console can recover Windows 2000 settings or fix a problem
> - Describe how the restoration process works to restore a server to its original condition

Chapter 13 discussed the fault tolerance mechanisms available in Windows 2000 Server (and the clustering available in Windows 2000 Advanced Server and Datacenter Server). As noted in that chapter, being fault-tolerant isn't always enough. Your entire cluster could be destroyed by a fire or flood. The disk controller on your mirror set could fail, leaving you with inaccessible disks. For example, George thinks he knows how to back up the server; unfortunately, he finds out—too late—that he didn't know the procedure as well as he imagined. In fact, the server hasn't been backed up in weeks. Although this case is a hypothetical example, it's really not far from reality. Things like this happen every day.

Not all of the tools that Windows 2000 offers to help you recover from disaster work in quite the same way. Each has a different function. Some tools reverse a single action that's causing a problem; others allow you to scrap all changes and start over. Which disaster recovery tool you use to get things back up and running again depends on both your understanding of what the problem is and the tools themselves. It's critical that you pick the right tool for the job. There's nothing magical about recovery tools, after all. They restore damaged or missing files. The tool you pick to fix a damaged system depends on which files you need to replace.

What's Happening During the Boot Process?

First, let's look at what happens behind the scenes when you boot a Windows 2000 computer. As you'll see, the boot process is simply the systematic loading of the base operating system, the files needed to support the devices attached to the computer, and the services running on the computer.

Loading Basic Hardware Support

Before considering the problem of whether Windows 2000 is even working, you need to get the hardware working. In the initial stages of the boot process, the computer reads the BIOS to discover the basic hardware configuration. It then reads the disk signature on the boot disk to find the location of the bootable partition (where the operating system is stored).

As a consequence, you will not be able to boot the server if the boot drive isn't working. Thus, the drive itself, the disk controller for the boot drive, and the cable connecting the two must be operational. Additionally, the CPU and the motherboard must be up and running, as must the system BIOS. The CPU handles all processing in the computer; the motherboard is the common interface for all hardware that allows the various parts of the computer to communicate; and the BIOS describes the computer to itself.

If any of these parts is not working, skip to the section on rebuilding the server from the backups. Other hardware can give you problems, but you need all of these pieces to get the server to respond.

If you are having low-level hardware problems, restart and observe the computer to see the point at which the problem appears. Here are some points at which problems may appear and some possible solutions:

- If the computer does not boot and makes no noise when you flip (or press) the On switch, the problem is power. Check the power cord to ensure that it is working and plugged into a live power outlet. If the power source isn't the problem, the power supply in the computer might be at fault.

- If the computer comes on for half a second and then switches off just as fast, the problem probably lies in the connection of the motherboard to the power supply. The motherboard must be plugged in properly with two connections; reverse the connections, and the motherboard will short out. Older computers would let you turn on the computer and kill the motherboard, but newer ones will just cut the power if they recognize that the power supply connections are reversed.

- If the fan starts but the computer doesn't do anything else, the motherboard is probably not working and needs to be replaced.

What's Happening During the Boot Process? 397

If you don't hear the fan when you start up the computer, double-check that the fan is working even if the rest of the computer boots normally. Electronic components are very delicate and can easily overheat. The fan circulates air within the computer to keep things cool. Even if the room is comfortable, the inside of the computer (typically 15–20 degrees warmer than the ambient temperature) may be too warm.

- If you can hear the computer boot but you can't see anything (remember that you need working video to use Windows 2000) and hear a beep, the problem probably lies with the video card. Verify that it's seated properly. If its seating is not the problem, you may need to replace the video card.

- If the computer boots and can find the CD-ROM drive and floppy drive but does not find the hard disk controller, the controller has failed and needs to be replaced.

- If the computer boots and finds the hard disk controller but no bootable hard disk, the hard disk may be damaged (possibly from a virus) or not working and may need to be replaced.

Loading Ntldr

Assuming that the computer parts are all working and the computer has found the bootable hard disk, the next step is to load the operating system. The first part of Windows 2000 that loads is **Ntldr**, a small program in the root directory of the boot partition of the server's hard disk. Ntldr announces itself by displaying the boot menu for your computer. It is also doing the following:

1. Shifting the processor into 386 mode
2. Starting a very simple file system that allows Windows 2000 to boot from the hard disk
3. Reading the contents of Boot.ini to display a menu of other possible boot options
4. Accepting the choice of which operating system to load

If you choose to load Windows 2000 Server, Ntldr passes control to Ntdetect.com, which detects the hardware on your server.

Detecting Hardware

Ntdetect.com is in charge of figuring out what hardware is present on your server. It checks for the following:

- The PC's machine ID type
- The bus type (PCI, ISA, MCA, EISA)
- The video board type
- The keyboard and mouse type

- The ports detected on the computer (USB, serial, and parallel)
- The floppy drives present on the computer

Once Ntdetect has run without problems, it takes the results of its survey and uses them to build the HKLM\Hardware key of the Registry, shown in Figure 14-1. This key is rebuilt each time you restart your computer, so it is always up to date. If Ntdetect doesn't run, it is either missing or a hardware conflict exists in the server.

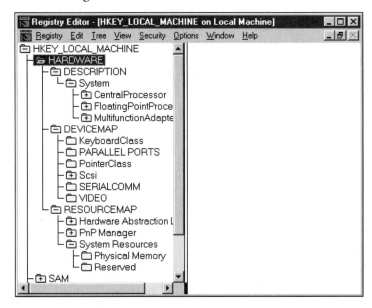

Figure 14-1 Contents of the Hardware key

Loading the Windows 2000 System Kernel

In Chapter 2, we noted that the core part of Windows 2000 is located in **Ntoskrnl.exe**, which is the "kernel" of the Windows 2000 operating system. When Ntdetect has located the hardware platform in use, it installs the hardware abstraction layer (HAL) appropriate to it and loads Ntoskrnl at the same time in four stages: loading the kernel, initializing the kernel, loading the services set to start automatically, and starting the Win32 subsystem.

Kernel Load Phase

Once Hal.dll and Ntoskrnl are loaded into memory, Windows 2000 loads the system settings into HKLM\System\CurrentControlSet\Services. It then refers to these settings to determine which drivers it must load and in what order. All services set to load during the boot phase are loaded at this time.

 Are you unsure which services load when? All services currently installed on the server have keys in HKLM\System\CurrrentControlSet\Services. To find out when a service loads, open its key and look at the start value. A start value of 0 means that the service loads during the kernel load phase; a value of 1 loads the service during the kernel initialization phase; a value of 2 loads the service automatically when the services are loading; a value of 3 indicates that the service is enabled but can be started only manually; and a value of 4 indicates that the service is disabled.

Kernel Initialization Phase

Once the kernel is loaded, it is initialized. The kernel scans for services with a start value of 1 and starts them. In addition, Windows 2000 builds a new current control set, but does not save it yet (it will not save this set until the next phase). Autochk.exe runs to verify that the file system on NTFS volumes is intact and notes the location of any bad sectors. Also, the page file is set up.

Services Load Phase

At this point, Windows 2000 loads the Services Manager and the Win32 subsystem, and starts all services with a start value of 2. Windows 2000 writes the current control set to HKLM\System.

Windows Subsystem Start Phase

The final stage of the Windows 2000 boot process involves initializing the Win32 subsystem, which supports the graphical interface for Windows 2000. Winlogon.exe, which handles interactive user logons and logoffs, starts and listens for the Ctrl+Alt+Delete sequence that means someone is trying to log on.

ADVANCED OPTIONS MENU

But what if the boot process doesn't work that way? Some of the most annoying problems that can plague an operating system are really simple. The **Advanced Options menu** can help you detect such flaws.

When you boot a Windows 2000 Server, you will see a short boot menu listing the operating systems installed on the computer or just Windows 2000 if it is the only operating system. If you press F8 when this menu appears, you will exit the standard boot menu and go to the Advanced Options menu, shown in the following code:

```
Windows 2000 Advanced Options Menu
Safe Mode
Safe Mode with Networking
Safe Mode with Command Prompt

Enable Boot Logging
Enable VGA Mode
Last Known Good Configuration
Directory Services Repair Restore Mode (Windows 2000 Domain
Controllers Only)
Debugging Mode

Boot Normally
Return to OS Choices Menu
```

Use the last two options to either just boot Windows 2000 Server or return to the main menu to see the available options. Starting from the top, let's look at what each of the other options can do to fix a broken Windows 2000 installation.

Safe Mode Options

Safe Mode is shorthand for "boot the operating system with the bare bones of the drivers and services it needs to run." Windows 2000 supports three kinds of Safe Mode: Ordinary Safe Mode, Safe Mode with Networking, and Safe Mode with Command Prompt.

Ordinary Safe Mode loads only the drivers and services required to boot the computer and to provide a simple operating environment. No network drivers are loaded, and network-dependent services (which normally start automatically) are set to start manually. In fact, these services are disabled—you can't turn them on from the Services tool in the Administrative Tools program group or from the Microsoft Management Console. This version of Safe Mode is useful when you need to fix problems related to network-dependent services, or when you are not sure what the problem is and don't want to take any chances, but need the GUI to resolve it.

Safe Mode with Networking is just like Safe Mode, except for the addition of network support. Choose this boot option when you want a pared-down version of the operating system, but need network support to fix something (for example, if the printer drivers you need to reload are installed on another computer, and the computer you are fixing is allowed to install printer drivers only from the trusted source).

Safe Mode (Command Prompt Only) works like Safe Mode—no networking support, basic VGA video, no extraneous drivers—except that it uses the command prompt (Cmd.exe) for a shell instead of Explorer (Explorer.exe). Use this mode if something is wrong with Explorer that keeps you from loading the graphical desktop. Although you can load any working part of the operating system from the command prompt if you know the name of the executable file that loads that component, none of the graphical pieces needs to work to start Windows 2000 in this mode. You can even receive a regular desktop if Explorer.exe works, but you're not dependent on it.

Boot Logging

Enabling **boot logging** sets up Windows 2000 to load normally, as it would if you had not interrupted the process. The only addition to the process is that Windows 2000 logs the boot process, listing all of the files loaded in support of the operating system in a file called Ntbtlog.txt. You can use this option to see which drivers did—and did not—load in the course of the boot process.

Boot logging is useful as a recovery tool only if you have previously logged the boot process at a time when everything is working properly. If you've done so, then if some component of Windows 2000 stops working, you can compare the two lists to see whether a particular file is missing. Boot logging is also turned on by default whenever you boot in Safe Mode.

Enable VGA Mode

Let us assume that you have just installed a new video card in your Windows 2000 computer. You install a new driver for it and select the video card. When testing it (Windows 2000 always has you test new resolutions to make sure that the monitor and card can support them), however, you can't see anything. You inadvertently press the Tab key and Enter, accidentally telling Windows 2000 that you want to keep these settings. Unfortunately, you can't see it well enough to restore it to a configuration that works.

Under the first version of Windows NT, you had to go through a long chain of keystrokes to fix this problem, essentially typing blind to get a vanilla video configuration. Under later versions of Windows NT and Windows 2000, however, **VGA Mode** is now a boot option.

With the VGA mode option, instead of loading the video driver that your computer is normally set to use, a plain VGA driver will be loaded that will work with any board that Windows 2000 supports. The screen may not have the high resolution to which you're accustomed, and the refresh rate (the rate at which the screen repaints itself—the higher the refresh rate, the less the screen flickers) may be uncomfortably low, but you will be able to edit the video settings so that a driver works. Fix the settings, reboot, and you have fixed the problem.

Last Known Good Configuration

Humans are fallible. So as long as they use operating systems, there should be some kind of undo feature. In Windows 2000, this feature is called the **Last Known Good Configuration**. It can't help you in every situation in which you change your system, or reboot, and then realize that the modification damaged the system. Nevertheless, it can sometimes help you reverse history by allowing you to load not the configuration that was in place when you logged off (which is normally what would happen), but the configuration that was in place the last time you successfully logged on.

The Last Known Good Configuration option in the Advanced Options menu works because of how Windows 2000 maintains configuration information. Every time you boot Windows 2000 and log on, the kernel loading phase stores the computer and operating system configuration information for the local machine in a Registry key called HKLM\System\CurrentControlSet. When Windows 2000 needs to find out its current settings, it refers to the values stored here.

To ensure that the computer can't be rendered unbootable by a single bad configuration, Windows 2000 also stores a backup copy of the configuration information. In fact, it stores a couple of copies of the computer's system settings in the Registry, as shown in Figure 14-2. (Look for CurrentControlSet001 and CurrentControlSet002.)

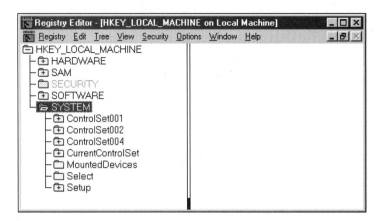

Figure 14-2 Copies of the Windows 2000 configuration settings in HKLM\System

These numbers are assigned to the configuration settings (and they're likely to be different on different machines). To find out which configuration set your Windows 2000 computer is using at the moment, look in HKLM\System\Select (see Figure 14-3).

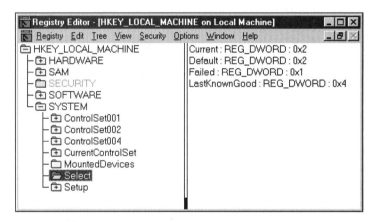

Figure 14-3 Possible values for configuration settings

Four values are shown in Figure 14-3: Current, Default, Failed, and LastKnownGood. If you restart the machine and boot normally (that is, without using the Advanced Options menu), the Default control set is used. The Failed value is the configuration set that was the default when you chose to start the machine from the Last Known Good Configuration menu. Because you instructed Windows 2000 to not start with that configuration set, it is now marked as Failed—even if nothing is actually wrong with it.

Note that this option applies only to the system configuration information, you must be able to load the Windows 2000 kernel, and its success is dependent on the settings used the last time you booted the computer and logged on. As a result, you can't always use the Last Known Good Configuration option to reverse an error. Specifically, you cannot use the Last Known Good Configuration option in the following situations:

- You must have logged on at least once successfully. Consequently, this option won't help you if you're installing Windows 2000.
- You must use this option *before* you log on again. The settings in place when you log on are saved as the Last Known Good value and are kept for only one generation. Even if the system hangs immediately when you log on, it is too late.
- If the change you want to reverse is not part of the control set information, you can't use the Last Known Good Configuration option to reverse it. Changes to user profiles and system policies are not kept in the control set information, nor are passwords or group accounts.
- If you can't even get to the boot menu, this option is useless.

Directory Services Restore Mode

The Directory Services Restore Mode is actually the second step for restoring a domain controller. Ordinarily, you can restore the Active Directory from Windows 2000 Backup (as described in the later section, "Restoring a Server") and then log back on again normally. The Active Directory (and Certificate Server) will recheck their indices and perform an integrity check. Then, you should again be up and running.

The **Directory Services Restore Mode** is intended for those times when you want to perform a more advanced verification. When you choose this option, it will kick you back to the main boot menu, with blue text at the bottom of the screen indicating that you are in Directory Services Restore Mode. The system will boot in Safe Mode with Networking, run CHKDSK on all the volumes, and then present the logon screen for you to log on as the administrator of the local domain.

As soon as you log on, run REGEDT32 and look in HKLM\System\CurrentControlSet\Service\NTDS for a subkey called Restore in Progress, which is created by Windows 2000 Backup. The presence of this key tells the Active Directory to check all of its indices the next time it starts up in normal mode.

Once you've ensured that the Active Directory was restored properly, you can restart the computer normally. The directory should work as intended.

Debugging Mode

Debugging mode is not actually a repair mode, but rather a way of moving the system boot log to another computer for evaluation. You can use this mode to debug a boot process from a computer that won't let you get far enough in the boot process to glean any useful information from the boot log. When you select this option, Windows 2000 sends all of the boot information to the serial port, transmitting it to another computer connected to the one you are debugging with a serial cable.

Repairing a Damaged Operating System

As you can see, the Advanced Options menu is helpful mostly for problems that are not too serious. Should you run into something more drastic, you will need to use either the Emergency Repair Disk or the Recovery Console to fix the problem.

Emergency Repair Disk

The **Emergency Repair Disk (ERD)** is a simple procedure for those times when you don't know precisely what the problem is, but you want to fix the server and get it back up and running again. If you've regularly backed up your system configuration data with the ERD option in the Backup program, you should be able to restore the server to a working configuration. Essentially, when you use the ERD during a repair of this kind, you tell Windows 2000 to read the configuration files stored in a Repair\Regback directory in your Windows 2000 installation and to copy those files back to their original locations. Any files that don't match the contents of the Regback folder may be replaced.

The Repair folder contains the original Windows 2000 configuration files, so you can use the ERD to restore your operating system to its original configuration without reinstalling the operating system.

If you don't update the contents of the Repair\Regback folder regularly, it will contain old Registry information. That isn't necessarily bad, but it will restore your Windows 2000 Server to an older state. In Windows 2000, Registry information is not stored on the ERD itself—unlike the Windows NT 4 ERD.

System Recovery Console

The ERD is designed for those times when you don't know what's wrong, but you want the problem fixed right away. In contrast, the **Recovery Console** is meant for those times when you've got a pretty good idea of what the problem is and how to fix it, but something about the Windows 2000 interface or the way it works makes it impossible to do so. In many ways, the Recovery Console acts like a command-line version of Windows 2000, but with a few limitations.

For example, imagine that you have a runaway network card service, set to run automatically when you boot Windows 2000, that doesn't work properly. While it is loaded, it repeatedly releases error messages and uses up nearly 100% of the CPU time by displaying these messages. You can grab a few cycles only during the seconds between when you click OK on the error message and the instant the next error message starts up. With great difficulty and a lot of determination, you could open the Services tool in the Administrative Tools folder, find the errant tool, and disable it. Doing so would take forever, however, because you would have only a few CPU cycles in which to move the mouse, go through the various folders to find the Services tool, find the tool in the list, and then disable it.

A better option would be to disable the service without ever giving it a chance to start. You can do so from the Windows 2000 Recovery Console.

In fact, you can do all of the following from the Recovery Console:

- Copy system files from a floppy disk or CD to a hard disk
- Start and stop services
- Read and write data in the system directory on the local hard disk
- Format and repartition disks
- Write boot sectors and master boot records to disks

To get a complete list of commands available in the Recovery Console, you can type **help** at the command prompt. Table 14-1 shows the available commands.

Table 14-1 Recovery Console commands

Command Name	Function
CD or CHDIR	Displays the name of the current directory, or changes directories. Typing CD.. closes the current directory and moves you up one in the tree.
CHKDSK	Runs CheckDisk.
CLS	Clears the screen of any previous output so that you can see better.
COPY or EXTRACT	Copies files from removable media to the system folders on the hard disk. By default, it does not accept wildcards.
DEL or DELETE	Deletes one or more files. By default, this command does not accept wildcards.
DIR	Lists the contents of the current or selected directory.
DISABLE	Disables the named service or driver.
ENABLE	Enables the named service or driver.
DISKPART	Creates or deletes disk partitions.
FIXBOOT	Writes a new partition boot sector on the system partition.
FIXMBR	Writes a new master boot record (MBR) for the partition boot sector.
FORMAT	Formats the selected disk.
LISTSVC	Lists all services running on the Windows 2000 installation.
LOGON	If you have multiple Windows 2000 (or Windows NT) installations on the local hard disk, allows you to pick the installation you want to repair.
MAP	Displays the drive letter mappings currently in place. This command is handy for getting the information you need to use DISKPART.
MD or MKDIR	Creates a directory.
MORE, TYPE	Displays the contents of the chosen text file.
RD or RMDIR	Deletes a directory.
RENAME or REN	Renames a single file.
SYSTEMROOT	Makes the current directory become the system root of the drive you are logged into.
ATTRIB	Changes the attributes of a selected file or folder.
EXTRACT	Extracts a compressed installation file to the local fixed disk. It works only if you're running the Recovery Console from the installation CD.

In addition to the commands listed in Table 14-1, the Recovery Console includes a BATCH command that you can use to create jobs. When you are finished with the Recovery Console, type "exit" to restart the computer.

Unlike the other Windows 2000 recovery tools, the Recovery Console is not set up by default. You can reach it either by running Setup from the Windows 2000 CD and choosing to repair an existing Windows 2000 installation or by installing it from Windows 2000 so that the Recovery Console is included in the boot menu that appears at system startup.

RESTORING A SERVER

You may need to rebuild your server from the ground up. To do so—and to prepare for such an eventuality—you need to understand the wedding cake of generic operating system data, system configuration data, and user data that makes up a server. Again, this restoration operation is not rocket science—it is nearly all about file replacement.

The first step to restoring a server is to reinstall the operating system from scratch. This step will replace any system executable files, DLLs, and other files that your operating system needs. If any service packs or bug fixes for Windows 2000 have been issued and you already had them installed, reinstall them after installing Windows 2000. If you don't have the same set of core operating system files available that was installed previously, you may not be able to restore the backups.

When the base operating system is available, use the Windows 2000 Backup Restore Wizard to restore the System State data from your backups. This step will restore the Active Directory certificate services (if you had them set up), the COM registration database, the system volume, the file replication service, boot files, and the Registry. When you restart the system, Active Directory should inspect its indices to verify that they're in order; it will then be ready to support the directory again. For a more hands-on approach to making sure that the system state data are ready to go, refer to the Active Directory Restore option in the Advanced Options menu.

You must watch out for the Authoritative Restore option in the Restore Wizard. If you have more than one domain controller in your domain and the Active Directory is replicated to any of these other domain controllers, you need to have that information replicated onto the other domain controllers. To ensure that the data you are restoring are replicated to these domain controllers, you must perform what's called an **authoritative restore**. Normally, the Backup Restore operation doesn't operate in authoritative mode, meaning that any data restored—including Active Directory objects—will retain the original update sequence number used by the Active Directory replication system to detect and spread Active Directory changes among the domain controllers. As a result, any data restored in nonauthoritative form look older than the other Active Directory entries and won't be replicated to the other domain controllers. In addition, the Active Directory replication system will replace the restored data with the newer data from the other domain controllers and wipe out your restore operation.

Authoritative restore solves this problem. After you've restored the system state data but before you've restarted the server, run the NTDSUTIL utility in the Windows 2000 System Tools. At the prompt, type "authoritative restore". The system state data you just restored will receive the highest update sequence number in the Active Directory replication system, so the information will be replicated throughout the domain.

If you like, you can restore user data at the same time that you restore the System State data. You don't have to restore the user data and configuration data separately, although you might want to do so if you have any doubts about restoring the System State data. Restoring in steps keeps you from wasting your time by restoring data that you can't yet use.

Chapter Summary

- You've now learned the basics of the Windows 2000 disaster recovery tools. As you can see, almost all of these tools are intended to replace files that are missing or corrupted. For this reason, it's very important that you back up your data and update the Registry backups in the Repair\Regback folder every time you make a change. You'll then be sure to have the files on hand that you need to get things back up and running.

Key Terms

Advanced Options menu — An alternative boot menu (accessible by pressing F8 when the boot menu is displayed) from which you can access the various specialized start modes available for troubleshooting purposes.

authoritative restore — A method of restoring the Active Directory information to make sure that it is the most recent copy of the information and the one that should be propagated throughout the domain.

boot logging — An advanced option that boots the computer normally but lists all files loaded during the boot process, and saving the list in a file called Ntbtlog.txt. Boot logging is enabled by default when you boot to any form of Safe Mode.

debugging mode — A mode that starts Windows 2000 normally while sending debugging information through a serial cable to another computer. It is useful when you want to examine the boot process carefully.

Directory Services Restore Mode — An advanced boot option that allows you to verify that the Active Directory has been restored from backups successfully.

Emergency Repair Disk (ERD) — A floppy disk that you can create with Windows 2000 Backup and that you can use to restore a previously saved set of configuration information (stored in %*systemroot*%\repair\regback). The ERD does not contain any configuration settings itself, just the files needed to restore the information saved on the hard disk.

Last Known Good Configuration — The configuration settings that were in place the last time you successfully booted Windows 2000. You can choose to load these settings if you boot from the Advanced Options menu and choose Last Known Good Configuration from the menu.

Ntdetect.com — A core file of Windows 2000 that inventories the computer's hardware and uses this inventory to build HKLM\Hardware. Every time you boot the machine, Ntdectect.com rechecks all hardware.

Ntldr — A core file of Windows 2000 that gets the computer ready to start running Windows 2000.

Ntoskrnl.exe — An executable image for the Windows 2000 kernel that contains the base operating system functionality.

Ordinary Safe Mode — An option that loads only the drivers and services required to boot the computer and to provide a simple operating environment.

Recovery Console — A command-line recovery interface that you can use to repair bits and pieces of Windows 2000 without replacing all configuration settings.

Safe Mode — A way of booting Windows 2000 with a minimal set of drivers. It displays the usual desktop (although using only the Vga.sys driver) and has no networking support.

Safe Mode (Command Prompt Only) — An option that works like Safe Mode—no networking support, basic VGA video, no extraneous drivers—except that it uses the command prompt (Cmd.exe) for a shell instead of Explorer (Explorer.exe).

Safe Mode with Networking — An option that is just like Safe Mode, except for the addition of network support. You would use this boot option when you want a pared-down version of the operating system, but need network support to fix something.

VGA Mode — An advanced boot option that boots Windows 2000 as usual, except that it uses the generic Vga.sys instead of the video driver you have installed. It is useful for fixing problems related to bad or incompatible video drivers.

REVIEW QUESTIONS

1. When using the Recovery Console, you can copy system files from a floppy disk to the hard disk, but not the reverse. True or False?

2. Which of the following is not required to boot Windows 2000?

    a. A working BIOS

    b. An operational floppy controller

    c. A functioning power supply

    d. A drive controller

3. When you turn the computer on, it powers up for a second and then shuts off. You can't keep it turned on. What is most likely the problem?

    a. The motherboard is connected to the power supply incorrectly.

    b. The power supply is not functioning.

    c. The BIOS is corrupted.

    d. The drive controller is not receiving power.

4. Which tool would you use to rewrite the MBR on a disk?
   a. Emergency Repair Disk
   b. Recovery Console
   c. Last Known Good Configuration
   d. Safe Mode (Command Prompt Only)
5. Which part of Windows 2000 displays the boot menu?
   a. Ntoskrl.exe
   b. Ntdetect.com
   c. Ntldr
   d. Boot.ini
6. Which piece of Windows 2000 builds HKLM\Hardware?
7. Which of the following is the start value of a service that is set up to start automatically during the kernel initialization phase?
   a. 1
   b. 2
   c. 3
   d. 4
8. What is the start value of the disabled service?
   a. 0
   b. 2
   c. 3
   d. 4
9. When does AUTOCHK run to check the integrity of NTFS file systems?
   a. During the kernel start phase
   b. During the kernel initialization phase
   c. During the services load phase
   d. After you log on
10. Mistakenly thinking that Explorer.exe was the filename of Internet Explorer, someone erases the file in an attempt to get rid of the Web browser. Which of the following Advanced Options could you use to fix the problem?
    a. Last Known Good Configuration
    b. Safe Mode
    c. Safe Mode (Command Prompt Only)
    d. Debugging Mode

11. Under what conditions does boot logging run?
12. Which of the following problems cannot be solved with the Last Known Good Configuration option? (Choose all that apply.)
    a. You've changed the Administrator password and now don't know what it is, so you want to go back to what it was before you rebooted.
    b. You inadvertently deleted a driver.
    c. You edited a group policy and want to reverse the edit.
    d. You reconfigured the printer settings.
13. You must run Directory Services Restore Mode after replacing System State data on the computer to reindex the Active Directory. True or False?
14. Why is it important to reinstall service packs before restoring System State data?
15. You must restore system state data before restoring user data. True or False?
16. What is the name of the key that the Active Directory looks for to see that it must reindex the directory?
17. Under what conditions must you use authoritative restore?
    a. When restoring data to the server while logged in with an account other than the Administrator account
    b. When restoring data to the server from an account that is not part of the Domain Administrators group
    c. When restoring the System State data
    d. When restoring the Active Directory to a computer that is not the only domain controller in the domain
18. Your Windows 2000 boot process keeps going to a certain point and then stops. You can't figure out the problem. Which of the following repair options can help you determine where loading Windows 2000 is failing?
    a. Recovery Console
    b. Last Known Good Configuration
    c. Boot logging
    d. Debugging
19. Where is repair information (in the form of updated Registry backups) for your Windows 2000 installation stored?
    a. On the Emergency Repair Disk
    b. In the \Repair folder
    c. In the \System32 folder
    d. None of the above
20. Which Advanced Options choices do *not* start the computer in some form of Safe Mode?

HANDS-ON PROJECTS

Project 14-1

To create a boot log for your computer and examine its contents:

1. Reboot the computer. When the boot menu appears, press **F8** to open the Advanced Options menu.

2. Choose **Enable Boot Logging** from the menu (use the arrow keys to move to this option and press **Enter** when it is highlighted). You'll return to the main boot menu.

3. Choose **Microsoft Windows 2000 Server** from the boot menu and press **Enter**. Windows 2000 will boot normally.

4. After you log onto Windows 2000, open the file **Ntbtlog.txt**, which is located in %*systemroot*%. You will see a list like the one in Figure 14-4.

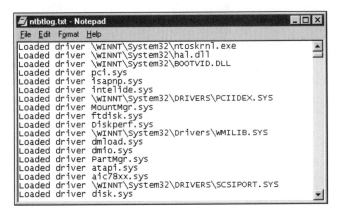

Figure 14-4 Contents of Ntbtlog.txt

Project 14-2

To change two configuration settings and see which you can restore with the Last Known Good Configuration boot option:

1. Open the **Display** applet in the **Control Panel**. Click the **Appearance** tab, and change the color scheme to something you are not currently using (in our example, we selected Rose (large)—see Figure 14-5). Apply the changes and close the applet so that you can see the new colors.

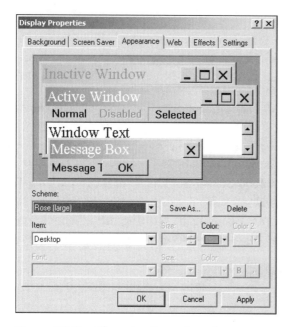

Figure 14-5 Changing the color scheme

2. From the **Date/Time Properties** applet in the Control Panel (also available if you double-click the clock on the Taskbar), change the time zone from its current setting (see Figure 14-6).

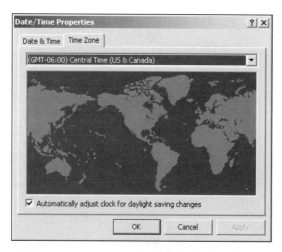

Figure 14-6 Changing the time zone

3. Restart the computer. When you reach the boot menu, press **F8** and choose **Last Known Good Configuration** from the Advanced Options menu.

4. You will be asked to choose a hardware profile (even if you haven't set one up; the default is called Profile 1). Press **Enter** or wait 30 seconds to let the default profile be chosen.
5. Windows 2000 will start normally, except that you'll see a message box indicating that Windows 2000 could not start as configured and a previous configuration was used instead. Close the message box.
6. You'll notice that the display is still a hideous shade of pink. Check the **Date/Time** properties, however, and you'll see that the time zone is back to its original setting.

 The reason why one setting changed and the other did not lies in the fact that one setting was in CurrentControlSet and the other was not. CurrentControlSet does not store display colors, but it does store the date and time settings. To see which settings are reversible with the Last Known Good Configuration option, run the Registry Editor and look at the keys contained within HKLM\System\CurrentControlSet (see Figure 14-7). These keys control the services settings, the drivers loaded, the Internet settings in the hardware profiles, and other information; they do not control system colors or the existence of files, however.

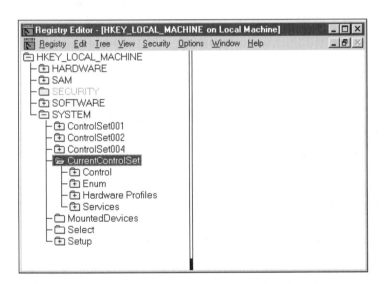

Figure 14-7   Contents of the Windows 2000 control set

Project 14-3

To install support for the Recovery Console from Windows 2000:

1. Open the **Run** tool in the Start menu, type **d:\i386\winnt32 /cmdcons** (assuming that the Windows 2000 setup files are available from drive D:), and press **Enter**. Windows 2000 will display the message box shown in Figure 14-8. Click **Yes**.

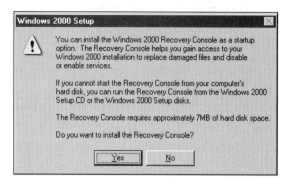

Figure 14-8 Initial screen for installing the Recovery Console (21.37)

2. Windows 2000 Setup will copy some files from the installation CD, and then prompt you to restart the computer.

3. The Recovery Console will be in the Startup menu (the text menu you see when you start up the computer) when you reboot, listed as Microsoft Windows 2000 Command Console. To start it, just choose that option before the 30-second timeout to whatever your default start-up option is.

Project 14-4

To use the Recovery Console to list services and then disable one of them, and then enable it and change its start value:

1. Reboot the system. From the boot menu, choose **Microsoft Windows 2000 Server Recovery Console**.

2. If more than one installation of Windows NT or Windows 2000 exists on the computer, choose the one you want to administer. Log into the Recovery Console using the Administrator's password.

3. In the Recovery Console, type **listsvc**. Windows 2000 will display a list of all services and drivers currently installed for that installation of Windows 2000, a short description of them, and their start type (Boot, Automatic, Manual, System, or Disabled).

Listing all of the services will probably take a few screen pages. The services are listed alphabetically, however, so you can find the one you want fairly easily. Write down its name (not case-sensitive).

4. Once you have found the suspected problem, it is time to use the disable command. The syntax is simple: **disable** *servicename* (choose a service and use it in place of *servicename*). Windows 2000 will then notify you that it found the Registry entry for this service (or tell you that it can't find an entry for this service, in which case you need to check your spelling and try again). It will also display the current start type and the new start type for the service. Write down the current start type for the service in case you want to start it again.

5. To make the change take effect, type **exit** to leave the Recovery Console and restart the computer.

Project 14-5

To reenable the service and then change its start type:

1. Restart the Recovery Console as described in Project 14-4. After you have logged in, refer to your notes and restart the service you disabled earlier by typing the following command: **enable** *servicename*.

2. To change the service's start type, you'll use the enable command again, but with an additional argument: **start_type**. For example, use **enable** *servicename* **start_type**. (If you apply this command to a disabled service, using this syntax will both enable the service and apply a start type to it.) Table 14-2 shows the available start types.

Table 14-2 Service start types available

Start Type	Meaning
Service_boot_start	Boot
Service_system_start	System
Service_demand_start	Manual
Service_auto_start	Automatic

CASE PROJECTS

1. You power up the server for the first time after rebuilding it. You can hear the drive spin up and the fan goes on, but the computer beeps at you and you cannot see any output on the screen. Which Windows 2000 disaster recovery tool should you apply to fix the problem? What do you think the problem is? Explain why the Last Known Good Configuration option can't help you if you deleted a driver that you need.

2. You attempt to start Windows 2000 one morning and see the following error message: "Windows 2000 could not start because the following file is missing or corrupt: \windows2000 root\system32\ntoskrnl.exe. Please reinstall a copy of the above file." Pressing Enter has no effect, and you see the same error message when you reboot the system. You've formatted the system partition with NTFS, so you can't get to it with a bootable floppy. What is the job of the missing file, and how can you use the Windows 2000 recovery tools to replace it?

3. Thinking that it's the executable for Internet Explorer, someone has gone to a lot of trouble to delete Explorer.exe from your Windows 2000 computer, booting to an alternative operating system so that he or she can delete the file. Now Windows 2000 won't run. What is the role of Explorer in Windows 2000, and what tool in the Advanced Options menu can you use to replace it?

4. You've restored the main domain controller (there are three) in your Active Directory structure. You notice that the information published in the Active Directory is now old—not the information that you restored to the main domain controller. What's happened, and how can you resolve this problem?

CHAPTER 15

TROUBLESHOOTING WINDOWS 2000

> **After reading this chapter and completing the exercises, you will be able to:**
> - Troubleshoot general problems with Windows 2000
> - Understand some of the Windows 2000 troubleshooting tools
> - Understand the Registry
> - Work with advanced boot options

Windows 2000 troubleshooting is an important and vast arena. In this chapter, we discuss several aspects of detecting, isolating, and eliminating problems. The discussion includes material on installation failures, repair tools, printing solutions, and a collection of other pertinent and related issues.

GENERAL PRINCIPLES OF TROUBLESHOOTING

Troubleshooting is a tedious process of systematically eliminating problems in a computer system. You'll soon discover that troubleshooting is more often an art than an exact science. You should follow several common-sense guidelines to improve your troubleshooting skills and reduce system downtime.

Over the years, we've discovered that information is the most valuable asset you can possess when troubleshooting. Two types of information are key to troubleshooting: details about the computer and details about previous troubleshooting activities.

Computer Information File

A **Computer Information File (CIF)** is a detailed collection of all information related to the hardware and software products that make up your computer (and even your entire intranet). Actually, a CIF is not just a single file, but an ever-expanding accumulation of data sheets sorted into related groupings, which are in turn stored in a fireproof storage vault. Obviously, constructing a CIF from scratch is a lengthy process, but one that will be rewarded with averted problems, easy reconfigurations, and simplified replacement of failed components.

The organization of a CIF is not important; what is important is that the file contains thorough, specific, and accurate information about the products, configuration, setup, and problems associated with your intranet. Some method of correlating the data sheets to the actual components must be derived, such as an alpha-numeric labeling system.

Some of the important items you'll want to include in your CIF are as follows:

- The platform, type, brand, and model number of each component
- Complete manufacturer specifications
- Configuration settings, including jumpers and DIP switches, plus what each setting means, including IRQs, DMA addresses, memory base addresses, port assignments, and so forth
- The manual, user's guide, or configuration sheets
- The version of BIOS, driver software, patches, fixes, and so on, with floppy copies
- Printed and floppy copies of all parameter and initialization files
- A detailed directory structure printout
- The names and versions of all software
- Network-assigned names, locations, and addresses
- The status of empty ports, upgrade options, or expansion capabilities
- System requirements
- Warranty information
- Complete technical support contact information

- An error log with detailed and dated entries of problems and solutions
- The date and location of the last complete backup
- The location of backup items and original software
- A network layout and cabling map
- A date and initials on everything

Your CIF is not complete with just hardware and software details. You should also include the nonphysical characteristics of your system in the CIF, such as the following:

- Information services present
- Important productivity services
- Plans for future service deployment
- Hardware and software matched with services
- The structure of authorized access and security measures
- A training schedule
- A maintenance schedule
- A backup schedule
- Contact information for all system administrators
- Personnel organization or management hierarchy
- Workgroup arrangements
- Online data storage locations
- In-house content and delivery conventions
- Authorship rights and restrictions
- Troubleshooting procedures

Neither of these lists is exhaustive. As you operate and maintain your systems, you'll undoubtedly discover numerous other important data to add to this collection of information. Remember—if you don't document it, then you won't be able to find it when you really need it.

We recommend maintaining both a printed/written version of this material and an electronic version. Every time a change, update, or correction occurs, it should be documented in the electronic version, and a new printout should be made and stored. Murphy's law guarantees that the moment at which you will need your electronic data most is when your system will not function.

Common-Sense Troubleshooting

Unfortunately, the point at which you need to be most clear-headed and have plenty of time to solve problems is usually the exact moment when you are overworked, have lots of stress, or are under serious deadlines. Troubleshooting is a process that rarely offers satisfactory results when pursued with impatience and hostility. Here are some common-sense rules for getting the most out of your troubleshooting efforts:

- *Be patient.* Anger, frustration, hostility, and frantic impatience usually cause problems to intensify rather than dissipate.

- *Be familiar with your system's hardware and software.* If you don't know what baseline normal is, you may not know when a problem is solved or when new problems surface.

- *Attempt to isolate the problem.* When possible, eliminate segments or components that are functioning properly, thereby narrowing the range of suspects.

- *Repeal the most recent change.* The simplest fix is to undo the problem you just caused; attempt to expunge the most recent alteration, upgrade, or change made to your system.

- *Investigate the most common points of failure.* The most active or sensitive components are the most common points of failure; they include hard drives, cables, and connectors.

- *Recheck items that have caused problems in the past.* As the axiom goes, history does repeat itself (and usually right in your own backyard).

- *Do the easy and quick first.* Why punish yourself early? Try the easy fixes before moving on to the more time-consuming, difficult, or even destructive measures.

- *Let the fault guide you.* The old adage, "Where there is smoke, there is fire," applies to computer problems just as much as real life. Investigate related components and system areas associated with the suspected fault.

- *Make changes one at a time.* A step-by-step process enables you to clearly distinguish the solution when you stumble upon it.

- *Repeat the failure if possible.* In many cases, being able to repeat an error is the only way to locate it. Transient and inconsistent faults are difficult to uncover because of their "now you see it, now you don't" nature.

- *Keep a detailed solution and attempted solution log.* Keep track of everything you do (both successful and failed attempts). This log will prove an invaluable resource when an error occurs again on the same or a different system, or when the same system experiences a related problem.

- *Learn from others' mistakes.* Others' failures, if you study them, can save you from making the same mistake.

- *Learn from your own mistakes.* A wise administrator is the one who can look at his or her failures, and better himself or herself through them.

This list of common-sense items shouldn't contain much that you didn't already know. The most difficult part is remembering these guidelines when you are in the heat of battle.

TROUBLESHOOTING INSTALLATION PROBLEMS

Unfortunately, the installation process of Windows 2000 is susceptible to several errors: media errors, domain controller communication difficulties, stop message errors or halt on blue screen, hardware problems, and dependency failures. The following list contains a short synopsis of each error type.

- *Media errors:* Media errors are problems with the distribution CD-ROM itself, the copy of the distribution files on a network drive, or the communication link between the installation and the distribution files. The only regularly successful solution to media errors is to switch media—for example, copying the files to a network drive, linking to a server's CD-ROM, or installing a CD-ROM on the workstation. If you encounter media errors, always restart the installation process from the beginning.

- *Domain controller communication difficulties:* Communication with the domain controller is crucial to some installations, especially when attempting to join a domain. Most often this problem is related to a typing error (such as a name, password, or domain name), but network failures and offline domain controllers can be causes as well. Verify the viability of the domain controller directly and from other workstations (if applicable).

- *Stop message errors or halt on blue screen:* Use of an incompatible or damaged driver controller is the most common cause of stop messages and halting on the blue screen during installation. If any information is presented to you about an error, try to determine whether you are using the proper driver. Otherwise, double-check your hardware and the drivers that are required to operate them under Windows 2000.

- *Hardware problems:* If you failed to verify your hardware with the Hardware Compatibility List (HCL) or a physical defect has surfaced in previously operational devices, very strange errors can arise. In such cases, replacing the device is the only viable solution. Before you go to that expense, double-check the installation and configuration of all devices within the computer.

- *Dependency failures:* The failure of a service or driver due to the failure of a foundational or prior service or driver is known as a dependency failure. For example, the server and workstation services may fail because the NIC does not initialize properly. Often Windows 2000 will boot in spite of these errors, so check the Event log for more details.

Just knowing about these installation problems can help you avoid them. Unfortunately, successfully installing Windows 2000 does not eliminate the possibility of further complications. Luckily, Microsoft has included several troubleshooting tools that can help locate and eliminate most system failures, are discussed in the next section.

TROUBLESHOOTING TOOLS

The repair and troubleshooting tools native to Windows 2000 are components with which you need to become familiar. They are applicable to most situations and can save you countless hours of troubleshooting digression. The next few sections detail how to use the Event Viewer and the Computer Management tools.

Event Viewer

The **Event Viewer** is used to view system messages regarding the failure or success of various key occurrences within the Windows 2000 environment (see Figure 15-1). The items recorded in the Event Viewer's logs inform you of system drivers or service failures as well as security problems or aberrant applications. Located in the Administrative Tools section of the Control Panel and Start menu, this tool is used to view the logs created automatically by Windows 2000. These logs are as follows:

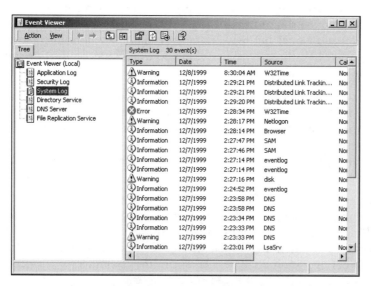

Figure 15-1 Event Viewer with System Log selected

- **Application Log**—Records application events, alerts, and system messages.
- **Directory Service Log**—Records events related to the Directory Service.
- **DNS Service Log**—Records events related to the DNS Service.

- **File Replication Service Log**—Records events related to the File Replication Service.

- **Security Log**—Records security-related events, including audit events.

- **System Log**—Records information and alerts about the Windows 2000 internal processes, including hardware and operating system errors, warnings, and general information messages.

Each log records a different type of event. All of the logs, however, collect the same meta-information about each event: date, time, source, category, event, user ID, and computer. Each logged event (see Figure 15-2) includes some level of detail about the error, ranging from an error code number to a detailed description with a memory HEX buffer capture. Most system errors, including stop errors that result in the blue screen, are recorded in the System log. You can therefore review the time and circumstances around a system failure. In many cases, the details in the Event Viewer can be used as pieces of evidence in your search for the actual cause of a problem. The event details offer little actual resolution information, however.

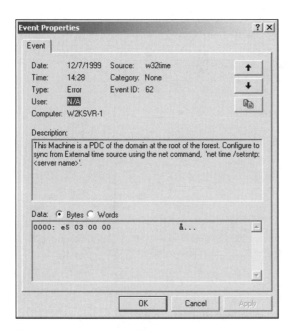

Figure 15-2 Event Viewer event detail

Computer Management

One of the most helpful advancements in the area of hardware support under Windows 2000 is the addition of Plug and Play capabilities to the robustness of Windows NT. A useful side effect of Plug and Play is greater simplicity of the troubleshooting tools, which can be brought to bear against nearly every aspect of Windows 2000. The bulk of these tools are collected into a single interface under the Computer Management tool found in the Administrative Tools section of the Control Panel and Start menu.

The Computer Management tool combines many tools from Windows NT, Windows 98, and several completely new utilities. This single interface (see Figure 15-3) makes locating and resolving problems on your key systems easier than ever before. The Computer Management collection of utilities is divided into three sections: System Tools, Storage, and Services and Applications. The Services and Applications section contains management controls for various installed and active services and applications. The actual contents of this section will depend on the state of your system. Some of the common controls are as follows:

- *Telephony*: For modem and remote communications
- *WMI Control*: For management of the Windows Management Instrumentation (WMI) service
- *Services:* For stopping and starting services as well as configuring the start-up parameters for services
- *Indexing Service:* For defining the corpus for Index Server
- *Internet Information Services:* For managing Internet services
- *DNS:* For managing the Domain Name Service

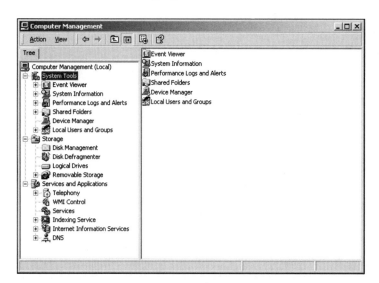

Figure 15-3 Computer Management

The System Tools section contains six tools. The Event Viewer is accessible here (as discussed earlier in this chapter). The System Information tool is used to access configuration information and status summaries for the computer and operating system environment. You can quickly discover information such as system model numbers, free IRQs, sharing conflicts, and component configurations. This tool is invaluable when attempting to add new hardware into your system. The third tool, the Performance Logs and Alerts tool, offers another means to access the Performance Monitoring tool of Windows 2000 (see Chapter 13 for details). Shared Folders is used to discover the shared folders existing on the local system. This interface shows hidden shares, current sessions, and open files. The Device Manager enables you to view and alter the current hardware configurations of all existing devices. The Local Users and Groups tool is disabled when Active Directory is present; otherwise, it is used to create and manage local user accounts and groups.

The Storage section of Computer Management includes four tools that simplify storage device administration. The Disk Management tool allows you to view and alter the partitioning and volume configuration of hard drives. The Disk Defragmenter improves the layout of stored data on drives by reassembling fragmented files and aggregating free space. Logical Drives is used to gain information about logical drives (that is, those that you've formatted and assigned drive letters to). Removable Storage enables you to manage removable media, from floppies to tapes to whatever.

THE REGISTRY

Windows 2000 uses a system component called the **Registry** which is a database that stores data about a system's configuration in a hierarchical form. The Registry holds information essential to Windows 2000 itself as well as native applications, added services, and most add-on software products from Microsoft and third-party vendors. The information stored in the Registry is comparable to information stored in initialization (.ini, .dat, .bat, .sys, and so on) files in Windows 3.x or even Windows 95/98. For native Windows 2000 applications, the Registry takes the place of .ini files, storing all of their configuration information in this database. Although the Control Panel applets and the Administration Tools utilities suffice to cover most Windows 2000 configuration needs, some settings can be established or changed only by editing the Registry directly.

One important fact to keep in mind about the Registry is that it is not an exhaustive collection of configuration settings. Instead, it holds only the exceptions to the defaults. Processes within Windows 2000 will operate with their own known internal defaults unless a **value** in the Registry specifically alters that default behavior. This fact makes working with the Registry difficult, as most often the control you need is not contained in the Registry because the internal defaults are being used. To alter such a setting, you must know the exact syntax, spelling, location, and valid values; otherwise, you will be unable to modify the default behavior. For Windows NT 4.0, the Resource Kit contains a help file named Regentry.hlp that lists all of the possible Registry entries and valid values.

Each Registry **key** is similar to a bracketed heading in an .ini file. Changes made to system configurations through Administrative Tools or Control Panel applets are applied to the Registry database. A special kind of administrative tool, the Registry Editor, allows you to make changes directly to the Registry database. Such tools understand the hierarchical nature of the Registry and are capable of manipulating each level in the hierarchy.

The structure and layout of the Registry are not exactly human-friendly. Instead, this database was designed for programming ease and speed of interaction for processes. Its structure, although a bit daunting, is understandable if broken down into its parts. The Registry is divided into five major groupings, called keys. Below each key are one or more levels of **subkeys**. A subkey is just another sublevel of grouping. Within each subkey, one or more values can exist. A **value entry** is a named parameter or placeholder for a control setting or configuration data. It can hold a single binary digit, a long string of ASCII characters, or a hexidecimal value. The actual data held by a value entry is known as the value. Figure 15-4 depicts the Registry's structure.

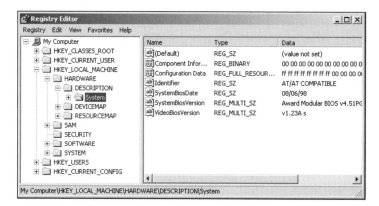

Figure 15-4 View of Registry hierarchy structure via the Registry Editor

Important points to keep in mind about the Registry include the following:

- Keys are the top-level or root divisions of the Registry.
- Keys can contain one or more subkeys.
- A subkey can contain one or more subkeys.
- A subkey can contain one or more value entries.

Each time Windows 2000 starts, the Registry is loaded into memory from files stored on the hard drive. Each time Windows 2000 shuts down, the Registry is written from memory back to the files. While Windows 2000 is operating, the Registry remains in memory. The Registry is therefore easy to access and quick to respond to control queries. Because it remains in memory, changes to the Registry take effect immediately. In most cases, any change made to the Registry immediately results in the use of that change as an operational parameter. Only in rare cases will Windows 2000 require a reboot to enforce changes.

As noted earlier, there are five top-level keys in the Registry. Each key has a unique purpose, as described in the following list:

- **HKEY_LOCAL_MACHINE**—This Registry key contains the value entries that control the local computer, including hardware devices, device drivers, and various operating system components. The data stored in this key is not dependent on a logged-on user or the applications or processes in use. (See Figure 15-5.)

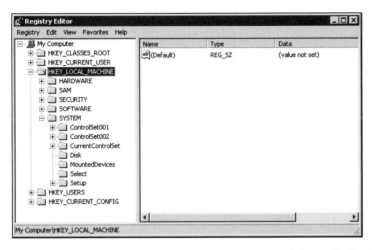

Figure 15-5 HKEY_LOCAL_MACHINE as viewed through the Registry Editor

- **HKEY_CLASSES_ROOT**—This Registry key contains the value entries that control the relationships between file extensions (and therefore file format types) and applications. It also supports the data used in object linking and embedding (OLE), COM object data, and file-class association data. This key actually points to another Registry key named HKEY_LOCAL_MACHINE\Software\Classes, and it provides multiple points of access to make itself easily accessible both to the operating system and to applications that need access to the compatibility information already mentioned. (See Figure 15-6.)

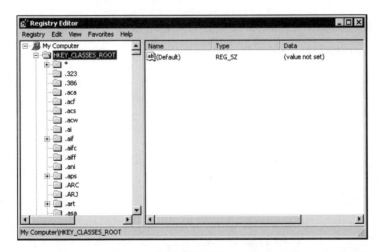

Figure 15-6 HKEY_CLASSES_ROOT as viewed through the Registry Editor

- **HKEY_CURRENT_CONFIG**—This Registry key contains the value entries that control the currently active hardware profile. Its contents are built each time the system starts up. This key is derived from data stored in the

HKEY_LOCAL_MACHINE\System\CurrentControlSet\HardwareProfiles subkey. It provides backward compatibility with Windows 95/98 applications. (See Figure 15-7.)

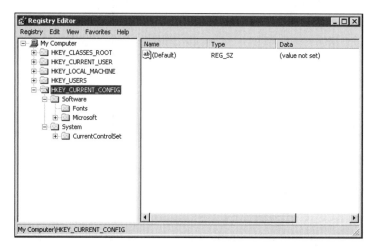

Figure 15-7 HKEY_CURRENT_CONFIG as viewed through the Registry Editor

- **HKEY_CURRENT_USER**—This Registry key contains the value entries that define the user environment for the currently logged-on user. It is built each time a user logs onto the system. The data in this key is derived from the HKEY_USERS key and the Ntuser.dat/.man file of a user's profile. (See Figure 15-8.)

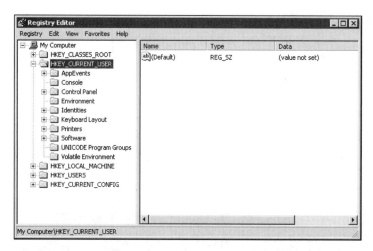

Figure 15-8 HKEY_CURRENT_USER as viewed through the Registry Editor

- **HKEY_USERS**—This Registry key contains the value entries that define the user environments for all users who have ever logged onto this computer. When a new user logs onto this system, a new subkey is added for that user which is either built from the default profile stored in this key or constructed from the roaming user profile associated with the domain user account. (See Figure 15-9.)

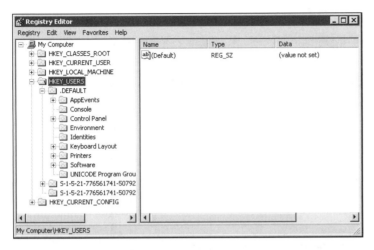

Figure 15-9 HKEY_USERS as viewed through the Registry Editor

 In some instances, a sixth key may appear on Windows 2000. The HKEY_DYN_DATA key is used by some Windows 95 applications. When these applications are installed on a Windows 2000 system, the Windows 2000 Registry creates a pseudo-key that redirects calls to this sixth key to the alternative areas of the Registry, such as HKEY_CLASSES_ROOT, where the data actually reside.

About Value Entries

Value entries within the Registry consist of three parts: name, data type, and value. A Registry value entry's name is typically a multiword phrase without spaces that uses title capitalization—for example; AutoAdminLogon (see Figure 15-10).

The data type of a value entry tells the Registry how to store the value. This information is extremely important because an ACSII text string is different from a hex value, which is in turn different from binary data. The data type specifies whether the data consist of a text string or a number and the numerical base or radix of that number. Radix types supported by Windows 2000 are decimal (base 10), hexadecimal (base 16), and binary (base 2). All hexadecimal values are listed with the prefix "0x" to identify them clearly (as in 0xF for 15).

The value of a value entry is the actual data contained by that value entry. It can be of any length, and its content is limited only by its data type. Windows 2000 supports five data types:

- **REG_BINARY**—Binary format
- **REG_DWORD**—Binary, hex, or decimal format
- **REG_EXPAND_SZ**—Expandable text-string format that contains a variable that is replaced by an application when it is used (for example, %Systemroot%\file.exe)

- **REG_MULTI_SZ**—Text-string format that contains multiple human-readable values separated by NULL characters
- **REG_SZ**—Text-string format

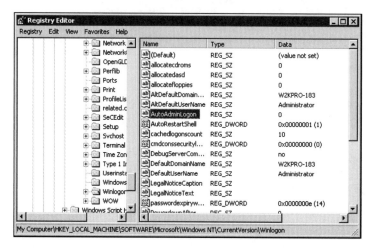

Figure 15-10 AutoAdminLogon as viewed through the Registry Editor

 Once a value entry is created and its data type defined, that data type cannot be changed. To alter the data type of a value, you must delete the value entry and then re-create it with a new data type.

Registry Storage Files

The files used to store the Registry are located in the %systemroot%\system32\config directory of the boot partition (see Figure 15-11). The Registry is not stored in files that match one-to-one with the top-level keys. Instead, it is stored in various subkey, logging, and backup files, as shown in Table 15-1.

The Registry

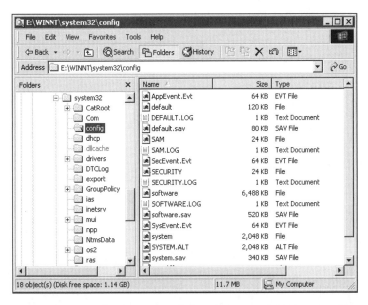

Figure 15-11 The contents of the %systemroot%\system32\config directory

Table 15-1 The storage files of the Registry

Registry hive	Filenames
HKEY_LOCAL_MACHINE\SAM	Sam, Sam.log, Sam.sav
HKEY_LOCAL_MACHINE\Security	Security, Security.log, Security.sav
HKEY_LOCAL_MACHINE\Software	Software, Software.log, Software.sav
HKEY_LOCAL_MACHINE\System	System, System.alt, System.log, System.sav
HKEY_USERS\.DEFAULT	Default, Default.log, Default.sav
(Not associated with a hive)	Userdiff, Userdiff.log
HKEY_CURRENT_USER	Ntuser.dat, Ntuser.dat.log

Notice that only four of the HKEY_LOCAL_MACHINE subkeys, the .DEFAULT subkey of the HKEY_USERS key, and the HKEY_CURRENT_USER key are stored in files. All of the other keys and subkeys are either built during the boot process or are copies of a subsection of HKEY_LOCAL_MACHINE.

The HKEY_USERS key is built from the default file (which represents the default user profile's Ntuser.dat file) and copies the profiles for all users who have ever logged onto the computer. These profiles are cached locally in \Documents and Settings\<username> directories. A copy of the Ntuser.dat or Ntuser.man file is copied into the repair directory for the currently logged-on user.

Notice that the Registry storage files use four extensions. The extension identifies the purpose or function of the particular file:

- *No extension:* The storage file for the subkey.
- *.alt:* The backup file of the subkey. Note that only the HKEY_LOCAL_MACHINE\System subkey has a backup file.
- *.log:* A file containing all changes made to a key. This file is used to verify that all modifications to the Registry are applied properly.
- *.sav:* Copies of a key in their original state as created at the end of the text portion of Windows 2000 installation.

The Registry Editors: REGEDIT and REGEDT32

Because the structure of the Registry is so complex, special tools are required to operate on it directly. In Windows 2000, you have two different Registry Editors from which to choose: **REGEDIT** and **REGEDT32**. The former is a 16-bit application, whereas the latter is a 32-bit application. REGEDIT (see Figure 15-12) offers global searching and combines all of the keys into a single display. REGEDT32 (see Figure 15-13) allows you greater control over key and value entry security, and displays each root key in a separate window. REGEDT32 also offers a read-only mode so you can explore without the possibility of accidentally altering value entries. Both editors can be used to perform searches, add new subkeys and value entries, alter the data in value entries, and import and export keys and subkeys. You'll need to get to know both editors to manipulate the Registry with great dexterity.

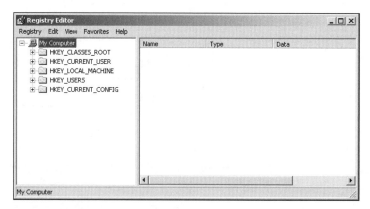

Figure 15-12 REGEDIT

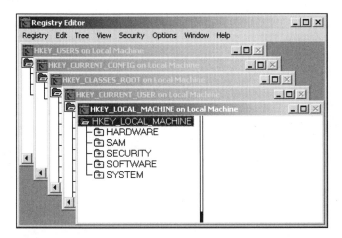

Figure 15-13 REGEDT32

Editing the Registry directly is a task that should not be undertaken without forethought and planning. It is easily possible to alter the Registry—whether on purpose or accidentally—in such a way as to render a system completely unrecoverable. If you don't know exactly what you are doing in the Registry, don't edit it! Even when you do think you know exactly what you wish to change in the Registry, it is always a good idea to take precautions.

- Back up all important data on the computer.
- Make a separate backup of all or part of the Registry. Saving each key or subkey individually is recommended. Store the backup files on local drives, network drives, and floppies or other removable media to ensure access.
- Restart the computer before editing the Registry.
- Perform only one Registry modification at a time. Test the results before proceeding.
- Reboot immediately after each change to force full system compliance. This step is not strictly necessary but has often proven a prudent measure.
- Always test the changes on a nonproduction system hosting noncritical services before deploying them on production systems.
- Use the REGEDT32 read-only mode to explore the Registry to ensure that accidental changes are not made.

Registry Size Limitations

As noted earlier, the Registry is stored in active memory, so it is quickly and easily accessible while the operating system is functioning. It resides in the paged pool portion of memory, which means it can be swapped out to disk when it is not in use. In contrast, the kernel resides in a nonpaged pool portion of memory, so it always stays in physical RAM. As your system ages, many changes will accumulate in the Registry, causing its size to grow. Its initial size on a Windows 2000 Professional system is approximately 10 MB. To prevent the

Registry from consuming too much memory, Windows 2000 imposes a maximum size for the Registry. This size ceiling is set at one-fourth of the current paged pool by default, although you can change it. When the page pool size changes, Windows 2000 will automatically adjust the Registry size ceiling as well.

To alter the Registry ceiling, open the Virtual Memory dialog box (the Change button appears on the Performance Options dialog box, which is accessed by clicking the Performance Options button on the Advanced tab of the System applet from the Control Panel). Then change the value in the number field beside Maximum registry size (MB) within the Registry size area (see Figure 15-14). This value sets the maximum boundary size only for the Registry; it does not allocate paged pool space or guarantee that paged pool space will even be available.

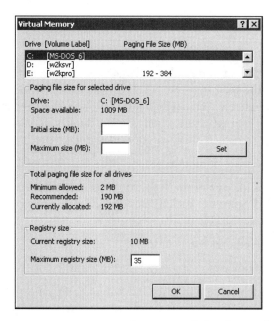

Figure 15-14 Virtual Memory dialog box, where the Registry size is defined

Backing Up the Registry

Even though Windows 2000 automatically manages the safety of the Registry via its fault-tolerance mechanisms (namely, .log and .alt files), it is still important for you to take proactive measures to back up the Registry. You can employ several methods to create reliable Registry backups:

- Most Windows 2000 backup applications include support for full Registry backups. With these products, you can back up the Registry as part of your daily automated backup or as a distinct Registry-only procedure.

- Either REGEDIT or REGEDT32 can be used to save all or part of the Registry to separate files.

- You can make a copy of the %systemroot%\System32\config directory manually.
- You can employ the *Windows 2000 Resource Kit* tools, Reg.exe or Regback.exe.

 Note No matter which method you employ, take the time to make two copies or perform the backup twice. This step will provide additional insurance just in case your first backup attempt failed for some reason. If you've ever destroyed a production machine by manipulating the Registry when you didn't have a recent backup, then you'll understand why this hopefully superfluous preparation work is so important. Nine times out of 10, when you don't make the backup, you'll need it.

Restoring the Registry

Obviously, if you intend to take the time to create backups of the Registry, you need to understand how to restore this database. You have several options for restoring the Registry, and maybe more, depending on the method used to make the backup. Windows 2000 itself will attempt to maintain a functional Registry using the fault-tolerance mechanisms already discussed. In cases where the automatic restoration process fails, however, you can first attempt to restore the **Last Known Good Configuration (LKGC)**.

To access this boot option, you press F8 during the initial startup of Windows 2000 when the boot menu is displayed. Don't worry—the basic boot menu even prompts you to press F8 if you need an alternative boot method. Pressing F8 reveals a new selection menu similar to the following:

```
OS Loader v5.0

Windows 2000 Advanced Options Menu
Please select an option:

Safe Mode
Safe Mode with Networking
Safe Mode with Command Prompt

Enable Boot logging
Enable VGA Mode
Last Known Good Configuration
Directory Services Restore Mode (Windows 2000 domain
controllers only)
Debugging Mode

Use [up] and [down] to move the highlight to your choice.
Press Enter to choose.
```

Just use the arrow keys to highlight the Last Known Good Configuration selection, then press Enter. The LKGC is the state of the Registry stored in one of the control sets (described earlier in this chapter) when the last successful user logon was performed. If the Registry becomes damaged in such a way that it will not fully boot or will not allow a user to log on, the LKGC option can restore the system to a previous state. Keep in mind that any changes made to the system between the time the LKGC was stored and when it was used to restore the system will be lost. If the LKGC fails to restore the system to a functioning state, then you have only two options:

1. Use your backup software to restore the Registry files. This operation is possible only if your backup application offers a DOS-based restoration mechanism, which can bypass NTFS write restrictions. In other words, the backup software must operate with a functioning Windows NT environment when launched from a bootable floppy. This type of software lets you restore files to the boot and system partitions (that is, the Registry) so that you can return to a functional operating system. Unfortunately, these applications are rare.

2. Reinstall Windows 2000 either fully or as an upgrade. An upgrade may replace the section of the Registry that is causing the problems, allowing you to retain most of your configuration, but this ability is just the luck of the draw. A full reinstallation of Windows 2000 will return the system to a preconfigured state, requiring you to perform all post-installation changes again.

If you are able to boot into the system but things do not function the way they should or services, drivers, or applications do not load or operate properly, you may need to restore the Registry in part or whole from your backup. Simply use the same tool employed to create the backup to restore the Registry state. Keep in mind that with some tools, you can restore portions of the Registry instead of the entire database at once.

Regardless of which method you choose to restore the Registry, it's always a good idea to restart the system to ensure that the restoration was completed successfully and that the system is using only the updated (or, more correctly, reverted) settings. It is also a good idea to retain the copies of the old Registry until you are confident that the system is functioning normally and you've had an opportunity to create new backups.

Windows 2000 Resource Kit Registry Tools

The **Windows 2000 Resource Kit** includes several utilities which can be brought to bear against the Registry. Because many of these tools are command-line tools or have significant ancillary materials, we recommend that you peruse the Support Tools documentation yourself before actually using them. Some of the key utilities to focus on include the following:

- *Reg.exe:* A tool used to perform command-line operations on the Registry, ideally suited for batch file operations. Functions include querying for value entry data, adding new value entries, changing current values, deleting values or keys, copying keys, backing up and restoring keys, and loading and unloading keys.

- *Regdump.exe:* A command-line tool used to dump all or part of the Registry to the STDOUT file. The output of this tool is suitable for the Regini.exe tool.

- *Regfind.exe:* A command-line tool used to search for a key, value name, or value data based on keywords.

- *Compreg.exe:* A GUI tool used to compare two local or remote Registry keys and highlight all differences between them.
- *Regini.exe:* A command-line scripting tool used to add keys to the Registry.
- *Regback.exe:* A command-line tool used to back up keys from the Registry.
- *Regrest.exe:* A command-line tool used to restore keys to the Registry.
- *Scanreg.exe:* A GUI tool used to search for a key, value name, or value data based on keywords.

TROUBLESHOOTING BOOT FAILURES

Troubleshooting **boot failures** is an essential skill you need to master. It is all too common for errors to occur that will cause a Windows 2000 system to fail to boot. Most of the tasks or actions used to correct problems are fairly simple and logical. In most cases, you'll start with simple solutions and continue to apply more drastic measures until the problem is resolved. The ability to restore a system to boot functionality does not exclude the requirement to maintain a regular and complete backup of your data.

The boot failure troubleshooting process requires four key elements:

- The four Windows 2000 setup boot disks (which can always be built from the CD's \bootdisk directory)
- The Windows 2000 CD and any applied service packs
- An ERD built via the Backup utility
- A recent backup of your Windows 2000 system

The ERD built via the Backup utility under Windows 2000 is not the same as the ERD built via the rdisk /s command under Windows NT 4.0. The Windows NT ERD contains a significant portion of the Registry duplicated by copying files from the systemroot%\repair folder. The Windows 2000 ERD does not contain these Registry files. Instead, its ERD repair process attempts to access the systemroot%\repair folder directly instead of relying on a floppy-based backup. Needless to say, this change on Microsoft's part places less faith in the ERD repair process under Windows 2000 than it did under Windows NT.

With these tools in hand, you can attempt to restore your system to boot functionality by taking the following actions. They are discussed in a general order of simplest to the most complex and drastic.

Advanced Start-up Options

Windows 2000 boasts numerous start-up options not found in Windows NT. These options were borrowed from Windows 95/98 and offer a wider range of capabilities to circumvent boot problems. To access the alternative boot methods, press F8 when the boot menu appears. You'll see a prompt for this action at the bottom of the screen. Pressing F8 reveals the Advanced Options Menu, which looks like the following:

```
OS Loader v5.0

Windows 2000 Advanced Options Menu
Please select an option:

Safe Mode
Safe Mode with Networking
Safe Mode with Command Prompt

Enable Boot Logging
Enable VGA Mode
Last Known Good Configuration
Directory Services Restore Mode (Windows 2000 domain
controllers only)
Debugging Mode

Use [up] and [down] to move the highlight to your choice.
Press Enter to choose.
```

From this menu, you can make the following selections:

- *Safe Mode*—Windows 2000 starts using only the minimal drivers and system files. No networking components are loaded.

- *Safe Mode with Networking*—Windows 2000 starts in Safe Mode with network support (this support does not include PC Card networking).

- *Safe Mode with Command Prompt*—Windows 2000 starts in Safe Mode but results in a text-only command prompt instead of the standard GUI desktop.

- *Enable Boot Logging*—This option configures the boot process to write details about loaded drivers and services to the %systemroot%\Ntbtlog.txt file.

- *Enable VGA Mode*—Windows 2000 starts normally but uses only the basic VGA video drivers and resets resolution to 640 × 480 at 256 or 16 colors.

- *Last Known Good Configuration*—Windows 2000 starts using the state of the Registry as stored at the moment of the last successful logon.

- *Directory Service Restore Mode*—Windows 2000 starts and rebuilds/restores the Active Directory. This selection functions on Windows 2000 domain controllers only.

- *Debugging Mode*—Windows 2000 starts and sends debugging information to another system connected by a serial cable. See the *Windows 2000 Resource Kit* for details.

Start-up File Repair

If one of the start-up options does not resolve your boot problems, or if you cannot even reach the boot menu, you may need to replace or repair your start-up files. Although boot failures are often caused by damaged start-up files, such as Boot.ini, Ntdetect.com, Ntldr, or Ntoskrnl.exe, a damaged **master boot record (MBR)** on the system drive can cause similar problems. The following Repair process can resolve all of these issues:

1. Start the system using the Windows 2000 setup boot disks. After you insert the fourth disk, you'll be prompted for a start-up option. Press the R key to select to Repair a damaged system.

2. Next, you'll be prompted with two additional choices: to repair Windows 2000 using the Recovery Console, or to repair Windows 2000 using the Emergency Repair Process. The Recovery Console option is meant only for advanced users; for details on it, consult the *Windows 2000 Resource Kit* or a Microsoft repair professional. Select the Emergency Repair Process by pressing the R key.

3. Next, you are prompted to decide whether to perform a manual or a fast repair. The manual option offers you the ability to walk through the repair functions one at a time (those functions consist of repair system files, partition and boot sector problems, and start-up and bootstrapping problems). The fast repair performs all of these functions without further prompting. Select either choice.

4. When prompted, provide your ERD or the Windows 2000 distribution CD.

5. Follow any additional prompts that may appear based on the repair process and the problems encountered.

6. Once the repair is complete, the repair process will attempt to restart your computer. Watch for this action, and make sure that all floppies are removed when the reboot occurs.

If your system is not repaired at this point, you have two more options. You can attempt a DOS-based restoration of your backed-up data to restore the system, or you can start over with a fresh installation.

TROUBLESHOOTING PRINTER PROBLEMS

Network printers are often the instigators of several affronts to normal productive activity. Printer problems can occur anywhere between the power cable of the printer to the application attempting to print. Systematic elimination of possible points of failure is the only reliable method of resolving printing errors. Here are some common and useful tips for printers:

- Always check the physical aspects of the printer—cable, power, paper, toner, and so on.
- Check the logical printer on both the client and the server.
- Check the print queue for stalled jobs.
- Reinstall the printer driver to make sure it has not become corrupted.
- Attempt to print from a different application or a different client.
- Print using Administrator access.

- Stop and restart the spooler using the Services tool found in Computer Management.
- Check the status and CPU usage of the Spoolss.exe using the Task Manager.
- Check the free space on the drive hosting the spooler file, and change its destination.

This list covers most of the more common print-related problems. For more tips on troubleshooting, consult the *Windows 2000 Resource Kit*.

TROUBLESHOOTING RAS PROBLEMS

RAS is another area that offers numerous points of failure—from the configuration of the computers on both ends, to the modem settings, to the condition of the communications line. Unfortunately, no ultimate RAS troubleshooting guide exists. Nevertheless, here are some solid steps in the right direction:

- Check all physical connections.
- Check the communications line itself, with a phone if appropriate.
- Verify the RAS installation, the port configurations, and the modem setup.
- Check that both the client and the server dial-up configurations match, including their speed, protocol, and security settings.
- Verify that the user account has RAS privileges.
- Inspect the RAS-related logs: Device.log and Modemlog.txt.
- Remember that multilink and callback will not work together.
- Recognize that autodial and persistent connections may cause the computer to attempt RAS connection upon logon.

Most RAS problems are related to misconfiguration. For more details on RAS, consult the *Windows 2000 Resource Kit*.

TROUBLESHOOTING NETWORK PROBLEMS

Network problems can range from faults in the media, to misconfigured protocols, to workstation or server errors. Attempt to eliminate the obvious and easy before moving on to more drastic, complex, or unreliable measures. Cabling, connections, and hardware devices are just as suspect as the software components of networking. Verifying hardware functionality involves more than just eyeballing it. You may need to perform some electrical test work, change physical settings, or even update drivers or /ROM BIOS.

TROUBLESHOOTING DISK PROBLEMS

The component on your computer that experiences the most activity is the hard drive, even when compared to your keyboard and mouse. It should not be surprising that drive failures are common. Windows 2000 is natively equipped to maintain the file system, but even a well-tuned system is subject to hardware glitches. Most partition, boot sector, and drive configuration faults can be corrected or recovered from by using the Disk Management tool. Ultimately, the only truly reliable means of protecting data on storage devices is to maintain accurate and timely backups.

MISCELLANEOUS TROUBLESHOOTING ISSUES

Several troubleshooting tips just don't fit well into the other categories described in this chapter. They are included here in a kind of grab bag of tips.

Permissions Problems

Permission problems typically occur when group memberships conflict or when permissions are managed on a per-account basis. To test for faulty permission settings, attempt to perform the same actions and activities with the Administrator account. Double-check group memberships to verify that no Deny access settings are causing the problem. This step requires examining the ACLs of the objects and the share, if applicable.

It is important to remember that any changes to the access permissions of the individual or groups will not affect those users until the next time they log in. The Access Token used by the security system is rebuilt each time a user logs in.

Master Boot Record

The MBR is the area of a hard drive that contains the data structure that initiates the boot process. If the MBR fails, the ERD cannot be used to repair it. Instead, you'll need to use a DOS 6.0+ bootable floppy and execute "FDISK /MBR". This command will re-create the drive's MBR and restore the system.

Dr. Watson

Windows 2000 includes an application error debugger called **Dr. Watson** that is a diagnostic tool that detects application failures and logs diagnostic details. Data that are captured by Dr. Watson are stored in the Drwtsn32.log file. This feature can also be configured to save a memory dump of the application's address space for further investigation. In reality, the information extracted and stored by Dr. Watson is useful only to a Microsoft technical professional who is well versed in the cryptic logging syntax used.

Windows 2000 automatically launches Dr. Watson when an application error occurs. To configure Dr. Watson, you'll need to launch it from the Start, Run command with "DRWTSN32".

Applying Service Pack Updates

At this point, Microsoft has not released any **service packs** for Windows 2000. But if the company's track record for Windows NT is used as a guide, a service pack will be released soon. A service pack is a collection of code replacements, patches, error corrections, new applications, version improvements, or service-specific configuration settings that correct, replace, or hide the deficiencies of the original product, preceding service packs, or **hot fixes**. A hot fix is similar to a service pack, except that it addresses only a single problem, or a small number of problems, and it may not be fully tested.

Service packs are cumulative, which means that Service Pack 3 (SP3) contains SP2 plus all post-SP2 hot fixes. Thus all you need to install is the latest service pack. You should apply a hot fix only if you are experiencing the problem it was created to resolve; otherwise the hot fix may cause other problems.

A few important points to remember about patches include the following:

- Always back up your system before applying any type of patch, as the backup will give you a way to restore your system if the fix destroys the operating system.
- Be sure to retrieve the correct CPU type and language version.
- Always read the readme and Knowledge Base Q documents for each patch before installing it.
- Update your ERD.
- Make a complete backup of the Registry using the Registry Editor or the REGBACK utility from the Support Tools.
- Export the disk configuration data from Disk Administrator.
- Because service packs rewrite many system-level files, you must disconnect all current users, exit all applications, and temporarily stop all unneeded services before installing any service pack or patch.

To locate Knowledge Base documents, visit or use one of these resources:

- Web site: *http://support.microsoft.com/*
- TechNet CD
- Microsoft Network
- CompuServe: GO MICROSOFT
- Resource Kit Documentation (online help file)

Service packs and hot fixes can be retrieved from the following sources:

- The Web/FTP: *ftp://ftp.microsoft.com/bussys/winnt/winnt-public/fixes/usa/*
- The Web's download section: *http://www.microsoft.com/windows/*

Installing and Uninstalling a Service Pack

To install a service pack:

1. Move the SP file into an empty directory.
2. Close all applications, especially debugging tools.
3. Locate and execute Update.exe with the Start, Run command (see Figure 15-15).

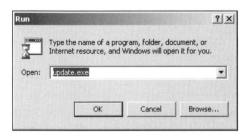

Figure 15-15 Running Update.exe

4. Follow any prompts that appear.
5. When instructed, restart your system.

To uninstall a service pack:

1. You must have selected the "save uninstall information" option during the initial application of the service pack. Whenever it's offered as an option, this choice is usually a good path to take.
2. Extract the original service pack archive into an empty directory.
3. Locate and execute Update.exe.
4. Click the "Uninstall a previously installed service pack" button.
5. Follow the prompts.
6. Restart the computer.

Verifying Service Packs

To determine which service packs have been applied to your system, you can use one of the following techniques:

- Type "WINVER" from a command prompt. This command launches the About Windows information screen, as shown in Figure 15-16.

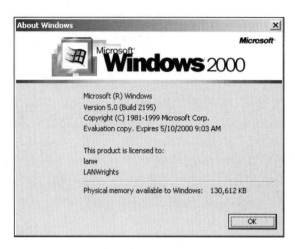

Figure 15-16 The About Windows information screen

- Select Help, About Windows 2000 from the menu bar of any native tool, such as Windows Explorer.

- Use the Registry Editor to view the CSDVersion value in the HKEY_LOCAL_MACHINE\SOFTWARE\Microsoft\WindowsNT\CurrentVersion.

USING MICROSOFT REFERENCES FOR TROUBLESHOOTING

Several Microsoft resources are available to aid you in troubleshooting and working with Windows 2000:

- Microsoft's Web site—*http://www.microsoft.com/windows/*.

- The Knowledge Base—The predecessor to, and a resource for, the TechNet CD is the online Knowledge Base. It can be accessed by several means, which were detailed earlier in this chapter.

- TechNet—The best periodic publication from Microsoft is TechNet. This multi-CD collection is an invaluable resource containing white papers, FAQs, troubleshooting documents, book excerpts, articles, and other written materials, plus utilities, patches, fixes, upgrades, drivers, and demonstration software. At only $300 for an annual subscription, it is well worth the cost. It is also available online in a limited form at *http://technet.microsoft.com/*.

- Resource Kits—Resource Kits are useful information sources that are available in electronic form through TechNet (in their entirety) and through the online services (in portions). Resource Kits document material outside that contained in Microsoft's manuals, and they often include add-on software utilities to enhance product use.

CHAPTER SUMMARY

- This chapter introduced Windows 2000 troubleshooting techniques, tools, and tips. No matter what problems or errors are discovered on your computer system, there are several common-sense principles of troubleshooting that you should always follow. These principles include performing one task at a time, remaining calm, isolating the problem, and performing the simplest fixes first.

- Information is the most valuable tool needed for troubleshooting. It includes the Computer Information File and a detailed history log of troubleshooting activities.

- Five installation problems are commonly encountered: media errors, domain controller communication difficulties, stop message errors or halt on blue screen, hardware problems, and dependency failures.

- Windows includes several utilities you can use for troubleshooting—most importantly, Event Viewer and the Computer Management tool.

- The Registry is a hierarchical structured database of configuration settings for Windows 2000. It is divided into five keys, each having a unique purpose. When alterations to a system are necessary, it is advisable to use the GUI administration tools first, instead of attempting to edit the Registry directly. Windows 2000 includes two Registry Editors; REGEDIT and REGEDT32. The former is useful for global searches, whereas the latter is useful for changing security settings on keys and value entries. As part of your normal system maintenance and administration, you should create copies of the Registry. Backing up the Registry often is the only way to ensure that you have a functional Registry to restore in the event of a failure.

- Most boot failures can be repaired through the use of a start-up/boot floppy repair process.

- Printer problems are most often associated with physical configuration or spooling problems.

- RAS and network problems are caused by several types of errors, the most common of which is misconfiguration.

- Service packs and hot fixes are used to repair portions of Windows 2000 after the release of the operating system.

- Microsoft has provided several avenues to gain access to information about the operation and management of its products, including a substantial collection of troubleshooting documents.

Key Terms

Application log — Records application events, alerts, and system messages.

boot failures — Problems that occur between powering up a computer and the logon prompt display.

Computer Information File (CIF) — A detailed collection of all information related to the hardware and software products that make up your computer (and even your entire network).

Directory Service log — Records events related to the Directory Service.

DNS Service log — Records events related to the DNS Service.

Dr. Watson — The Windows 2000 application error debugger. This diagnostic tool detects application failures and logs diagnostic details.

Event Viewer — The utility used to view the three logs automatically created by Windows 2000.

File Replication Service log — Records events related to the File Replication Service.

HKEY_CLASSES_ROOT — A Registry key that contains the value entries that control the relationships between file extensions (and therefore file format types) and applications. It also supports the data used in object linking and embedding (OLE), COM object data, and file-class association data. This key actually points to another Registry key named HKEY_LOCAL_MACHINE\Software\Classes, and it provides multiple points of access to make itself easily accessible both to the operating system itself and to applications that need access to compatibility information.

HKEY_CURRENT_CONFIG — A Registry key that contains the value entries that control the currently active hardware profile. Its contents are built each time the system is started. This key is derived from data stored in the HKEY_LOCAL_MACHINE\System\CurrentControlSet\HardwareProfiles subkey. It provides backward compatibility with Windows 95/98 applications.

HKEY_CURRENT_USER — A Registry key that contains the value entries that define the user environment for the currently logged-on user. It is built each time a user logs onto the system. The data in this key are derived from the HKEY_USERS key and the Ntuser.dat/.man file of a user's profile.

HKEY_LOCAL_MACHINE — A Registry key that contains the value entries that control the local computer, including its hardware devices, device drivers, and various operating system components. The data stored in this key are not dependent on a logged-on user or the applications or processes currently in use.

HKEY_USERS — A Registry key that contains the value entries that define the user environments for all users who have ever logged into this computer. When a new user logs into the system, a new subkey is added for that user which is either built from the default profile stored in this key or constructed from the roaming user profile associated with the domain user account.

hot fix — Similar to a service pack, except that it addresses only a single problem, or a small number of problems, and may not be fully tested.

key — A top-level division of the Registry. The Windows 2000 Registry contains five keys. Each key can contain subkeys.

Last Known Good Configuration (LKGC) — A configuration recording made by Windows 2000 of all Registry settings that exist at the time when a user successfully logs onto the computer.

master boot record (MBR) — The area of a hard drive that contains the data structure that initiates the boot process.

REG_BINARY — A Registry value entry data type that stores data in binary format.

REG_DWORD — A Registry value entry data type that stores data in binary, hex, or decimal format.

REG_EXPAND_SZ — A Registry value entry data type that stores data in an expandable text-string format that contains a variable that is replaced by an application when it is used (for example, %Systemroot%\file.exe).

REG_MULTI_SZ — A Registry value entry data type that stores data in text-string format that contains multiple human-readable values separated by null characters.

REG_SZ — A Registry value entry data type that stores data in text-string format.

REGEDIT — The 16-bit Registry Editor. REGEDIT offers global searching and combines all of the keys into a single display. It can be used to perform searches, add new subkeys and value entries, alter the data in value entries, and import and export keys and subkeys.

REGEDT32 — The 32-bit Registry Editor. REGEDT32 offers control over key and value entry security but displays each root key in a separate window. It also offers a read-only mode so that you can explore without accidentally altering value entries. REGEDT32 can be used to perform searches, add new subkeys and value entries, alter the data in value entries, and import and export keys and subkeys.

Registry — The hierarchical database of system configuration data that is essential to the health and operation of a Windows 2000 system.

Security log — An Event Viewer log that records security-related events.

service pack — A collection of code replacements, patches, error corrections, new applications, version improvements, or service-specific configuration settings that correct, replace, or hide the deficiencies of the original product, preceding service packs, or hot fixes.

subkey — A sublevel division of a Registry key. A subkey can contain other subkeys and value entries.

System log — An Event Viewer log that records information and alerts about the internal processes of Windows 2000.

value — The actual data stored by a value entry.

value entry — A named Registry variable that stores a specific value or data string. A Registry value entry's name is typically a multiword phrase without spaces that uses title capitalization.

Review Questions

1. When approaching a computer problem, which of the following should you keep in mind? (Choose all that apply.)
   a. How the last problem was solved
   b. What changes were recently made to the system
   c. Information about the configuration state of the system
   d. Your ability to repeat the failure

2. If a media error occurs during installation, which of the following are steps you should take to eliminate the problem? (Choose all that apply.)
   a. Attempt to recopy or reaccess the file that caused the failure.
   b. Switch media sources or types.
   c. Open the Control Panel and reinstall the appropriate drivers.
   d. Restart the installation from the beginning.

3. Which of the following Windows 2000 repair tools can be used to gain information about drivers or services that failed to load?
   a. Event Viewer
   b. Registry
   c. System applet
   d. Dr. Watson

4. The Last Known Good Configuration is useful for which of the following?
   a. Returning the system to the state it was in immediately after the initial installation
   b. Recording a system state for future use
   c. Returning the system to the state it was in at the time of the last successful user logon
   d. Loading a configuration file from floppy disks to use as the current boot parameter file

5. Which Registry Editor should you use if you need to modify the access permissions on a specific key?
   a. REGEDIT
   b. REGEDT32

6. Which of the following are possible troubleshooting techniques for eliminating printer problems? (Choose all that apply.)
   a. Check the physical aspects of the printer—cable, power, paper, toner, and so on.
   b. Check the print queue for stalled jobs.
   c. Attempt to print from a different application or a different client.
   d. Stop and restart the spooler using the Services tool.

7. What is the most common cause of RAS problems?
   a. Telecommunications service failures
   b. Misconfiguration
   c. User error
   d. Communications device failure
8. A user's ability to access a resource is controlled by access permissions. If you suspect a problem with a user's permission settings, what actions can you take? (Choose all that apply.)
   a. Attempt the same actions and activities with the Administrator account.
   b. Delete the user's account and create a new one from scratch.
   c. Double-check group memberships to verify that no Deny access settings are causing the problem.
   d. Grant the user full access to the object directly.
9. Which application automatically loads to handle application failures?
   a. Event Viewer
   b. System applet
   c. Computer Management
   d. Dr. Watson
10. After installing a new SCSI driver, Windows 2000 will not start. No other changes have been made to the system. What is the easiest way to return the system to a state where it will start properly?
    a. Use the repair process with the ERD.
    b. Use the Last Known Good Configuration.
    c. Configure Dr. Watson.
    d. Boot to DOS, and run the setup utility to change the installed drivers.
11. Which of the following are important actions to perform before installing a service pack or a hot fix? (Choose all that apply.)
    a. Make a backup of your system.
    b. Read the readme and Knowledge Base Q documents.
    c. Make a complete backup of the Registry.
12. The Registry is the primary data storage mechanism for Windows 2000. Which of the following are data storage files used by other Microsoft operating systems that may still exist on Windows 2000 for backward compatibility purposes? (Choose all that apply.)
    a. Win.ini
    b. Autoexec.bat
    c. System.ini
    d. Config.sys

13. The Registry is used only to store configuration data for native Windows 2000 applications, services, and drivers. True or False?

14. Which of the following tools are most highly recommended by Microsoft for editing the Registry? (Choose all that apply.)
    a. Control Panel applets
    b. REGEDIT
    c. Reg.exe
    d. Administrative Tools

15. The Registry is an exhaustive collection of system control parameters. True or False?

16. When editing the Registry, and especially when attempting to alter the unseen defaults, which of the following pieces of information are important? (Choose all that apply.)
    a. Syntax
    b. Spelling
    c. Subkey location
    d. Valid values
    e. Time zone

17. Changes made to the Registry never go into effect until the system restarts. True or False?

18. Which of the following can host subkeys or value entries?
    a. Data type
    b. Key
    c. Subkey
    d. Value data

19. Each of the five keys of the Registry is stored in a distinct file on the hard drive. True or False?

20. Which Registry key contains the value entries that control the local computer?
    a. HKEY_LOCAL_MACHINE
    b. HKEY_CLASSES_ROOT
    c. HKEY_CURRENT_CONFIG
    d. HKEY_USERS

21. Which Registry key contains the value entries that define the user environment for the currently logged-on user?
    a. HKEY_LOCAL_MACHINE
    b. HKEY_CLASSES_ROOT
    c. HKEY_CURRENT_CONFIG
    d. HKEY_CURRENT_USER

22. Which Registry key contains the value entries that control the relationships between file extensions (and therefore file format types) and applications?
    a. HKEY_LOCAL_MACHINE
    b. HKEY_CLASSES_ROOT
    c. HKEY_CURRENT_CONFIG
    d. HKEY_USERS

23. Which Registry key contains the value entries that control the currently active hardware profile?
    a. HKEY_LOCAL_MACHINE
    b. HKEY_CLASSES_ROOT
    c. HKEY_CURRENT_CONFIG
    d. HKEY_CURRENT_USER

24. From which key can you delete subkeys using the System applet?
    a. HKEY_LOCAL_MACHINE
    b. HKEY_CLASSES_ROOT
    c. HKEY_CURRENT_CONFIG
    d. HKEY_USERS

25. The files used to load the Registry at startup are stored where on a Windows 2000 system?
    a. %systemroot%\config
    b. %systemroot%\system32\config
    c. %systemroot%\system\config
    d. %systemroot%\system32\repair

HANDS-ON PROJECTS

Project 15-1

To use the Event Viewer:

1. Open the **Event Viewer** from the Start menu (Start, Programs, Administrative Tools, Event Viewer).
2. Select the **System log** from the list of available logs in the left pane (refer back to Figure 15-1).
3. Notice the various types of events that appear in the right pane.
4. Select an event in the right pane.
5. Select the **Properties** command from the **Action** menu.
6. Review the information presented by the event detail (refer back to Figure 15-2).

7. Click the up and down arrows to view other event details.
8. Click **OK** to close the event detail.
9. Close the Event Viewer by clicking the **X** button in the upper-right corner of the title bar.

Project 15-2

To view the Registry through REGEDIT:

1. Open the Run command by selecting **Start**, **Run**.
2. Type **regedit**, then click **OK**. The Registry Editor opens (refer back to Figure 15-4).
3. Double-click **HKEY_LOCAL_MACHINE** (refer back to Figure 15-5).
4. Locate and double-click **SOFTWARE** under HKEY_LOCAL_MACHINE.
5. Locate and double-click **Microsoft** under SOFTWARE.
6. Locate and double-click **Windows NT** under Microsoft.
7. Locate and double-click **CurrentVersion** under Microsoft.
8. Locate and select **Winlogon** under CurrentVersion.
9. In the right pane, locate and select **DefaultUserName** (see Figure 15-17).

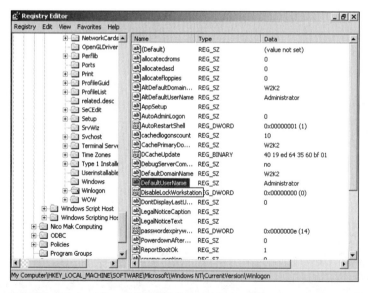

Figure 15-17 The HKEY_LOCAL_MACHINE\SOFTWARE\Microsoft\Windows NT\CurrentVersion\Winlogin key, DefaultUserName value

10. Select **Modify** from the **Edit** menu.
11. Notice that the value of this value entry is the name of the user account you are currently using (see Figure 15-18).

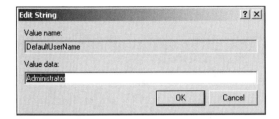

Figure 15-18 The Edit String window

12. Click **Cancel**.
13. In the left pane, scroll up until you see HKEY_LOCAL_MACHINE.
14. Double-click **HKEY_LOCAL_MACHINE**.

Project 15-3

To search for a value entry with REGEDIT:

 This Hands-on Project requires that Hands-on Project 15-2 be completed.

1. Select **Find** from the **Edit** menu.
2. In the **Find what** field, type **DefaultUserName** (see Figure 15-19).

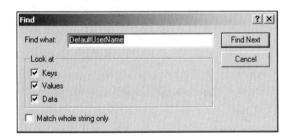

Figure 15-19 The Find window in Registry Editor

3. Click **Find Next**.
4. After a few seconds of searching, REGEDIT will locate the first key, value, or data containing that string. Notice that the first found match is AltDefaultUserName.
5. Select **Find Next** from the **Edit** menu.
6. Notice that item found now is the actual DefaultUserName value entry that you viewed in Hands-on Project 15-2.
7. In the left pane, scroll up and double-click **HKEY_LOCAL_MACHINE**.

Project 15-4

To save a Registry key:

1. Make sure that the **HKEY_USERS** key is selected.
2. Select **Export Registry File** from the **Registry** menu.
3. Select a destination folder of your choice.
4. Provide a filename, such as **HUsave.reg** (see Figure 15-20).

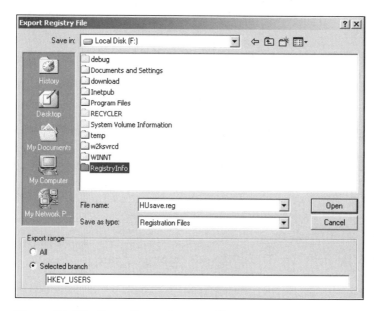

Figure 15-20 Exporting a Registry file

5. Make sure that the **Selected branch** radio button at the bottom of the Export Registry File dialog box is selected and that **HKEY_USERS** is listed in the text field, as shown in Figure 15-20.
6. Click **Save**. REGEDIT will create a backup file of the selected key.

Project 15-5

To restore a Registry key:

Note: This Hands-on Project requires that Hands-on Project 15-4 be completed.

Note: If you have made any change to the system or Registry since you completed Hands-on Project 15-3, you may not want to do this project as it will discard those changes by restoring the state of the Registry from the saved file.

1. Select **Import Registry File** from the **Registry** menu.
2. Locate and select your **HUsave.reg** file.
3. Click **Open**.

4. After a few moments of importing, a message stating whether the import succeeded is displayed. Click **OK**.
5. Select **Exit** from the **Registry** menu.

Project 15-6

To use REGEDT32:

1. Open the Run command by selecting **Start**, **Run**.
2. Type **regedt32**, then click **OK**. The Registry Editor opens.
3. Notice that each key is displayed in a separate window within the Registry editor.
4. Select **HKEY_LOCAL_MACHINE** from the **Window** menu.
5. Select **Find Key** from the **View** menu.
6. Type **DefaultUserName**.
7. Click **Find Next**.
8. Notice that you are back in the same subkey as was viewed in Hands-on Project 15-1.
9. Select **Read Only Mode** from the **Options** menu.

Project 15-7

To view security with REGEDT32:

Note: This Hands-on Project requires that Hands-on Project 15-6 be completed.

1. Select **HKEY_USERS** from the **Window** menu.
2. Select **Permissions** from the **Security** menu.
3. A notice may appear indicating that you can only view permissions for this key. Click **OK**.
4. Notice that the Permissions dialog box for the Registry is identical to that used elsewhere in Windows 2000.
5. Click **Cancel**.
6. Select **Exit** from the **Registry** menu.

CASE PROJECTS

1. After you installed a new drive controller and a video card, along with their associated drivers, Windows 2000 refuses to start and the LKGC does not result in an operational system.

   Required Result:

   Return the system to a bootable and operational state.

Optional Desired Results:

Retain the security ID.

Retain most, if not all, of the system's configuration.

Proposed Solution:

Perform a complete reinstallation of Windows 2000.

a. The proposed solution produces the desired result and both of the optional desired results.

b. The proposed solution produces the desired result, but only one of the optional desired results.

c. The proposed solution produces the desired result, but neither of the optional desired results.

d. The proposed solution does not produce the desired result.

2. After you install a new drive controller and a video card, along with their associated drivers, Windows 2000 refuses to start and the LKGC does not result in an operational system.

Required Result:

Return the system to a bootable and operational state.

Optional Desired Results:

Retain the security ID.

Retain most, if not all, of the system's configuration.

Proposed Solution:

Perform an upgrade reinstallation of Windows 2000.

a. The proposed solution produces the desired result and both of the optional desired results.

b. The proposed solution produces the desired result, but only one of the optional desired results.

c. The proposed solution produces the desired result, but neither of the optional desired results.

d. The proposed solution does not produce the desired result.

3. You need to perform several Registry modifications to fine-tune an application. You'll be following detailed instructions from the vendor. What steps can you take to ensure that even if the vendor's instructions fail, you'll still be able to return to a functioning Windows 2000 system?

4. Describe the common problems associated with installing Windows 2000 and the steps you can take to either avoid these problems or resolve them once encountered.

Appendix

Windows Scripting Host

Talk to any UNIX administrator for long enough, and he or she will mention that the Windows operating system lacks a good method of scripting programs. Until recently, this statement was true, but then Microsoft released Windows Scripting Host (WSH).

Before WSH became available, scripted programs were extremely difficult to work with. You could easily create a script via a batch file that displayed information on the screen or executed some internal programs. But if you tried to create one that uses variables and then pass those variables to and from the system, you would notice that the batch file is lacking in some functionality. Although third-party tools are available to improve the ability to create logon scripts, they still lack some network connectivity, such as choosing the server to log into or the domain controller to use for authentication purposes.

The Microsoft WSH engine is a language-independent scripting tool. It runs on all 32-bit Windows platforms and is built into Windows 2000. Best of all, it's free. WSH relies on scripting engines, which provide its power and flexibility. When WSH ships from Microsoft, it includes two scripting engines: Visual Basic Scripting Edition and JavaScript. Microsoft has designed this tool so that third-party developers can also develop their own scripting engines for it, such as Perl, REXX, and Python.

This appendix describes some of the capabilities of WSH. Unfortunately, the actual scripting languages are beyond the scope of this book; therefore, these languages will not be covered in detail.

WSH comes in two flavors: a text-based, DOS-like version (Cscript.exe) and a Windows-based version (Wscript.exe). These versions are covered in the next sections.

COMMAND-BASED SCRIPTING

The command line-based version of WSH, called Cscript.exe, is located in the %systemroot%\system32 directory. The application is executed using the following syntax:

```
CScript scriptname.extension [option...] [arguments...]
```

The Cscript switches are as follows:

- **Scriptname.extension** This switch consists of the name of the script file and its extension—for example, script.js (for JavaScript) or script.vbs (for Visual Basic). This script is a text file that can be edited with any basic text editor. Other extensions exist for third-party scripting languages that might be installed in the system.

- **Option** Options allow you to customize how your script will be executed. You can enable or disable any of the options, as noted in Table A-1. Be aware that any option must be preceded by two forward slashes (//). You may sometimes find these options referred to as *host parameters*.

- **Arguments** Some options have the ability to receive information from the operating system and send it through to the script. These are called arguments.

For example, to execute a JavaScript script that shuts down a server (it is named shutdown.js), with it being given a maximum of 30 seconds to execute with no input from any users, you would issue the following command:

```
Script shutdown.js //B //T:30
```

The "//B" option sets the script into batch mode and suppresses all errors and messages. The "//T:30" option passes an argument of 30 seconds to the //T option (which will time the script out after 30 seconds).

Table A-1 Options for Cscript.exe

Option	Description
//B	Sets the WSH into batch mode. All script errors and prompts are suppressed and do not display.
//D	Enables Active Debugging mode.
//E:engine	Allows you to set the engine to be used for executing the script.
//H:Cscript	Changes the default script host to Cscript.exe.
//H:Wscript	Changes the default script host to Wscript.exe (the default).
//I	Puts WSH into Interactive mode (the default and the opposite of //B). All script errors and messages are displayed.
//Job:xxxx	Executes a WSH job.
//Logo	Displays the logo (the default). A banner will be shown at the execution time of the script.
//Nologo	Prevents the logo from displaying. No banner will be shown at the execution time of the script.

Table A-1 Options for Cscript.exe (continued)

Option	Description
//S	Saves the current command-line options for this user.
//T:nn	Time out in seconds. Sets a maximum amount of time that a script is permitted to run before WSH terminates it.
//U	Redirects the output from the script.
//X	Executes the script in the debugging mode.

WINDOWS-BASED SCRIPTING

Windows-based scripting is slightly more intuitive. The command line is pretty much the same:

```
Wscript scriptname.extension [option...] [arguments...]
```

Table A-2 lists all of the available options. Notice that, except for lacking the //X option, all of the options exist in both types of WSH scripts.

Table A-2 Options for Wscript.exe

Option	Description
//B	Sets the WSH into batch mode. All script errors and prompts are suppressed and do not display.
//D	Enables Active Debugging mode.
//E:engine	Allows you to set the engine to be used for executing the script.
//H:Cscript	Changes the default script host to Cscript.exe.
//H:Wscript	Changes the default script host to Wscript.exe (the default).
//I	Puts WSH into Interactive mode (the default and the opposite of //B). All script errors and messages are displayed.
//Job:xxxx	Executes a WSH job.
//Logo	Displays the logo (the default). A banner will be shown at the execution time of the script.
//Nologo	Prevents the logo from displaying. No banner will be shown at the execution time of the script.
//S	Saves the current command-line options for this user.
//T:nn	Time out in seconds. Sets a maximum amount of time that a script is permitted to run before WSH terminates it.
//U	Redirects the output from the script.

Manually Registering Script Engines

Sometimes, you may find that you need to manually configure a new scripting engine or reconfigure an existing one. This section deals with how your would register such an engine, assuming that:

- The scripting engine is called **NewScriptEngine**.
- The file extension used for the script engine is **.nsf**.
- The scripting identifier is **NewScriptFile**.

Table A-3 lists all of the Registry entries that must be added to register the new script.

Table A-3 Manually registering a new script engine

Registry Key	Key Type	Key Value
.nsf	REG_SZ	NewScriptFile
NewScriptFile	REG_SZ	NewScriptEngine Script File
NewScriptFile\ScriptEngine	REG_SZ	NewScriptEngine
NewScriptFile\Shell Open\	REG_SZ	&Open
NewScriptFile\Shell Open\Command	REG_EXPAND_SZ	%systemroot%\system32\wscript "%1" %*
NewScriptFile\Shell Open2	REG_EXPAND_SZ	Open &with command console
NewScriptFile\Shell Open2\Command	REG_SZ	%systemroot%\system32\wscript "%1" %*
NewScriptFile\ShellEx\PropertySheetHandlers\WSHProps	REG_SZ	{60254CA5-953B-11CF-8C96-00AA00B8708C}

Sample Script

The following is a simple script using Visual Basic Script to display a message and then count to 10.

```
Dim Counter
Wscript.Echo "Welcome to my first Windows Scripting Host program"
Wscript.Echo "Here is a script that will count from 1 to 10"
For Counter = 1 to 10
Wscript.Echo Counter
Next
```

GLOSSARY

access control list (ACL) — A list associated with an object that defines the rights that groups and individuals have to the object. The ACL is used by the Security Reference Monitor to protect objects from unauthorized access.

access token — An identifier given to an object upon its creation. Based on the identity of the person who created it (or who created the object that created it), an object has certain rights, which are listed in its access token. The Security Reference Monitor compares the data in the access token with that required by the ACL to determine what kind of access the object may have to a particular object.

Active Directory — A hierarchical directory database used in Windows 2000 to store all object information, including information about users, groups, and computers.

Active Directory domain — A logical domain of Windows 2000 computers that share the same security and user information.

Active Directory-integrated zone — A zone that allows for Active Directory security to control replication of the database information.

active/active cluster — A type of cluster found in Windows 2000 Advanced Server and Windows 2000 Datacenter in which both nodes in the cluster are serving client requests all the time. If one node fails, the cluster service moves its resources to the other node and the second node manages both workloads. The two nodes do not have to be identical.

active/standby cluster — A type of cluster in which one node is serving client requests and the other is dormant, or doing work that may be discarded. When the active node fails, the cluster service moves its resources to the standby node, and the standby node drops whatever it had been doing and takes over the active server's workload. The two nodes do not have to be physically identical.

Add/Remove Hardware Wizard — A Control Panel applet introduced in Windows 2000 that was badly missed in Windows NT. This applet allows the operating system to detect and install new hardware devices.

Address (A) resource record — An address resolution from a regular name to a TCP/IP address.

address translation — The act of converting virtual addresses to physical addresses. This conversion is necessary because the operating system deals entirely in virtual addresses, leaving physical memory addresses to hardware. The two types of addresses don't necessarily bear any relation to each other.

Advanced Configuration and Power Interface (ACPI) specification — Defines Advanced Power Management features and is an integral part of the OnNow system built into Windows 2000. For more information, see the Microsoft Web site: *http://www.microsoft.com/hwdev/onnow/*.

Advanced Options menu — An alternative boot menu (accessible by pressing F8 when the boot menu is displayed) from which you can access the various specialized start modes available for troubleshooting purposes.

Advanced Power Management (APM) — The legacy specification that implements power management in machine-specific BIOS code.

affinity — The term used when a process is set up to prefer using one processor over another.

AppleTalk Remote Access Protocol (ARAP) — A protocol that allows Apple Macintosh computers to connect to a remote access server.

Application layer — The layer of the OSI model that allows access to networking services.

application license — A license that allows you to run a particular application.

Application log — Records application events, alerts, and system messages.

application programming interface (API) — The entire set of DLLs that an environmental subsystem supports to request kernel-mode services.

application service provider (ASP) — A service running applications from a terminal server and making them available to anonymous users via the Internet for a fee.

archive attribute — A simple attribute that identifies a file as having changed since the last full backup.

archive bit — An attribute that allows the backup program to determine which files have been modified. Any file that has the archive bit set has been modified.

assigned software — Software that is installed automatically when a user reboots his or her computer. The feature is often used for software patches and service packs.

attribute — A characteristic associated with a file object (file or folder). Different file systems have different attributes.

authentication — The process that a computer undertakes to determine that you are who you say you are.

authoritative restore — A method of restoring the Active Directory information to make sure that it is the most recent copy of the information and the one that should be propagated throughout the domain.

Automatic Caching for Documents — The caching option that automatically caches only those files that are accessed by the user. This setting does not cache the entire contents of the directory, nor does it require user intervention.

Automatic Caching for Programs — The caching option that automatically copies the entire contents of the folder to the user's local cache.

background application — An application that is running but not currently receiving user input.

backup domain controller (BDC) — A Windows NT Server that maintains a read-only version of the directory database to authenticate users.

balance set manager — The part of Win2K responsible for trimming process working sets to free physical memory as well as for identifying low-priority threads that aren't receiving CPU cycles.

base priority — The priority with which a thread starts after its creation. The base priority of a thread is always equal to that of the process that created it.

basic disk — A disk that has been partitioned and formatted using Windows NT 4.0. Basic disks can support primary and extended partitions as well as logical disks.

basic storage — A hard disk designed to support primary and extended partitions and logical drives. Any operating system can recognize disks set up to use basic storage.

batch jobs — Sequences that are submitted for execution on a computer as a single task.

batch system — A runtime environment in which one program or application follows another in sequence.

bit mask — The result of an XOR function. The bit mask contains a 1 for every mismatch between numbers and a 0 for every match.

boot failures — Problems that occur between powering up a computer and the logon prompt display.

boot logging — An advanced option that boots the computer normally but lists all files loaded during the boot process, and saving the list in a file called Ntbtlog.txt. Boot logging is enabled by default when you boot to any form of Safe Mode.

boot partition — On a Windows 2000 system, the partition that contains the main operating system directory and the pagefile. The boot partition can be the same as the system partition, but most often is located elsewhere, either on the same drive or on a different physical drive.

boot sector — An area at the beginning of each partition that names the files to be loaded to run the operating system stored on that partition.

boot virus — Malicious software that targets the master boot record of a disk to make the disk unbootable. Until the advent of macro viruses, boot viruses were the most common virus type.

Boot.ini — A file that defines the host partitions and the primary executables of the operating systems present on the computer. Boot.ini also defines the default operating system that loads when the customizable boot menu display timer expires.

Bootsect.dos — On a multiboot system with another Microsoft, clone, or near-equivalent operating system such as DOS or Windows 95/98, a file that is used to establish a start-up environment more conducive to these older Microsoft operating systems.

bootstrapping — The initialization process that a computer goes through to inspect its hardware and locate the boot files for an operating system on the active partition of a hard drive.

bootstrapping files — Computer files required to initiate loading and launching an operating system. Also called boot files.

breaking the mirror set — Reverting both halves of a mirror set to independent simple volumes.

broadcast — The signal sent across the network by a resource to notify users of its availability.

bus class driver — One of the native Windows 2000 driver layers, which provides all basic driver functionality for bus devices.

bus minidriver — A small device driver that implements manufacturer-specific features not included in the bus class driver. It works in conjunction with the bus class driver.

Canonical Name — An alias that can be assigned to a TCP/IP host.

CardBus — A high-speed bus specification based on the PCMCIA technology found on laptop computers. This hardware interface supports PC Card peripheral technologies.

central processing unit (CPU) — The "brains" of the computer. The components that complete most of the calculations on a system.

certificate — A portable method of authentication that demonstrates the identity of a user or service. Certificates are files that may be imported or exported, so you can move or copy them if necessary.

certificate authority — A server entrusted with the task of creating certificates for users and services.

change journal — A list of all changes made to files in the volume. Some Windows 2000 functions, such as the remote storage service, can refer to the change journal to know when to do their jobs. The change journal is a more efficient way of looking for changes than browsing the volume looking for the desired difference.

ciphertext — Encrypted data.

Circular Logging — A process by which older log files are overwritten as the current log file fills to capacity. When this option is enabled, data recovery is greatly minimized.

client — The computer or user that requests information from a server.

client access license — A type of license that permits the holder to access a server from the network.

cluster — A logical grouping of sectors, with the number of sectors per cluster depending on the size of the partition and the file system being used. A cluster is the smallest storage unit that Windows 2000 file systems can recognize.

cluster resource — An object that can be moved between servers in a server cluster.

cluster service — A Windows 2000 service running on all nodes of a cluster, facilitating communication and failover between nodes.

clustering — A technique that involves logically combining two or more servers for redundancy.

clustering — The ability of multiple servers to function as a single, logical server. A clustering facility allows tasks and threads to be distributed among the servers in a cluster in much the same way that an operating system that supports multiple CPUs distributes threads and tasks on a single multiprocessor machine.

command language — A collection of terms that allow a user to tell the operating system what to do.

committed memory — Memory allocated to a process that is backed with the necessary amount of space in the paging file. Processes must commit memory before they can store data in it.

Computer Information File (CIF) — A detailed collection of all information related to the hardware and software products that make up your computer (and even your entire network).

console license — A type of license that comes with an operating system and represents permission to install the operating system on a single machine and use it from that machine.

context — The information describing the operating environment for all threads in a particular process.

context switch — The action that takes place when a processor switches from kernel mode to user mode.

context switching — The act of setting aside one thread's context for that of another thread, when the second thread starts using the CPU.

context switching — The process of saving the state of the running task, loading the state of the pending task, and then starting execution of that pending task.

control object — A kernel object that controls various operating system functions, such as running the kernel process.

control set — A hardware-profile-specific collection of boot process parameters.

cooperative multitasking — A type of multitasking in which all applications in turn get some CPU time and are supposed to relinquish the processor when their time is up.

copy backup — A backup method that copies the data to the backup media without changing the archive bit of the files.

copy backup — A type of backup that works like a normal backup in that it copies all selected files to the backup media, regardless of whether the archive bit is set. A copy backup does not reset the archive bit.

copy-on-write data sharing — A form of shared memory protection. Copy-on-write allows multiple processes to read the same bit of data stored in physical memory. If one of the processes attempts to change the data, however, the Virtual Memory Manager copies the edited data to a new location and the process uses the copy. This approach keeps the editing process from corrupting the data that other processes are using.

core system files — Those files that make up the core components of an operating system. If these files become corrupted or damaged, the operating system cannot function.

cycles — Discrete chunks of time that the CPU can dedicate to any given application's needs.

cyclic redundancy check (CRC) — A mathematical recipe that generates a specific value, called a checksum, based on the contents of a data frame. The CRC is calculated before a data frame is transmitted and then is included with the frame; on receipt, the CRC is recalculated and compared with the sent value. If the two agree, the data frame is assumed to have been delivered intact; if they disagree, the data frame must be retransmitted.

cylinder — All of the parallel tracks on all surfaces. For example, Track 10 on all surfaces creates Cylinder 10 for the disk.

daily backup — A type of backup that copies only those files that have changed on the day of the backup.

Data Link layer — The layer of the OSI model that uses the hardware address of the system to communicate.

data stream — Chunks of data that may be associated with more than one file. Data streaming allows you to deal with several distinct pieces of data as one unit.

Dcpromo.exe — The Active Directory Installation Wizard, which is found in the windir\system32 directory. This wizard allows you to install your server as a domain controller or to remove it as one.

debugging mode — A mode that starts Windows 2000 normally while sending debugging information through a serial cable to another computer. It is useful when you want to examine the boot process carefully.

default gateway — A device (a multihomed computer or a router) that can communicate between two different networks.

delegation of administration — A Windows 2000 feature that allows you to implement users having different permissions. For example, you can create an organizational unit and assign an administrator who will have the right to modify the objects within that organizational unit, but not in organizational units that exist above it.

deleting the mirror set — Removing the mirror set volume and thus discarding all of its data.

device class driver — A layer of built-in device support that implements basic support for a class of hardware, such as modems. A device class driver supports all generic or standard features of a particular type of peripheral, thereby easing the development burden for hardware manufacturers.

device class driver — A piece of software that supplies basic driver interfaces and functions that define broad parameters for specific types of devices.

device driver — A kernel-mode module that acts as a go-between for the I/O subsystem and the hardware abstraction layer.

device driver interfaces (DDIs) — Interfaces that define how device drivers interact with the operating system components, such as OnNow.

Device Manager — An internal Windows 2000 device management routine that handles enumeration, Plug and Play configuration, and device support.

device minidriver — A small device driver that implements manufacturer-specific features not included in the device class driver. It works in conjunction with the device class driver.

DFS link — A pointer to an additional share included in the DFS configuration.

DFS root — The local server share that acts as the starting point for users to access resources on the DFS share.

DHCP lease — An IP address, subnet mask, and optional parameters that are given to a DHCP client for a configured amount of time.

DHCP scope — A logical grouping of TCP/IP addresses that can be assigned to DHCP clients by the server.

differential backup — A backup method that backs up all data added or modified since the last full backup. This method resets the archive bit.

differential backup — A type of backup that copies to the backup media every selected file that has the archive bit set, but does not reset the archive bit.

Directory Service log — Records events related to the Directory Service.

Directory Services Restore Mode — An advanced boot option that allows you to verify that the Active Directory has been restored from backups successfully.

disk duplexing — A mirror set that incorporates two disks attached to different disk controllers, so they are not affected by controller failure.

disk duplication — A feature that allows for the duplication of system hard drives for use with third-party disk imaging software.

disk mirroring — A RAID type that combines space on two physical disks to create a mirror image; that is, when data are written to one disk, the same information is written to the other disk.

disk quotas — A feature available with Windows 2000 Server's new NTFS file system (Version 5). As an administrator, you can now assign users quotas on folders, volumes, or disks. This feature ensures that a single user does not monopolize the hard disk space that exists on your server.

disk quotas — A method of preventing users from using more than a predetermined amount of space in a volume. When a user exceeds his or her quota, he or she will be denied write access to the volume until some files have been deleted to go below the quota.

Glossary

disk striping with parity — See *RAID 5 volume*.

dispatcher — A set of routines in the Win2K kernel that governs thread scheduling.

DNS Service log — Records events related to the DNS Service.

domain — A group of computers that shares a centralized security database.

domain controller — A Windows 2000 Server that authenticates users in a Windows 2000 network.

domain controller — The computer that stores the domain's security database. A domain can have more than one domain controller to ease the burden of authenticating users.

Domain Name Service (DNS) — A dynamic method for resolving TCP/IP addresses to Internet names, and vice versa.

Dr. Watson — Windows 2000's application error debugger. This diagnostic tool detects application failures and logs diagnostic details.

driver stack — The entire device driver layer in Windows 2000, including the HAL, bus class and minidrivers, and device class and minidrivers.

duplexed volume — A volume that uses two disks on two separate controllers. The data are written to both disks at the same time.

dynamic disk — A new type of disk introduced with Windows 2000. It allows for an unlimited number of volumes to be created on a single disk.

Dynamic Host Configuration Protocol (DHCP) — A protocol that allows for the automatic configuration of TCP/IP properties for clients.

dynamic link library (DLL) — A specific set of function calls that allows executable routines to be stored as files and to be loaded only when needed by a program that calls them.

dynamic routing — The process used by routers to dynamically learn about the routes that they can take to connect to remote networks.

dynamic storage — A new type of storage in Windows 2000 that designs disks to support multidisk volumes. Volumes on dynamic disks may be added, resized, and deleted without rebooting.

Emergency Repair Disk (ERD) — A floppy disk that you can create with Windows 2000 Backup and that you can use to restore a previously saved set of configuration information (stored in %*systemroot*%\repair\regback). The ERD does not contain any configuration settings itself, just the files needed to restore the information saved on the hard disk.

emulation — A mechanism by which an environmental subsystem supports applications for which it doesn't have an API.

Encrypted File System (EFS) — A system for encrypting files on a Windows 2000 system to protect them from unauthorized access. Intended mainly for people with laptops and for removable storage that's vulnerable to theft.

encryption — A blanket term for any method of systematically obscuring the meaning of data by applying an encryption key to it.

End User License Agreement (EULA) — Paper or software text accompanying software that defines the conditions under which the licensee may use the software.

enumeration — The process by which Plug and Play adapters are recognized by the operating system and a device tree is built.

environmental subsystem — The part of an operating system that provides an interface to the functions that an application needs to support user requests. Win2K supports three environmental subsystems: Win32, POSIX 1.0a, and OS/2 1.0.

Event Viewer — The utility used to view the three logs automatically created by Windows 2000.

exclusive OR (XOR) arithmetic — The function that RAID 5 volumes use to calculate the parity information for their data. When calculating the XOR for two binary numbers, you compare them side by side. The result will have a 0 in every place where the numbers match and a 1 in every place where they do not.

executable image — The name of an application or a logical construct for the processes and threads that actually execute the application.

executive services — The collection of all intermediary and management components for all resources, security, and communications in the Windows 2000 environment. User-mode processes do not actually interact with executive services; rather, they interact with APIs defined for their application subsystems. The virtual machine in which the calling application runs then redirects such API calls to the kernel, where they are routed to the appropriate executive service.

extended partition — A disk partition on a basic disk that's designed to hold logical drives. Extended partitions can't hold any data on their own—they're just areas of free space in which you can create logical drives. A hard disk may hold one extended partition, but you can make as many logical drives within that partition as you like.

FAT (file allocation table) — A catalog at the beginning of a volume that notes each file and folder in the volume and lists the clusters in which each file is stored.

FAT16 — A file system first used with DOS and supported in Windows 2000 for compatibility reasons—only Windows 2000 can read NTFS volumes, so if you need to support dual-boot machines or write data to floppy disks, you need FAT. FAT16 uses a 16-bit addressing scheme for clusters and can support only fairly small volumes without wasting space from overlarge clusters, but it has little overhead.

FAT32 — A version of FAT that uses a 32-bit addressing scheme, so that it can address more clusters than FAT16.

fault tolerance — An aspect of an operating system that ensures high availability of both user and system data and of the computing resources.

fault-tolerant cluster — A cluster type in which two physically identical nodes operate in tandem, performing the same functions. If one node fails, the other takes over for it almost instantly because no resource transfer is needed.

fault-tolerant volume — Any volume designed to reduce the risk of data loss due to disk failure. Fault-tolerant volumes either keep a copy of data or maintain information from which that data may be regenerated.

File Replication Service log — Records events related to the File Replication Service.

file system — A method of logically organizing the physical disk space in a partition for use by the operating system. Different file systems catalog data differently and support different file attributes.

file system cache — A range of virtual memory addresses reserved for storing recently used data related to storage I/O.

file system driver — A device driver that translates file-oriented I/O requests for the hardware abstraction layer to pass to storage media.

filter driver — A device driver that intercepts file I/O requests and processes the request to make it intelligible to the receiving device.

First In, First Out (FIFO) — An algorithm that marks the oldest data in RAM to be sent to the paging file. The balance set manager uses this algorithm on Alpha and multiprocessor x86 computers.

foreground application — The application currently receiving user input.

forest — A collection of two or more trees with noncontiguous namespace.

forward lookup zone — The zone in charge of Internet name to TCP/IP address resolution.

frame — The basic package of bits that represents a protocol data unit (PDU) sent from one computer to another across a network. In addition to its contents, a frame includes the sender's and receiver's network addresses as well as control information at the head and a CRC at the tail.

free space — An area of an extended partition not yet made into a logical drive.

full backup — A backup method that completely backs up the data to the backup media and resets the archive bit.

Full Zone Transfer (AXFR) — A complete transfer of all zone information from the primary site to the secondary sites.

function call — A predefined request for a kernel-mode action that the environmental subsystem can call at the request of an application.

Gateway Services for NetWare (GSNW) — A service that allows multiple Windows clients to access file and print resources on one or more Novell NetWare servers without the need to reconfigure all clients to log into the NetWare network.

Grandfather/Father/Son (GFS) — A backup scheme that uses a monthly normal backup, a weekly normal backup, and a daily incremental or differential backup to create a three-month record of server data.

group — A collection of like cluster resources that the cluster service can manage as a group.

group policies — A service that allows an administrator to control the amount of access that users have to applications and systems based on the users' permissions.

group policies — Policies that control the security settings for computers and users in the domain.

groupware — Multiuser applications that come with a group license and are used by several people simultaneously, such as e-mail servers.

handle — A connection to an object that allows one object to manipulate another.

hardware abstraction layer (HAL) — The only module of Windows 2000 that is hardware-specific. The HAL is built to match the type and state of the hardware during installation.

hardware address — See *Media Access Control (MAC) address*.

hardware device driver — A module that writes data to or retrieves data from a physical device or network, manipulating the hardware via the hardware abstraction layer.

hardware devices — Physical hardware, features, and interfaces installed in a PC.

head — The read-write mechanism in a disk. Each surface has its own head.

helper — Parts of the operating system that allow applications to communicate with hardware. Originally, these parts were lumped together in a single unit and communicated with each other in a separate area of memory, away from applications.

hidden attribute — A simple attribute that hides a file. If the hidden attribute is set, the file will not show up in a DIR listing of the folder's contents, or in Windows Explorer unless hidden files are visible.

hive — A section of the Registry that is stored in a separate file. Hives are permanent structures that are saved each time the system is shut down, and reloaded each time the system is powered up.

HKEY_CLASSES_ROOT — A Registry key that contains the value entries that control the relationships between file extensions (and therefore file format types) and applications. It also supports the data used in object linking and embedding (OLE), COM object data, and file-class association data. This key actually points to another Registry key named HKEY_LOCAL_MACHINE\Software\Classes, and it provides multiple points of access to make itself easily accessible both to the operating system itself and to applications that need access to compatibility information.

HKEY_CURRENT_CONFIG — A Registry key that contains the value entries that control the currently active hardware profile. Its contents are built each time the system is started. This key is derived from data stored in the HKEY_LOCAL_MACHINE\System\CurrentControlSet\HardwareProfiles subkey. It provides backward compatibility with Windows 95/98 applications.

HKEY_CURRENT_USER — A Registry key that contains the value entries that define the user environment for the currently logged-on user. It is built each time a user logs onto the system. The data in this key are derived from the HKEY_USERS key and the Ntuser.dat/.man file of a user's profile.

HKEY_LOCAL_MACHINE — A Registry key that contains the value entries that control the local computer, including its hardware devices, device drivers, and various operating system components. The data stored in this key are not dependent on a logged-on user or the applications or processes currently in use.

HKEY_USERS — A Registry key that contains the value entries that define the user environments for all users who have ever logged into this computer. When a new user logs into the system, a new subkey is added for that user which is either built from the default profile stored in this key or constructed from the roaming user profile associated with the domain user account.

hot fix — Similar to a service pack, except that it addresses only a single problem, or a small number of problems, and may not be fully tested.

human interface device class — One of the Windows 2000 driver classes devoted to handling input devices such as mice, keyboards, and game controllers.

idle thread — A low-priority thread that runs whenever no other threads are running on the CPU. The idle thread watches for events that will require CPU time, but doesn't actually do anything with the CPU itself.

IEEE 1394 Serial Bus (FireWire) — A high-speed serial bus that supports 63 devices per bus, allows interconnection of 1023 buses, and features automatic device recognition.

in-place upgrade — An upgrade to Windows 2000 in which all current domain configurations are maintained.

incremental backup — A type of backup that copies to the backup media every selected file that has the archive bit set and then resets the archive bit to show that the file has been backed up.

incremental backup — A type of backup that will back up all data added or modified since the last backup without resetting the archive bit.

Incremental Zone Transfer (IXFR) — A partial transfer of modified zone information between the primary and secondary sites.

index — A list of all files in a folder in an NTFS volume.

individual device driver — A device- and model-specific program that defines the exact capabilities and functions of a particular device down to the make and model level, and allows the operating system to access the device's functions.

interactive logon — The act of typing your name and password into the login screen of a Windows 2000 computer.

Internet client license (ICL) — A type of license that permits an anonymous user to log onto a terminal server via the Internet. ICLs are restricted for anonymous use; people with domain accounts can't use them.

Internet Information Services (IIS) — Microsoft's Web Services software that is included with Windows 2000 and is used to make information available on the World Wide Web.

Internet Printing Protocol (IPP) — A new protocol that allows clients to connect to a printer that is connected to a Windows 2000 network using a URL, to download and install drivers over the Internet, and to view the printer status in a Web browser, such as Internet Explorer.

Internet Protocol Security (IPSec) — A new, secure, industry standard implementation of the popular TCP/IP protocol.

Internet Services Manager (ISM) — The application used to manage and maintain IIS applications.

Internetwork Packet Exchange/Sequenced Packet Exchange (IPX/SPX) — A protocol developed by Novell for its NetWare operating system. It may be used in routed environments.

interrupt request (IRQ) — A special, high-priority communications channel through which a hardware device informs the CPU that it needs to perform some action or respond to some condition.

job — A collection of processes with certain common characteristics, such as the working set and the amount of CPU time that the threads in the process get.

Kerberos — The native Windows 2000 authentication protocol. Kerberos relies on a system of shared secrets for mutual authentication of client and server.

Kerberos security — An industry standard form of security authentication that is used by Windows 2000.

kernel mode — A processing mode that gives complete access to all writable addresses in the system process area. Kernel objects run in kernel mode. Because this mode allows access to the operating system, only code that must interact with the operating system directly runs in kernel mode.

kernel object — An object that exists only in kernel mode and with which the kernel manipulates executive-level objects such as processes and threads. Kernel objects contain no security information or other attributes, so they don't incur the same kind of policy-based overhead that executive objects do.

key — A top-level division of the Registry. The Windows 2000 Registry contains five keys. Each key can contain subkeys.

key — An algorithm used to encrypt or decrypt data. Sometimes, the same key may do both; at other times, the encryption key may be different from the decryption key.

Key Distribution Center (KDC) — A secure server in a Windows 2000 domain that's responsible for generating the cryptographic keys and tickets that are the basis of Kerberos security.

Last Known Good Configuration — The configuration settings that were in place the last time you successfully booted Windows 2000. You can choose to load these settings if you boot from the Advanced Options menu and choose Last Known Good from the menu.

Last Known Good Configuration (LKGC) — A configuration recording made by Windows 2000 of all Registry settings that exist at the time when a user successfully logs onto the computer.

launch — The process of executing an application.

Layer Two Tunneling Protocol (L2TP) — A protocol that relies on other encryption methods (such as IPSec) for communication. It creates the secure connection, but other methods of encryption must be used.

Least Recently Used (LRU) — An algorithm that marks the least recently used data in RAM to be sent to the paging file. The balance set manager uses this algorithm on single-processor x86 computers.

legacy virtualization drivers layer — A layer in the driver stack that supports legacy VxD-style device drivers.

load balancing — Distributing client requests among grouped (but not necessarily clustered) servers so that the least busy server always services the next client request.

local area network (LAN) — A group of computers that are connected to form a network within a small area, such as a floor or a building.

local print device — A printing device directly connected to the computer.

local procedure call (LPC) facility — The Win2K messaging mechanism that allows client and server processes to communicate.

Local Security Authority (LSA) — The component that checks whether a user logging on has an account on a local or a trusted domain. When you are logging onto another domain, the LSA must communicate with that domain's domain controller to see whether the domain controller has an account for you in its security database.

local user profile — A user profile stored on the local computer; the default setting for all user profiles. Local user profiles exist on a per-computer basis, so a user may have different environment settings depending on which computer he or she logs onto. Changes to the profile are saved to the local computer when the user logs off.

logical drive — A formattable division of an extended partition, created from an area of free space. An extended partition may hold as many logical drives as you like.

Mail Exchanger — A DNS record used to resolve which server in the domain takes charge of e-mail.

mandatory user profile — A roaming user profile that is not user-definable. If the user changes the environment settings, those changes are not saved at logoff. A mandatory user profile has a .man extension.

Manual Caching for Documents — The caching setting that requires users to manually transfer files to be used offline from the server to their local computer; this is the default setting for shares.

master boot record (MBR) — A file stored in the first sector of a hard disk. It contains the partition table and links to the boot sectors for all partitions.

master boot record (MBR) — The area of a hard drive that contains the data structure that initiates the boot process.

master boot record (MBR) — The section on a hard drive where the partition table and other key descriptive information are stored.

master file table (MFT) — A file in each NTFS volume that contains a 2 KB entry for each file and folder in the volume. If the file plus all attributes (including the data attribute) is smaller than 2 KB, then it may be stored in the MFT itself; otherwise, the file's entry in the MFT contains a pointer to the rest of the file's attributes that wouldn't fit.

master zone — See *standard primary zone*.

Media Access Control (MAC) address — A unique number that is assigned to each network device. It ensures that no two devices exist with the same addressing information.

metropolitan area network (MAN) — A network of computers that exist within the same metropolitan area, such as a city.

mirror set — A fault-tolerant volume that exists in two identical, linked volumes on two dynamic disks. When you write data to a mirror set, the information is written to both volumes so that if one disk fails, the data will be recoverable from the other volume.

mirror set — The name for the combined disk space that is turned into a disk mirror.

mirrored volume — A volume on a dynamic disk that uses two disks and writes the same data to both of them.

mixed mode — A mode in which Windows 2000 runs so as to maintain backward compatibility with Windows NT domains.

modular architecture — A method of programming where multiple separate components are combined into a single logical whole. Each component handles a specific task or a small set of related tasks. Windows 2000 uses such architecture in its kernel mode, particularly for the components that make up its executive services.

mounting a partition — Logically linking a volume to an empty folder on another NTFS volume. It means that you can write data to the path on one volume and have that data actually stored on the mounted volume.

MSInfo32 — A system configuration and documentation utility that reports numerous hardware and software settings. Also called the System Information tool.

multiboot system — A computer that contains two or more operating systems and allows the user to select which operating system to start during each initial system start-up cycle.

multicast scope — A scope that is used to send collaborative information to a group of computers without the need to manually configure the clients.

multimaster replication — A situation in which all domain controllers maintain a read-write copy of the database that they replicate to all other domain controllers.

multiple display support — Native support within Windows 2000 that allows definition and use of as many as nine display monitors.

multiprocessing — A system with multiple CPUs installed.

My Network Places — The starting point for accessing network resources on a Windows 2000 computer.

name resolution — The method of converting between human-readable names and computer names and addresses.

Name Server — A DNS record that defines which server in the domain acts as the name server.

native mode — The way in which Windows 2000 Systems communicate with other Windows 2000 Systems.

near-line backup — Data are migrated from the hard disk to a slower, but easily accessible media such as CD-ROMs. This backup technique allows the data to be accessible without using up disk space.

NetBIOS Enhanced User Interface (NetBEUI) — A protocol that can be used in small, nonrouted environments.

network — Two or more computers connected so that they can share information and resources.

network computers — See thin clients.

Network layer — The layer of the OSI model that addresses the messages for delivery.

network load balancing — A feature that allows you to configure your network so that some network-based servers, such as Web services, are available most of the time. These services can therefore be shared between two or more Windows 2000 Advanced Server systems and fail over between them automatically.

Network Place — A resource on the network, generally accessed through a shortcut from the My Network Places dialog box.

network redirectors and servers — File system drivers that transfer data to and from network-accessible drives.

network-interface print device — A printing device attached to a special network interface card that does not require a direct computer connection.

nodes — Individual servers in a cluster.

nonroutable protocol — A network protocol that cannot be used in a routed network environment.

normal backup — A type of backup that copies every selected file to the backup media and resets the archive bit on the original files. This backup type is the core of a backup strategy.

NT LAN Manager (NTLM) — The default authentication protocol used in Windows NT 4.

NTBACKUP — The backup program that comes with Windows 2000. It is accessed by selecting Start, Run, and typing NTBACKUP.

Ntbootdd.sys — A file that appears on Windows 2000 and Windows NT systems with SCSI controllers that do not have an on-board BIOS translation enabled or present. It enables the drive controller system on the motherboard to control a SCSI adapter and its attached hard drives.

Ntdetect.com — A core file of Windows 2000 that inventories the computer's hardware and uses this inventory to build HKLM\Hardware. Every time you boot the machine, Ntdectect.com rechecks all hardware.

Ntdetect.com — A file that is invoked just prior to loading the Windows 2000 executable files from the boot partition. It performs a hardware inspection to create an inventory of devices and their configurations. The configuration that is detected is used to select a hardware profile, which in turn determines which device drivers are loaded.

NTFS (New Technology File System) — The native file system for Windows NT that is extended in Windows 2000. NTFS has many advanced features that make it more efficient and faster on large drives, supports volume mounting, and offers other features such as disk compression, file quotas, and a native encryption system.

Ntldr — The operating system initialization file that the computer launches upon the completion of the bootstrapping process. It is responsible for loading Windows NT or other operating systems when it appears on a multiboot system. Ntldr uses the Boot.ini file to present a boot menu, which in turn is used to select the operating system to be launched.

Ntoskrnl.exe — A file that contains the Windows 2000 kernel, which is the core of the Windows 2000 operating environment. It controls the loading of all other files involved in establishing the computing environment. Ntoskrnl.exe resides on the boot partition in the \Winnt\System32 folder (assuming the default name for the system root is accepted during installation).

object — A component of the Active Directory, such as a user, group, computer, or application.

object attributes — Configuration variables for objects.

object classes — The definitions for new objects and for object classes within the Active Directory, which are stored within the schema.

object manager — The part of the executive that creates the objects representing executive-level structures such as processes and threads.

offline backup — A backup method in which data are copied to removable media, such as a tape.

Offline Files and Folders — The Windows 2000 feature that allows users to cache files on their local drives for access when they are not connected to the network.

offline folder — A new feature in Windows 2000 that allows you to store commonly accessed network documents on your workstation so that they are available when your system is not connected to the network. Modified files are automatically synchronized when you reconnect to the network and log on.

online — In terms of fault tolerance, when a resource provides its service on its node.

online backup — A backup technique in which a copy of the data is maintained at all times on a separate and remote system.

OnNow system — A Microsoft specification that supports hibernation, "instant-on," and sophisticated power management features. For more information, see the Microsoft Web site: *http://www.microsoft.com/hwdev/onnow/*.

Open Shortest Path First (OSPF) — A protocol used by routers to learn about different routes to remote networks.

Ordinary Safe Mode — An option that loads only the drivers and services required to boot the computer and to provide a simple operating environment.

organizational unit (OU) — A way to maintain a set security model for several objects within a domain. Similar to Windows NT domains.

Organizationally Unique Identifier (OUI) — A unique number that is assigned to each network device vendor to ensure that hardware addresses do not overlap.

Osloader.exe — A file that appears only on Alpha systems. It replaces all of the various files found on Intel machines by combining their functions into a single file.

page directory — A collection of page tables for a particular process.

page fault — An event in which the Virtual Memory Manager must retrieve data from disk to put it back into RAM for a process.

page fault handler — The part of the Virtual Memory Manager that finds the data that's been paged to disk so as to put that data back into RAM.

page table — A list of page table entries, used to map virtual addresses to storage areas in physical memory.

page table entry (PTE) — The entry on a page table that contains the mapping of physical storage to virtual memory addresses.

pagefile — Temporary storage space on a hard drive.

pages — Sections of memory used by an operating system to transfer data from the physical memory to the swap file and back. Because physical memory is much faster than hard disks, paging slows down the system considerably.

paging file — See *pagefile*.

partition — A logical division of disk space. A disk must be partitioned, and the partitions formatted, before it can be used. Disks can have a maximum of four partitions without the help of an operating system.

partition table — A table stored in the first sector of a hard disk, noting the location and size of every partition on the disk and indicating whether those partitions are bootable.

PC Card — Laptop peripheral technology based on the CardBus specification. Similar in design to PCMCIA cards but operating at a higher bus speed.

PCI bus — High-performance personal computer bus that allows component-to-component communication without the need for CPU intervention.

PDC emulator — A service that runs on a Windows 2000 system that emulates the single-master replication method used in Windows NT. This service is used until all servers have been upgraded to Windows 2000.

per-seat license — A type of license that permits a predefined number of computer connections to the operating system or application being licensed.

per-session license — A type of license that permits a predefined number of simultaneous user connections to the operating system or application being licensed.

Physical layer — The layer of the OSI model that defines the physical structure of the network (copper, fiber, and so on).

physical memory — The memory chips installed in the computer that are used for temporary storage of process data. Synonymous with random access memory (RAM).

plaintext — Unencrypted data.

platter — A magnetized metal disk within a hard disk—the actual storage medium.

Plug and Play — A hardware specification that allows automatic discovery and configuration of hardware devices.

Plug and Play Manager — The Windows 2000 component that handles operating system recognition of Plug and Play hardware.

Point-to-Point Tunneling Protocol (PPTP) — A protocol that is used to encrypt data between a server and a client.

Pointer — A DNS record that resolves a TCP/IP address to its Internet name.

power management — The Windows 2000 component that provides operating system power management features and controls hardware power management features.

Power On, Self-Test (POST) — An internal diagnostic that a computer performs during the earliest phases of the bootstrapping process.

preemptive multitasking — A type of multitasking in which the Virtual Memory Manager controls who has control of the CPU, rather than giving this responsibility to the applications.

preemptive multitasking — Type of multitasking in which the memory manager controls who has control of the CPU, rather than giving the responsibility to the applications.

Presentation layer — The layer of the OSI model that translates data from a format understood by the application into a generic format that can be understood by other systems.

primary domain controller (PDC) — The Windows NT Server that maintains the master copy of the database.

primary partition — A disk partition on a basic disk that's designed to hold an operating system (although it doesn't have to do so—a primary partition might hold only data). One primary partition is marked active, meaning that the computer will boot from it. A disk may hold a maximum of four primary partitions. Primary partitions may not be subdivided.

print device — A physical printing device.

print driver — A software component that is used to translate print jobs into the language used by the print device.

print server — A computer configured to manage the printing activities of one or more print devices.

printer — A software interface between the operating system and the physical printing device.

priority interrupts — A way for hardware devices to notify the CPU that they need its attention.

private key — A key devoted to decrypting data for a particular person. Private keys should be kept secure.

process — The environment defining the resources available to threads, which are the executable parts of an application. Processes define the memory available, any processor affinities, the location where the process page directory is stored in physical memory, and other information that the CPU needs to work with a thread.

processor affinity — In multiprocessor systems, a feature that may be used to tell all threads in a process that they should use one processor in preference to another, even if the preferred processor is busier than the alternative processors.

protocol — A common language that allows heterogeneous systems to communicate and share information on a network.

public key — A key devoted to encrypting data for a particular person. A public key only encrypts; it does not decrypt.

published software — Software made available to users on an as-needed basis. Users can select from the list of published software to determine whether they want to install available applications.

quantum — The number of CPU cycles that a thread gets to use when executing. During its quantum, a thread gets all of the CPU's attention.

quorum resource — A cluster resource that is used as a tiebreaker when two servers are trying to form a cluster at once. The one with control of the quorum resource controls the cluster.

quota — The amount of disk space to which a user has access on a quota-enabled volume.

RAID 5 volume — A fault-tolerant volume extending over 3–32 disks. It works like a stripe set, except that in addition to writing data in stripes across the disks in the volume, it also writes parity information for the volume. If one disk in the RAID 5 volume fails, then the data on that disk may be regenerated from the parity information on the other disks.

RAID 5 volume — An elaboration of disk striping in which parity information for the data written to the volume is also written to the volume. If one disk in a RAID 5 volume fails, the data that it contained may be reconstructed from the parity information on the remaining disks.

read-only attribute — A simple attribute that makes it impossible to edit a file.

Recovery Console — A command-line recovery interface that you can use to repair bits and pieces of Windows 2000 without replacing all configuration settings.

redirector — An Application layer software component that captures application output and redirects it to a different location.

Redundant Array of Independent Disks (RAID) — The technique of logically combining physical disks to make fault-tolerant disk volumes. If one disk in a RAID array fails, the other disk or disks can take over until the broken disk may be replaced.

REGEDIT — The 16-bit Registry Editor. REGEDIT offers global searching and combines all of the keys into a single display. It can be used to perform searches, add new subkeys and value entries, alter the data in value entries, and import and export keys and subkeys.

REGEDT32 — The 32-bit Registry editor. REGEDT32 offers control over key and value entry security but displays each root key in a separate window. It also offers a read-only mode so that you can explore without accidentally altering value entries. REGEDT32 can be used to perform searches, add new subkeys and value entries, alter the data in value entries, and import and export keys and subkeys.

REG_BINARY — A Registry value entry data type that stores data in binary format.

REG_DWORD — A Registry value entry data type that stores data in binary, hex, or decimal format.

REG_EXPAND_SZ — A Registry value entry data type that stores data in an expandable text-string format that contains a variable that is replaced by an application when it is used (for example, %Systemroot%\file.exe).

REG_MULTI_SZ — A Registry value entry data type that stores data in text-string format that contains multiple human-readable values separated by Null characters.

REG_SZ — A Registry value entry data type that stores data in text-string format.

Registry — The hierarchical database of system configuration data that is essential to the health and operation of a Windows 2000 system.

Remote Computer Management — A service, also included with Windows 2000 Professional, that adds the capability to configure the properties of any server service or application that might be installed on a remote system.

Remote Display Protocol (RDP) — The specialized protocol developed for Terminal Services that facilitates communication between the client and the server.

Remote Installation Service (RIS) — A service that allows for the remote installation of Windows 2000 Professional systems from a central networked location.

remote storage — A service that an administrator can configure to automatically migrate files that are not commonly accessed to a remote storage device, such as a tape backup system, so as to free up disk space for applications and services that require it.

removing the mirror set — Discarding one half of a mirror set's data (converting the volume to unallocated space) and reverting the other half to a simple volume.

reparse points — NTFS pointers that may be set into a file path to redirect the path from one volume to another. Reparse points make mounted volumes work.

replica — A copy of part of the directory.

reserved memory — Virtual memory addresses set aside for a particular process but not yet committed—that is, no space in the paging file has been reserved for them.

resident — Attributes that are stored in the master file table instead of being pointed to are known as resident attributes. Some attributes are required to be resident.

resources — Name resolution information for a zone.

resources — Part of a cluster (hardware or software) that the cluster software manages. The cluster service includes DLLs that represent some common potential resources, and developers can build their own.

reverse lookup zone — A zone that maintains the pointer records and resolves IP addresses to names.

roaming user profile — A user profile stored on a network server and downloaded to whichever computer a user is currently logged into. Changes to the profile are saved to the network server when the user logs off.

root domain — The top-level domain in Active Directory (for example, microsoft.com).

root folder — The folder in the FAT that lists all folders in the volume and all files in the root directory. A root folder can contain a maximum of 512 entries.

routable protocol — A network protocol that can be used in a routed environment to communicate with remote networks.

routing — The process of transferring packets of information from one network to another network.

Routing Information Protocol for Internet Protocol (RIP for IP) — A protocol used by routers to learn about different routes to remote networks.

routing table — A list of available networks and interfaces over which a system must communicate to contact a remote system.

runtime environment — The packaging of common control elements for applications to use.

Safe Mode — A way of booting Windows 2000 with a minimal set of drivers. It displays the usual desktop (although using only the Vga.sys driver) and has no networking support.

Safe Mode (Command Prompt Only) — An option that works like Safe Mode—no networking support, basic VGA video, no extraneous drivers—except that it uses the command prompt (Cmd.exe) for a shell instead of Explorer (Explorer.exe).

Safe Mode with Networking — An option that is just like Safe Mode, except for the addition of network support. You would use this boot option when you want a pared-down version of the operating system, but need network support to fix something.

schema — The way in which the Active Directory recognizes different objects. You can modify the schema to add information, such as a user's picture.

secret key communication — The method of authentication on which Kerberos is based, where a client and server must both know and use the same cryptographic key to protect the network.

sector — The smallest physical unit of storage on a hard disk.

security ID (SID) — The unique identifier that is determined by the security restrictions of the user group to which you belong and any settings that the administrator has applied directly to your account.

security identification (SID) number — A unique number assigned by Windows 2000 to each user account.

Security log — An Event Viewer log that records security-related events.

security principal — A Windows 2000 computer in a domain using Kerberos.

selection information file — The file in which backups are stored. This file has a .bks extension.

service — A software component that exists on servers that run in the background so as to perform normal server operations, such as file and print sharing, Web and FTP services, and DNS services.

Service Location — Allows you to configure services that are located on remote systems.

service pack — A collection of code replacements, patches, error corrections, new applications, version improvements, or service-specific configuration settings that correct, replace, or hide the deficiencies of the original product, preceding service packs, or hot fixes.

Services for Macintosh — A service that connects Apple Macintosh systems to a Windows 2000 system and allows file and print sharing.

Session layer — The layer of the OSI model that initiates and maintains communication between different systems on the network.

simple volume — A volume on a dynamic disk that exists on a single disk. Simple volumes may be expanded on the same disk or made into spanned volumes that extend to another physical disk.

smart terminal — A computer that has only a monitor and a keyboard with a network attachment.

spanned volume — A volume that extends over two or more dynamic disks.

sparse files — Files marked with an attribute that says, "Only provide space in the paging file for the parts of this file that actually have data in them, instead of strings of 0s." The data have pointers to the places where the long strings of 0s can be, so that they can be filled in as necessary, but sparse files save room in the paging file and in memory by allocating only the storage that's actually needed.

spawn — Same as *launch*. The process of executing an application.

standard primary zone — The authority for the zone. It is in charge of all changes to the domains.

standard secondary zone — A read-only copy of the standard primary zone database. It is used for fault tolerance and load balancing.

Start of Authority (SOA) — A DNS record that defines the different timeout and TTL values for the domain.

static routing — A system in which the network administrator must manually configure all paths from one network to another.

stripe set — A volume that extends over two or more dynamic disks, but which reduces disk read and write times by writing data to all disks in stripes, instead of filling up the volume from back to front as normal volumes do.

stripe set with parity — See *RAID 5 volume*.

striped volume — Same as a stripe set, but for dynamic disks.

subkey — A sublevel division of a Registry key. A subkey can contain other subkeys and value entries.

subnet — A logical boundary on a network.

superscope — A process of combining two or more scopes to group them into a single administrative unit.

surface — The side of a disk platter. Each platter has two surfaces.

symmetric encryption — A method of data encryption that uses the same algorithm to encrypt and decrypt plaintext.

system attribute — A simple attribute that identifies a file as part of the operating system.

system buses — The Windows 2000 component that recognizes and controls system buses such as PCI, CardBus, FireWire, and USB.

System log — An Event Viewer log that records information and alerts about Windows 2000's internal processes.

system page — Chunks of memory, as viewed by a processor. The system page for an x86 machine is 4 KB in size; for an Alpha machine, it is 8 KB in size.

system partition — The partition that contains the files used to initialize the Windows 2000 loading process.

System State — An option that allows you to choose which components to back up, such as the Active Directory, the boot files, and the Registry.

System State data — Windows 2000's name for system configuration information. System state data include the Registry, the boot files, the class registration database, and, if applicable, the certificate services database, Active Directory structure, and SYSVOL.

task switching — A method of multitasking in which the user may switch between applications. The application in the foreground gets all CPU cycles; the background applications get none.

terminal server client access license (TSCAL) — A type of license that permits the computer to which it's assigned to run a session from a terminal server.

Terminal Services — The Windows 2000 component that provides access to the Windows 2000 console for many types of clients. Similar to terminal functions in a mainframe environment.

terminal services — A service that provides Windows 2000 Server systems with the ability to support multiple client sessions running on a single computer. This feature greatly reduces TCO by minimizing the amount of hardware and software upgrades needed for each individual client system.

thin clients — A low-cost, low-powered desktop environment with just enough CPU power and memory to handle local input and output tasks.

thread — An entity within a process for which Win2K schedules CPU time to execute a function of some kind. When a thread has finished its job, it terminates.

thread — The executable element of an application.

thread state — Any one of five states that a thread may be in, defining its readiness to use the CPU.

threading — A way for a single task to operate multiple related activities in parallel without imposing the delays associated with a typical context switch.

ticket — A data structure generated by the KDC when a client computer asks the KDC for a secret key. The server's half of the secret key is embedded in the ticket and encrypted with the key that the KDC and the server have in common.

time slicing — A fixed length of time that the system allows a single task to occupy the CPU.

Tower of Hanoi (ToH) — A backup scheme that uses five tapes in rotation to create a 32-week record of normal backups. Because this backup scheme does not include differential or incremental backups, it should not be used as the sole backup plan.

track — A concentric circle traced on the surface of a platter, used to physically divide storage space.

transaction log — A list of changes to the volume structure maintained by NTFS. When changes are complete, they're listed in the transaction log as being committed. If the disk stops working, when it restarts, NTFS rolls back the volume structure to its form at the last committed change. This technique prevents the volume structure from being corrupted by half-made changes.

transitive trust — A relationship that states that if domain A trusts domain B, and domain B trusts domain C, then domain A will automatically trust domain C.

Transmission Control Protocol/Internet Protocol (TCP/IP) — The protocol for the Internet. It allows for the connection of large networks in different geographical locations.

Transport Driver Interface (TDI) — The specification to which all transport protocols must be written so that they can be used by higher-layer services, such as programming interfaces, file systems, and interprocess communication mechanisms.

Transport layer — The layer of the OSI model that is responsible for ensuring error-free transmission and reception of data.

tree — A collection of domains that use the same contiguous namespace.

trim — The procedure in which some of a process's working set is moved to the paging file to free room in physical memory.

trust relationship — A relationship that is set up between domains so that one domain can trust resources from another domain.

tunnel — A communication mechanism used by VPNs to establish a second, secure session between a client and remote server.

unallocated space — An area of a physical disk that has not yet been partitioned.

Universal Serial Bus (USB) — A new high-speed serial bus that supports 127 peripheral devices and automatic device configuration.

user mode — A restricted kind of access to CPU functions and virtual memory. User mode limits user applications to using per-process virtual memory addresses and a subset of CPU functions, allowing them to request kernel-mode functions but not to read or write data in system areas.

user profile — A file containing environment settings, which is loaded when a person logs onto a computer or domain. User profiles may be stored on the local computer or on a server, and may be either user-definable or locked down.

value — The actual data stored by a value entry.

value entry — A named Registry variable that stores a specific value or data string. A Registry value entry's name is typically a multiword phrase without spaces that uses title capitalization.

variable priority thread — A thread with a base priority from 1 to 15 that may have a higher priority if the dispatcher thinks it appropriate. A variable priority thread may never have a priority higher than 15.

VGA Mode — An advanced boot option that boots Windows 2000 as usual, except that it uses the generic Vga.sys instead of the video driver you have installed. It is useful for fixing problems related to bad or incompatible video drivers.

virtual directories — Folders used by the Web service to provide content to the Internet.

Virtual DOS Machine — A software environment within Windows 2000 that supports legacy DOS programs running in a protected environment space.

virtual machine — A software construct that creates a computer environment for each process, so that the process appears to be the exclusive resident of the physical machine. In Windows 2000, application subsystems construct virtual machines for processes. When a process requests access to a resource (whether memory, CPU time, keyboard input, display changes, or hard drive resources), the virtual machine relays that request to the application subsystem in which the virtual machine resides. This subsystem, in turn, passes the request to the appropriate executive service in the kernel mode.

Glossary

virtual machines — A way for Windows 2000 to let non-Windows 2000 applications run on the system. It emulates the native operating system of the application.

virtual memory — A mechanism by which RAM is supplemented with disk space to make it appear that the computer has more memory installed than it really does.

virtual memory — A method of using both hard disk space and physical RAM to make it appear as though a computer has as much as 4 GB of RAM.

virtual multitasking — A way of making a computer appear as if it is executing more than one thing at a time.

virtual private network (VPN) — A secure connection between a client and a private network over the Internet.

virtual server — The name by which the nodes in a cluster are collectively known. Clients connect to the virtual server, not to the individual nodes within the server.

volume — Another name for a partition—a logical division of physical disk space. Most often, volumes refer to areas on dynamic disks, whereas partitions refer to the division of basic disks.

VxD driver — The legacy device driver model, still supported under Windows 2000, that requires much more development effort than corresponding WDM drivers.

wide area network (WAN) — A group of computers that are networked over great distances, such as between cities.

Win32 Driver Model (WDM) — The new Windows driver model that allows simplified device driver development such that one driver can be used on both Windows 2000 and Windows 98 systems.

Windows clustering — A feature that allows for the implementation of Windows 2000 clusters. A cluster can automatically detect if an application, service, or server fails and then migrate the failed component to another system in the cluster. It is designed for mission-critical applications and servers.

Windows Internet Name Service (WINS) — A service that resolves NetBIOS names (or computer names) to TCP/IP addresses.

Windows NT domain — A logical collection of Windows NT computers that share the same user database and security models.

WINS — A DNS record that defines the TCP/IP address of one or more WINS servers on the network.

working set — Data that the thread in a process is currently using and that is stored in RAM.

working set — The data that the threads in a process have stored in physical memory. The working set may grow or shrink depending on how much physical memory is available, but the process may not use any data that is not in its working set.

zone — A logical group of addresses.

zone database file — A simple text file in a standard zone that is used by DNS to resolve TCP/IP names and addresses.

zone transfer — The process of transferring information between standard primary and standard secondary servers.

INDEX

A

access control lists (ACLs), 34, 107
access tokens, 106
ACLs (access control lists), 34, 107
ACPI (Advanced Configuration and Power Interface) specification, 125
active/active clusters, 376
Active Directory, 242, 271–284
   DHCP, 254
   directory structures, 280–281
   domains, 274–275
   files, 282–283
   forests, 276–277
   objects, 272–273
   organizational units, 273–274
   preparing for, 277–280
   trees, 276
   troubleshooting. *See* troubleshooting Active Directory
Windows 2000 Server, 15
Active Directory Installation Wizard, 279–280
Active Directory-integrated zones, 243
Active Directory Users and Computers tool, Windows 2000 Server, 73
active/standby clusters, 376–377
Add Printer Wizard, 307–309
Add/Remove Hardware Wizard
   Windows 2000 Professional, 14
   Windows 2000 Server, 73
Add/Remove Programs tool, Windows 2000 Server, 73
Address (A) resource record, 245–247
address translation, 103–105
administration, delegation, 281
Administration Tool, Terminal Services, 317–318
administrative templates, 339
Advanced Attributes dialog box, 343–344
Advanced Configuration and Power Interface (ACPI) specification, 125
Advanced Options menu, 399–403
   boot logging, 400
   Debugging mode, 403
   Directory Services Restore Mode, 403
   Last Known Good Configuration, 401–403
   Safe Mode, 400
   VGA mode, 401
affinity of processes, 88, 91
allocating
   CPU time, 68–69
   memory, 67–68
   resources, 12, 124–125
APIs (application program interfaces), 30
AppleTalk Remote Access Protocol (ARAP), 227
application(s)
   background, 89
   clustered, requirements, 379
   foreground, 89
   IntelliMirror for distribution, 311
   licensing. *See* licenses
   Web, IIS development tools, 312
Application layer, OSI reference model, 213
application licenses, 332
application program interfaces (APIs), 30
application service providers (ASPs), 332
ARAP (AppleTalk Remote Access Protocol), 227
archive attribute, 156
archive bits, 194, 363
ASPs (application service providers), 332
assigned software, 311
asymmetric encryption, 341
ATTRIB command, 405
attribute(s)
   FAT16 file system, 156
   NTFS, 158–159, 161–163, 342
attribute bytes, FAT16 file system, 156
authentication of users. *See* user authentication
authoritative restore, 406–407
Automatic Caching for Documents option, offline access, 303
Automatic Caching for Programs option, offline access, 303
automatic DHCP lease renewal, 253
AXFR (Full Zone Transfer), 247

B

background applications, 89
backing up
   Active Directory, 283–284
   data. *See* backing up data
   Registry, 65–66, 434–435
backing up data, 194–196, 360–367
   creating schemes, 365–366

media supported in Windows 2000, 367
methods, 195–196
schemes, 363–367
tools, 361–363
types, 194–195, 366
backup domain controllers (BDCs), 274
Backup feature, Windows 2000 Professional, 14
backup methods, 195–196
  near-line, 196
  offline, 196
  online, 195
balance set manager, 99
base priority, 92
basic disks, 182–184
basic storage, 151, 152
batch jobs, 4
batch systems, 4
BDCs (backup domain controllers), 274
bit masks, 371
Boot.ini file, 56
boot logging, 400
boot process, 53–54, 396–399
  base operating system loaders, 55–57
  detecting hardware, 397–398
  detecting problems with Advanced Options menu. *See* Advanced Options menu
  loading basic hardware support, 396–397
  loading Ntldr, 397
  loading Windows 2000 system kernel, 398–399
  troubleshooting. *See* troubleshooting boot process
Bootsect.dos file, 56
boot sector, 150
bootstrapping files, 53, 55–57
breaking the mirror set, 372

broadcasts, 296
bus(es), 131–133. *See also* IEEE 1394 Serial Bus (FireWire); PCI bus; Universal Serial Bus (USB)
bus class drivers, 127
bus minidrivers, 127

C

Cache Manager, 34–35
Caching dialog box, 302
CALs. *See* client access licenses (CALs)
CardBus, 131
CD command, 405
central processing units (CPUs), 9–10
  allocating CPU time, 68–69
  distributing cycles. *See* distributing CPU cycles; thread scheduling
  multiple, 5–6
  starvation, priority boosts to rectify, 99–100
  Windows 2000 Professional requirements, 15
  Windows 2000 Server requirements, 17
certificate(s), user authentication, 336
certificate authority, 336
change journal, NTFS, 162
CHDIR command, 405
checkpoint file, Active Directory, 283
CHKDSK command, 405
CIF (Computer Information File), troubleshooting, 418–419
ciphertext, 341
circular logging, Active Directory, 283
client(s), 28
  client-cluster communications, 378–379
  connecting to resources from, 298
  thin, 72

client access licenses (CALs), 330, 331
  Internet, 332
  terminal server, 331–332, 333
client licensing. *See* licenses
client roles, 228
client/server model, operating systems, 28
cluster(s), 151
  size in FAT16 volumes, 157
  size in NTFS, 161
clustering, 6, 373–380
  client-cluster communications, 378–379
  client's perception of servers and applications, 373–375
  cluster types, 375–377
  parts of cluster service, 375
  process, 378
  requirements for clustered applications, 379
  Windows 2000 Advanced Server, 18
cluster resources, 379
cluster service, 374
  parts, 375
command(s)
  embedded, 3–4
  Recovery Console, 405
command-based scripting, App 2–3
command languages, 4
comments, sharing network resources, 300, 301
committed memory, 101
common-sense troubleshooting, 420–421
Communications Manager, cluster service, 375
Component Services tool, 219
  dependencies, 222–223
  general settings, 219–220
  log on preferences, 220–221
  recovery options, 222

Compreg.exe, 437
compression, NTFS, 343
computer(s)
 identification, 242. *See also*
  Domain Naming Service
  (DNS); Dynamic Host
  Configuration Protocol
  (DHCP); Windows Internet
  Name Service (WINS)
 network, 72
Computer Information File
 (CIF), troubleshooting, 418–419
Computer Management tool
 troubleshooting, 423–424
 Windows 2000 Server, 73
Configuration Database Manager,
 cluster service, 375
configuring display and input
 devices, 133–134
consistency, interfaces, 12
console licenses, 331
context, threads, 90
context switch, 39
context switching, 8, 90
control objects, 36
Control Panel, 133
control programs, 4
control sets, 63
cooperative multitasking, 68–69, 89
copy backups, 194, 366
COPY command, 405
copy-on-write data sharing, 102
core system files, 53, 55–57
CPUs. *See* central processing units
 (CPUs)
CRCs (cyclic redundancy
 checks), 214
Cscript.exe, App 2–3
cycles, CPU, distributing. *See* distributing CPU cycles; thread
 scheduling
cyclic redundancy checks
 (CRCs), 214
cylinders, 148

D

daily backups, 366–367
database files
 Active Directory, 282
 zone, 243
data encryption. *See* encryption;
 encryption keys
Data Link layer, OSI reference
 model, 214–215
data packets, 214
data-processing requests,
 handling, 69
data stream attributes, NTFS, 162
data types, Registry, 60
Dcpromo.exe, 279
DDIs (device driver interfaces), 130
Debugging mode, 403
decryption, 344
default gateways, 252, 256
DEL (DELETE) command, 405
delegation of administration, 281
deleting the mirror set, 372
Dependencies tab, Service
 Properties dialog box, 222–223
dependency failures, troubleshooting, 421
device(s)
 hardware versus, 123–124
 management, 124–125
device class drivers, 54, 127
device driver(s), 37–38, 54–55
 class, 54, 127
 individual, 54–55
 minidrivers, 127
device driver interfaces
 (DDIs), 130
Device Manager, 123–124, 125
device minidrivers, 127
device sharing, 299–303
DFS. *See* Distributed File System
 (DFS)
DFS links, 305
DFS roots, 304–306

DHCP. *See* Dynamic Host
 Configuration Protocol (DHCP)
DHCPDISCOVER message, 251
DHCP leases, 251–254
 DHCPDISCOVER phase, 251
 DHCPOFFER phase, 251–252
 DHCPPACK phase, 252
 DHCPREQUEST phase, 252
 renewal, 252–254
DHCPOFFER message, 251–252
DHCPPACK message, 252
DHCPREQUEST message, 252
DHCP scopes, 254–255
differential backups, 195, 365
DIR command, 405
directories
 Active Directory, structure,
  280–281
 NTFS, 157–160
 virtual, 314
Directory Services Restore
 Mode, 403
DISABLE command, 405
disk(s)
 architecture. *See* disk architecture
 basic, 182–184
 duplication, Windows 2000
  Professional, 14
 dynamic. *See* dynamic disks
 fault-tolerant configurations. *See*
  fault-tolerant disk configurations
 groups, 367
 quotas. *See* disk quotas
 space. *See* disk space
 troubleshooting problems, 441
 writing to, 67
disk architecture, 148–154
 logical disk divisions, 150–154
 master boot record, 150
 partition table, 149–150
 physical disk divisions, 148–150
 volume types, 151–154

Disk Management tool, 182
    creating fault-tolerant volumes, 372
disk mirroring, 368–369
DISKPART command, 405
disk quotas
    NTFS, 157, 162, 191–194
    Windows 2000 Server, 15
disk space
    Windows 2000 Professional requirements, 15
    Windows 2000 Server requirements, 17
disk striping with parity, 153–154, 369–371
dispatcher, 90–91
displays
    configuring, 133
    multiple, 130–131
    Windows 2000 Professional requirements, 15
    Windows 2000 Server requirements, 17
Distributed File System (DFS), 304–306
    creating DFS roots, 305–306
    managing, 304–305
    Windows 2000 Server, 73
distributing CPU cycles, 88–100
    multitasking types, 89
    thread scheduling. *See* thread scheduling
DLLs. *See* dynamic link libraries (DLLs)
DNS. *See* Domain Naming Service (DNS)
documenting current settings, troubleshooting devices, 137–138
domain(s), 256
    Active Directory, 274–275
    monitoring available licenses, 331
    root, 281
    Windows NT, 274–275

domain accounts, server accounts versus, 333–334
domain controllers, 274–275, 333–334
    troubleshooting communication difficulties, 421
domain names, Active Directory domains, 280
Domain Naming Service (DNS), 241, 242–247
    SOA, 245–247
    zones, 243–244
    zone transfers, 247
DOS, 3
Dr. Watson, troubleshooting, 441
drive(s)
    logical, 152
    mapping, 298
driver stack, 128
duplexed volumes, 190
dynamic disks, 183, 184–191
    fault-tolerant volumes, 188–189, 190–191
    mirrored volumes, 189–190
    RAID 5 volumes, 190–191
    simple volumes, 185–186
    spanned volumes, 186–187
    striped volumes, 187–188
Dynamic Host Configuration Protocol (DHCP), 241, 250–255
    Active Directory, 254
    leases. *See* DHCP leases
    scopes, 254–255
dynamic link libraries (DLLs), 30
    clustering, 374–375
dynamic routes, 225, 227
dynamic storage, 151, 152–154

E

editors, Registry, 66–67, 432–433
EFS. *See* Encrypted File System (EFS)
embedded commands, 3–4

Emergency Repair Disk (ERD), 404
    Windows 2000 versus Windows NT, 437
emulation, 28–29
ENABLE command, 405
Encrypted File System (EFS), 14
    NTFS support, 162
encryption, 341–344
    enforcing, 344
    public key (asymmetric), 341
    symmetric, 341
    tools, 343–344
    Windows 2000, 344
encryption keys, 341
    protecting, 344
    public and private, 341
End User License Agreements (EULAs), 330
end user operating systems, 13
enumeration, 124–125
environmental subsystems, 28–32
    OS/2, 32
    POSIX, 31
    Registry values, 29
    Win32, 30–31
ERD. *See* Emergency Repair Disk (ERD)
error handling, 69–70
EULAs (End User License Agreements), 330
Event Processor, cluster service, 375
Event Viewer, 422–423
exclusive OR (XOR)
    arithmetic, 371
executable images, 32
executive, 32–35
    Cache Manager, 34–35
    I/O Manager, 34
    local procedure call facility, 35
    Object Manager, 35
    Process and Thread Manager, 32–33

Security Reference Monitor, 34
Virtual Memory Manager, 33–34
executive objects, 106–107
   names, 107
executive services, 67
Expire Interval, SOA, 245
extended partitions, 152
EXTRACT command, 405

F

fatal exception errors, troubleshooting, 139
FAT16 file system, 151, 155–157
   cluster sizes, 157
FAT32 file system, 151, 157
   file and folder sharing, 303–304
   Windows 2000 Professional support, 14
fault tolerance, 359–380
   backing up data. *See* backing up data
   clusters, 377
   definition, 359
   disk configurations. *See* fault-tolerant disk configurations
   server clustering. *See* clustering
   volumes. *See* fault-tolerant volumes
fault-tolerant clusters, 377
fault-tolerant disk configurations, 367–373
   creating fault-tolerant volumes with Disk Management tool, 372–373
   RAID levels supported in Windows 2000, 368–371
fault-tolerant volumes, 153–154, 184
   dynamic disks, 188–189, 190–191
FIFO (First In, First Out) algorithm, 103
file(s), 52. *See also specific files*
   Active Directory, 282–283
   attributes. *See* attribute(s)

boot process, 55–57
checkpoint, Active Directory, 283
database. *See* database files
decryption. *See* decryption
encryption. *See* encryption
finding under NTFS, 160
log, Active Directory, 283
paging, 103
Registry storage, 430–432
sharing, 302–306
sparse, 162
start-up, repairing, 438–439
volumes formatted with NTFS, 161
file system(s), 151, 155–163
   DFS. *See* Distributed File System (DFS)
   EFS, NTFS support, 162
   FAT16, 151, 155–157
   FAT32, 151, 157, 303–304
   file and folder sharing, 303–304
   NTFS. *See* NTFS (New Technology File System)
file system cache, 34–35
file system drivers, 38
File Transfer Protocol (FTP) server, IIS, 312
filter drivers, 38
FireWire. *See* IEEE 1394 Serial Bus (FireWire)
First In, First Out (FIFO) algorithm, 103
FIXBOOT command, 405
FIXMBR command, 405
folders
   decryption. *See* decryption
   encryption. *See* encryption
   NTFS, 160
   sharing, 302–306, 315
foreground applications, 89
forests, Active Directory, 276–277
FORMAY command, 405

forward lookup zones, 245–247
frames, 214
free space, 152
Front Page 2000 server extensions, IIS, 313
FTP (File Transfer Protocol) server, IIS, 312
full backups, 195
Full Zone Transfer (AXFR), 247
function calls, 29–30

G

Game Controllers applet, 133–134
gateways, default, 252, 256
Gateway Services for NetWare (GSNW), Windows 2000 Server, 15
General tab, Service Properties dialog box, 219–220
GFS (Grandfather/Father/Son) backup scheme, 365, 366
Global Update Manager, cluster service, 375
Grandfather/Father/Son (GFS) backup scheme, 365, 366
graphical backup tool, 360–361
group(s), disks, 367
group policies, 338–340
   applying, 340
   types, 339–340
   Windows 2000 Server, 15
group rights and permissions, 333–334
groupware, 332
GSNW (Gateway Services for NetWare), Windows 2000 Server, 15

H

HAL (hardware abstraction layer), 37, 54, 122–123
halts, troubleshooting, 421
handles, executive objects, 107
hard disks, signatures, 183

hardware
  detecting, 397–398
  devices versus, 123–124
  kernel-level support, 36–37
  loading basic hardware support, 396–397
  supported under WDM specification, 127–128
  troubleshooting, 396–397, 421
hardware abstraction layer (HAL), 37, 54, 122–123
hardware addresses, 215
hardware device(s), 121
hardware device drivers, 37
hardware management, 122–124
  components, 126
Hardware subkey, HKEY_LOCAL_MACHINE subtree, 62
helper parts of operating systems, 26
hidden attribute, 156
hives, Registry, 60–61
HKEY_CLASSES_ROOT key, 59, 63, 427
HKEY_CURRENT_CONFIG key, 59, 63–64, 427–428
HKEY_CURRENT_USER key, 59, 64
HKEY_LOCAL_MACHINE key, 59, 61–63, 426–427, 431, 432
  subkeys, 62–63
HKEY_USERS key, 60, 65, 428–429, 431
hot fixes, 442442
HTTP (Hypertext Transfer Protocol), IIS support, 312
human interface device class, 128
Hypertext Transfer Protocol (HTTP), IIS support, 312

I

ICLs (Internet client licenses), 332
identifying
  computers, 242. *See also* Domain Naming Service (DNS); Dynamic Host Configuration Protocol (DHCP); Windows Internet Name Service (WINS)
  partitions, 154
  volumes, 154
IEEE 1394 Serial Bus (FireWire), 123, 131
  troubleshooting, 139
IIS. *See* Internet Information Service (IIS) 5.0
incremental backups, 195, 364–365
Incremental Zone Transfer (IXFR), 247
indexes, NTFS, 160
individual device drivers, 54–55
initialization of kernel, 399
in-place upgrades, 279
input devices
  configuring, 133–134
  Windows 2000 Professional requirements, 15
  Windows 2000 Server requirements, 17
input/output (I/O) devices, 11. *See also* input devices
installing
  service pack updates, 443
  Terminal Services, 316–317
  troubleshooting problems, 421–422
  Windows 2000 networks, 279–280
IntelliMirror, 311
interactive logon, 334
interfaces, consistency, 12
Internet client licenses (ICLs), 332
Internet Information Service (IIS) 5.0, 312–315
  components, 312–313
  configuring folders for IIS access, 313–315
  features, 312
Internet Protocol Security (IPSec), 14
Internet Services Manager (ISM), 313
Internetwork Packet Exchange/Sequences Packet Exchange (IPX/SPX), 217, 218
interprocess communications (IPCs), 70–71
interrupt requests (IRQs), 53
I/O (input/output) devices, 11. *See also* input devices
I/O Manager, 34
IPCs (interprocess communications), 70–71
IP routing, 225–227
  dynamic routes, 225, 227
  static routes, 225–226
IPSec (Internet Protocol Security), 14
IPX/SPX (Internetwork Packet Exchange/Sequences Packet Exchange), 217, 218
IRQs (interrupt requests), 53
ISM (Internet Services Manager), 313
IXFR (Incremental Zone Transfer), 247

J

jobs, 33

K

KDC (Key Distribution Center), 336
Kerberos, 14, 334, 335–336
kernel, 35–37
  dispatcher, 90–91
  hardware support, 36–37
  loading, 398–399
kernel initialization phase, 399
kernel load phase, 398–399

kernel mode, 38–40
  services, 40
kernel objects, 36
key(s). *See* encryption keys; HKEY *entries*
Key Distribution Center (KDC), 336
Knowledge Base, 444

L

LANs (local area networks), 212
Last Known Good Configuration (LKGC), 401–403, 435–436
launching tasks, 8
layered operating systems, 27
Layer Two Tunneling Protocol (L2TP), 228
leases, DHCP. *See* DHCP leases
Least Recently Used (LRU) algorithm, 103
legacy virtualization drivers layer, 128–129
licenses
  application, 332
  client access, 330, 331–332, 333
  console, 331
  EULAs, 330
  per-seat, 330–331
  per-seat and per-session, 330–331
  per-session, 330–331
  terminal server, 331–332, 333
  types required, 331–333
LISTSVC command, 405
LKGC (Last Known Good Configuration), 401–403, 435–436
load balancing. *See* network load balancing
loading. *See* boot process
local area networks (LANs), 212
local print devices, 307
local procedure call facility, 35
Local Security Authority (LSA), 334

local user profiles, 337
log(s)
  boot process, 400
  Event Viewer, 422–423
  transaction. *See* transaction logs
logical drives, 152
logon
  interactive, 334
  preferences, 220–221
LOGON command, 405
Log On tab, Service Properties dialog box, 221
lookup zones, 245–247
LRU (Least Recently Used) algorithm, 103
LSA (Local Security Authority), 334
L2TP (Layer Two Tunneling Protocol), 228

M

MAC (Media Access Control) addresses, 215
Macintosh services, Windows 2000 Server, 15
mandatory user profiles, 337, 338
MANs (metropolitan area networks), 212
Manual Caching for Documents option, offline access, 303
manual DHCP lease renewal, 253–254
manually registering script engines, App 4
MAP command, 405
mapping network drives, 298
master boot record (MBR), 53, 150
  troubleshooting, 441
master file table (MFT), NTFS, 158–161
master zones, 243
MBR. *See* master boot record (MBR)
MD command, 405

media
  backup, supported in Windows 2000, 367
  troubleshooting errors, 421
Media Access Control (MAC) addresses, 215
memory, 10
  allocating, 67–68
  committed, 101
  management. *See* memory management
  physical, 88
  reserved, 101
  virtual, 33, 100–101
  Windows 2000 Professional requirements, 15
  Windows 2000 Server requirements, 17
memory management, 100–105
  earmarking memory for processes, 101–102
  paging file, 103
  reading data from memory, 103–105
  sharing memory among processes, 102–103
messaging, 71
metropolitan area networks (MANs), 212
MFT (master file table), NTFS, 158–161
Microsoft Management Console (MMC), 72–73
Microsoft references for troubleshooting, 444
Minimum Time-to-Live, SOA, 245
mirrored volumes, 184
  dynamic disks, 189–190
mirroring data, discarding mirror set, 372
mirror sets, 153
mixed mode, 277–278
MKDIR command, 405

MMC (Microsoft Management Console), 72–73
modifying the Registry, 66–67
modular architecture, 52
MORE command, 405
mounting partitions to folders, 154
Mouse applet, 134
MSInfo32 tool, 137
multiboot system, 53
multicast scopes, DHCP, 255
multimaster replication, 275
multiple display support, 130–131
multiprocessing, 5–9
    multiple CPUs, 5–6
    multiple tasks, 7–8
    multiple threads, 8–9
    multiple users, 6–7
multitasking
    cooperative, 89, 68069
    preemptive, 68, 89
    virtual, 7
My Computer, sharing devices, 299
My Network Places, 296–297
    sharing devices, 299–303

N

name(s)
    domain, Active Directory domains, 280
    NetBIO(s), 242
name resolution. See DHCP leases; Domain Naming Service (DNS); Dynamic Host Configuration Protocol (DHCP); Windows Internet Name Service (WINS)
native mode, 277, 278–279
nbstat parameters, 249
near-line backups, 196
NetBEUI. See NetBIOS Enhanced User Interface (NetBEUI)
NetBIOS Enhanced User Interface (NetBEUI), 217
    names, 242

network(s)
    installing, 279–280
    organization, 255–256
    troubleshooting, 440
    upgrading from Windows NT to Windows 2000, 277–279
Network and Dial-Up Connections tool, Windows 2000 Server, 73
network computers, 72
network functionality, operating systems, 70
network identification
    name resolution. See DHCP leases; Domain Naming Service (DNS); Dynamic Host Configuration Protocol (DHCP); Windows Internet Name Service (WINS)
    user identification versus computer identification, 242
networking, 211–229
    network types, 212
    operating systems, 223–224
    OSI reference model. See OSI reference model
    principles, 212
    protocols, 212, 217–218
    remote access, 227–228
    routing, 225–227
    server versus client roles, 228
    services. See service(s)
    Windows 2000 model, 224–225
    Windows 2000 Professional requirements, 15
    Windows 2000 Server requirements, 17
network-interface print devices, 307
Network layer, OSI reference model, 214
network load balancing, 378
    Windows 2000 Advanced Server, 17
Network Neighborhood, 297

Network News Transfer Protocol (NNTP), IIS support, 312, 313
network operating systems (NOSs), 223–224
Network Places, 296–297
network redirectors and servers, 38
network resources, sharing. See sharing network resources; sharing printers
New Scope Wizard, 254–255
New Technology File System. See NTFS (New Technology File System)
NNTP (Network News Transfer Protocol), IIS support, 313
node(s), in clusters, 373
Node Manager, cluster service, 375
nonroutable protocols, 217
normal backups, 195, 364
NOSs (network operating systems), 223–224
NTBACKUP utility, 195, 361
Ntbootdd.sys file, 56
Ntdetect.com file, 56, 397–398
NTFS (New Technology File System), 151, 157–163
    attributes, 158–159, 161–163, 342
    cluster sizes, 161
    directory organization, 157–160
    disk quotas, 157, 162, 191–194
    encryption, 342
    file and folder sharing, 303, 304
    limitation, 163
    system files, 161
NT LAN Manager (NTLM), 334, 335
Ntldr file, 56
    loading, 397
NTLM (NT LAN Manager), 334, 335
Ntoskrnl.exe file, 57, 398

O

object(s)
    Active Directory, 272–273

control, 36
executive. *See* executive objects
kernel, 36
object attributes, Active Directory, 272–273
object classes, Active Directory, 273
Object Manager, 35, 105–107
  executive objects, 106–107
  object security, 107
offline backups, 196
Offline Files and Folders feature, 302
offline folder feature, Windows 2000 Professional, 14
online backups, 195
online resources, 374
OnNow system, 129–130
Open Shortest Path First (OSPF) protocol, 227
Open Systems Interconnection (OSI) reference model. *See* OSI reference model
operating system(s) (OSs), 1–19, 25–41
  architecture. *See* operating system architecture
  batch systems, 4
  client/server model, 28
  control programs, 4
  damaged, repairing. *See* repairing damaged operating systems
  design objectives, 2–3
  DOS, 3
  embedded commands, 3–4
  essential operations, 67–72
  evolution, 3–9
  interface consistency, 12
  key functions, 9–12
  layered, 27
  multiple users, 5
  multiprocessing. *See* multiprocessing
  network, 223–224
  repairing. *See* repairing damaged operating systems
  resource allocation, 12
  security, 11–12
  types, 13
  Windows, 3
operating system architecture, 26–40
  device drivers, 37–38
  environmental subsystems, 28–32
  executive component, 32–35
  hardware abstraction layer, 37
  kernel, 35–37
  user space and kernel space, 38–40
Ordinary Safe Mode, 400
organizational units (OUs)
  Active Directory, 273–274
  applying group policies, 340
OSI reference model, 212–216
  Application layer, 213
  Data Link layer, 214–215
  functioning, 215–216
  Network layer, 214
  Physical layer, 215
  Presentation layer, 213–214
  Session layer, 214
  Transport layer, 214
  Windows 2000 networking model compared, 224–225
Osloader.exe file, 56
OSPF (Open Shortest Path First) protocol, 227
OS/2 subsystem, 32
OUs. *See* organizational units (OUs)

P

page(s), 10
  system, 102
page directories, 104
page fault(s), 104
page fault handlers, 104
page table(s), 104
page table entries (PTEs), 104
paging file, 103
parity, disk striping with, 153–154, 369–371
partitions, 149
  extended, 152
  identifying, 154
  mounting to folders, 154
  primary, 152
  system, 53
partition table, 149–150
PCI bus, 124
  troubleshooting, 139
PDC(s) (primary domain controllers), 274
PDC emulator, 278
permissions, 333–334
  troubleshooting problems, 441
Permissions dialog box, 301–302, 303
per-seat licenses, 330–331
per-session licenses, 330–331
Physical layer, OSI reference model, 215
physical memory, 88
plaintext, 341
platters, 148
  sectors, 148
  surfaces, 148
Plug and Play Manager, 124
Plug and Play standard, 122
Point-to-Point Tunneling Protocol (PPTP), 228
Portable Operating System Interface (based on) UNIX (POSIX), 31
POSIX (Portable Operating System Interface [based on] UNIX), 31
POSIX subsystem, 31
POST (Power On, Self-Test), 53
power management, 121, 129–130, 135
Power On, Self-Test (POST), 53

Power Options applet, 135
PPTP (Point-to-Point Tunneling Protocol), 228
preemption of threads, 94–95
preemptive multitasking, 68, 89
Presentation layer, OSI reference model, 213–214
primary domain controllers (PDCs), 274
primary partitions, 152
print devices, definition, 307
print drivers, 307
printers
  definition, 307
  sharing. *See* sharing printers
  troubleshooting, 439–440
Printers dialog box, 307
print servers, 307
priority
  processes, 92
  threads. *See* thread priority
priority interrupts, 8
private keys, 341
privileged mode, 39
process(es), 88–89
  affinity, 88, 91
  earmarking memory for, 101–102
  priority, 92
  Process and Thread Manager, 32
  sharing memory among, 102–103
  threads, 89
Process and Thread Manager, 32–33
programs. *See also* application(s)
  control, 4
Properties dialog box, 299–301, 315
  sharing printers, 310
protecting system memory, 102–103
protocols, 212, 217–218
  nonroutable and routable, 217
PTEs (page table entries), 104
public key encryption, 341
published software, 311

Q

quantum, 90
  end, 93
queries, WINS, 249
quorum resources, 374

R

RAID (redundant array of independent disks), 367–371
  disk mirroring, 368–369
  disk striping, 369–371
  levels, 188–189, 368–371
RAID 5 volumes, 153–154, 184, 190–191, 370–371
RAS (Remote Access Service), troubleshooting, 440
RD command, 405
RDP (Remote Display Protocol), 316
reading data from memory, 103–105
read-only attribute, 156
read/write head, 148
ready threads, 91
recovering Active Directory, 284
Recovery Console, 404–406
  commands, 405
Recovery tab, Service Properties dialog box, 222
redirector, Presentation level of OSI reference model, 213–214
redundant array of independent disks. *See* RAID (redundant array of independent disks)
Refresh Interval, SOA, 245
regback.exe, 437
Regback folder, 404
REG_BINARY data type, 429
Regdump.exe, 436
REG_DWORD data type, 429
REGEDIT, 66, 432–433
REGEDIT32, 66, 67, 432–433
Reg.exe, 436
REG_EXPAND_SZ data type, 429

Regfind.exe, 436
Regini.exe, 437
Registry, 58–67, 425–437
  backing up, 65–66, 434–435
  data types, 60
  editors, 66, 67, 432–433
  environmental subsystem values, 29
  hives, 60–61
  keys, 425–429
  modifying, 66–67
  Resource Kit tools, 436–437
  restoring, 435–436
  size limitations, 433–434
  storage files, 430–432
  subtrees, 59–60, 61–65
  value entries, 425, 426, 429–430
REG_MULTI_SZ data type, 430
Regrest.exe, 437
REG_SZ data type, 430
remote access, 227–228
Remote Access Service (RAS), troubleshooting, 440
Remote Computer Management, Windows 2000 Server, 15
Remote Display Protocol (RDP), 316
Remote Installation Service (RIS), Windows 2000 Server, 15
remote process communication (RPC), 71
remote storage, Windows 2000 Server, 15
removing the mirror set, 372
RENAME command, 405
REN command, 405
Repair folder, 404
repairing
  ERD. *See* Emergency Repair Disk (ERD)
  operating systems. *See* repairing damaged operating systems
  start-up files, 438–439

repairing damaged operating systems, 404–406
  ERD, 404
  Recovery Console, 404–406
reparse points, NTFS, 162
replicas, Active Directory, 274–275
reserved log files, Active Directory, 283
reserved memory, 101
resident attributes, NTFS, 159
resource(s), 374
  allocating, 12, 124–125
  DNS, 243, 244–247
  sharing. *See* sharing network resources; sharing printers
Resource Kits, 436–437, 444
Resource Manager/Failover Manager, cluster service, 375
Resource Monitor, cluster service, 375
restoring
  Active Directory, 284
  Registry, 435–436
  servers, 406–407
Retry Interval, SOA, 245
reverse lookup zones, 245
rights, 333–334
RIP for IP (Routing Information Protocol for Internet Protocol), 227
RIS (Remote Installation Service), Windows 2000 Server, 15
RMDIR command, 405
roaming user profiles, 337
root domain, 281
routable protocols, 217
routing. *See* IP routing
Routing and Remote Access tool, 226
  Windows 2000 Server, 73
Routing Information Protocol for Internet Protocol (RIP for IP), 227
routing tables, 225

RPC (remote process communication), 71
running threads, 91
runtime environments, 4

S

Safe Mode, 400
Safe Mode (Command Prompt Only), 400
Safe Mode with Networking, 400
SAM (Security Accounts Manager) subkey, HKEY_LOCAL_MACHINE subtree, 62
Scanreg.exe, 437
schemas, Active Directory, 273
scopes, DHCP, 254–255
scripting. *See* Windows Scripting Host (WSH)
sectors, platters, 148
security
  operating systems, 11–12
  Windows 2000 Professional, 14
Security Accounts Manager (SAM) subkey, HKEY_LOCAL_MACHINE subtree, 62
security IDs (SIDs), 34, 360–361
security principals, 336
Security Reference Monitor, 34, 107
Security subkey, HKEY_LOCAL_MACHINE subtree, 62
Serial Number, SOA, 245
server(s)
  clusters. *See* clustering
  restoring, 406–407
  virtual, 373
server accounts, domain accounts versus, 333–334
server clustering. *See* clustering
server-oriented operating systems, 13

server roles, 228
service(s), 218–223
  cluster. *See* cluster service
  configuring properties, 219–223
  kernel mode, 40
  user mode, 40
  Web, IIS, 312–315
service pack updates, 442–444
  installing and uninstalling, 443
  verifying, 443444
Service Properties dialog box, Log On tab, 221
services load phase, 399
service statuses, 220
Session layer, OSI reference model, 214
sharing network resources, 295–318
  connecting to resources from client, 298
  devices, 299–303
  files and folders, 303–306, 315
  finding resources, 296–298
  IIS, 312–315
  IntelliMirror, 311
  printers. *See* sharing printers
  Terminal Services. *See* Terminal Services
sharing printers, 306–310
  creating printers, 307–309
  existing Windows 2000 printers, 310
Sharing tab, Properties dialog box, 299–301
SIDs (security IDs), 34, 360–361
signatures, hard disks, 183
Simple Mail Transfer Protocol (SMTP), IIS support, 312, 313
simple volumes, 152
  dynamic disks, 185–186
single user operating systems, 13
16-bit addresses, 157
Smart Card, 14

12   Index

smart terminals, 71
SMP (Symmetric Multiple
   Processor) systems,
   Windows 2000 Server, 15
SMTP (Simple Mail Transfer
   Protocol), IIS support, 312, 313
snap-ins, IIS, 313
sneaker-nets, 212
SOA (Start of Authority), 245
software
   assigned, 311
   published, 311
software settings group policies, 339
Software subkey,
   HKEY_LOCAL_MACHINE
   subtree, 62–63
spanned volumes, 152, 184
   dynamic disks, 186–187
sparse files, 162
spawning tasks, 8
standard primary zones, 243
standard secondary zones, 243
standby threads, 91
Start of Authority (SOA), 245
start up
   advanced options, 437–438
   file repair, 438–439
   service startup types, 219–220
static route(s), 225–226
Static Route dialog box, 226
stop message errors, troubleshooting, 421
storage, 10–11. *See also* disk *entries;*
   file system(s)
   basic, 151, 152
   dynamic, 151, 152–154
   Registry files, 430–432
   Windows 2000 Server, 15
striped volumes, 184
   dynamic disks, 187–188
stripe sets, 152–153
   with parity, 153–154
subnets, 255–256
superscopes, DHCP, 255

surfaces, platters, 148
symmetric encryption, 341
Symmetric Multiple Processor
   (SMP) systems, Windows 2000
   Server, 15
system attribute, 156
system buses, 121, 131–133
System dialog box, Windows 2000
   Server, 73
system files, core, 53, 55–57
system pages, 102
system partition, 53
SYSTEMROOT command, 405
System State, Active Directory,
   283–284
system state data, 360–361
System subkey,
   HKEY_LOCAL_MACHINE
   subtree, 63

T

TAPI (Telephony API), 30
tasks
   launching (spawning), 8
   multiple, 7–8
task switching, 89
TCP/IP (Transmission Control
   Protocol/Internet Protocol),
   217, 218
TDI (Transport Driver
   Interface), 224
TechNet, 444
Telephony API (TAPI), 30
terminal server client access
   licenses (TSCALs), 331–332, 333
Terminal Services, 71–72, 316–318
   Administration Tool, 317–318
   setting up, 316–317
   Windows 2000 Server, 15
Terminal Services Licensing service, 332, 333
termination of threads, 95
   terminated threads, 91
thin clients, 72
32-bit addresses, 157

thread(s), 89
   context, 90
   multiple, 8–9
   priority. *See* thread priority
   Process and Thread Manager, 32
   quantum. *See* quantum
   scheduling. *See* thread scheduling
   termination, 91, 95
   thread states, 91–92
threading, 8–9
thread priority, 92
   boosting, 96–100
thread scheduling, 90–100
   adjusting, 95–100
   scheduling scenarios, 93–95
   thread and process priority, 92
   thread states, 91–92
thread states, 91–92
Time Service, cluster service, 375
time slicing, 7
time-to-live (TTL), SOA, 245
Tower of Hanoi (ToH) backup
   scheme, 365–366
tracks, 148
transaction logs
   Active Directory, 283
   NTFS, 162–163
transition threads, 91
Transmission Control
   Protocol/Internet Protocol
   (TCP/IP), 217, 218
Transport Driver Interface
   (TDI), 224
Transport layer, OSI reference
   model, 214
trees, Active Directory, 276
trimming working sets, 103
Troubleshoot button, 135–316
troubleshooting, 417–445
   Active Directory. *See* trou-
      bleshooting Active Directory
   boot process. *See* troubleshooting
      boot process
   CIF, 418–419

common-sense troubleshooting, 420–421
devices. *See* troubleshooting devices
disk problems, 441
Dr. Watson, 441
fatal exception errors, 139
hardware, 396–397
installation problems, 421–422
MBR, 441
Microsoft references, 444
network problems, 440
permissions problems, 441
printer problems, 439–440
RAS problems, 440
Registry. *See* Registry
service pack updates, 442–444
tools, 422–425
troubleshooting Active Directory, 281–284
  backing up, 283–284
  files, 282–283
  recovering and restoring Active Directory, 284
troubleshooting boot process, 437–439
  advanced start-up options, 437–438
  start-up file repair, 438–439
troubleshooting devices, 136–139
  changing single parameter at a time, 136–137
  documenting current settings, 137–138
  tips, 138–139
  universal serial bus, 138
trust relationships, Active Directory, 276
TSCALs (terminal server client access licenses), 331–332, 333
TTL (time-to-live), SOA, 245
tunnels, 228
TYPE command, 405

U

unallocated space, 152
uninstalling service pack updates, 443
Universal Serial Bus (USB), 123, 131, 132
  troubleshooting, 138
upgrading networks
  in-place upgrades, 279
  from Windows NT to Windows 2000, 277–279
USB. *See* Universal Serial Bus (USB)
user(s)
  authentication. *See* user authentication
  identification, 242
  multiple, 6–7
  number allowed to share devices, 301
  single-user operating systems, 13
user authentication, 334–336
  certificates, 336
  Kerberos, 334, 335–336
  NTLM, 334, 335
user input, priority boosts after waiting for, 97–98
user messages, priority boosts after waiting for, 97–98
user mode, 38–40
  services, 40
user profiles, 337–338
user rights and permissions, 333–334

V

value entries in Registry, 425, 426, 429–430
variable priority threads, 92
verifying service pack updates, 443, 444
VGA Mode, 401
virtual directories, 314

Virtual Directory Creation Wizard, 314
Virtual DOS Machine, 128
virtual machines, 11–12
virtual memory, 33, 100–101
  management. *See* memory management
Virtual Memory Manager, 33–34
virtual multitasking, 7
virtual private networks (VPNs), 228
  Windows 2000 Professional support, 14
virtual servers, 373
Visual InterDev RAD remote deployment, IIS support, 313
volumes, 151–154
  duplexed, 190
  fault-tolerant. *See* fault-tolerant volumes
  identifying, 154
  mirrored, 184, 189–190
  NTFS, files contained in, 161
  RAID 5, 153–154, 184, 190–191, 370–371
  simple, 152, 185–186
  spanned, 152, 184, 186–187
  striped, 184, 187–188
voluntary switching of threads, 93–94
VPNs. *See* virtual private networks (VPNs)
VxD driver, 122

W

waiting threads, 91
WANs (wide area networks), 212
WDM. *See* Win32 Driver Model (WDM)
Web application development tools, IIS, 312
Web services, IIS, 312–315
Web Sharing tab, Properties dialog box, 315

wide area networks (WANs), 212
Windows 2000 Advanced Server, 16–17
　services, 16–17
Windows-based scripting, App 3
Windows 2000 Datacenter Server, 17
Windows Explorer, sharing devices, 299–303
Windows Internet Name Service (WINS), 241, 247–250
　name query, 249
　name registration, 248–249
　name release, 249–250
　name renewal, 250
Windows 2000 networks
　installing, 279–280
　mixed mode, 277–278
　native mode, 277, 278–279
　upgrading existing Windows NT networks to, 277–279
Windows NT
　domains, 274–275
　ERD, 437
　upgrading existing networks for Active Directory, 277–279
Windows operating system, 3

Windows 2000 Professional, 14–15
　component requirements, 15
　new features, 14
　Windows 2000 Server compared, 13–18
Windows 2000 Resource Kit, 436–437
Windows Scripting Host (WSH), App 1–4
　command-based scripting, App 2–3
　manually registering script engines, App 4
　sample script, App 4
　Windows-based scripting, App 3
Windows 2000 Server, 15–16
　component requirements, 15–16
　features, 15
　tools, 72–74
　Windows 2000 Professional compared, 13–18
Windows settings group policies, 339
Windows subsystem start phase, 399
Win32 Driver Model (WDM), 121, 122, 126–129
　hardware devices supported, 127–128

　layered approach, 127–129
　legacy virtualization drivers layer, 128–129
WINS. *See* Windows Internet Name Service (WINS)
Win 32 subsystem, 30–31
working sets, 33, 103
　trimming, 103
World Wide Web server, IIS support, 313
Write Signature and Upgrade Disk Wizard, 183
writing to disk, 67
WSH. *See* Windows Scripting Host (WSH)

X
XOR (exclusive OR arithmetic), 371

# Z
zone(s), DNS. *See* Domain Naming Service (DNS)
zone database files, 243
zone transfers, 247